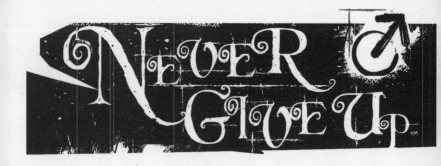

Volume 5
by
Hiromu Mutou

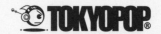

HAMBURG // LONDON // LOS ANGELES // TOKYO

Never Give Up Volume 5
Created by Hiromu Mutou

Translation - Mike Kiefl
Retouch and Lettering - Star Print Brokers
Production Artist - Bowen Park
Graphic Designer - James Lee

Editor - Katherine Schilling
Digital Imaging Manager - Chris Buford
Pre-Production Supervisor - Erika Terriquez
Art Director - Anne Marie Horne
Production Manager - Elisabeth Brizzi
Managing Editor - Vy Nguyen
VP of Production - Ron Klamert
Editor-in-Chief - Rob Tokar
Publisher - Mike Kiley
President and C.O.O. - John Parker
C.E.O. and Chief Creative Officer - Stuart Levy

A 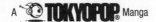 Manga

TOKYOPOP and are trademarks or registered trademarks of TOKYOPOP Inc.

TOKYOPOP Inc.
5900 Wilshire Blvd. Suite 2000
Los Angeles, CA 90036

E-mail: info@TOKYOPOP.com
Come visit us online at www.TOKYOPOP.com

NEBAGIBA! by Hiromu Mutou. © 2000 Hiromu Mutou. All rights reserved. First published in Japan in 2000 by HAKUSENSHA, INC.,TOKYO. English language translation rights in the United States of America and Canada arranged with HAKUSENSHA, INC., Tokyo through Tuttle-Mori Agency Inc., Tokyo.
English text copyright © 2007 TOKYOPOP Inc.

All rights reserved. No portion of this book may be reproduced or transmitted in any form or by any means without written permission from the copyright holders. This manga is a work of fiction. Any resemblance to actual events or locales or persons, living or dead, is entirely coincidental.

ISBN: 978-1-59816-169-4

First TOKYOPOP printing: July 2007
10 9 8 7 6 5 4 3 2 1
Printed in the USA

NEVER GIVE UP™

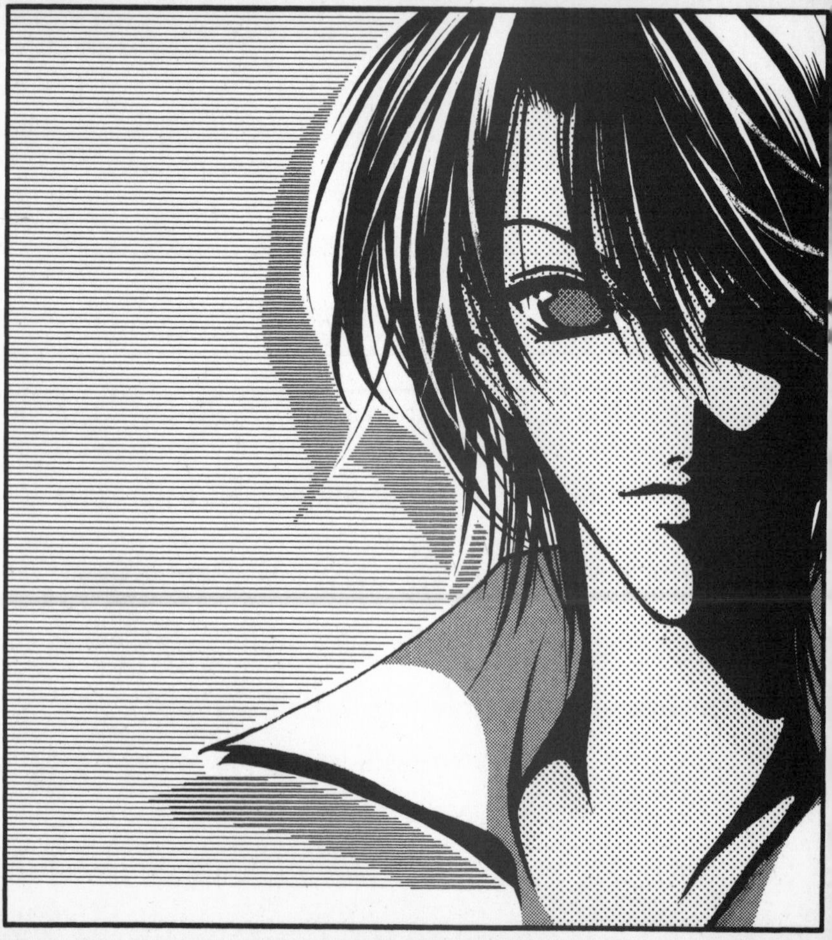

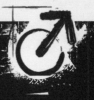

Contents

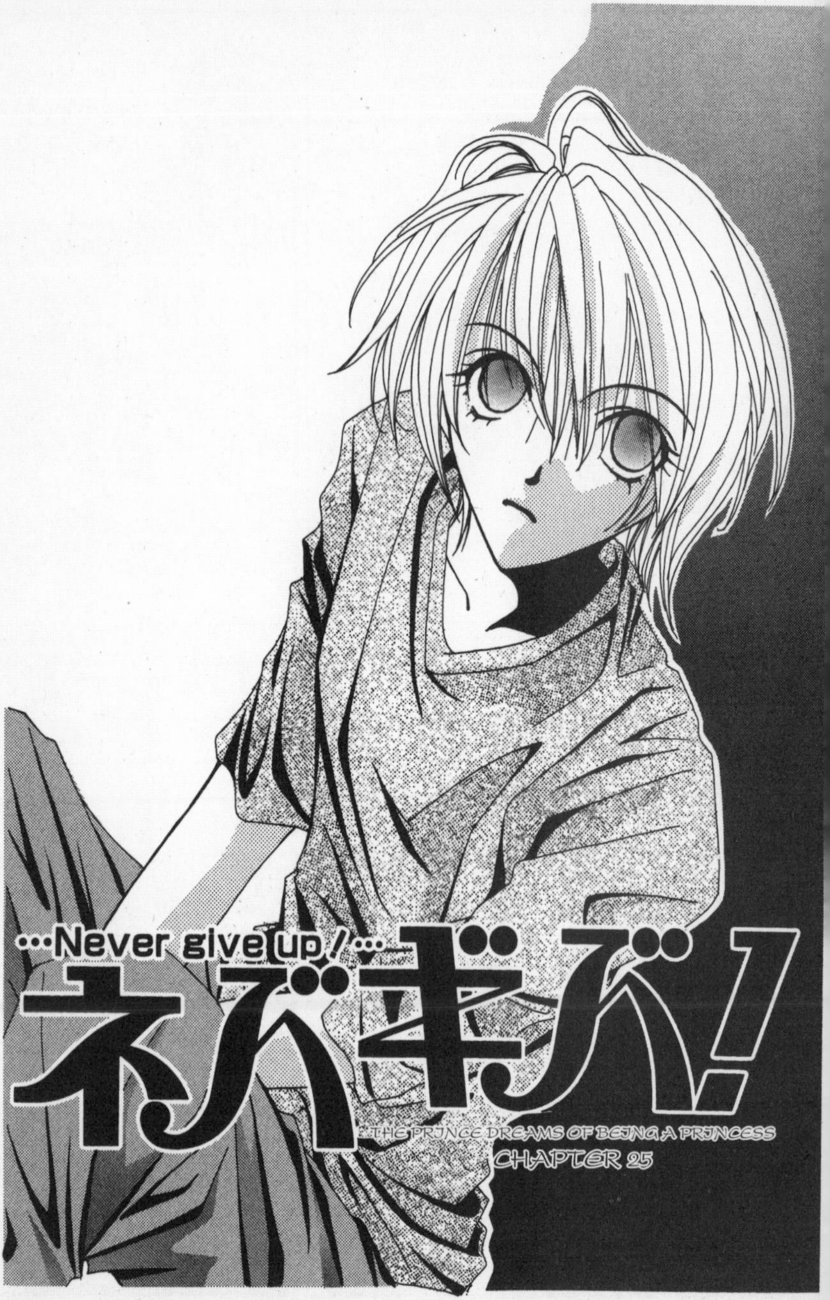

...Never give up!...
ネバギバ!
THE PRINCE DREAMS OF BEING A PRINCESS
CHAPTER 25

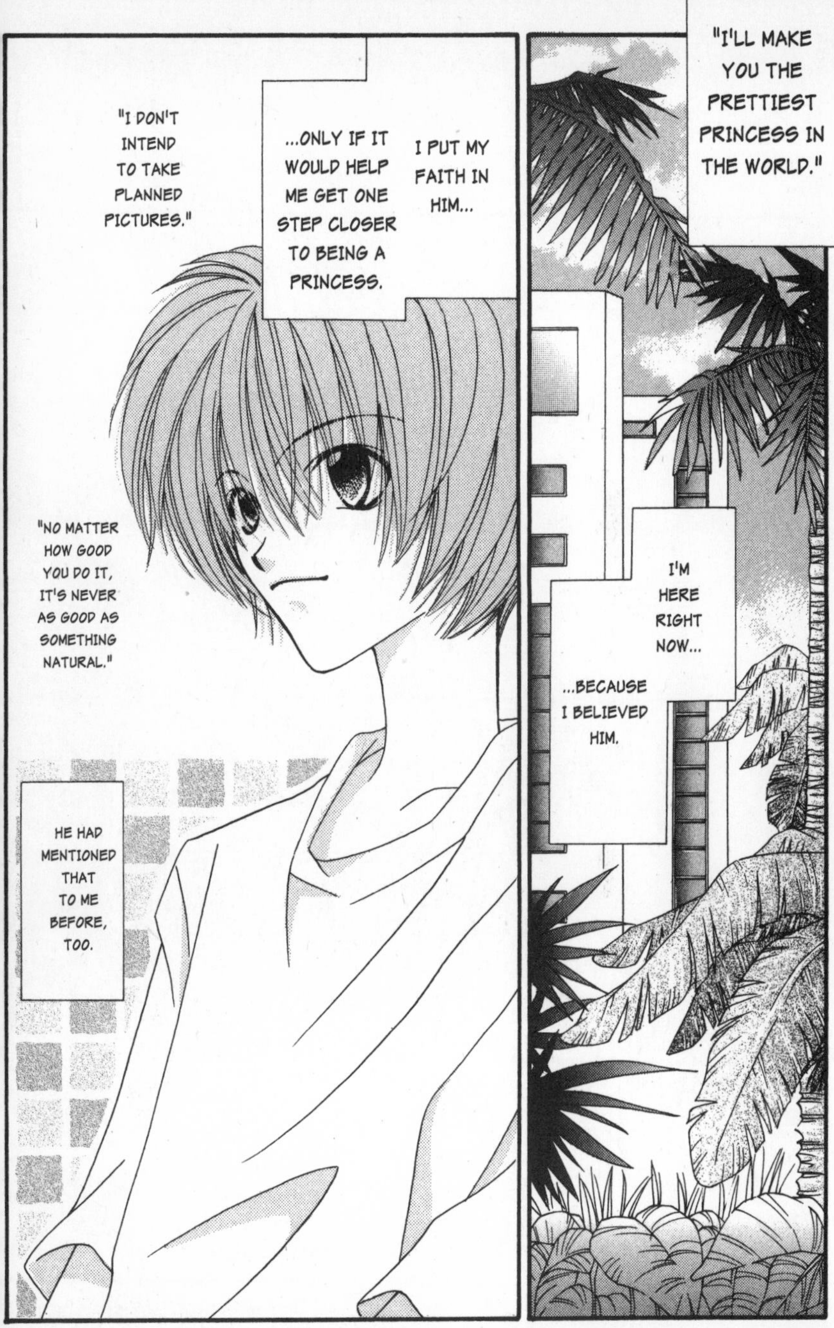
"I'LL MAKE YOU THE PRETTIEST PRINCESS IN THE WORLD."
I'M HERE RIGHT NOW...
...BECAUSE I BELIEVED HIM.
I PUT MY FAITH IN HIM...
...ONLY IF IT WOULD HELP ME GET ONE STEP CLOSER TO BEING A PRINCESS.
"I DON'T INTEND TO TAKE PLANNED PICTURES."
"NO MATTER HOW GOOD YOU DO IT, IT'S NEVER AS GOOD AS SOMETHING NATURAL."
HE HAD MENTIONED THAT TO ME BEFORE, TOO.

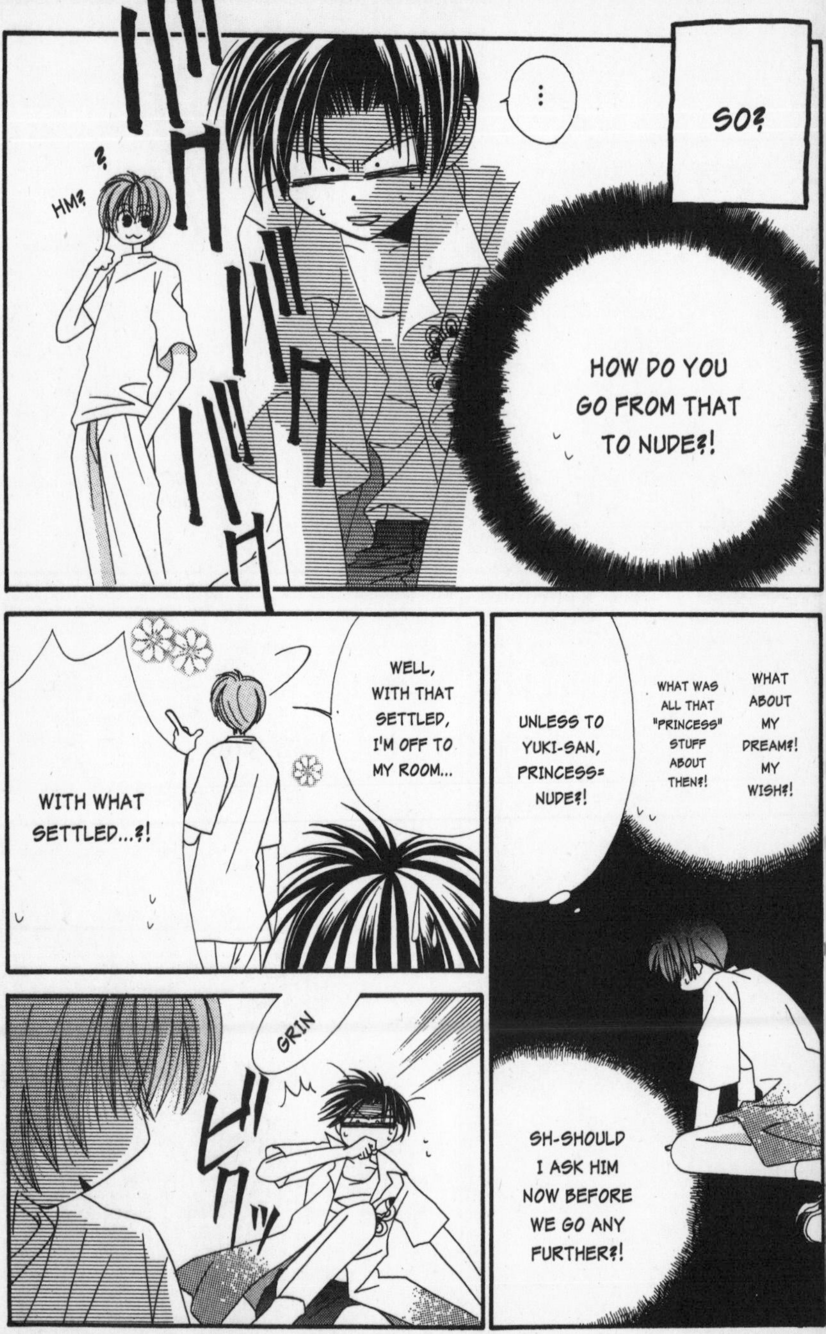
SO?
...
HOW DO YOU GO FROM THAT TO NUDE?!
HM?
WHAT ABOUT MY DREAM?! MY WISH?!
WHAT WAS ALL THAT "PRINCESS" STUFF ABOUT THEN?!
UNLESS TO YUKI-SAN, PRINCESS= NUDE?!
SH-SHOULD I ASK HIM NOW BEFORE WE GO ANY FURTHER?!
WELL, WITH THAT SETTLED, I'M OFF TO MY ROOM...
WITH WHAT SETTLED...?!
GRIN

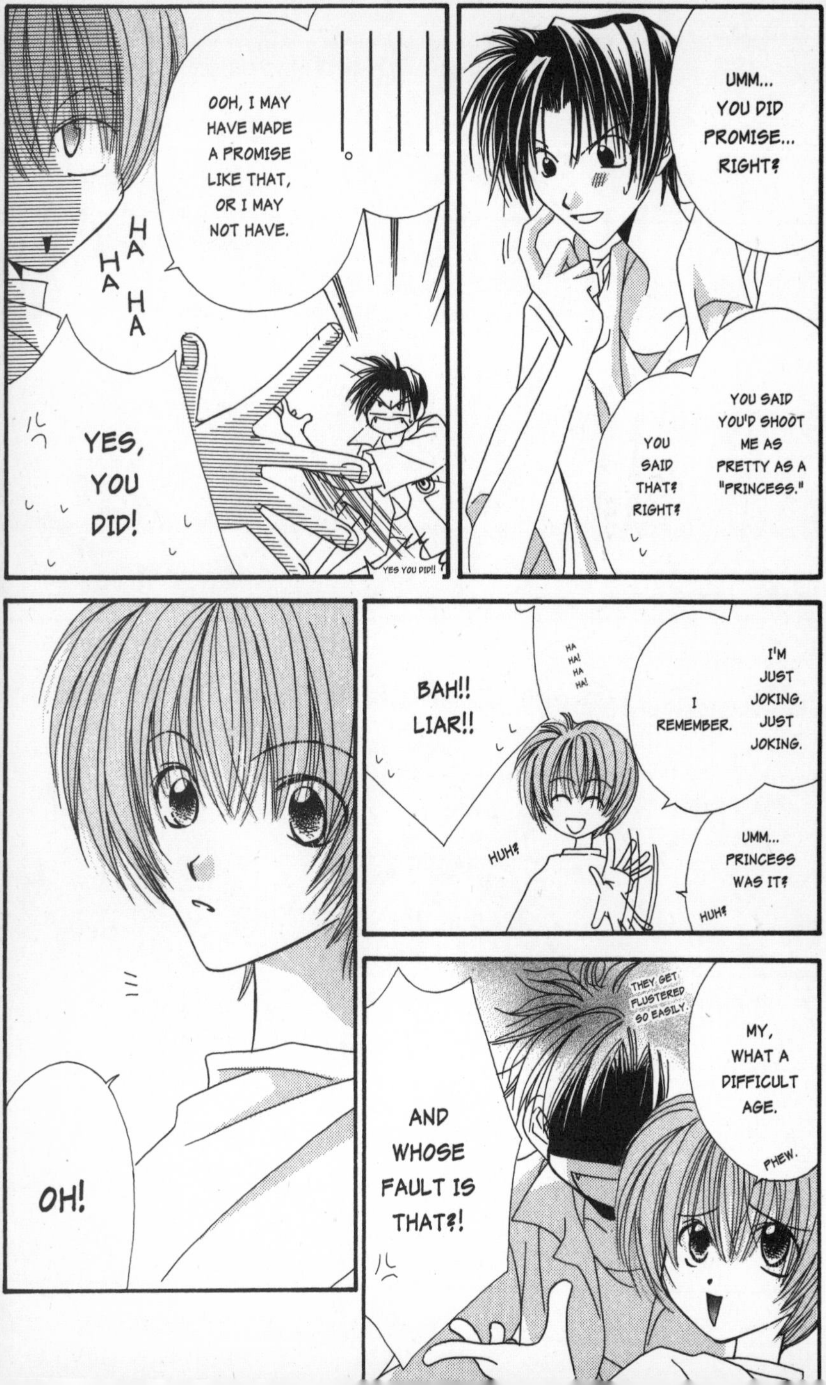
UMM... YOU DID PROMISE... RIGHT?
YOU SAID YOU'D SHOOT ME AS PRETTY AS A "PRINCESS."
YOU SAID THAT? RIGHT?
OOH, I MAY HAVE MADE A PROMISE LIKE THAT, OR I MAY NOT HAVE.
HA HA HA HA
YES, YOU DID!
YES YOU DID!!
I'M JUST JOKING. JUST JOKING.
I REMEMBER.
HA HA! HA HA!
BAH!! LIAR!!
UMM... PRINCESS WAS IT?
HUH?
HUH?
MY, WHAT A DIFFICULT AGE.
PHEW.
THEY GET FLUSTERED SO EASILY.
AND WHOSE FAULT IS THAT?!
OH!

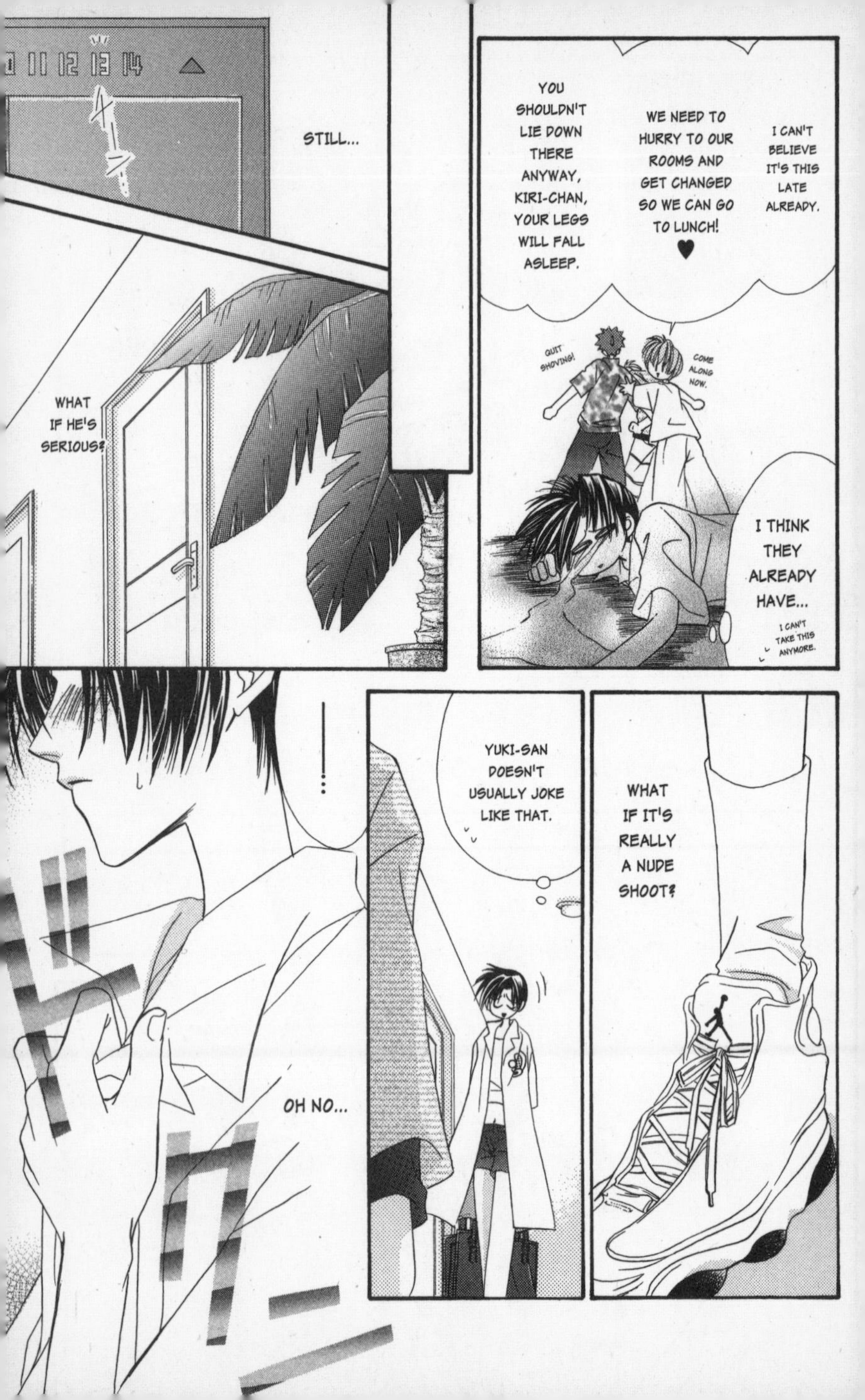
I CAN'T BELIEVE IT'S THIS LATE ALREADY.
WE NEED TO HURRY TO OUR ROOMS AND GET CHANGED SO WE CAN GO TO LUNCH! ♥
YOU SHOULDN'T LIE DOWN THERE ANYWAY, KIRI-CHAN, YOUR LEGS WILL FALL ASLEEP.
COME ALONG NOW.
QUIT SHOVING!
I THINK THEY ALREADY HAVE...
I CAN'T TAKE THIS ANYMORE.
STILL...
WHAT IF HE'S SERIOUS?
WHAT IF IT'S REALLY A NUDE SHOOT?
YUKI-SAN DOESN'T USUALLY JOKE LIKE THAT.
OH NO...

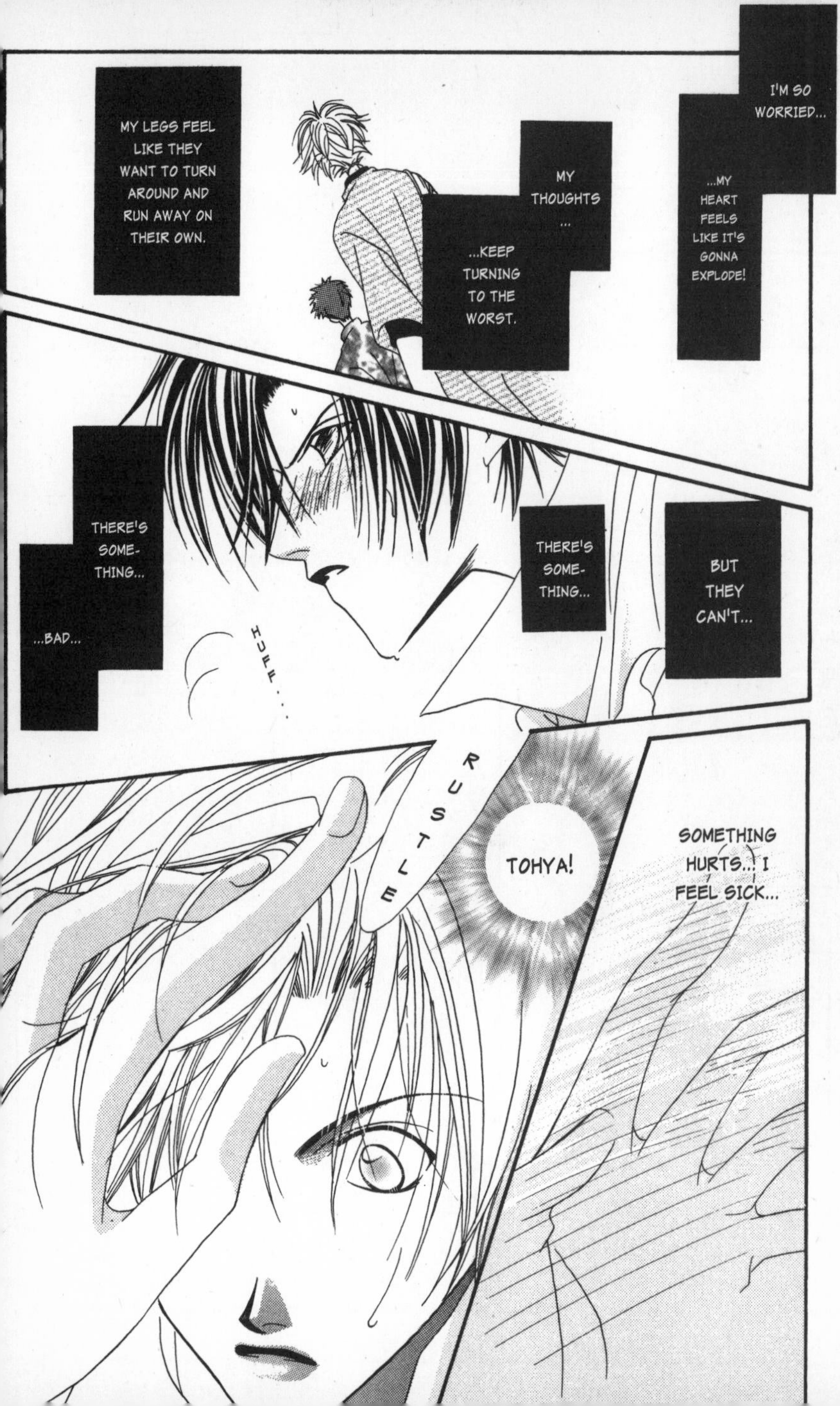
I'M SO WORRIED...
...MY HEART FEELS LIKE IT'S GONNA EXPLODE!
MY THOUGHTS ...
...KEEP TURNING TO THE WORST.
MY LEGS FEEL LIKE THEY WANT TO TURN AROUND AND RUN AWAY ON THEIR OWN.
BUT THEY CAN'T...
THERE'S SOME-THING...
HUFF...
THERE'S SOME-THING...
...BAD...
SOMETHING HURTS... I FEEL SICK...
TOHYA!
RUSTLE

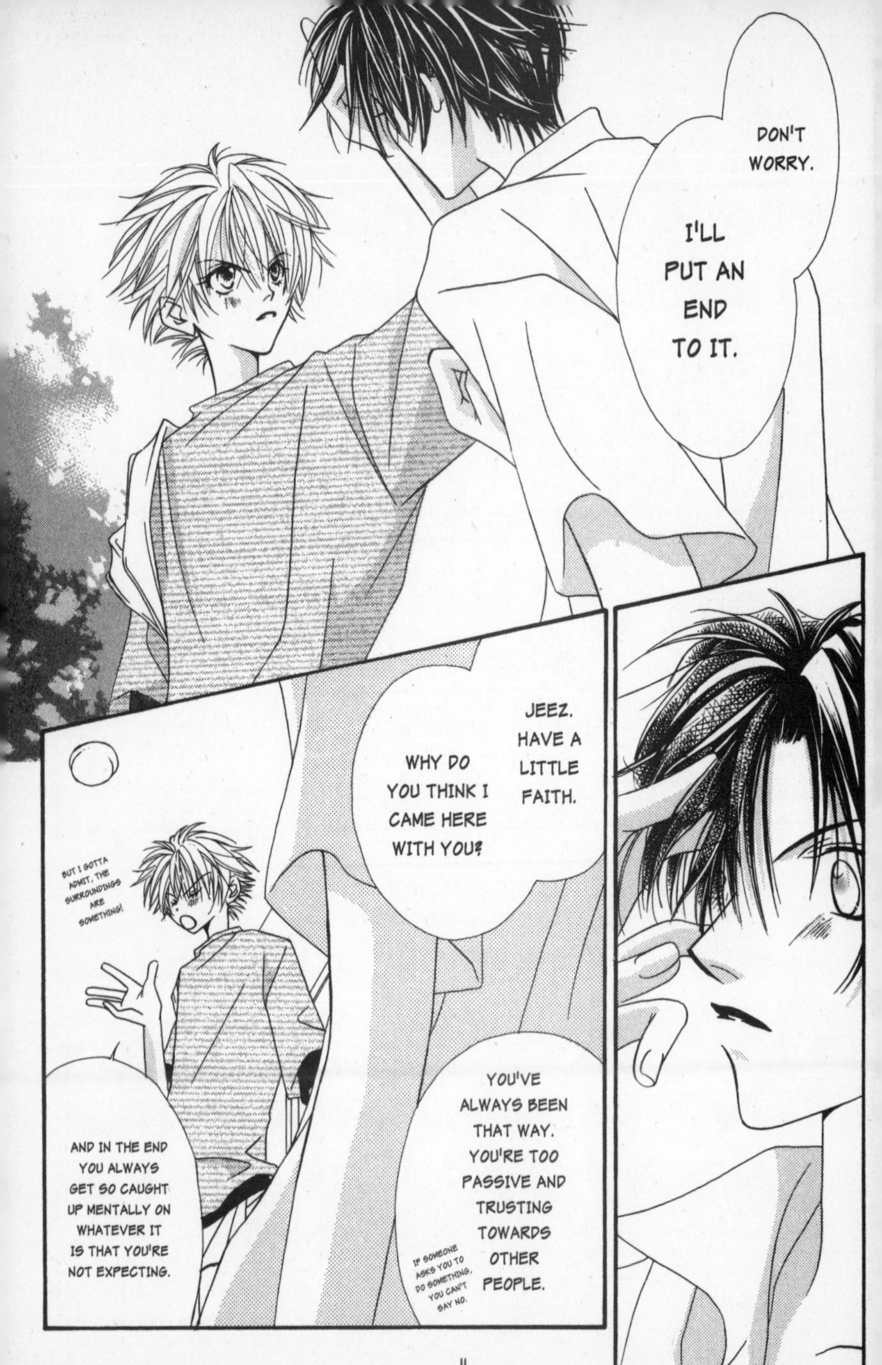
DON'T WORRY.
I'LL PUT AN END TO IT.
JEEZ. HAVE A LITTLE FAITH.
WHY DO YOU THINK I CAME HERE WITH YOU?
BUT I GOTTA ADMIT, THE SURROUNDINGS ARE SOMETHING!
YOU'VE ALWAYS BEEN THAT WAY. YOU'RE TOO PASSIVE AND TRUSTING TOWARDS OTHER PEOPLE.
IF SOMEONE ASKS YOU TO DO SOMETHING, YOU CAN'T SAY NO.
AND IN THE END YOU ALWAYS GET SO CAUGHT UP MENTALLY ON WHATEVER IT IS THAT YOU'RE NOT EXPECTING.

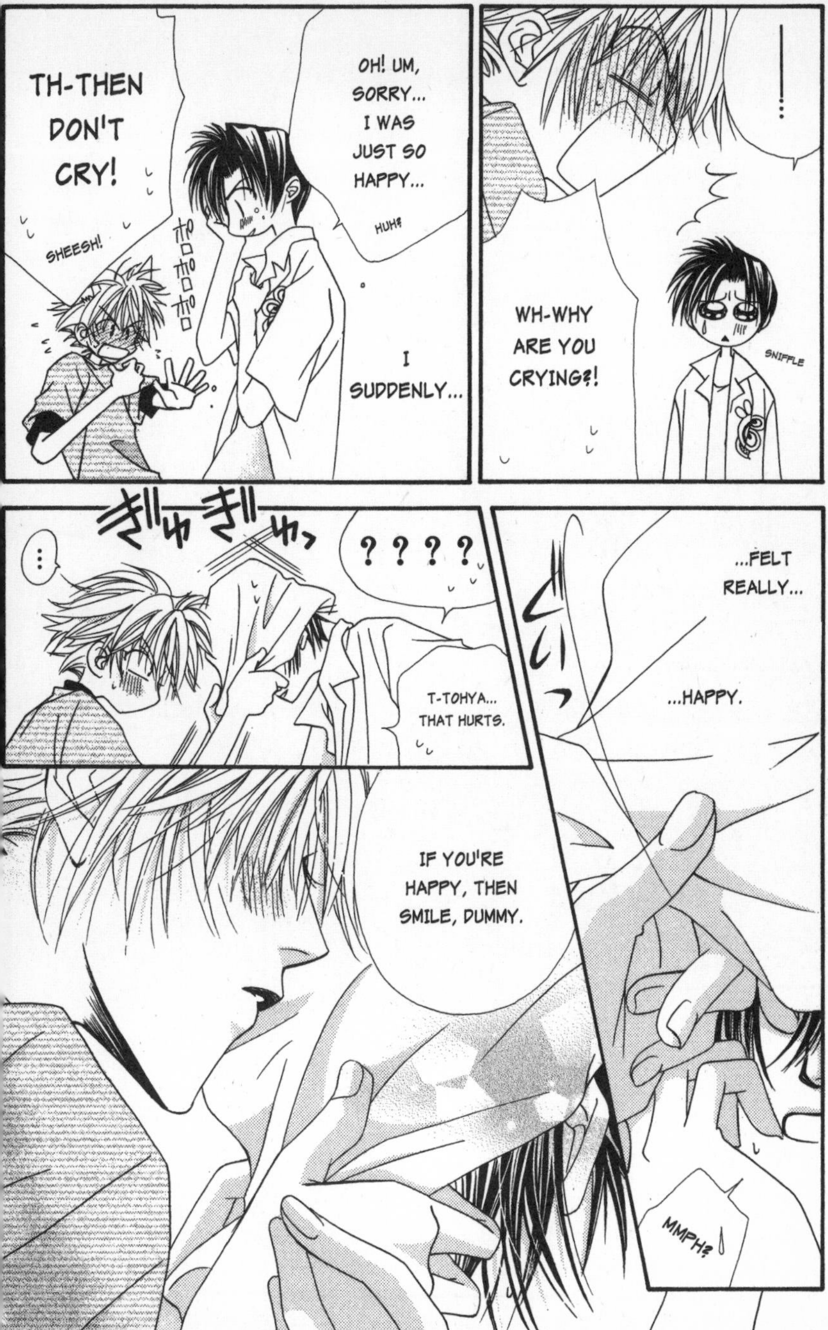
!...
WH-WHY ARE YOU CRYING?!
SNIFFLE
OH! UM, SORRY... I WAS JUST SO HAPPY...
HUH?
I SUDDENLY...
TH-THEN DON'T CRY!
ポロポロポロ
SHEESH!
...FELT REALLY...
...HAPPY.
ぐいっ
MMPH?
????
ぎゅぎゅっ
...
T-TOHYA... THAT HURTS.
IF YOU'RE HAPPY, THEN SMILE, DUMMY.

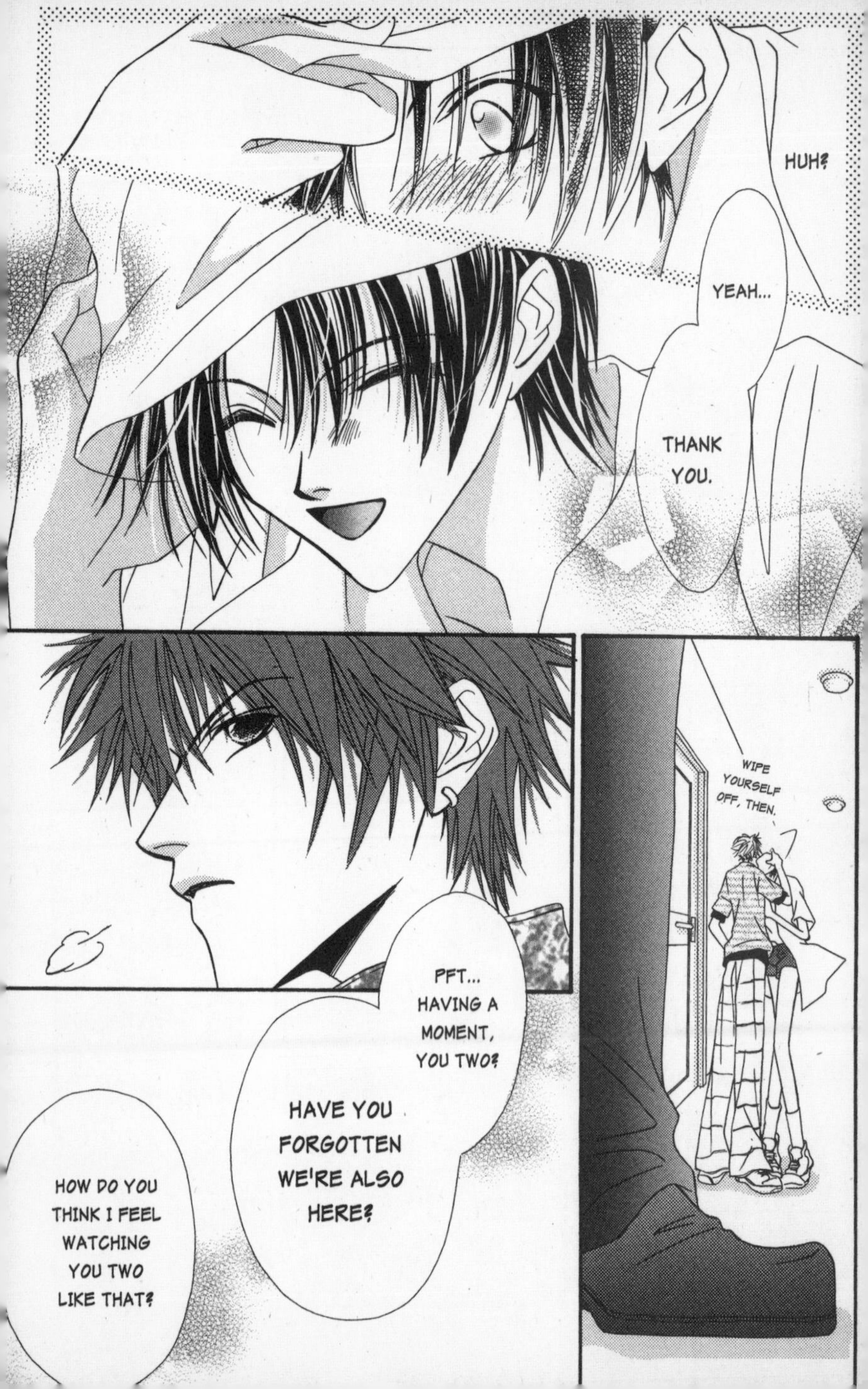
HUH?
YEAH...
THANK YOU.
WIPE YOURSELF OFF, THEN.
PFT... HAVING A MOMENT, YOU TWO?
HAVE YOU FORGOTTEN WE'RE ALSO HERE?
HOW DO YOU THINK I FEEL WATCHING YOU TWO LIKE THAT?

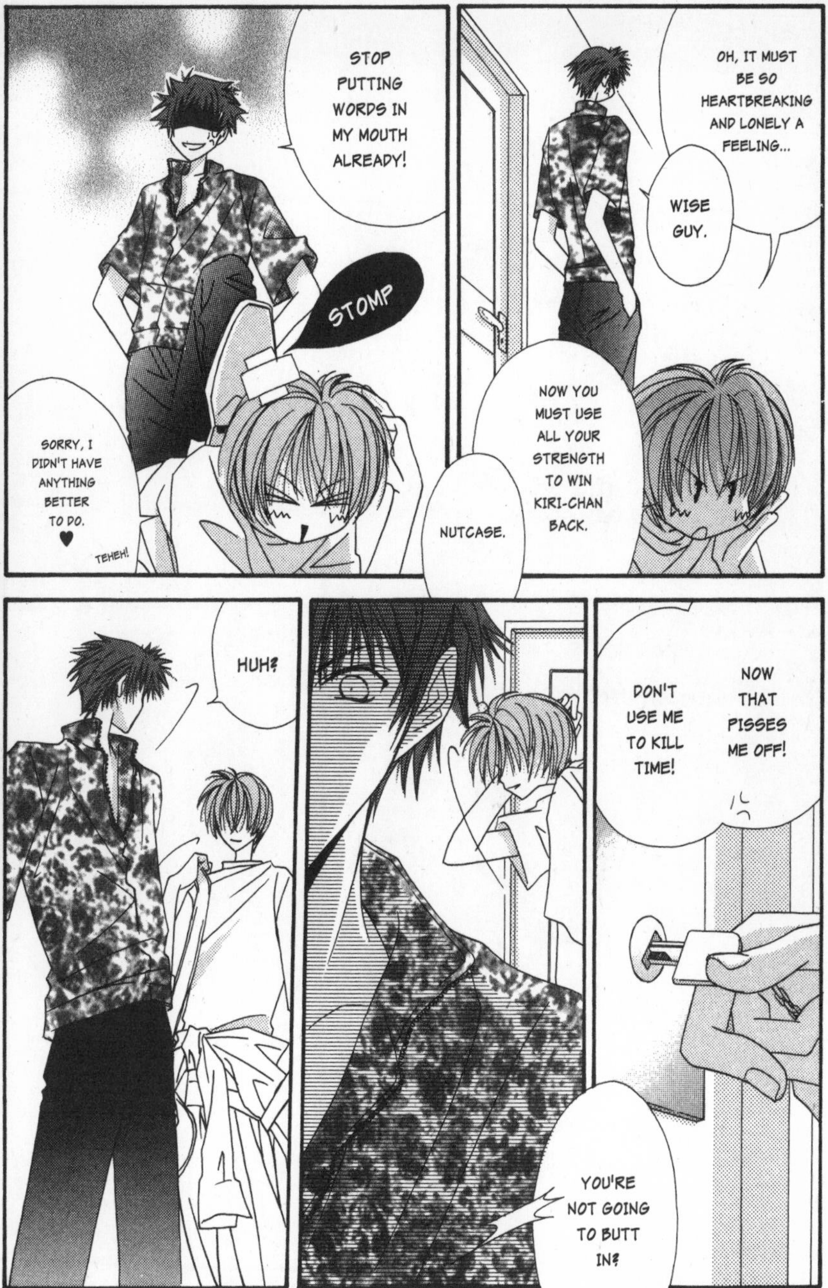
OH, IT MUST BE SO HEARTBREAKING AND LONELY A FEELING...
WISE GUY.
NOW YOU MUST USE ALL YOUR STRENGTH TO WIN KIRI-CHAN BACK.
NUTCASE.
STOP PUTTING WORDS IN MY MOUTH ALREADY!
STOMP
SORRY, I DIDN'T HAVE ANYTHING BETTER TO DO. ♥
TEHEH!
NOW THAT PISSES ME OFF!
DON'T USE ME TO KILL TIME!
YOU'RE NOT GOING TO BUTT IN?
HUH?

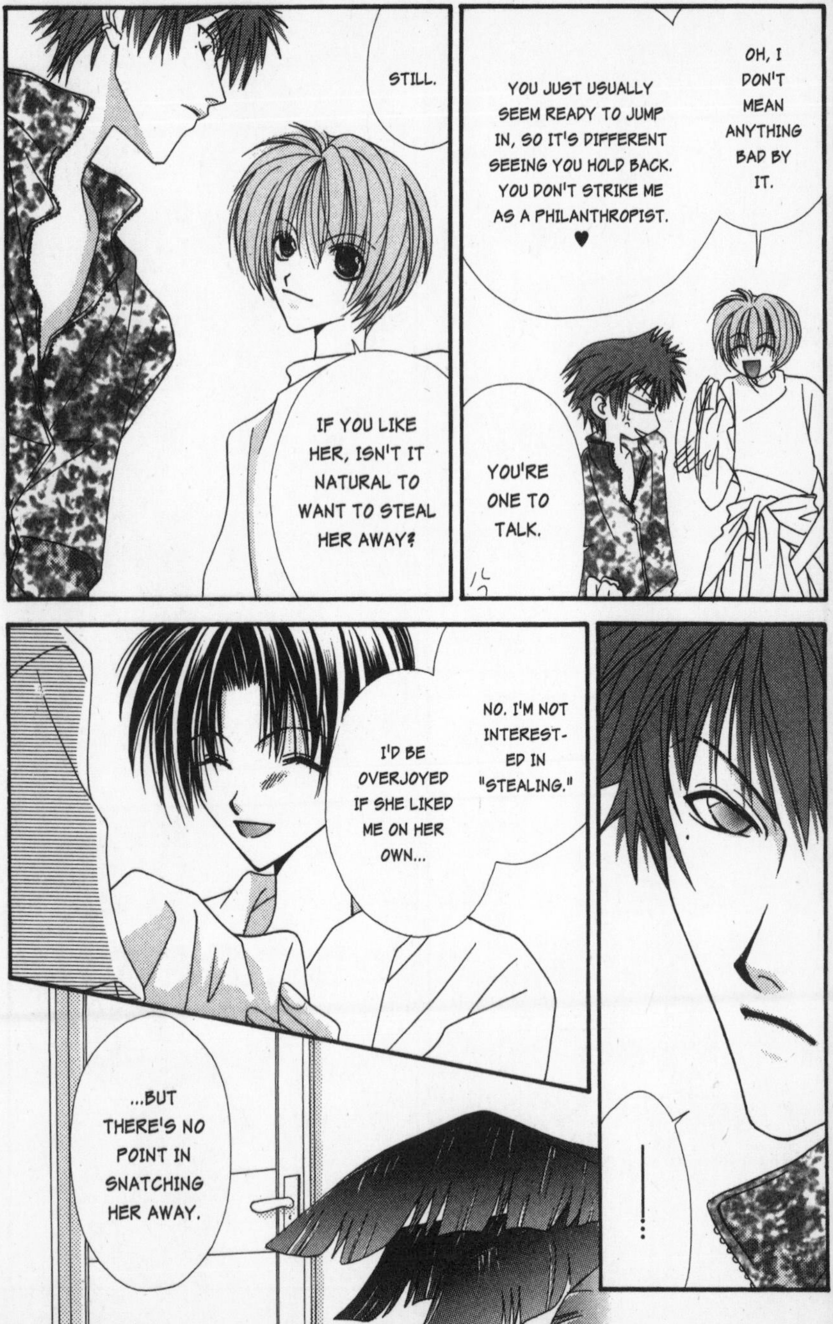
OH, I DON'T MEAN ANYTHING BAD BY IT.
YOU JUST USUALLY SEEM READY TO JUMP IN, SO IT'S DIFFERENT SEEING YOU HOLD BACK. YOU DON'T STRIKE ME AS A PHILANTHROPIST. ♥
YOU'RE ONE TO TALK.
STILL.
IF YOU LIKE HER, ISN'T IT NATURAL TO WANT TO STEAL HER AWAY?
......
NO. I'M NOT INTEREST-ED IN "STEALING."
I'D BE OVERJOYED IF SHE LIKED ME ON HER OWN...
...BUT THERE'S NO POINT IN SNATCHING HER AWAY.

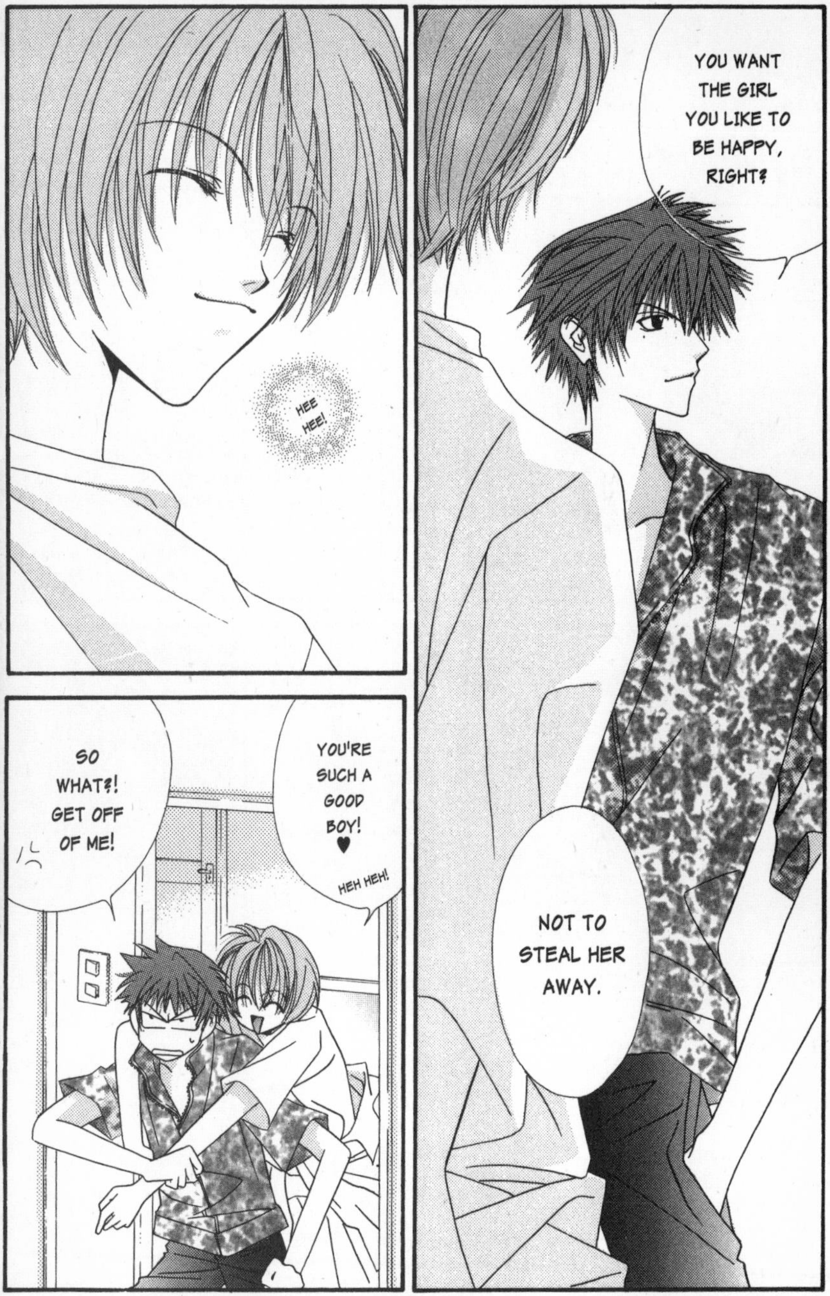
YOU WANT THE GIRL YOU LIKE TO BE HAPPY, RIGHT?
NOT TO STEAL HER AWAY.
HEE HEE!
YOU'RE SUCH A GOOD BOY! ♥
HEH HEH!
SO WHAT?! GET OFF OF ME!

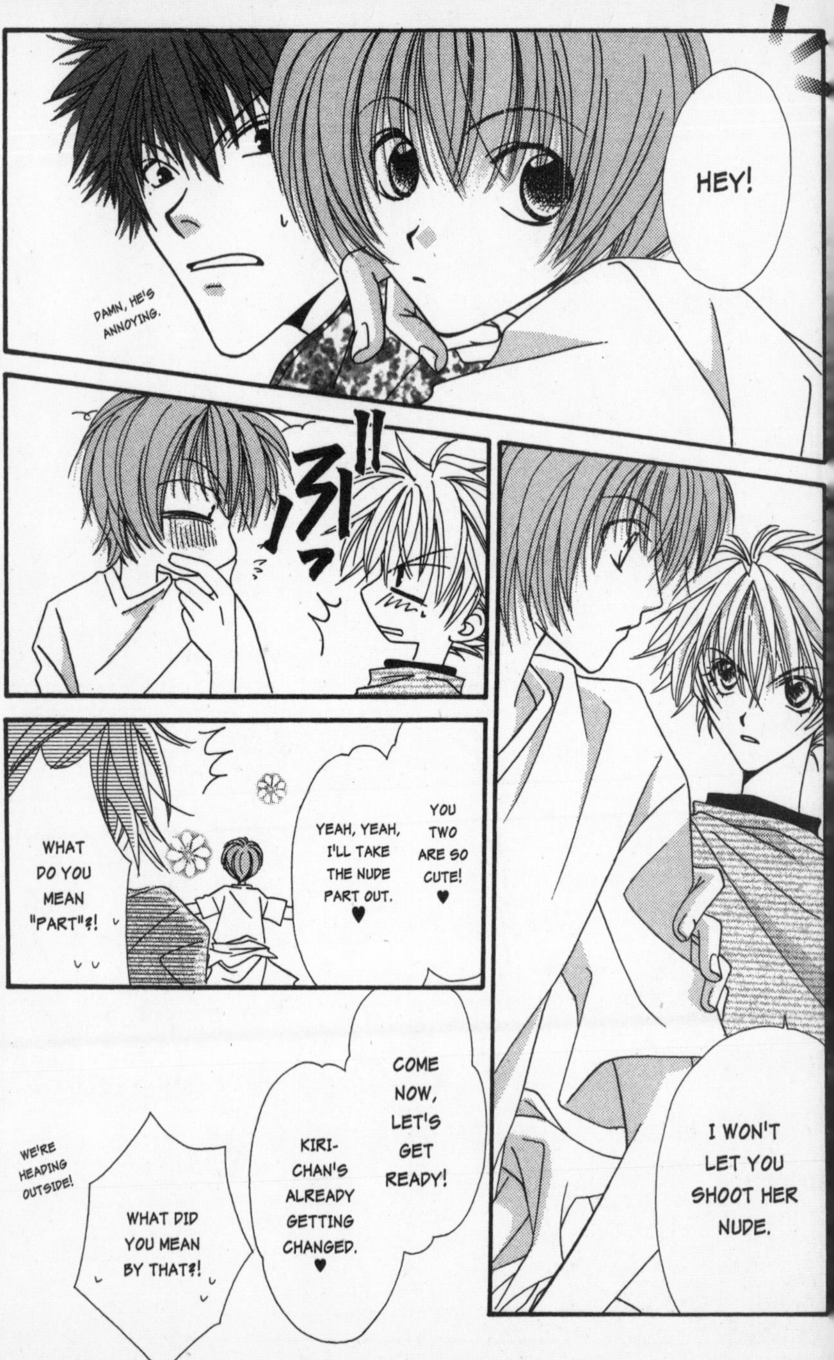
HEY!
DAMN, HE'S ANNOYING.
I WON'T LET YOU SHOOT HER NUDE.
YOU TWO ARE SO CUTE! ♥
YEAH, YEAH, I'LL TAKE THE NUDE PART OUT. ♥
WHAT DO YOU MEAN "PART"?!
COME NOW, LET'S GET READY!
KIRI-CHAN'S ALREADY GETTING CHANGED. ♥
WHAT DID YOU MEAN BY THAT?!
WE'RE HEADING OUTSIDE!

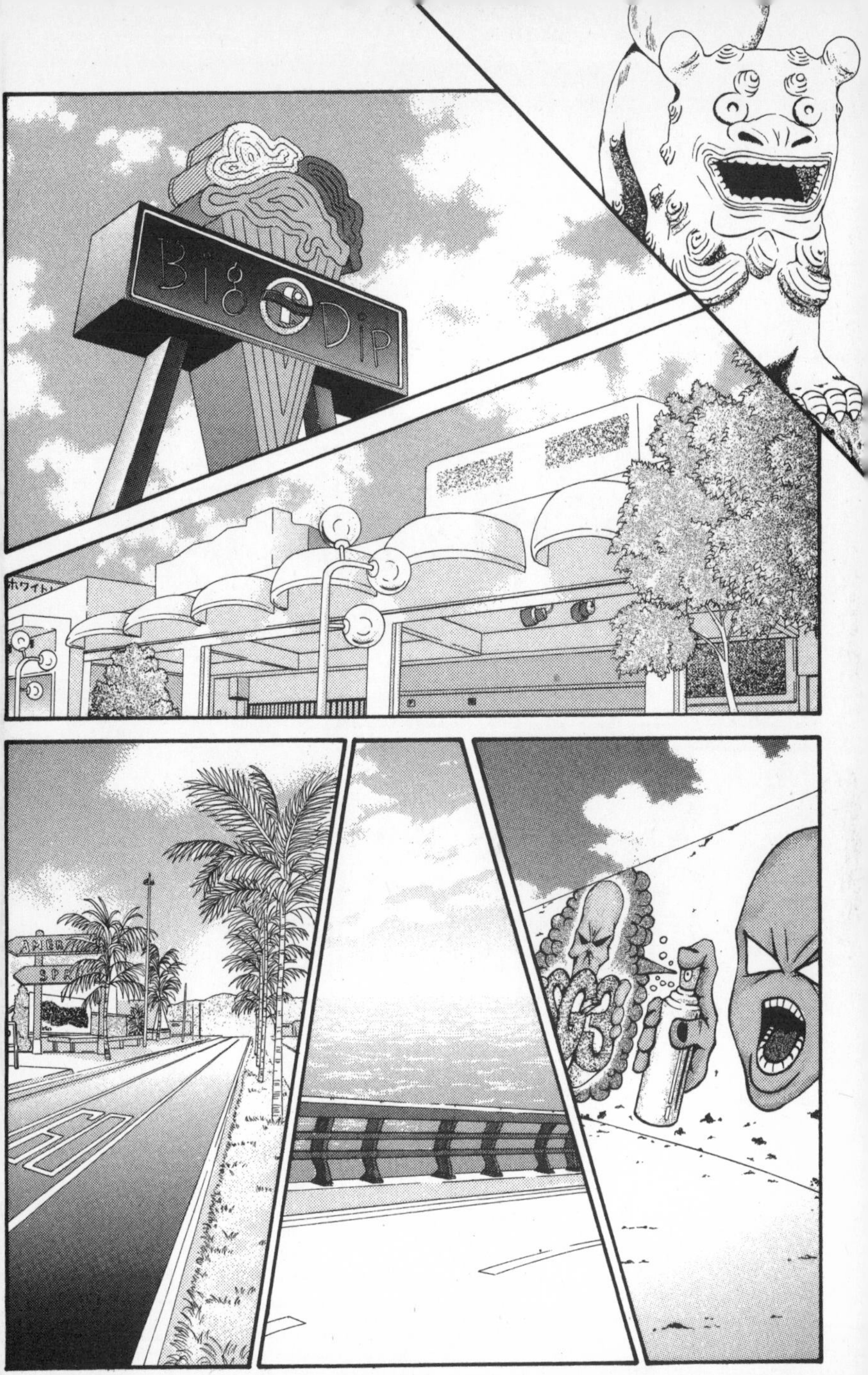
Big Dip

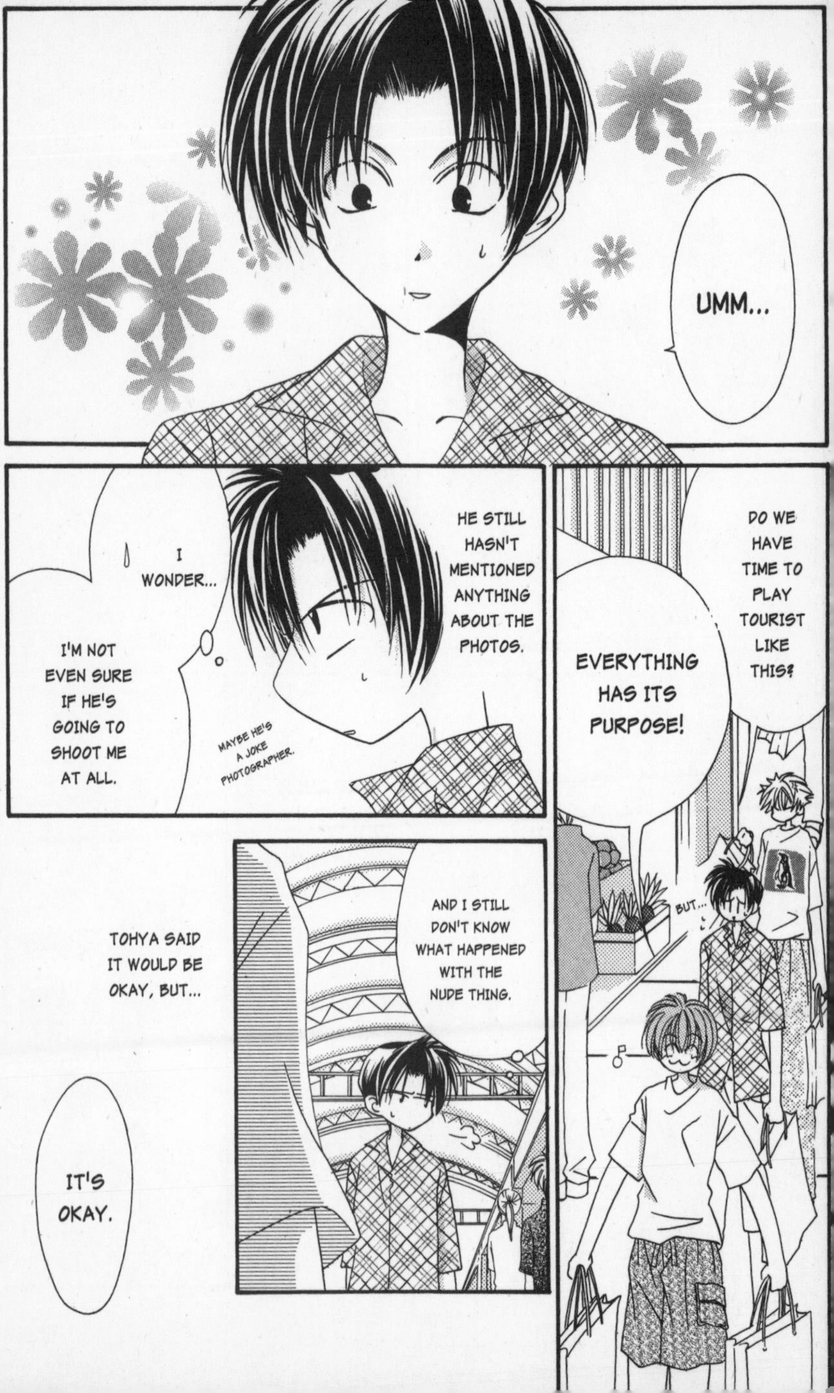
UMM...
DO WE HAVE TIME TO PLAY TOURIST LIKE THIS?
EVERYTHING HAS ITS PURPOSE!
BUT...
HE STILL HASN'T MENTIONED ANYTHING ABOUT THE PHOTOS.
I WONDER...
I'M NOT EVEN SURE IF HE'S GOING TO SHOOT ME AT ALL.
MAYBE HE'S A JOKE PHOTOGRAPHER.
AND I STILL DON'T KNOW WHAT HAPPENED WITH THE NUDE THING.
TOHYA SAID IT WOULD BE OKAY, BUT...
IT'S OKAY.

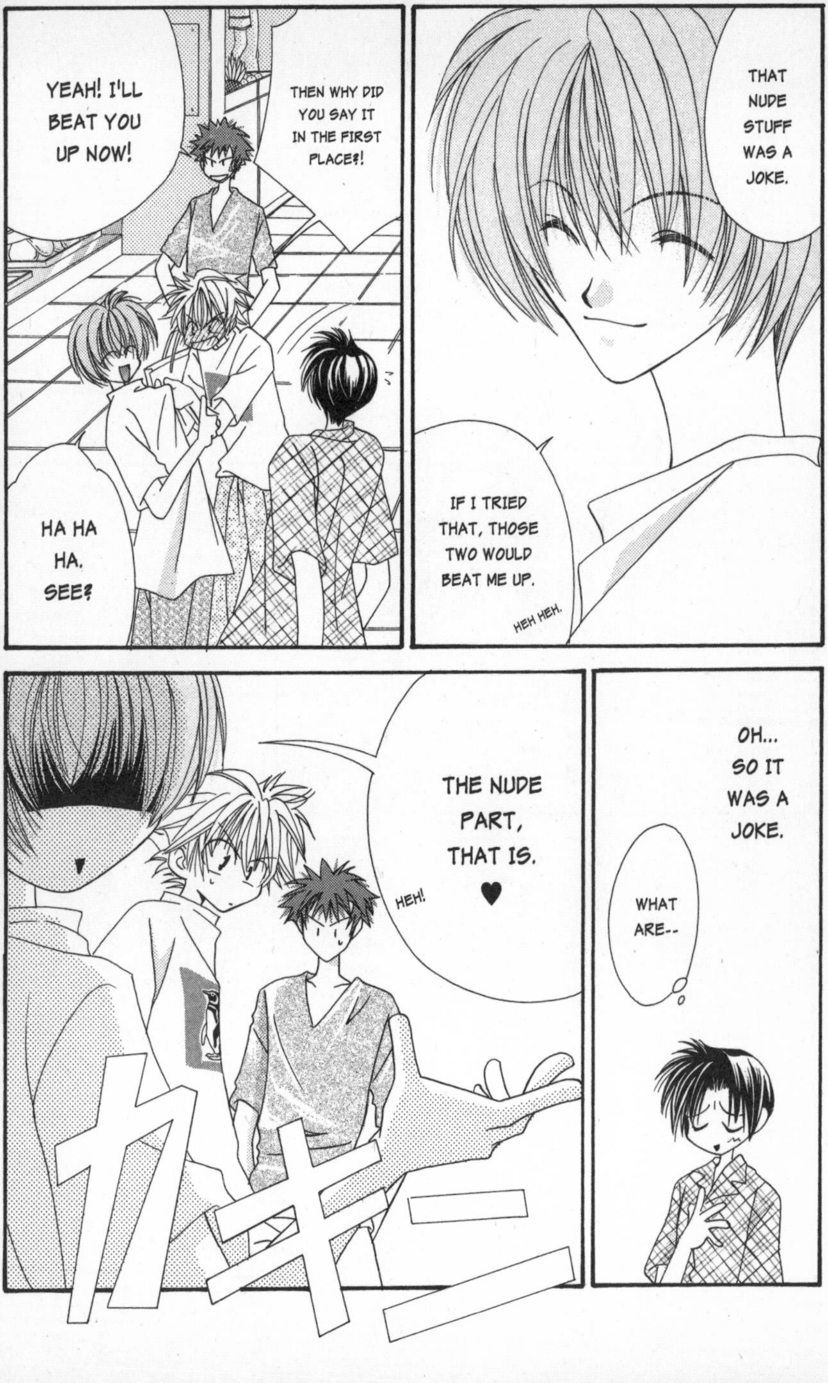
THAT NUDE STUFF WAS A JOKE.
IF I TRIED THAT, THOSE TWO WOULD BEAT ME UP.
HEH HEH.
THEN WHY DID YOU SAY IT IN THE FIRST PLACE?!
YEAH! I'LL BEAT YOU UP NOW!
HA HA HA. SEE?
OH... SO IT WAS A JOKE.
WHAT ARE--
THE NUDE PART, THAT IS. ♥
HEH!
カキーー

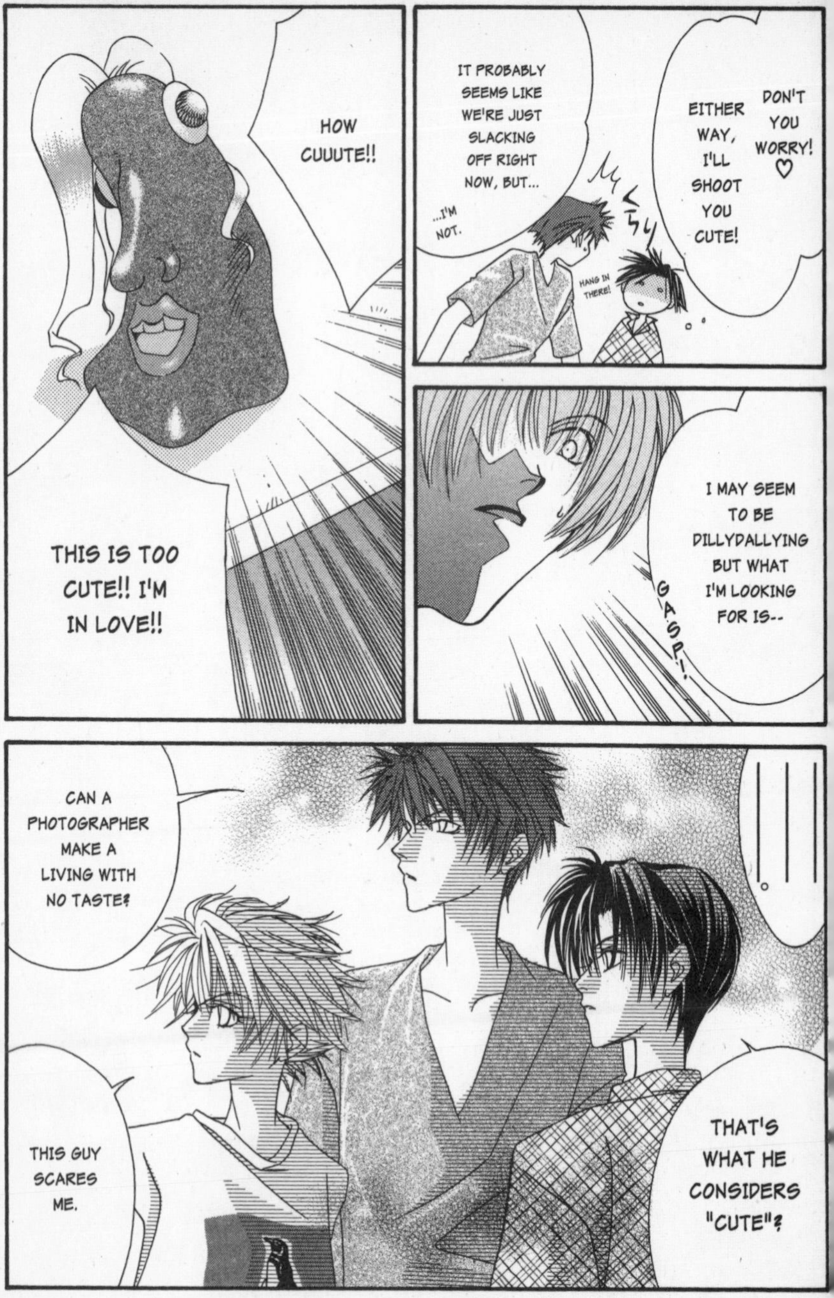
DON'T YOU WORRY! ♡ EITHER WAY, I'LL SHOOT YOU CUTE!
IT PROBABLY SEEMS LIKE WE'RE JUST SLACKING OFF RIGHT NOW, BUT...
...I'M NOT.
HANG IN THERE!
I MAY SEEM TO BE DILLYDALLYING BUT WHAT I'M LOOKING FOR IS--
GASP!!
HOW CUUUTE!!
THIS IS TOO CUTE!! I'M IN LOVE!!
!!!
THAT'S WHAT HE CONSIDERS "CUTE"?
CAN A PHOTOGRAPHER MAKE A LIVING WITH NO TASTE?
THIS GUY SCARES ME.

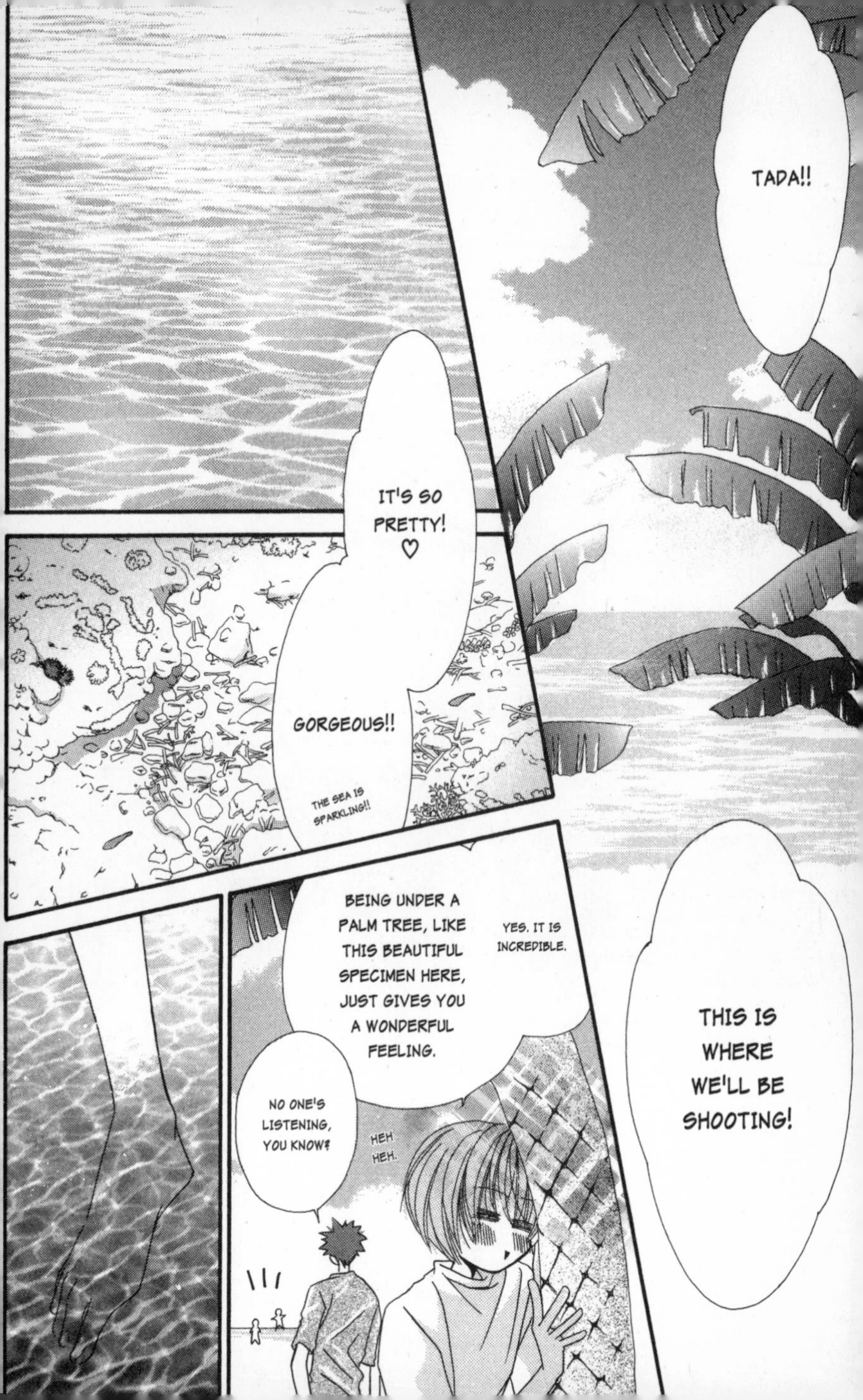
TADA!!
THIS IS WHERE WE'LL BE SHOOTING!
IT'S SO PRETTY! ♡
GORGEOUS!!
THE SEA IS SPARKLING!!
BEING UNDER A PALM TREE, LIKE THIS BEAUTIFUL SPECIMEN HERE, JUST GIVES YOU A WONDERFUL FEELING.
YES. IT IS INCREDIBLE.
HEH HEH.
NO ONE'S LISTENING, YOU KNOW?

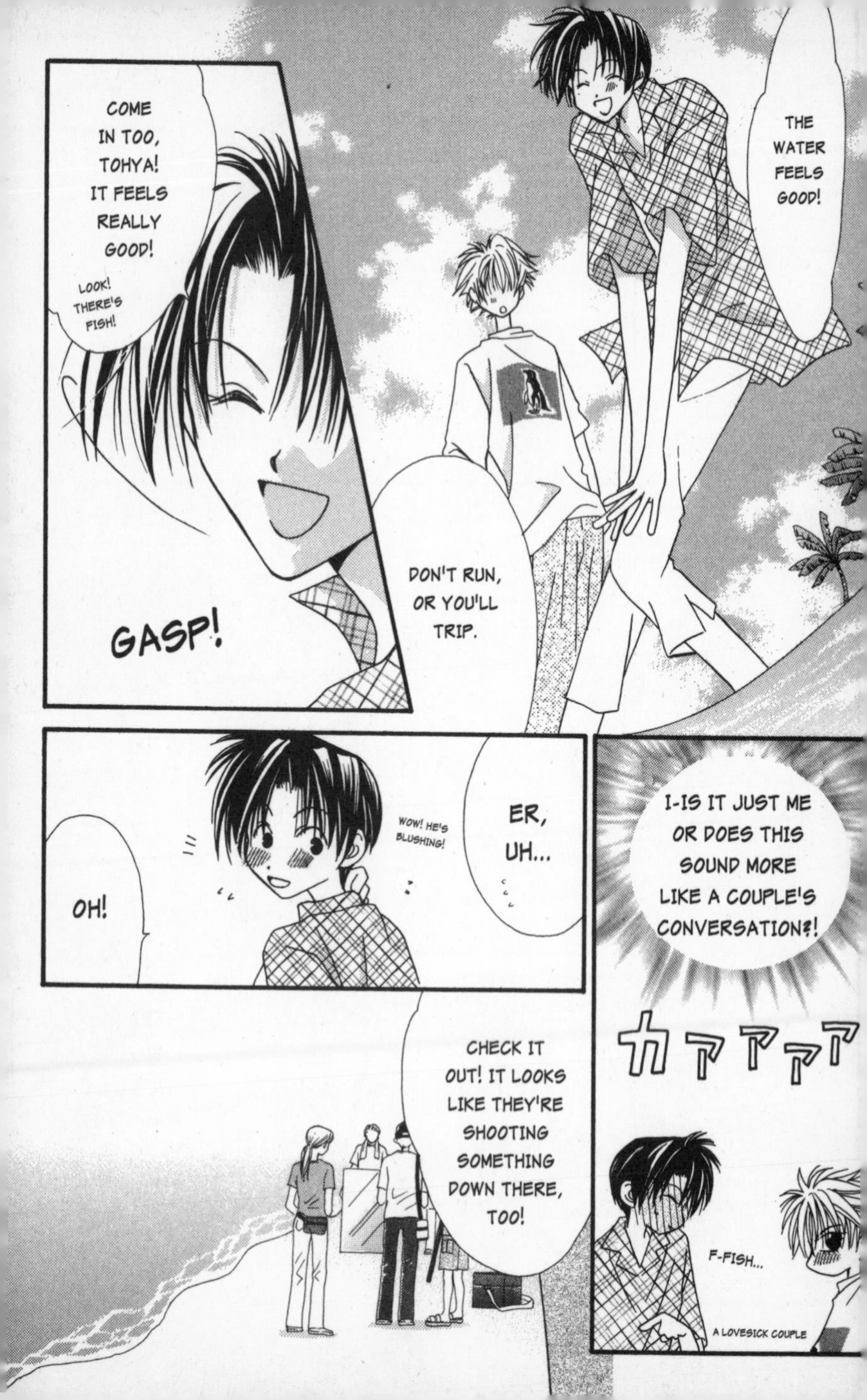
THE WATER FEELS GOOD!
COME IN TOO, TOHYA! IT FEELS REALLY GOOD!
LOOK! THERE'S FISH!
DON'T RUN, OR YOU'LL TRIP.
GASP!
I-IS IT JUST ME OR DOES THIS SOUND MORE LIKE A COUPLE'S CONVERSATION?!
カァァァア
F-FISH...
A LOVESICK COUPLE
ER, UH...
WOW! HE'S BLUSHING!
OH!
CHECK IT OUT! IT LOOKS LIKE THEY'RE SHOOTING SOMETHING DOWN THERE, TOO!

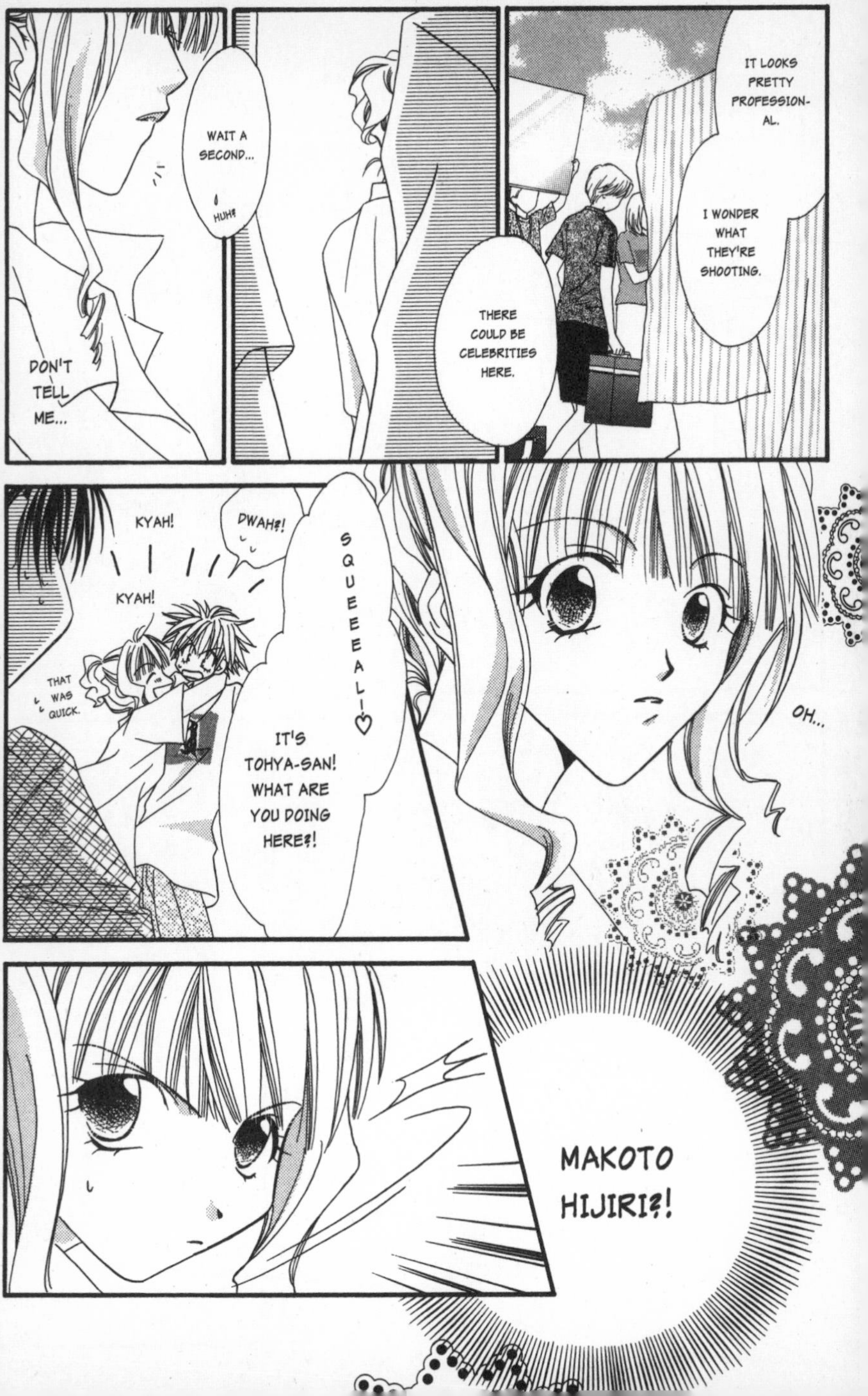
IT LOOKS PRETTY PROFESSION-AL.
I WONDER WHAT THEY'RE SHOOTING.
THERE COULD BE CELEBRITIES HERE.
WAIT A SECOND...
HUH?
DON'T TELL ME...
OH...
SQUEEEAL!♡
IT'S TOHYA-SAN! WHAT ARE YOU DOING HERE?!
DWAH?!
KYAH!
KYAH!
THAT WAS QUICK.
MAKOTO HIJIRI?!

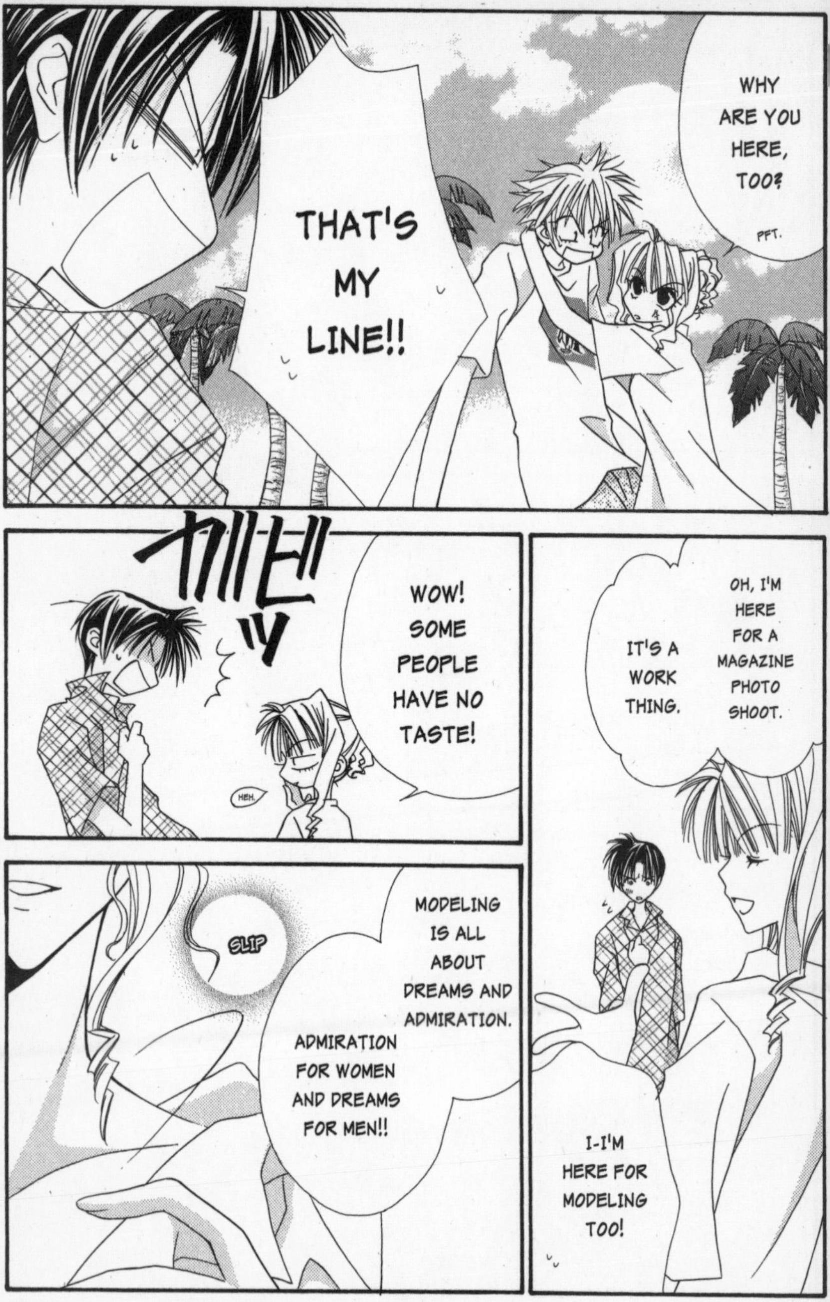
WHY ARE YOU HERE, TOO?
PFT.
THAT'S MY LINE!!
OH, I'M HERE FOR A MAGAZINE PHOTO SHOOT.
IT'S A WORK THING.
I-I'M HERE FOR MODELING TOO!
WOW! SOME PEOPLE HAVE NO TASTE!
HEH.
MODELING IS ALL ABOUT DREAMS AND ADMIRATION.
ADMIRATION FOR WOMEN AND DREAMS FOR MEN!!
SLIP

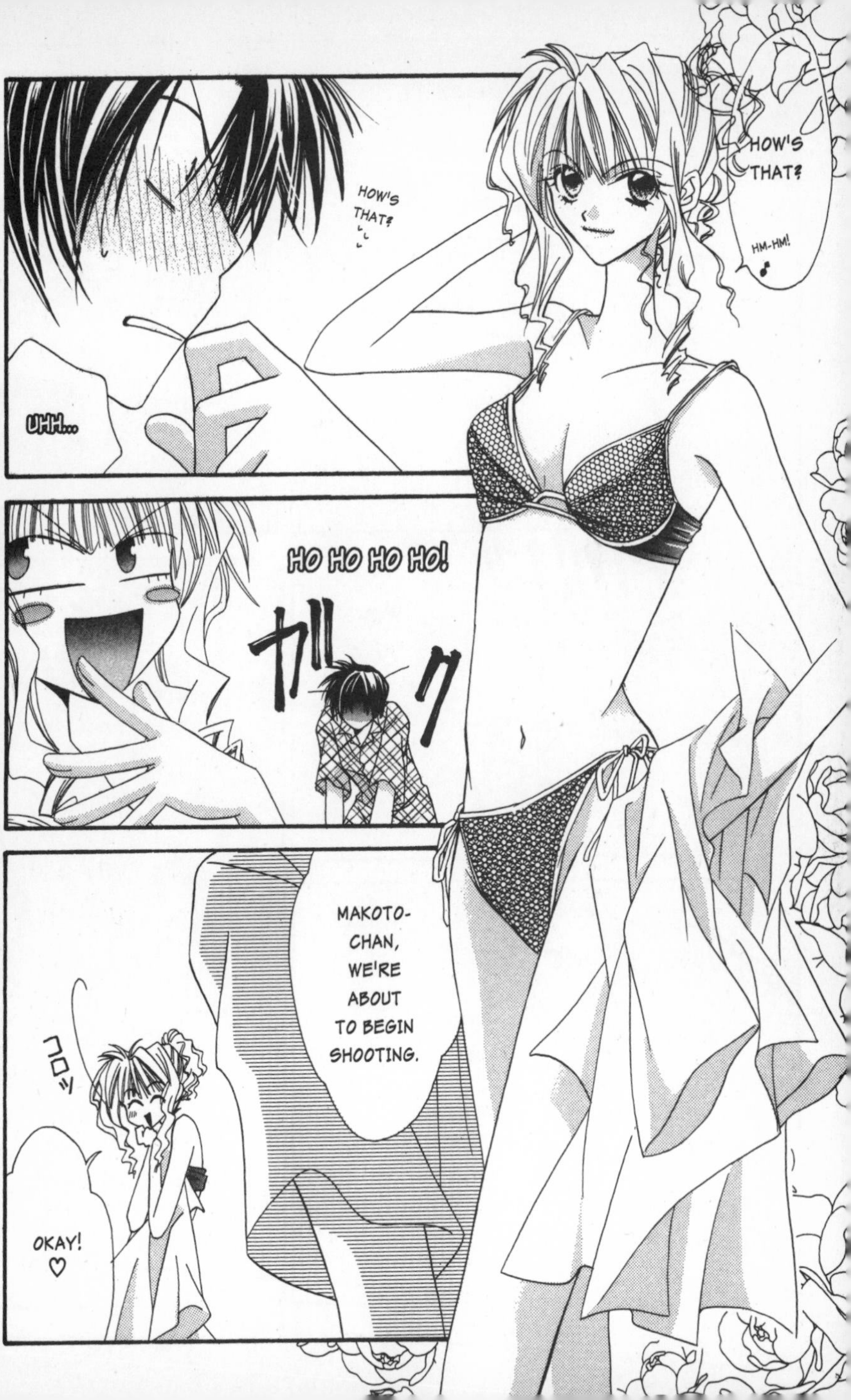
HOW'S THAT?
HM-HM!
HOW'S THAT?
UHH...
HO HO HO HO!
MAKOTO-CHAN, WE'RE ABOUT TO BEGIN SHOOTING.
コロッ
OKAY! ♡

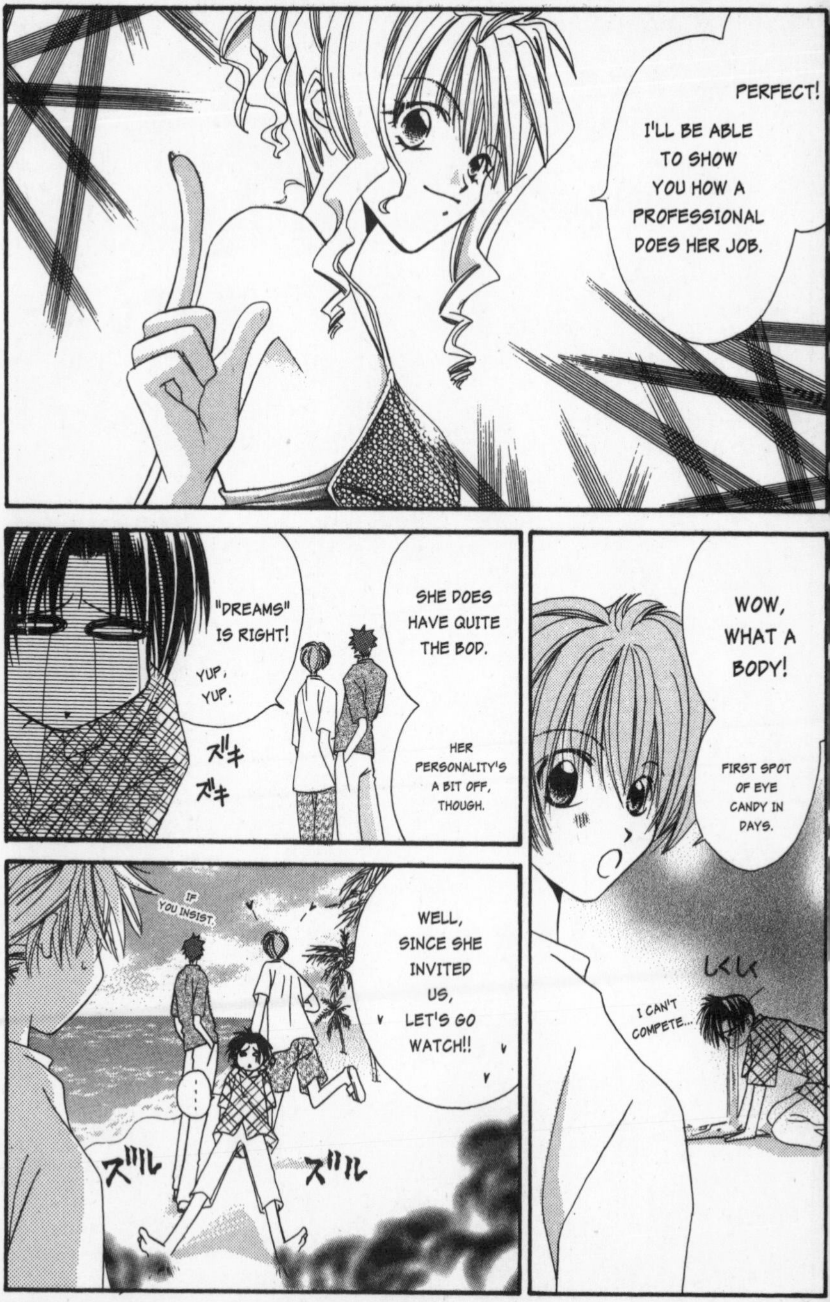
PERFECT!
I'LL BE ABLE TO SHOW YOU HOW A PROFESSIONAL DOES HER JOB.
WOW, WHAT A BODY!
FIRST SPOT OF EYE CANDY IN DAYS.
しくしく
I CAN'T COMPETE...
SHE DOES HAVE QUITE THE BOD.
HER PERSONALITY'S A BIT OFF, THOUGH.
"DREAMS" IS RIGHT!
YUP, YUP.
ズキ ズキ
WELL, SINCE SHE INVITED US, LET'S GO WATCH!!
IF YOU INSIST.
...
ズル ズル

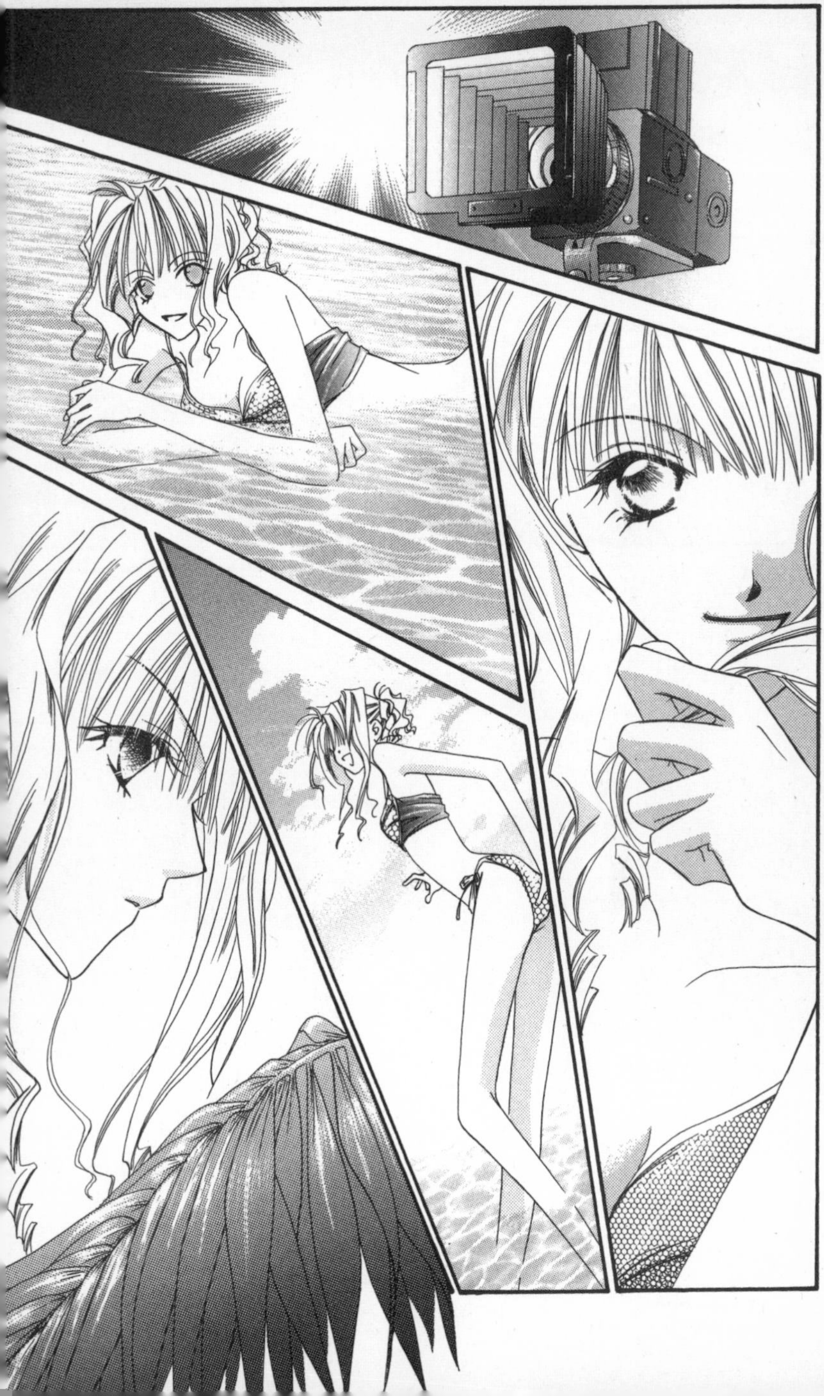

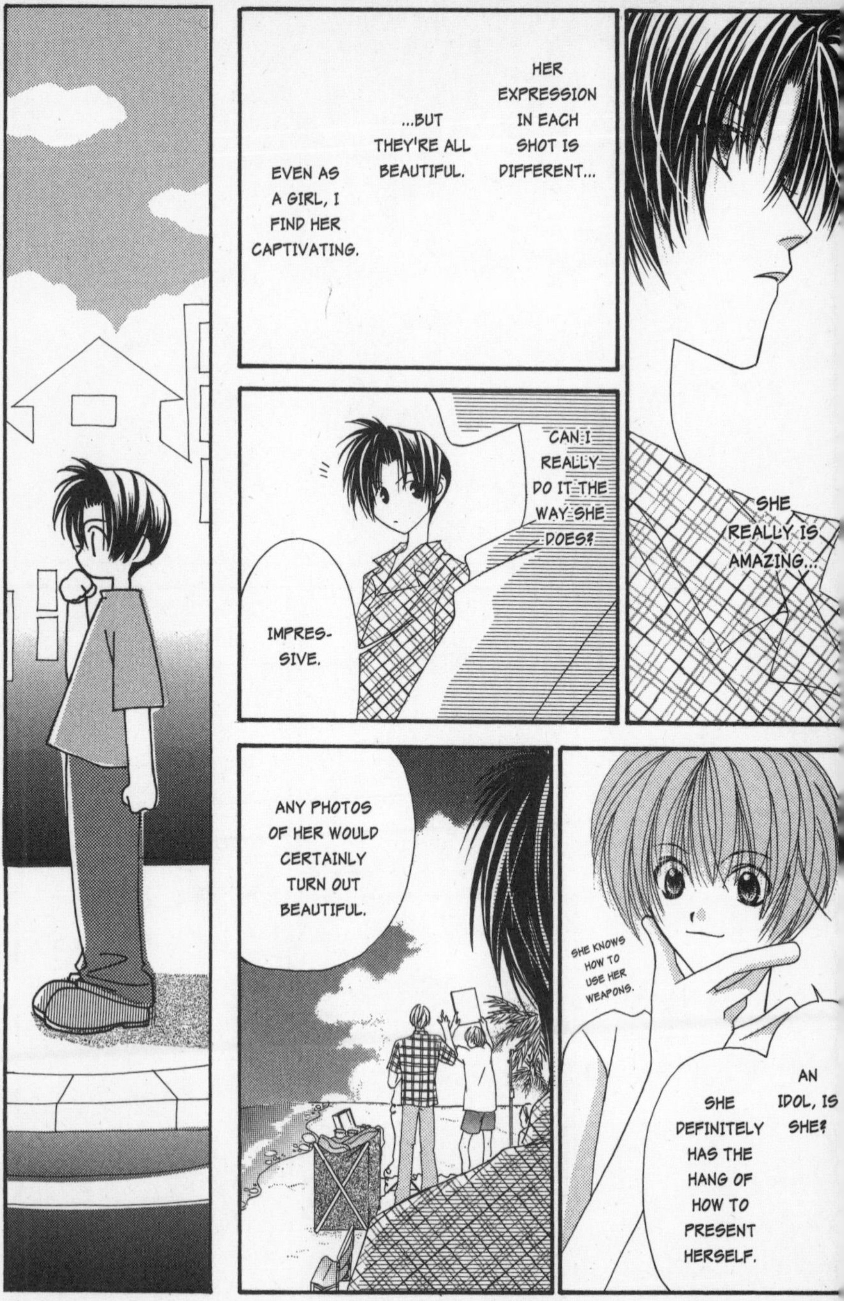
SHE REALLY IS AMAZING...
HER EXPRESSION IN EACH SHOT IS DIFFERENT...
...BUT THEY'RE ALL BEAUTIFUL.
EVEN AS A GIRL, I FIND HER CAPTIVATING.
CAN I REALLY DO IT THE WAY SHE DOES?
IMPRESSIVE.
AN IDOL, IS SHE?
SHE DEFINITELY HAS THE HANG OF HOW TO PRESENT HERSELF.
SHE KNOWS HOW TO USE HER WEAPONS.
ANY PHOTOS OF HER WOULD CERTAINLY TURN OUT BEAUTIFUL.

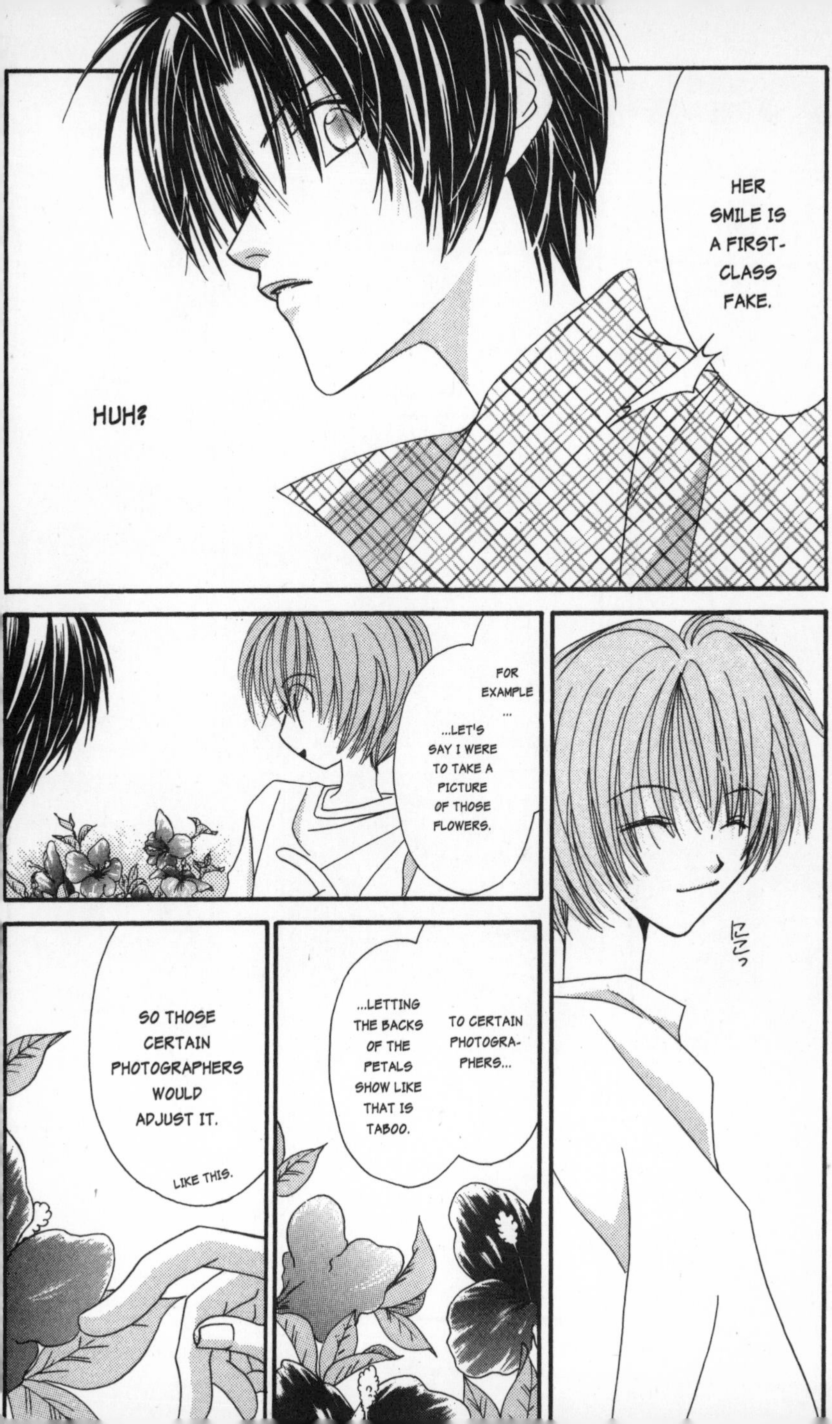
HER SMILE IS A FIRST-CLASS FAKE.
HUH?
にこっ
FOR EXAMPLE ...
...LET'S SAY I WERE TO TAKE A PICTURE OF THOSE FLOWERS.
TO CERTAIN PHOTOGRAPHERS...
...LETTING THE BACKS OF THE PETALS SHOW LIKE THAT IS TABOO.
SO THOSE CERTAIN PHOTOGRAPHERS WOULD ADJUST IT.
LIKE THIS.

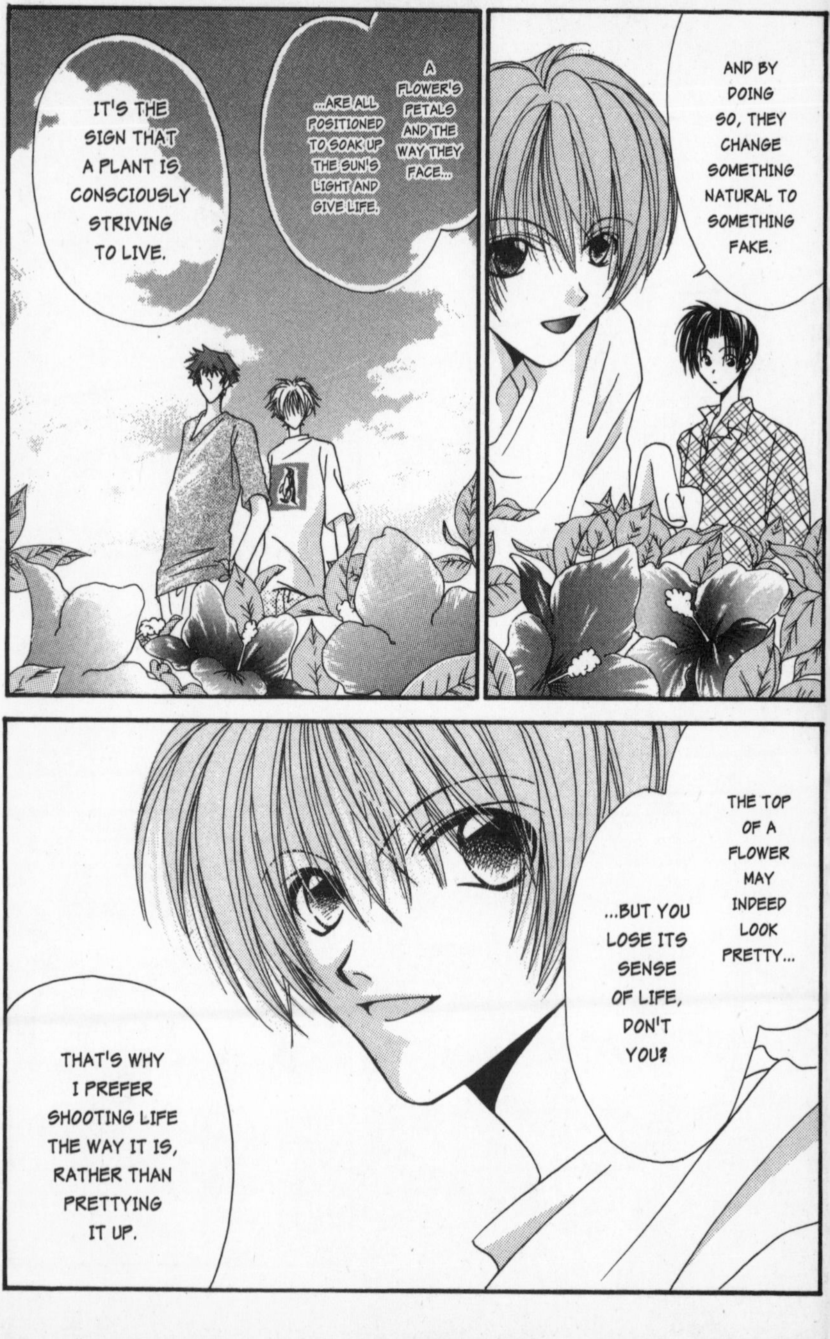
AND BY DOING SO, THEY CHANGE SOMETHING NATURAL TO SOMETHING FAKE.
A FLOWER'S PETALS AND THE WAY THEY FACE...
...ARE ALL POSITIONED TO SOAK UP THE SUN'S LIGHT AND GIVE LIFE.
IT'S THE SIGN THAT A PLANT IS CONSCIOUSLY STRIVING TO LIVE.
THE TOP OF A FLOWER MAY INDEED LOOK PRETTY...
...BUT YOU LOSE ITS SENSE OF LIFE, DON'T YOU?
THAT'S WHY I PREFER SHOOTING LIFE THE WAY IT IS, RATHER THAN PRETTYING IT UP.

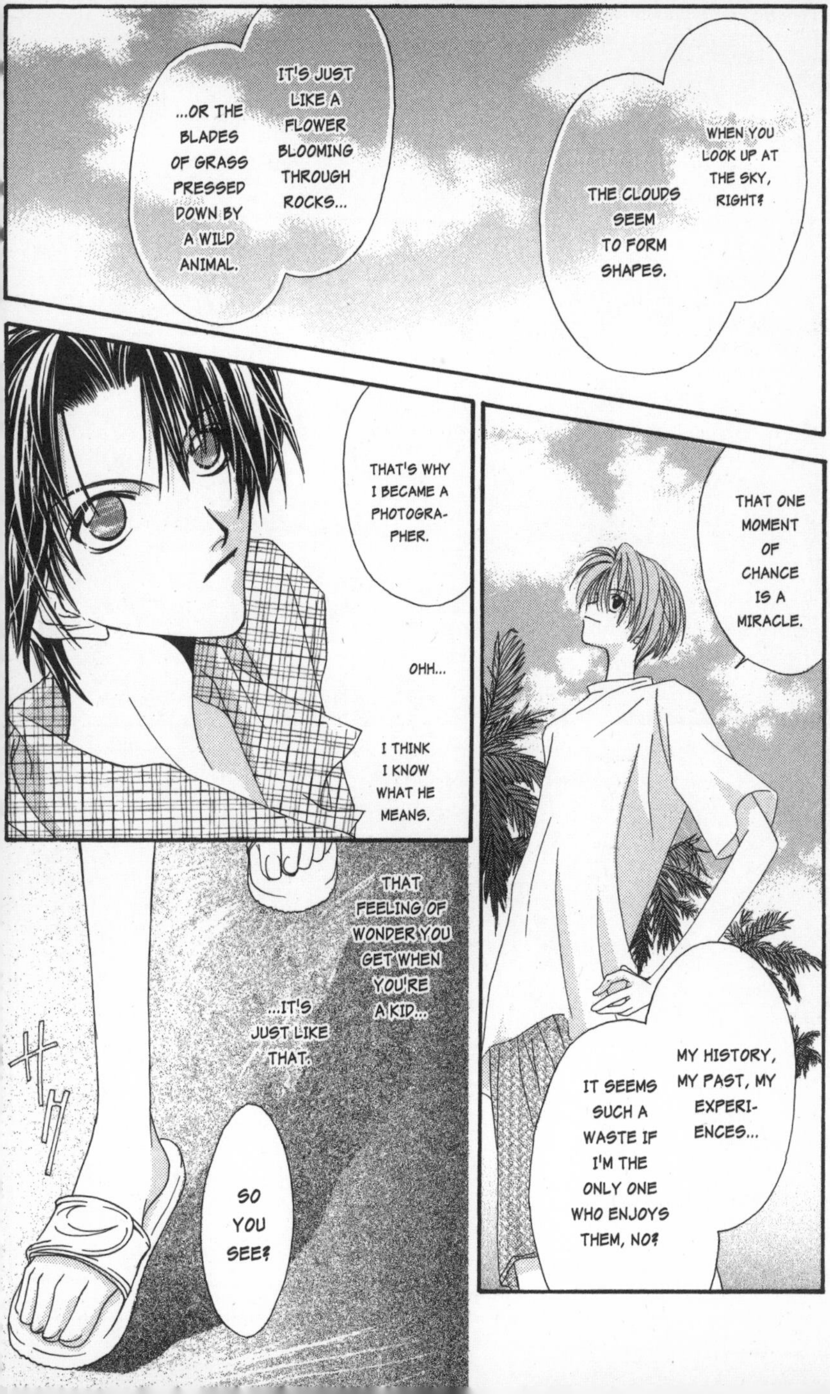
WHEN YOU LOOK UP AT THE SKY, RIGHT?
THE CLOUDS SEEM TO FORM SHAPES.
IT'S JUST LIKE A FLOWER BLOOMING THROUGH ROCKS...
...OR THE BLADES OF GRASS PRESSED DOWN BY A WILD ANIMAL.
THAT ONE MOMENT OF CHANCE IS A MIRACLE.
MY HISTORY, MY PAST, MY EXPERI-ENCES...
IT SEEMS SUCH A WASTE IF I'M THE ONLY ONE WHO ENJOYS THEM, NO?
THAT'S WHY I BECAME A PHOTOGRA-PHER.
OHH...
I THINK I KNOW WHAT HE MEANS.
THAT FEELING OF WONDER YOU GET WHEN YOU'RE A KID...
...IT'S JUST LIKE THAT.
SO YOU SEE?

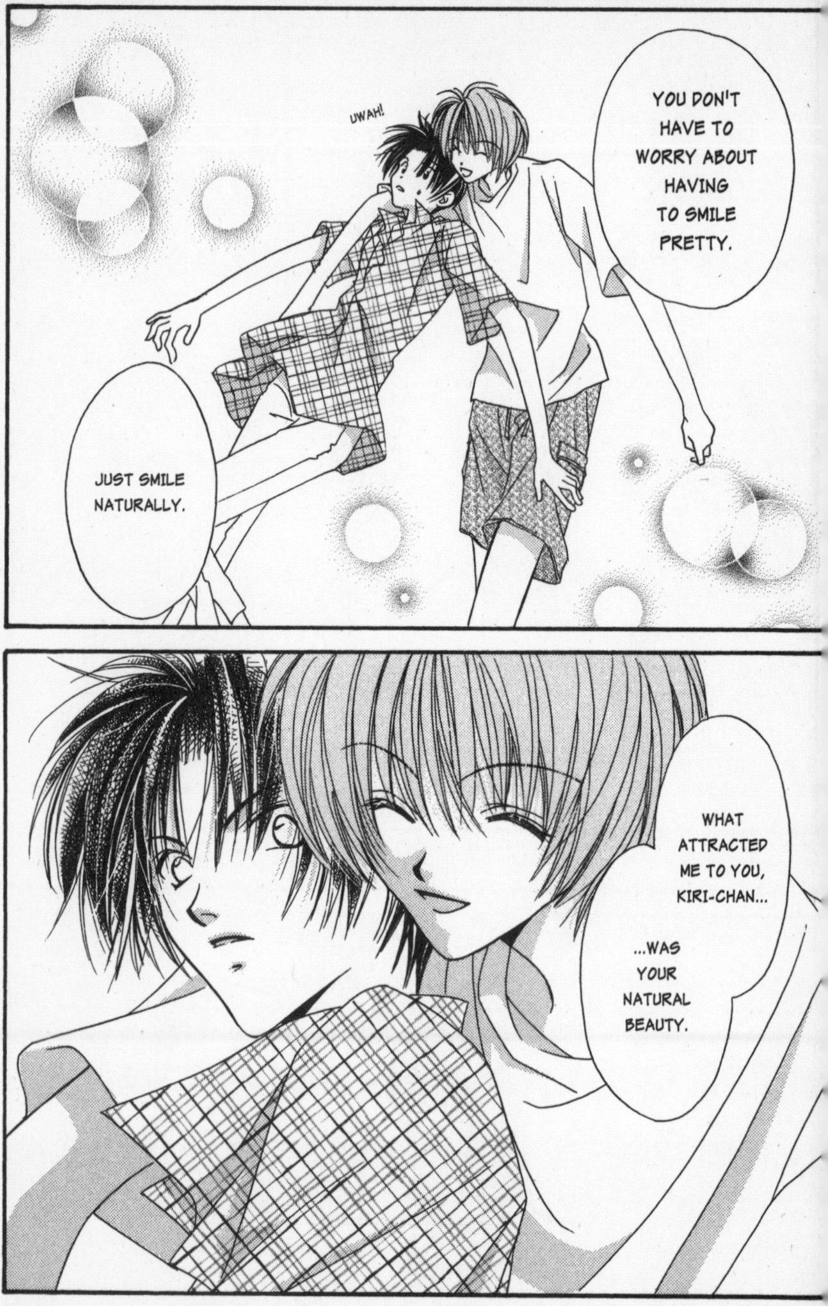
YOU DON'T HAVE TO WORRY ABOUT HAVING TO SMILE PRETTY.
UWAH!
JUST SMILE NATURALLY.
WHAT ATTRACTED ME TO YOU, KIRI-CHAN...
...WAS YOUR NATURAL BEAUTY.

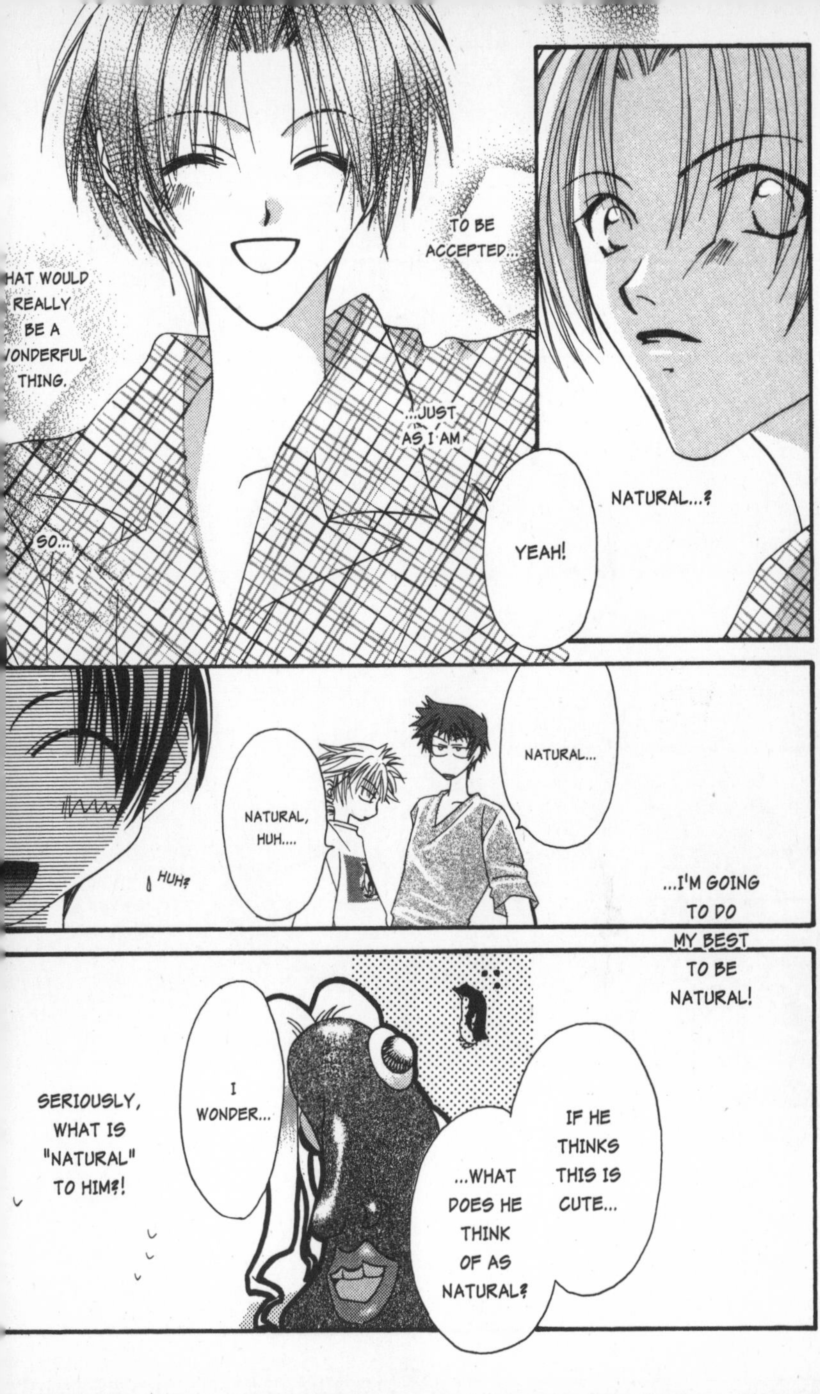
NATURAL...?
YEAH!
TO BE ACCEPTED...
...JUST AS I AM
HAT WOULD REALLY BE A WONDERFUL THING.
SO...
...I'M GOING TO DO MY BEST TO BE NATURAL!
NATURAL...
NATURAL, HUH....
HUH?
IF HE THINKS THIS IS CUTE...
...WHAT DOES HE THINK OF AS NATURAL?
I WONDER...
SERIOUSLY, WHAT IS "NATURAL" TO HIM?!

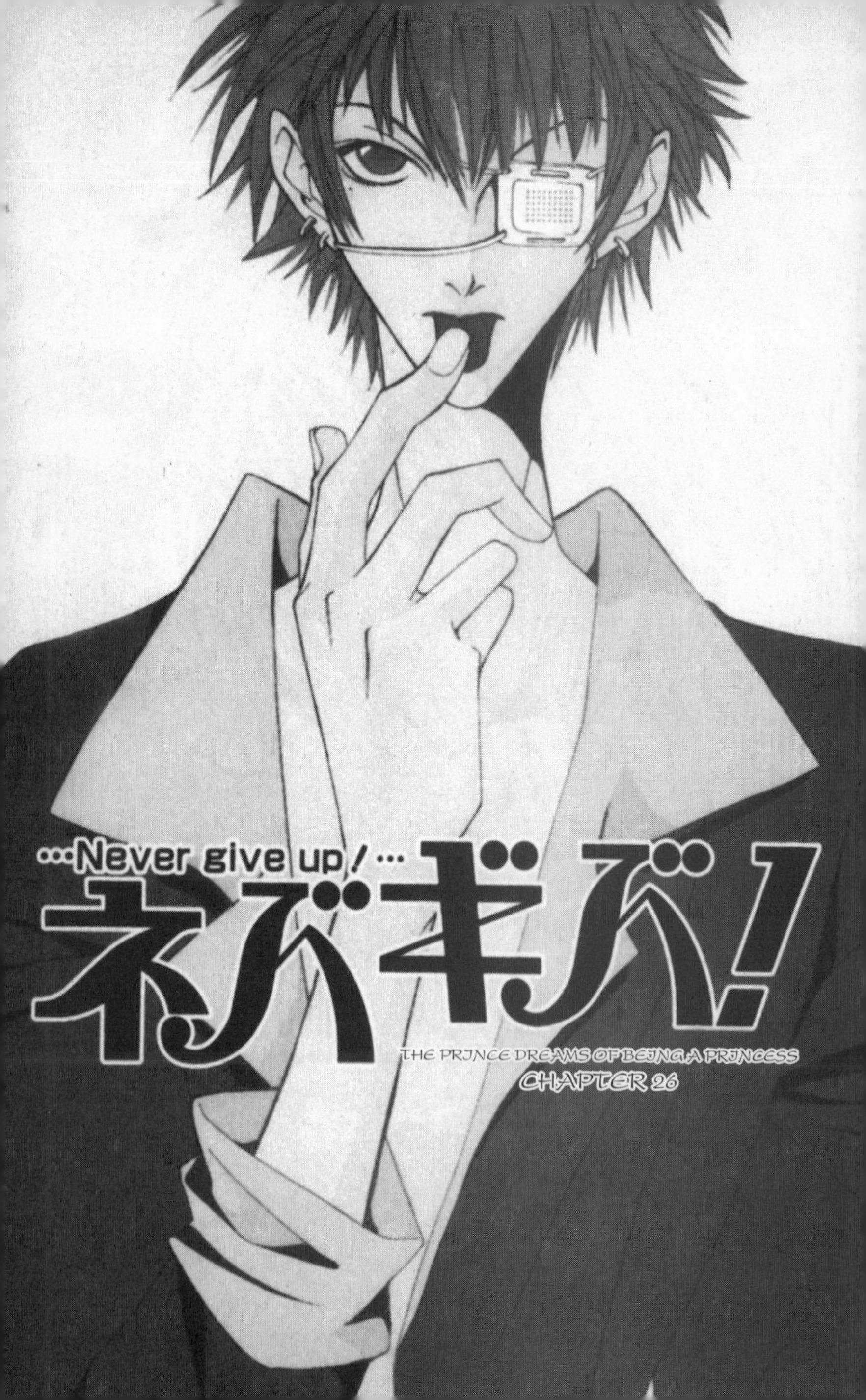
…Never give up!…
ネバギバ!
THE PRINCE DREAMS OF BEING A PRINCESS
CHAPTER 26

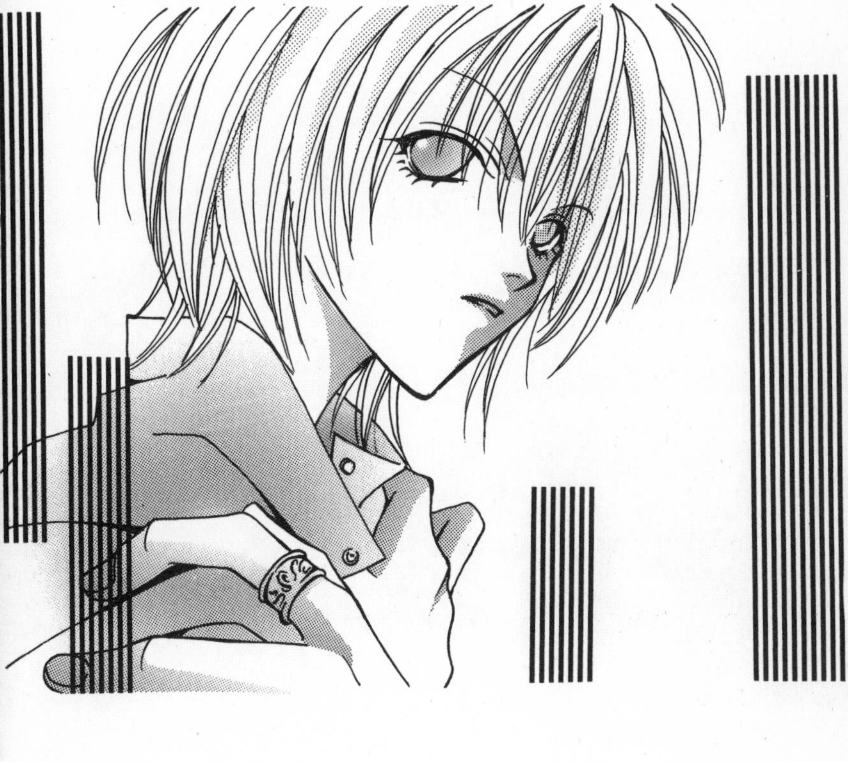

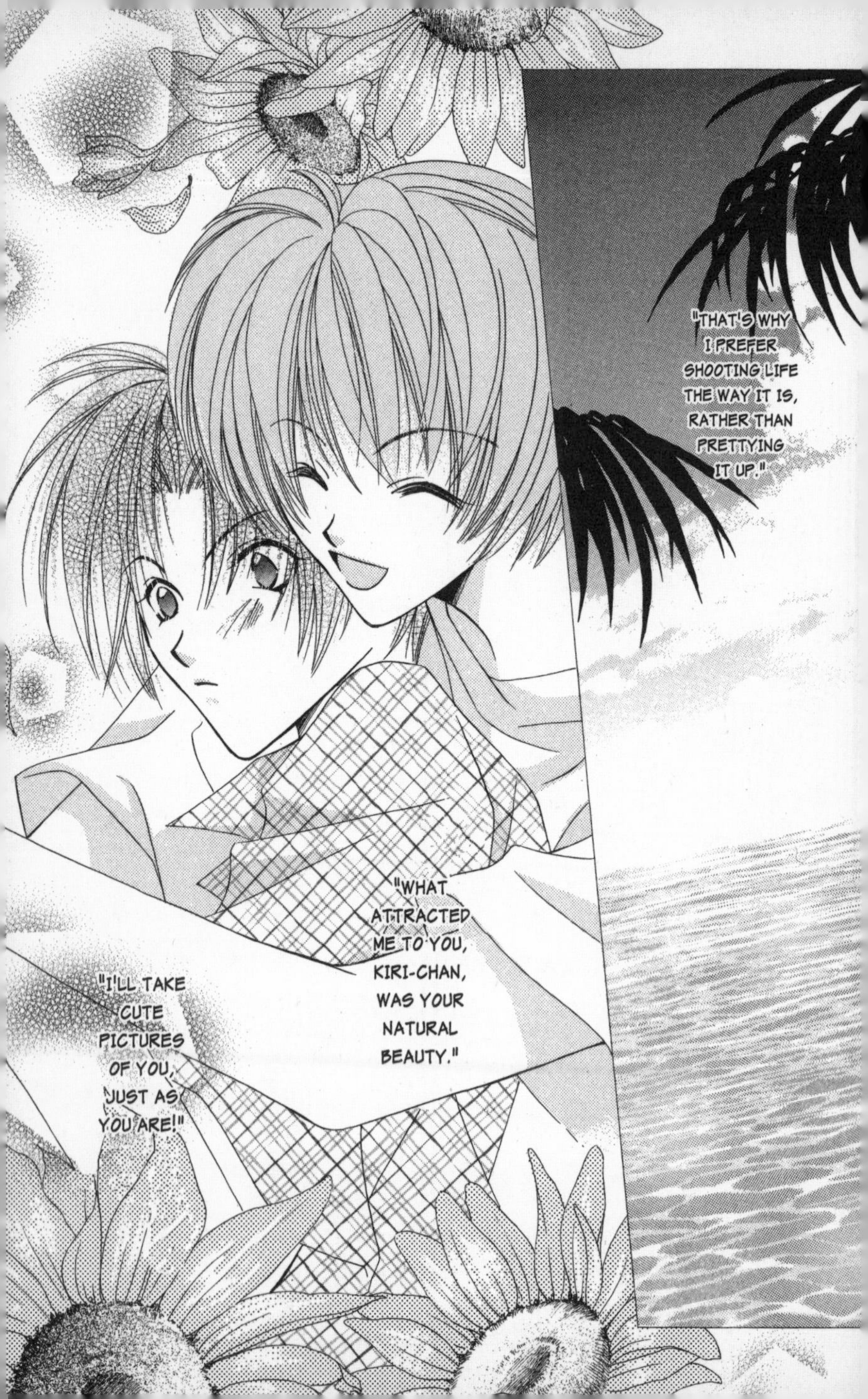
"THAT'S WHY I PREFER SHOOTING LIFE THE WAY IT IS, RATHER THAN PRETTYING IT UP."
"WHAT ATTRACTED ME TO YOU, KIRI-CHAN, WAS YOUR NATURAL BEAUTY."
"I'LL TAKE CUTE PICTURES OF YOU, JUST AS YOU ARE!"

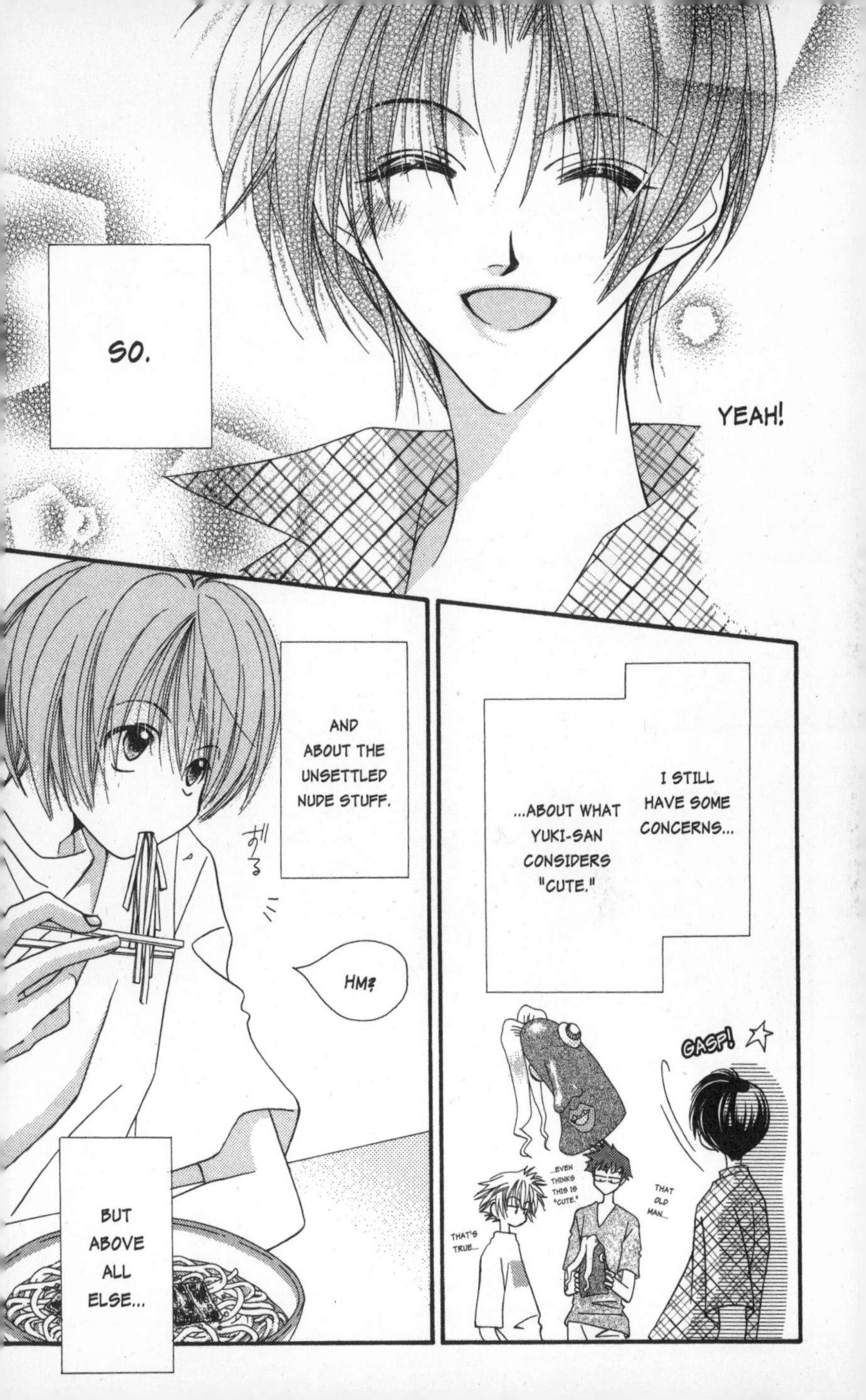
YEAH!
SO.
I STILL HAVE SOME CONCERNS...
...ABOUT WHAT YUKI-SAN CONSIDERS "CUTE."
GASP!
THAT OLD MAN...
...EVEN THINKS THIS IS "CUTE."
THAT'S TRUE...
AND ABOUT THE UNSETTLED NUDE STUFF.
ずる
HM?
BUT ABOVE ALL ELSE...

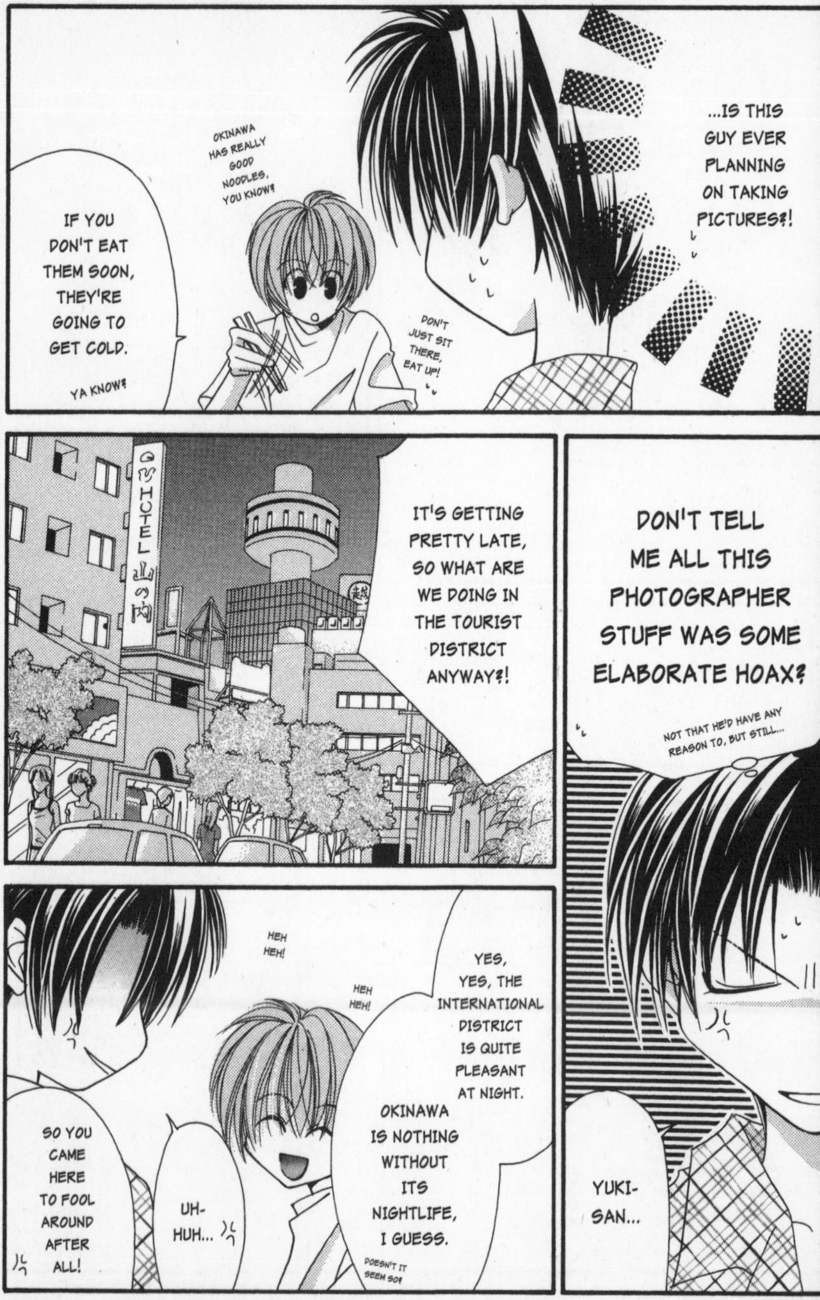
...IS THIS GUY EVER PLANNING ON TAKING PICTURES?!
DON'T JUST SIT THERE, EAT UP!
OKINAWA HAS REALLY GOOD NOODLES, YOU KNOW?
IF YOU DON'T EAT THEM SOON, THEY'RE GOING TO GET COLD.
YA KNOW?
DON'T TELL ME ALL THIS PHOTOGRAPHER STUFF WAS SOME ELABORATE HOAX?
NOT THAT HE'D HAVE ANY REASON TO, BUT STILL...
YUKI-SAN...
HOTEL
IT'S GETTING PRETTY LATE, SO WHAT ARE WE DOING IN THE TOURIST DISTRICT ANYWAY?!
YES, YES, THE INTERNATIONAL DISTRICT IS QUITE PLEASANT AT NIGHT.
HEH HEH!
HEH HEH!
OKINAWA IS NOTHING WITHOUT ITS NIGHTLIFE, I GUESS.
DOESN'T IT SEEM SO?
UH-HUH...
SO YOU CAME HERE TO FOOL AROUND AFTER ALL!

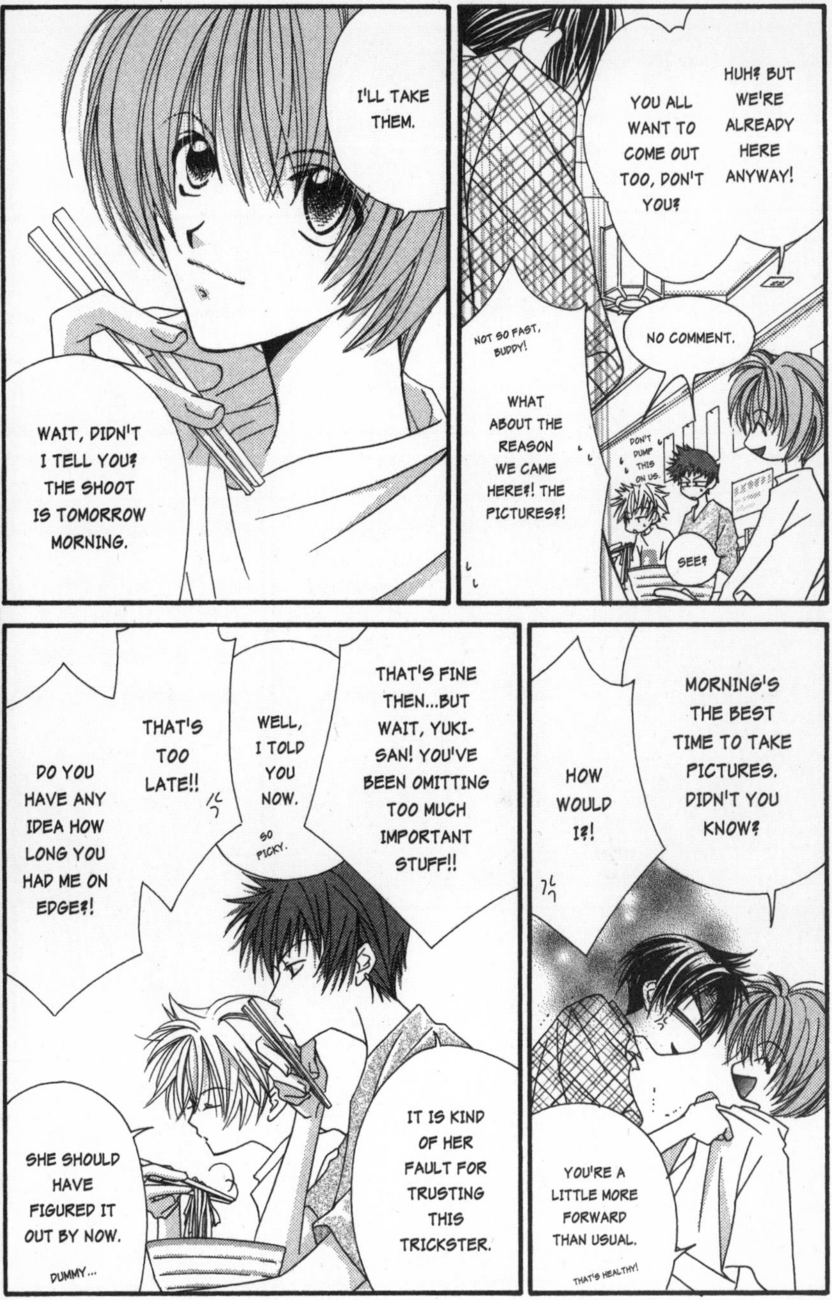
HUH? BUT WE'RE ALREADY HERE ANYWAY!
YOU ALL WANT TO COME OUT TOO, DON'T YOU?
NO COMMENT.
NOT SO FAST, BUDDY!
WHAT ABOUT THE REASON WE CAME HERE?! THE PICTURES?!
DON'T DUMP THIS ON US.
SEE?
I'LL TAKE THEM.
WAIT, DIDN'T I TELL YOU? THE SHOOT IS TOMORROW MORNING.
MORNING'S THE BEST TIME TO TAKE PICTURES. DIDN'T YOU KNOW?
HOW WOULD I?!
YOU'RE A LITTLE MORE FORWARD THAN USUAL.
THAT'S HEALTHY!
THAT'S FINE THEN...BUT WAIT, YUKI-SAN! YOU'VE BEEN OMITTING TOO MUCH IMPORTANT STUFF!!
WELL, I TOLD YOU NOW.
SO PICKY.
THAT'S TOO LATE!!
DO YOU HAVE ANY IDEA HOW LONG YOU HAD ME ON EDGE?!
IT IS KIND OF HER FAULT FOR TRUSTING THIS TRICKSTER.
SHE SHOULD HAVE FIGURED IT OUT BY NOW.
DUMMY...

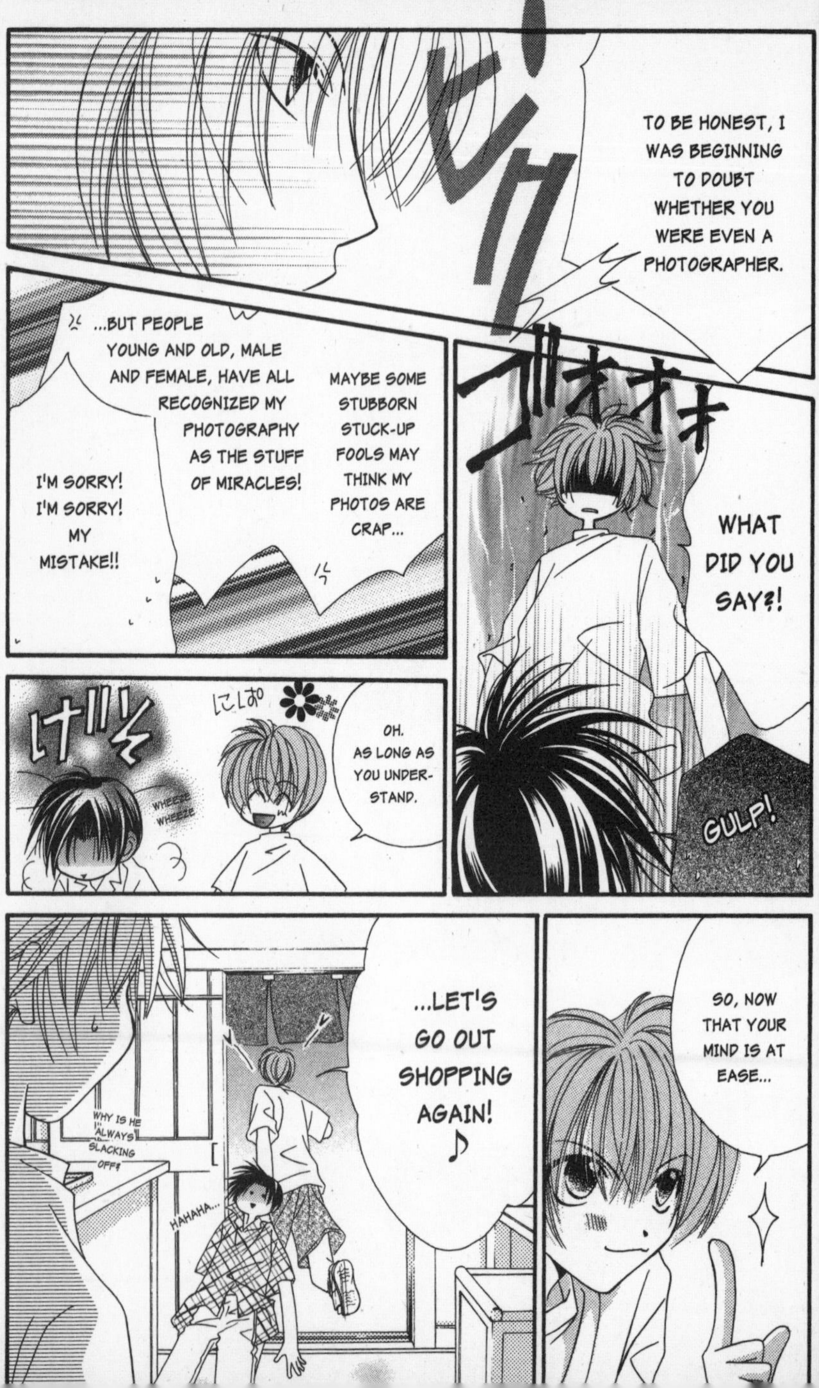
TO BE HONEST, I WAS BEGINNING TO DOUBT WHETHER YOU WERE EVEN A PHOTOGRAPHER.
WHAT DID YOU SAY?!
GULP!
MAYBE SOME STUBBORN STUCK-UP FOOLS MAY THINK MY PHOTOS ARE CRAP...
...BUT PEOPLE YOUNG AND OLD, MALE AND FEMALE, HAVE ALL RECOGNIZED MY PHOTOGRAPHY AS THE STUFF OF MIRACLES!
I'M SORRY! I'M SORRY! MY MISTAKE!!
OH. AS LONG AS YOU UNDER-STAND.
WHEEZE WHEEZE
SO, NOW THAT YOUR MIND IS AT EASE...
...LET'S GO OUT SHOPPING AGAIN! ♪
WHY IS HE ALWAYS SLACKING OFF?
HAHAHA...

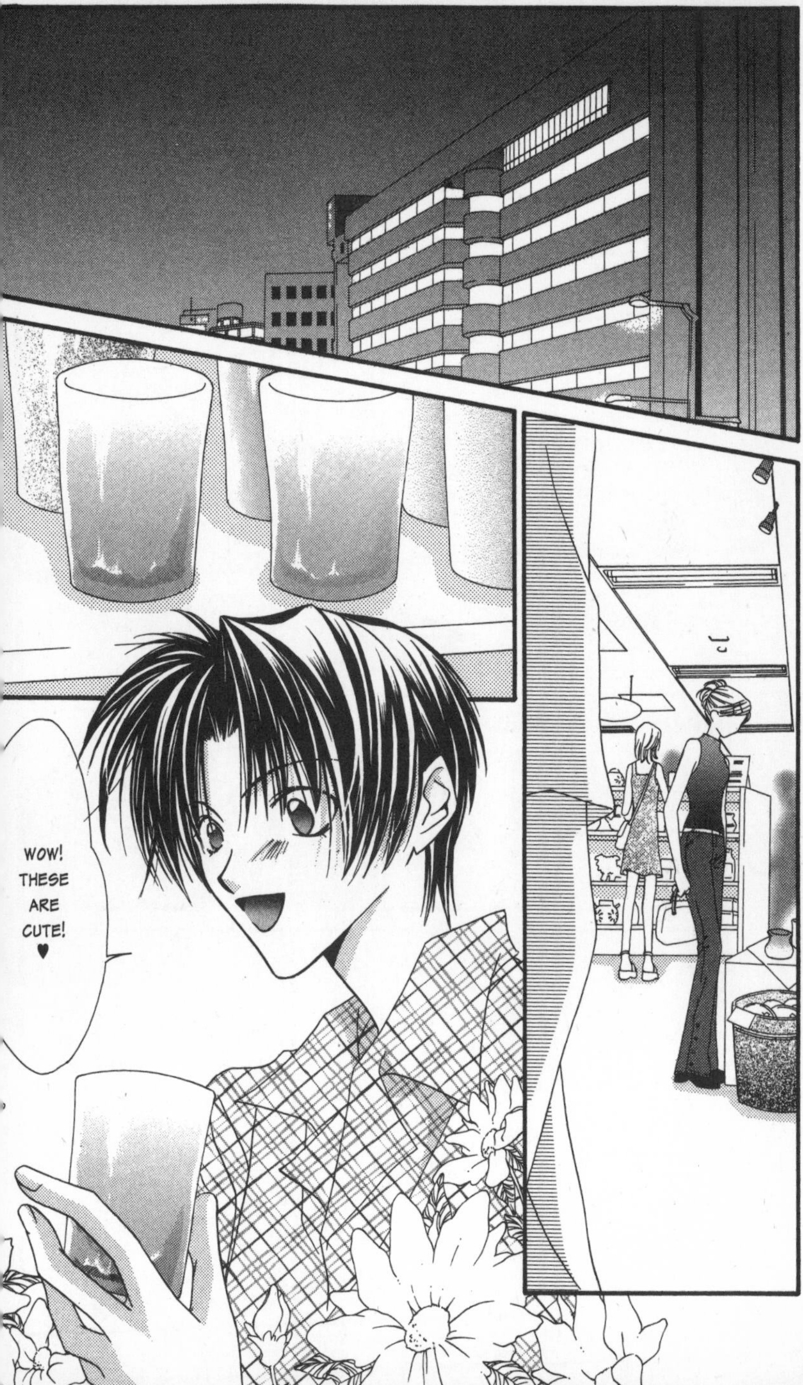
WOW! THESE ARE CUTE! ♥

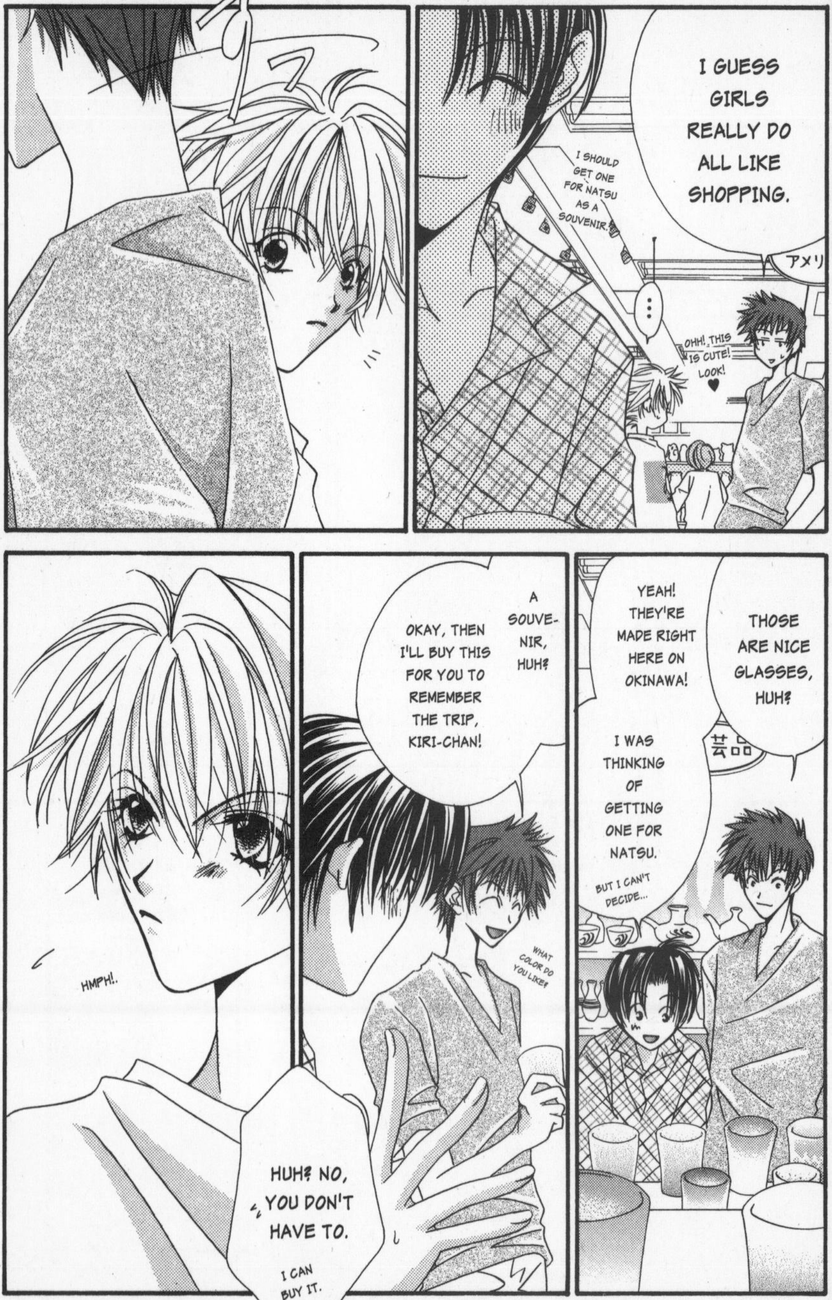
I GUESS GIRLS REALLY DO ALL LIKE SHOPPING.
アメリ
I SHOULD GET ONE FOR NATSU AS A SOUVENIR.
...
OHH! THIS IS CUTE! LOOK! ♥
THOSE ARE NICE GLASSES, HUH?
YEAH! THEY'RE MADE RIGHT HERE ON OKINAWA!
芸品
I WAS THINKING OF GETTING ONE FOR NATSU.
BUT I CAN'T DECIDE...
A SOUVENIR, HUH?
OKAY, THEN I'LL BUY THIS FOR YOU TO REMEMBER THE TRIP, KIRI-CHAN!
WHAT COLOR DO YOU LIKE?
HUH? NO, YOU DON'T HAVE TO.
I CAN BUY IT.
HMPH!.

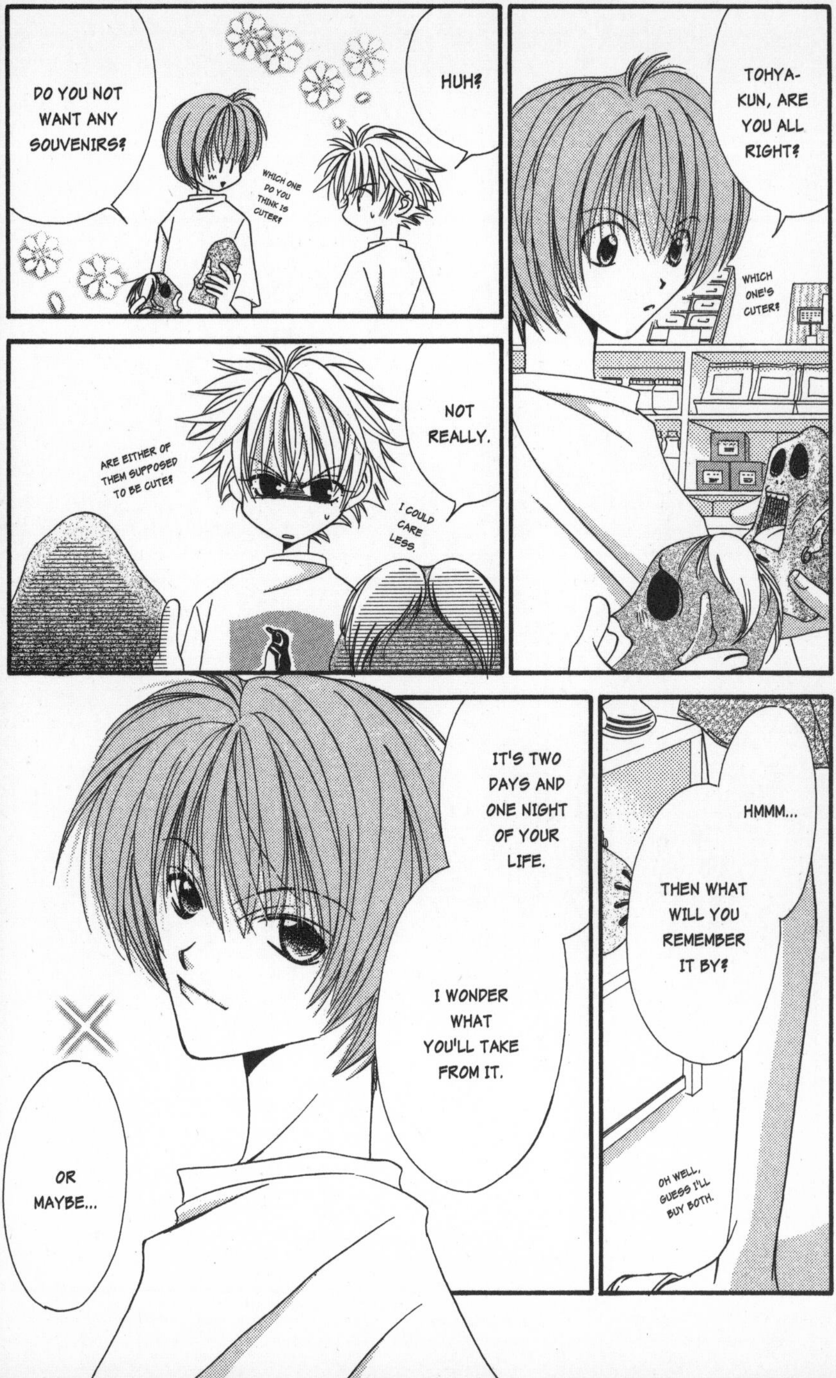
TOHYA-KUN, ARE YOU ALL RIGHT?
WHICH ONE'S CUTER?
HUH?
WHICH ONE DO YOU THINK IS CUTER?
DO YOU NOT WANT ANY SOUVENIRS?
NOT REALLY.
I COULD CARE LESS.
ARE EITHER OF THEM SUPPOSED TO BE CUTE?
HMMM...
THEN WHAT WILL YOU REMEMBER IT BY?
OH WELL, GUESS I'LL BUY BOTH.
IT'S TWO DAYS AND ONE NIGHT OF YOUR LIFE.
I WONDER WHAT YOU'LL TAKE FROM IT.
OR MAYBE...

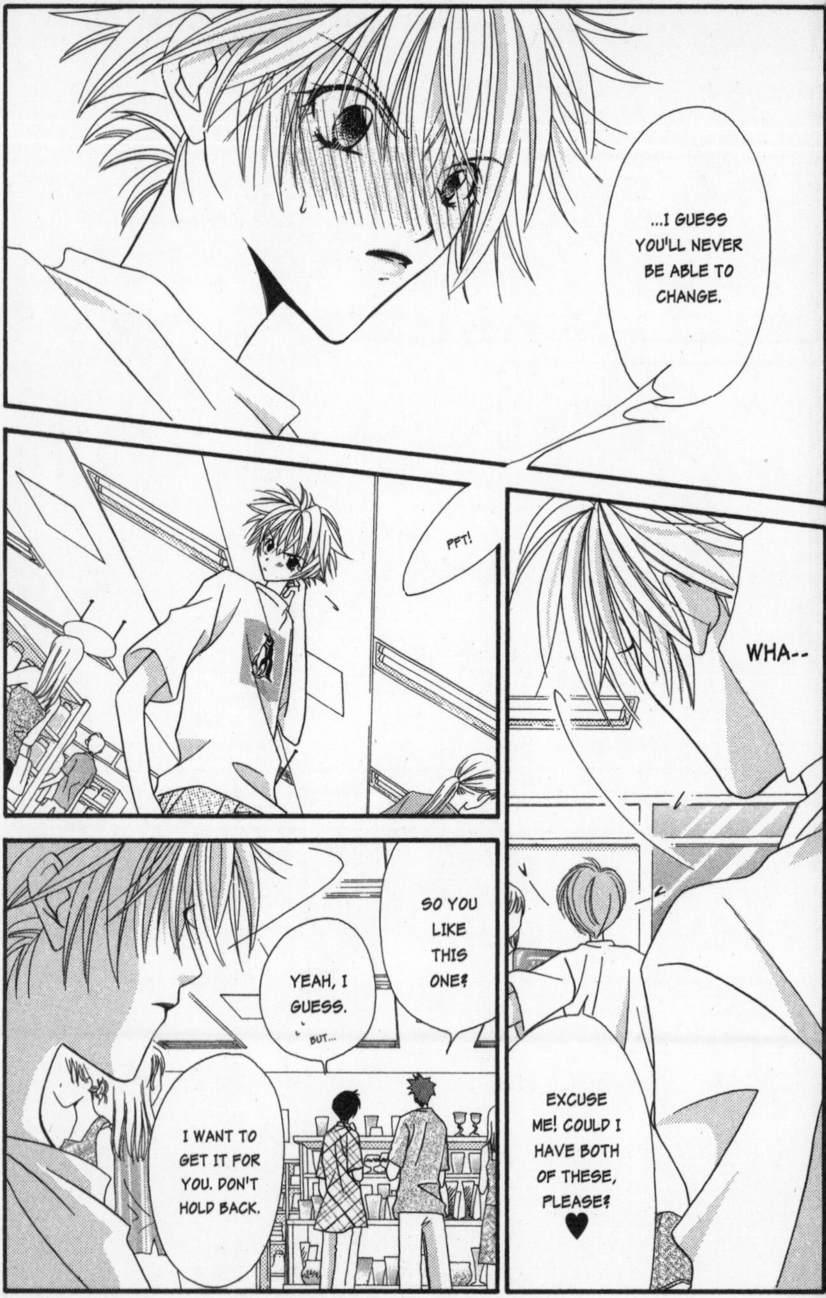
...I GUESS YOU'LL NEVER BE ABLE TO CHANGE.
WHA--
EXCUSE ME! COULD I HAVE BOTH OF THESE, PLEASE? ♥
PFT!
SO YOU LIKE THIS ONE?
YEAH, I GUESS.
BUT...
I WANT TO GET IT FOR YOU. DON'T HOLD BACK.

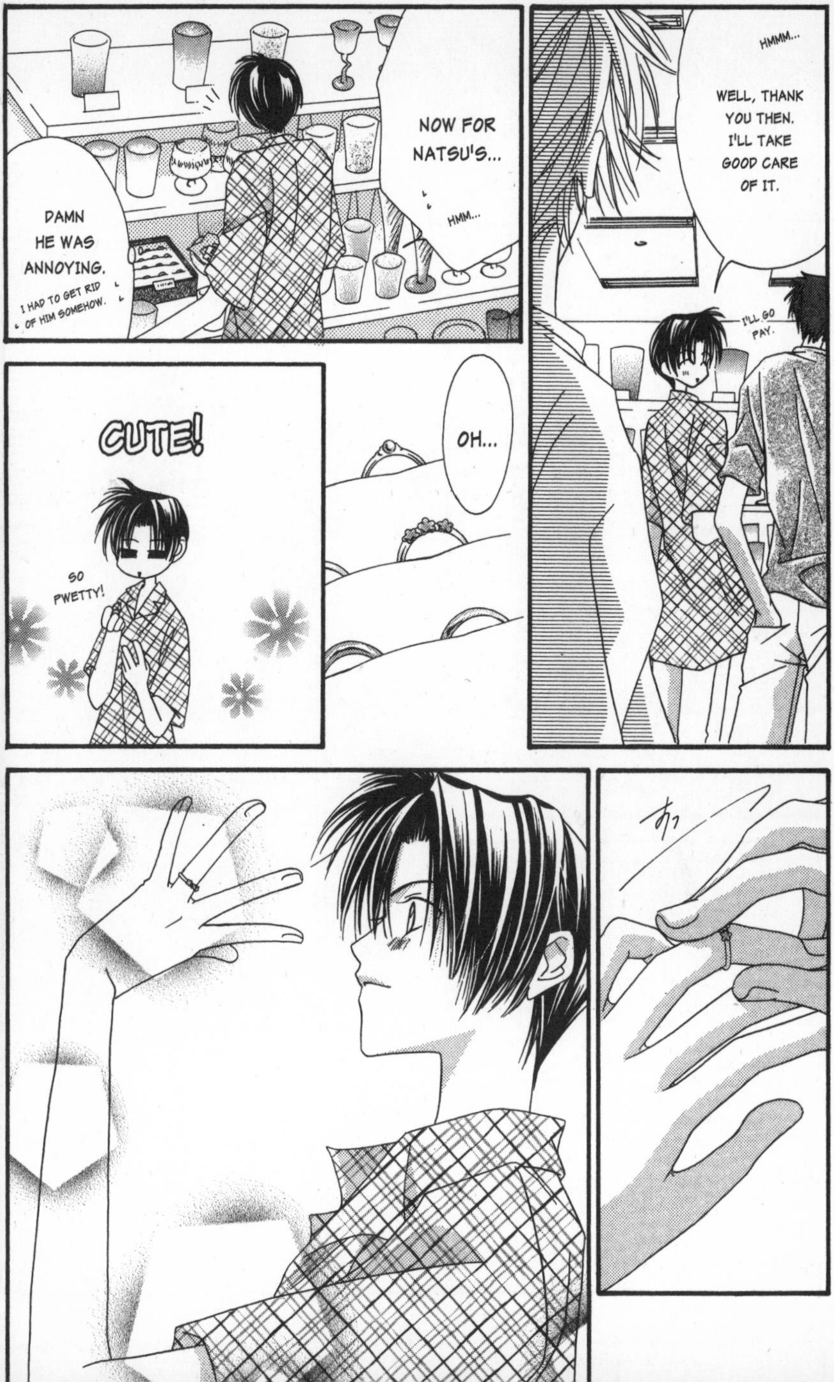
HMMM...
WELL, THANK YOU THEN. I'LL TAKE GOOD CARE OF IT.
I'LL GO PAY.
NOW FOR NATSU'S...
HMM...
DAMN HE WAS ANNOYING.
I HAD TO GET RID OF HIM SOMEHOW.
OH...
CUTE!
SO PWETTY!
あっ

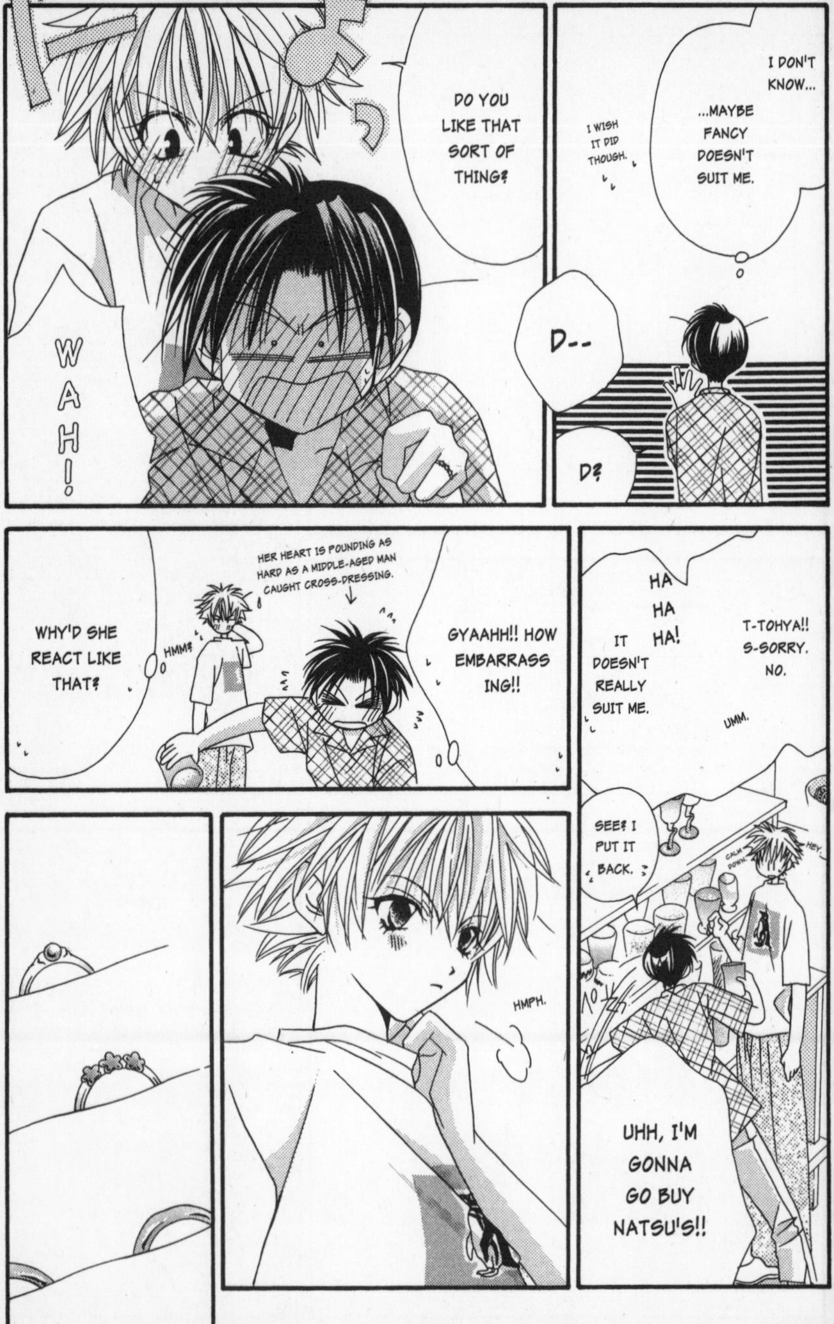
DO YOU LIKE THAT SORT OF THING?
WAH!
I DON'T KNOW...
...MAYBE FANCY DOESN'T SUIT ME.
I WISH IT DID THOUGH.
D--
D?
HER HEART IS POUNDING AS HARD AS A MIDDLE-AGED MAN CAUGHT CROSS-DRESSING.
WHY'D SHE REACT LIKE THAT?
HMM?
GYAAHH!! HOW EMBARRASS ING!!
HMPH.
HA HA HA!
IT DOESN'T REALLY SUIT ME.
T-TOHYA!! S-SORRY. NO.
UMM.
SEE? I PUT IT BACK.
CALM DOWN.
HEY.
UHH, I'M GONNA GO BUY NATSU'S!!

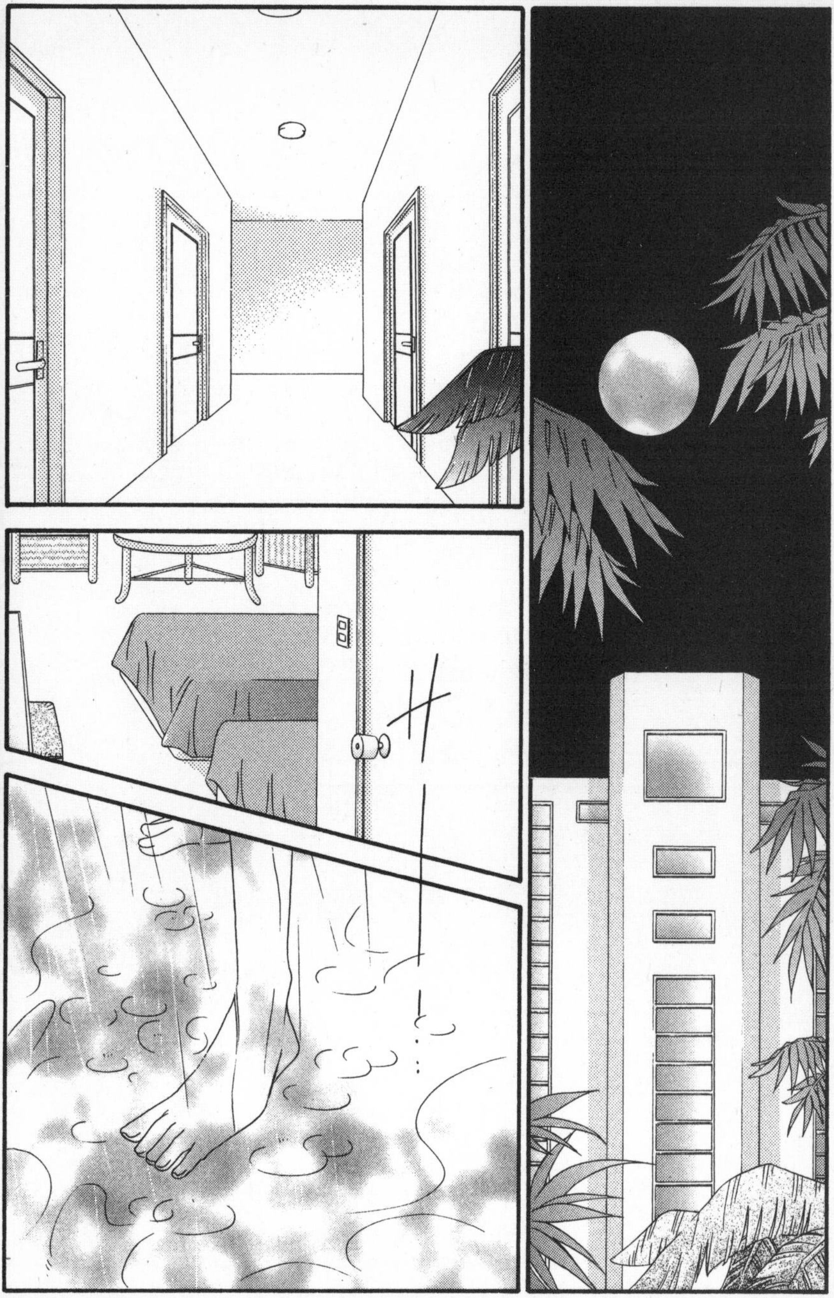

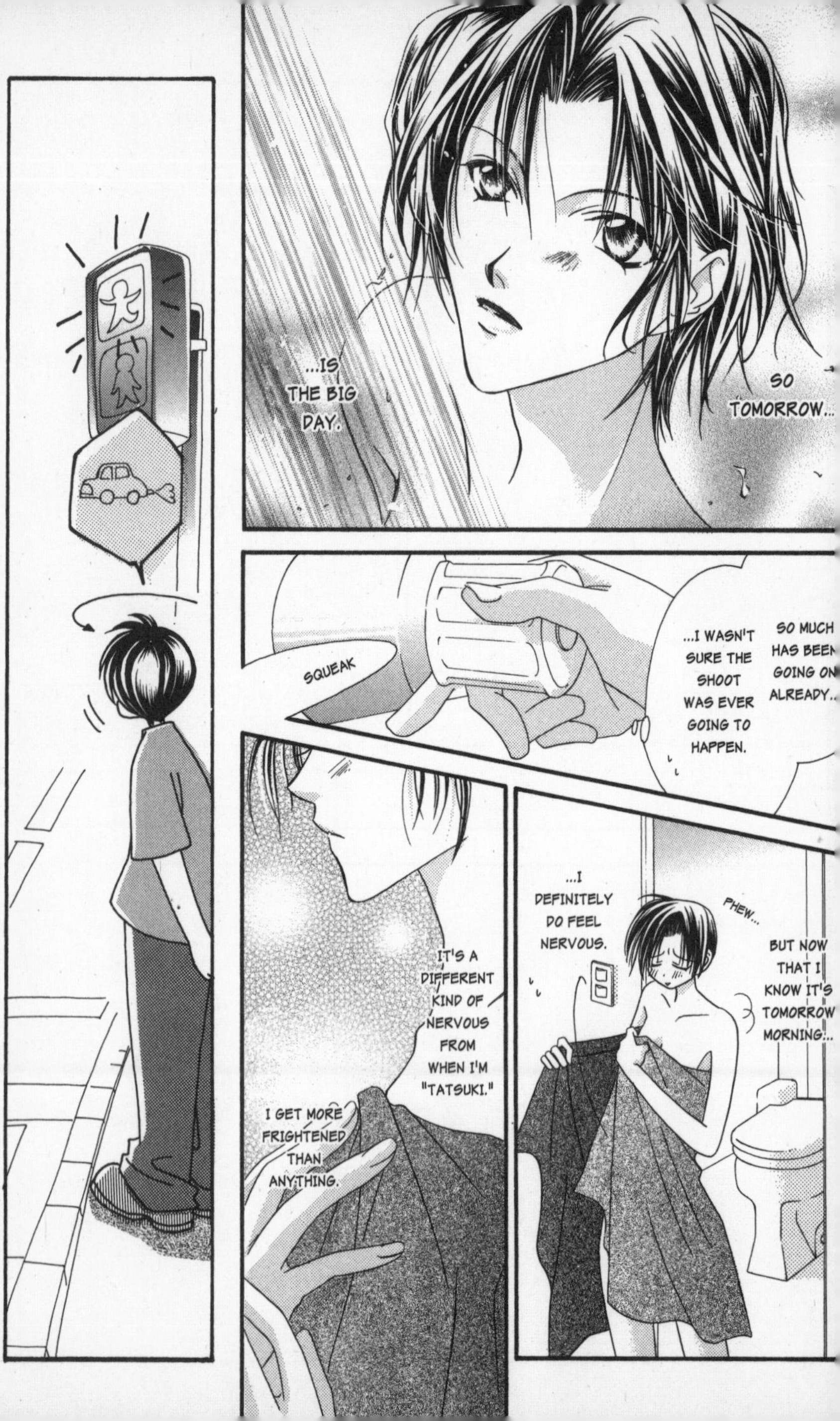
SO TOMORROW...
...IS THE BIG DAY.
SO MUCH HAS BEEN GOING ON ALREADY...
...I WASN'T SURE THE SHOOT WAS EVER GOING TO HAPPEN.
SQUEAK
PHEW...
BUT NOW THAT I KNOW IT'S TOMORROW MORNING...
...I DEFINITELY DO FEEL NERVOUS.
IT'S A DIFFERENT KIND OF NERVOUS FROM WHEN I'M "TATSUKI."
I GET MORE FRIGHTENED THAN ANYTHING.

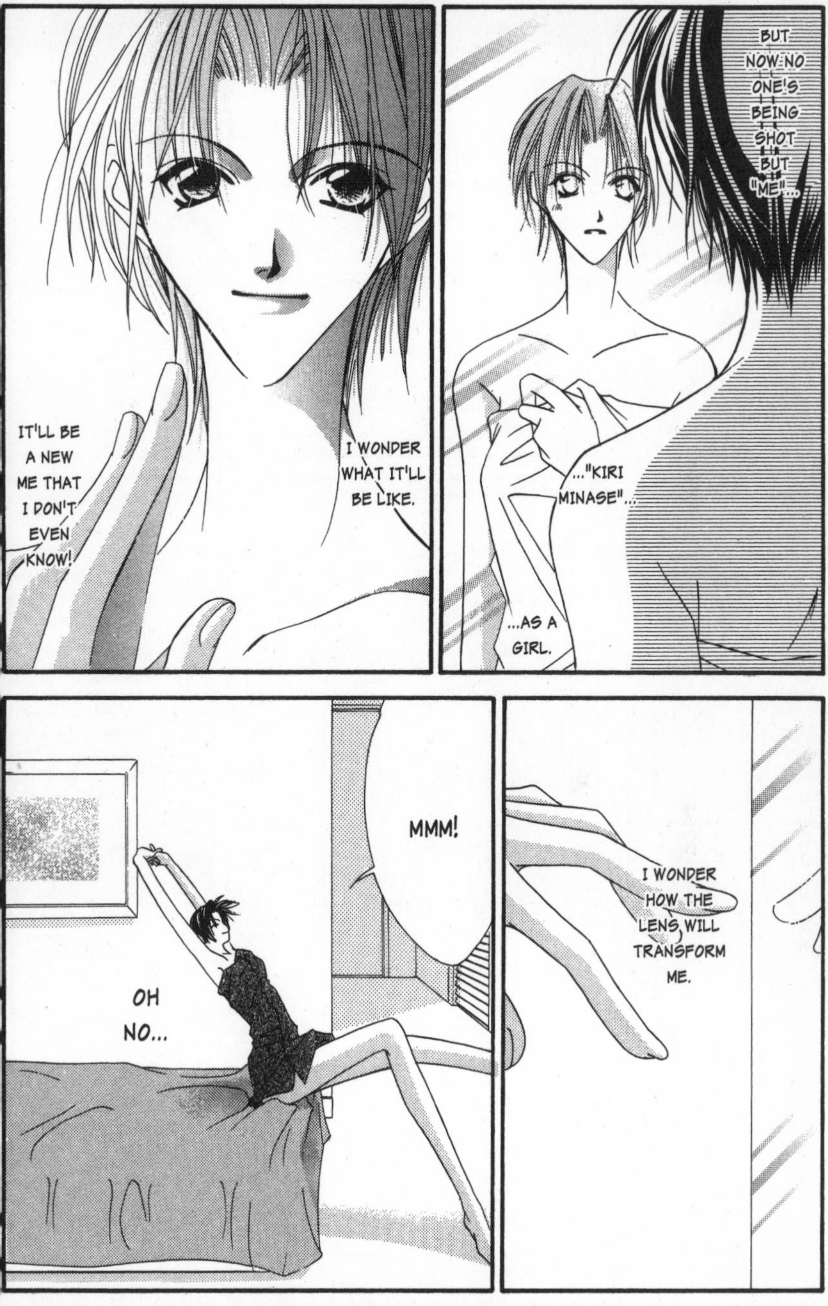
BUT NOW NO ONE'S BEING SHOT BUT "ME"...
..."KIRI MINASE"...
...AS A GIRL.
I WONDER WHAT IT'LL BE LIKE.
IT'LL BE A NEW ME THAT I DON'T EVEN KNOW!
I WONDER HOW THE LENS WILL TRANSFORM ME.
MMM!
OH NO...

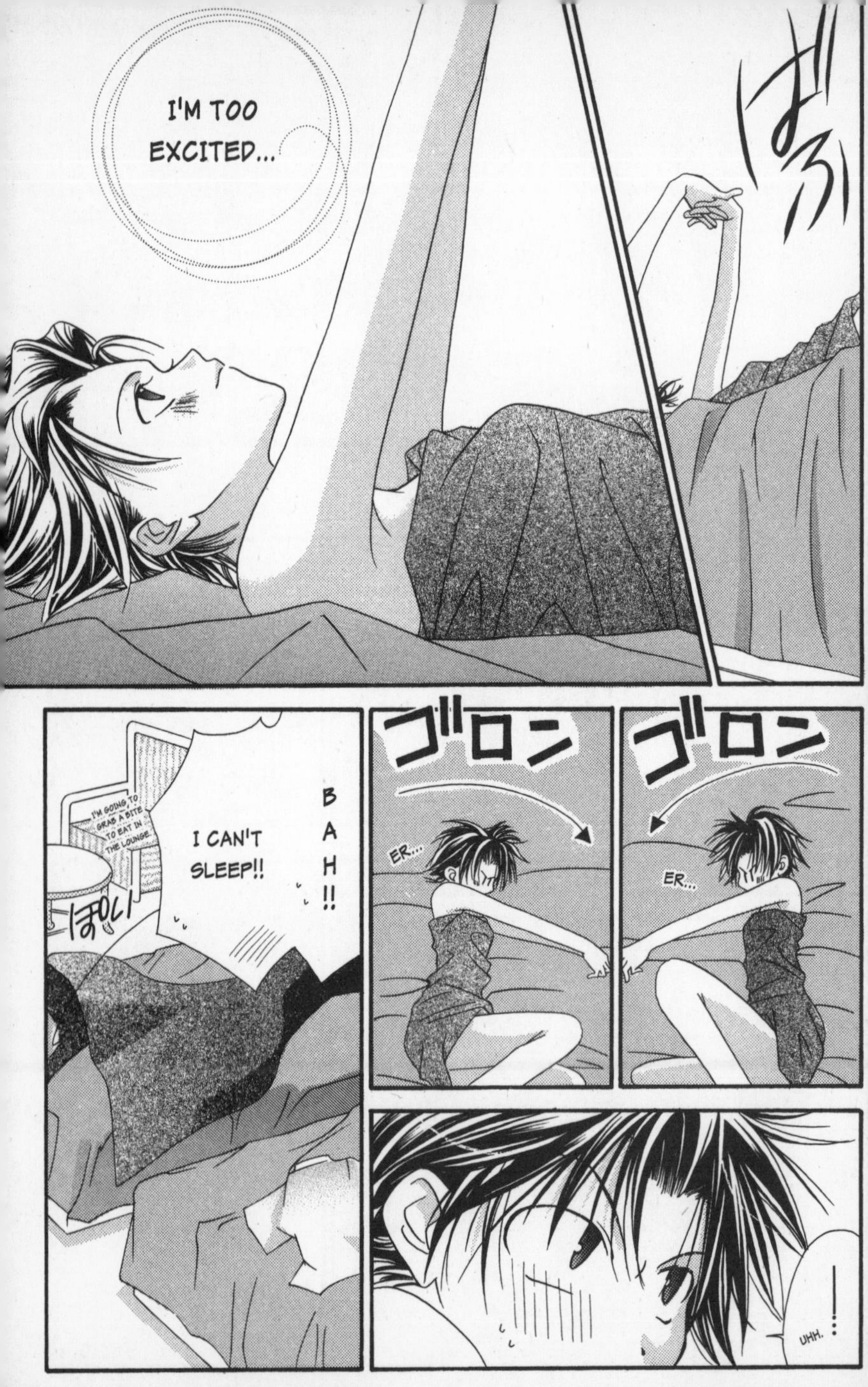
I'M TOO EXCITED...
ゴロン
ER...
ゴロン
ER...
UHH...!
BAH!!
I CAN'T SLEEP!!
ぽいっ
I'M GOING TO GRAB A BITE TO EAT IN THE LOUNGE.

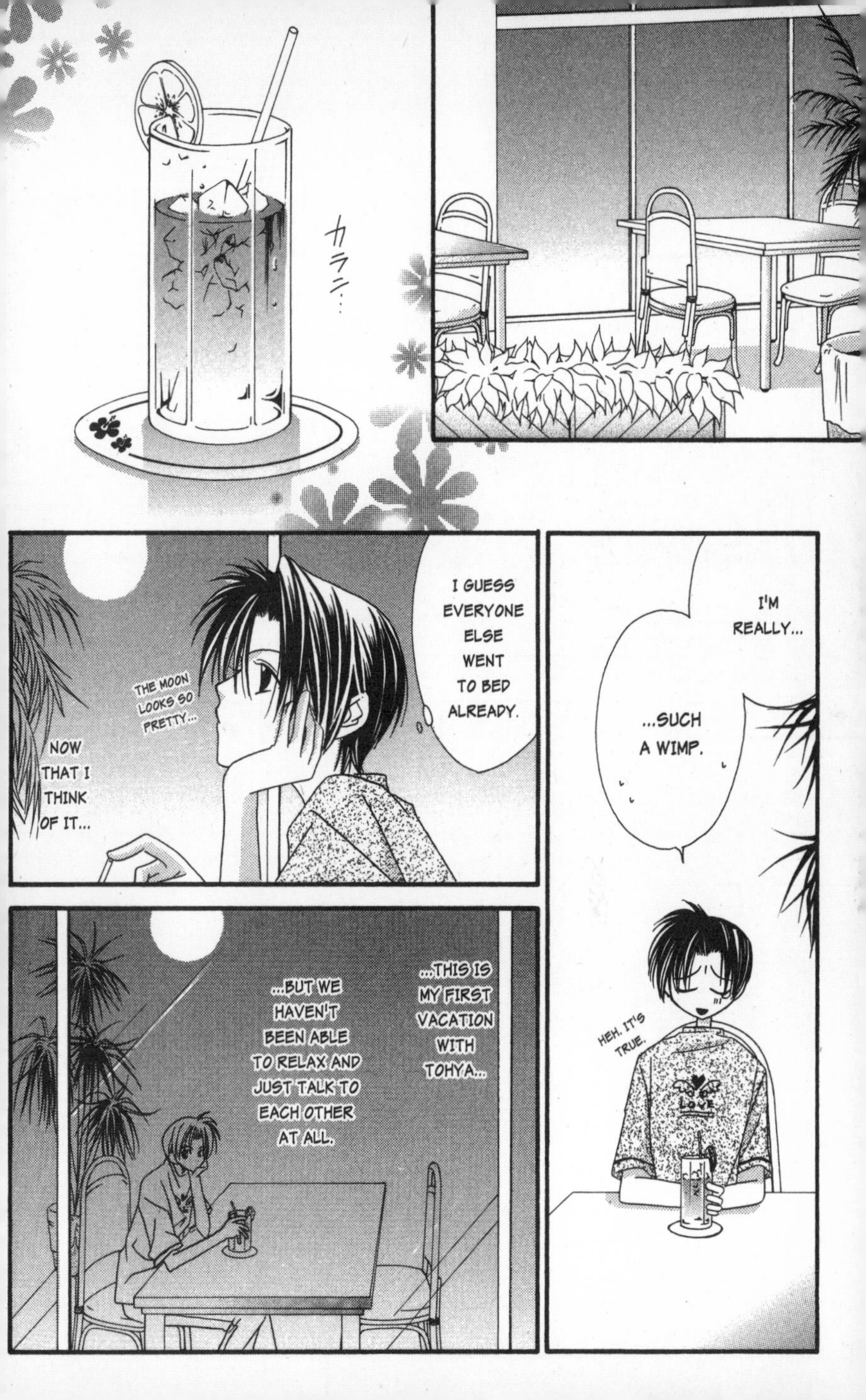
カラン…
I'M REALLY...
...SUCH A WIMP.
HEH. IT'S TRUE.
I GUESS EVERYONE ELSE WENT TO BED ALREADY.
THE MOON LOOKS SO PRETTY...
NOW THAT I THINK OF IT...
...THIS IS MY FIRST VACATION WITH TOHYA...
...BUT WE HAVEN'T BEEN ABLE TO RELAX AND JUST TALK TO EACH OTHER AT ALL.

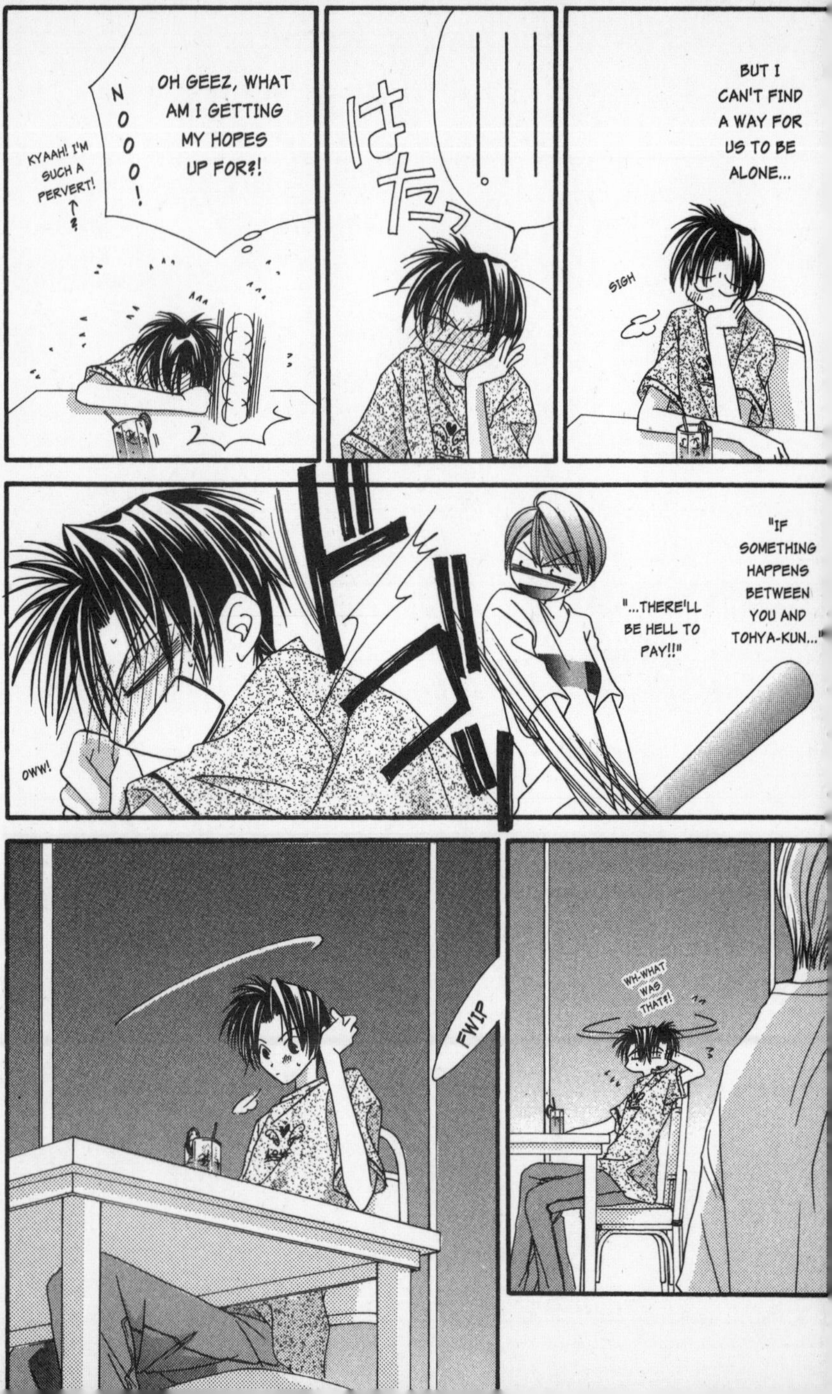
BUT I CAN'T FIND A WAY FOR US TO BE ALONE...
SIGH
はたっ
OH GEEZ, WHAT AM I GETTING MY HOPES UP FOR?!
NOOOO!
KYAAH! I'M SUCH A PERVERT!
"IF SOMETHING HAPPENS BETWEEN YOU AND TOHYA-KUN..."
"...THERE'LL BE HELL TO PAY!!"
ドゴッ
OWW!
WH-WHAT WAS THAT?!
FWIP

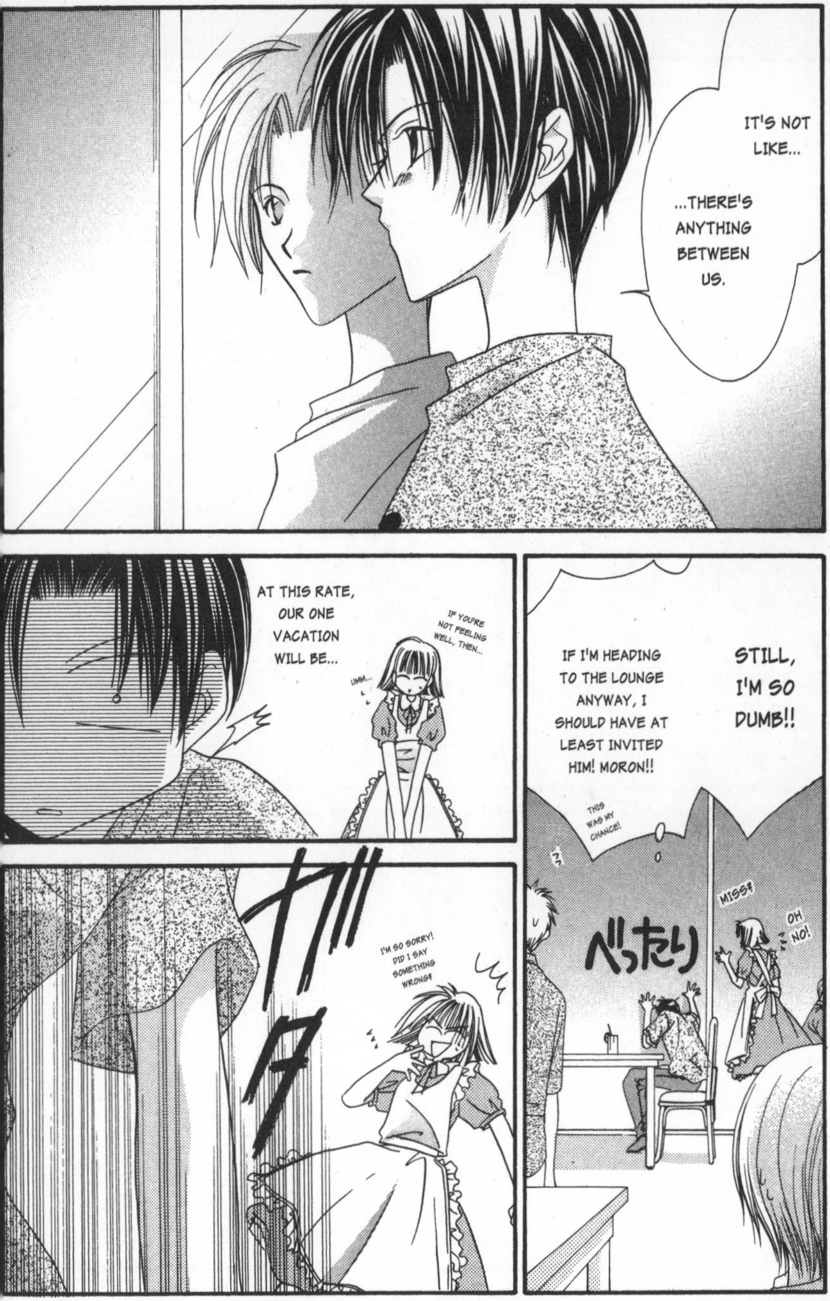
IT'S NOT LIKE...
...THERE'S ANYTHING BETWEEN US.
STILL, I'M SO DUMB!!
IF I'M HEADING TO THE LOUNGE ANYWAY, I SHOULD HAVE AT LEAST INVITED HIM! MORON!!
THIS WAS MY CHANCE!
MISS?
OH NO!
べったり
AT THIS RATE, OUR ONE VACATION WILL BE...
IF YOU'RE NOT FEELING WELL, THEN...
UMM...
ガタ
I'M SO SORRY! DID I SAY SOMETHING WRONG?

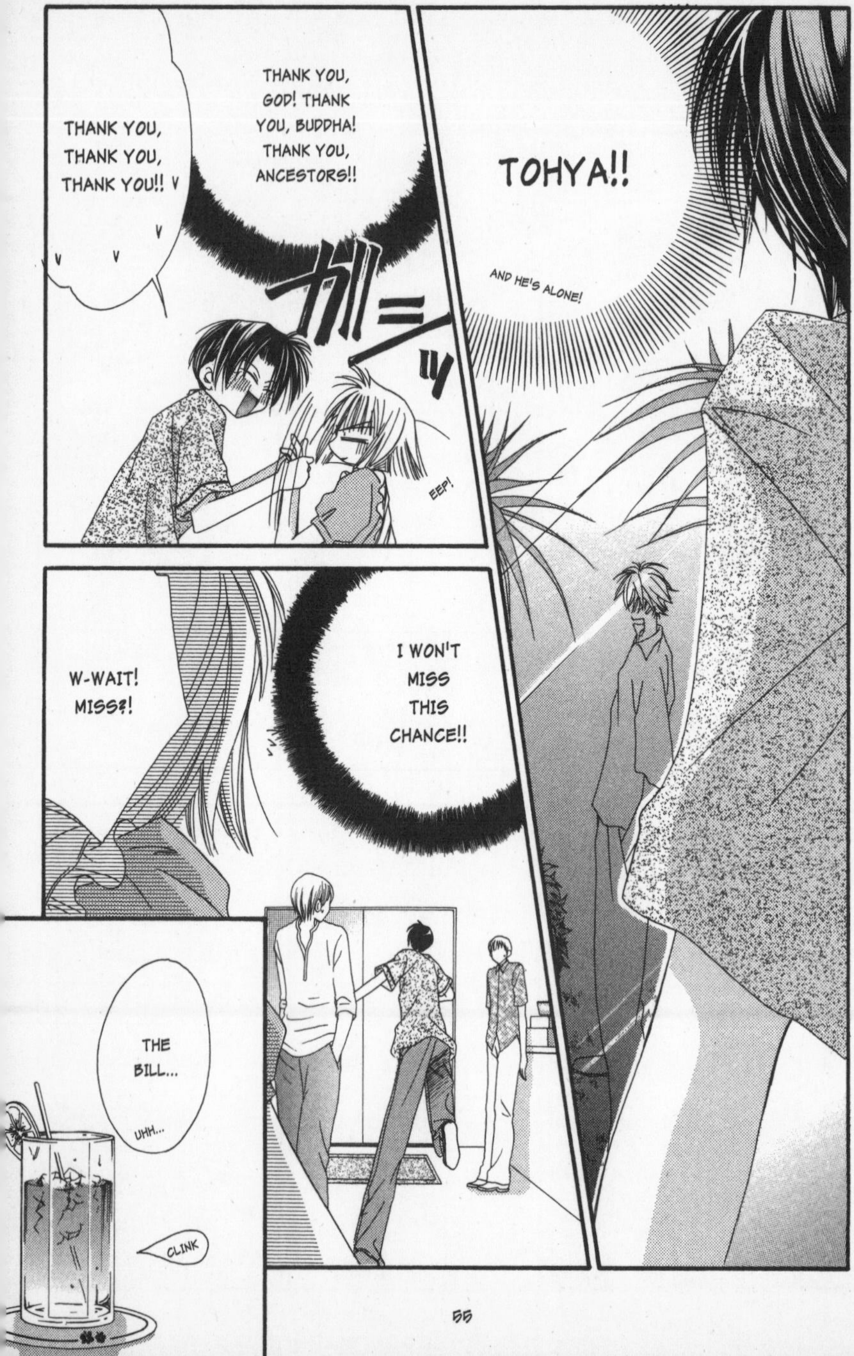
TOHYA!!
AND HE'S ALONE!
THANK YOU, GOD! THANK YOU, BUDDHA! THANK YOU, ANCESTORS!!
THANK YOU, THANK YOU, THANK YOU!!
EEP!
I WON'T MISS THIS CHANCE!!
W-WAIT! MISS?!
THE BILL...
UHH...
CLINK

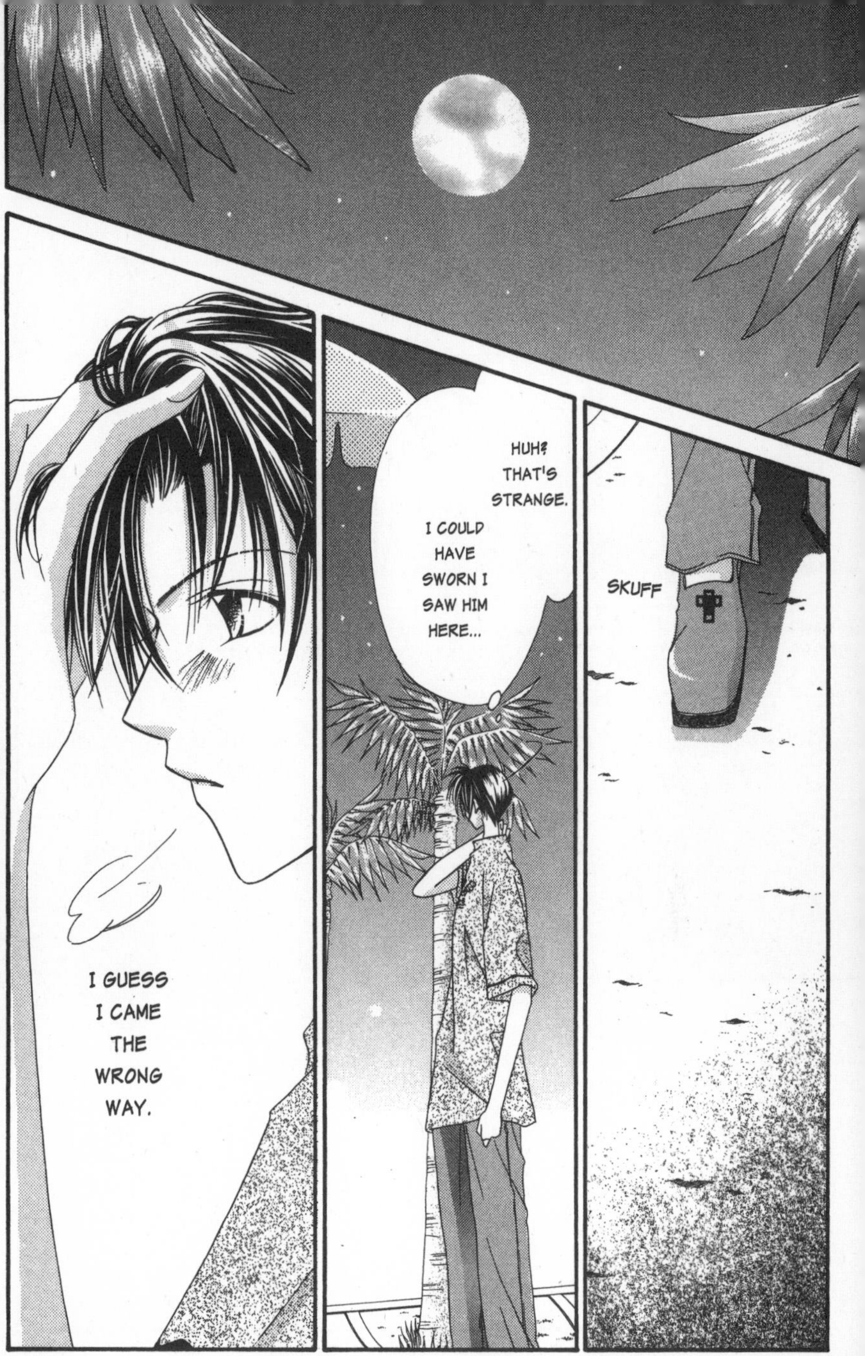
SKUFF
HUH? THAT'S STRANGE.
I COULD HAVE SWORN I SAW HIM HERE...
I GUESS I CAME THE WRONG WAY.

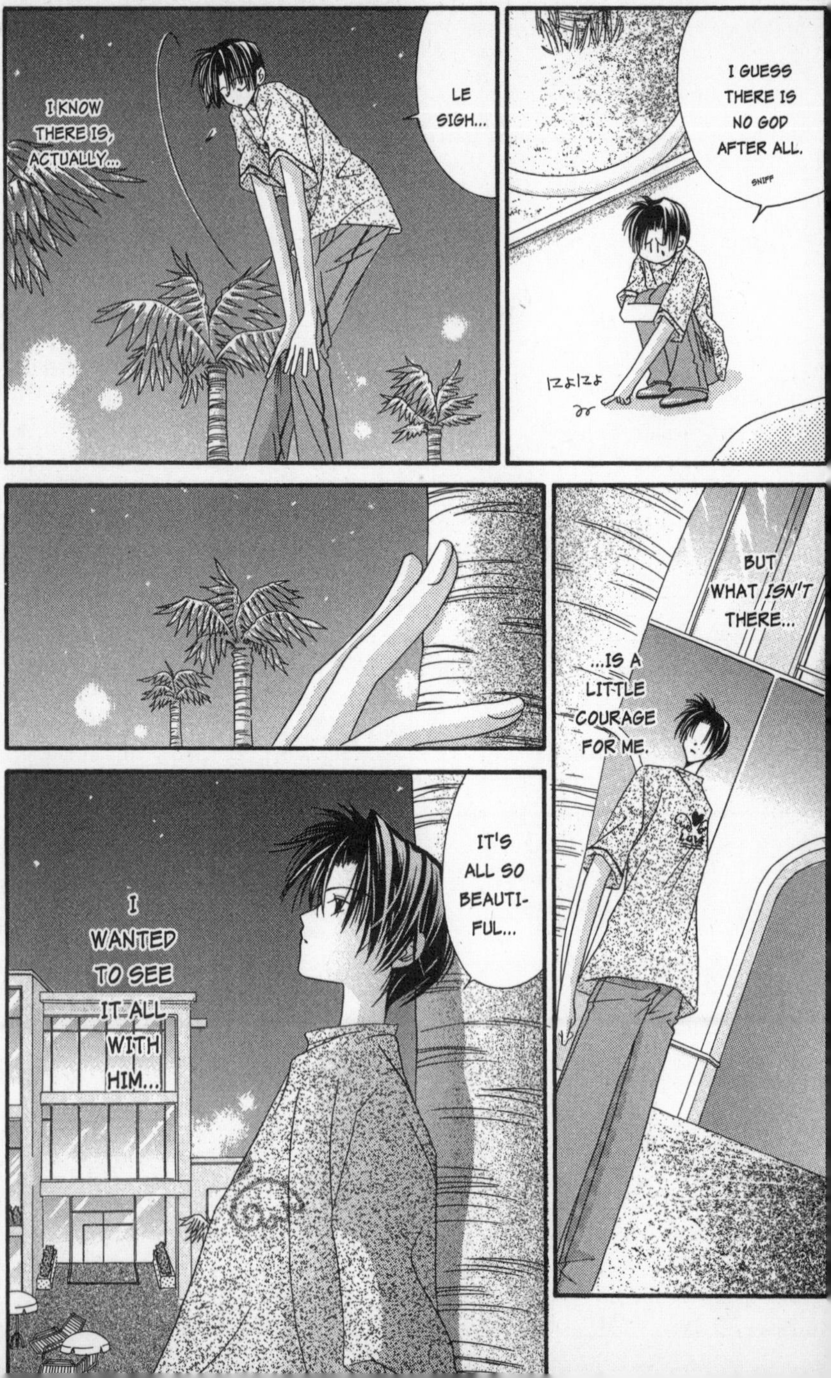
I GUESS THERE IS NO GOD AFTER ALL.
SNIFF
にょにょ
LE SIGH...
I KNOW THERE IS, ACTUALLY...
BUT WHAT ISN'T THERE...
...IS A LITTLE COURAGE FOR ME.
IT'S ALL SO BEAUTI-FUL...
I WANTED TO SEE IT ALL WITH HIM...

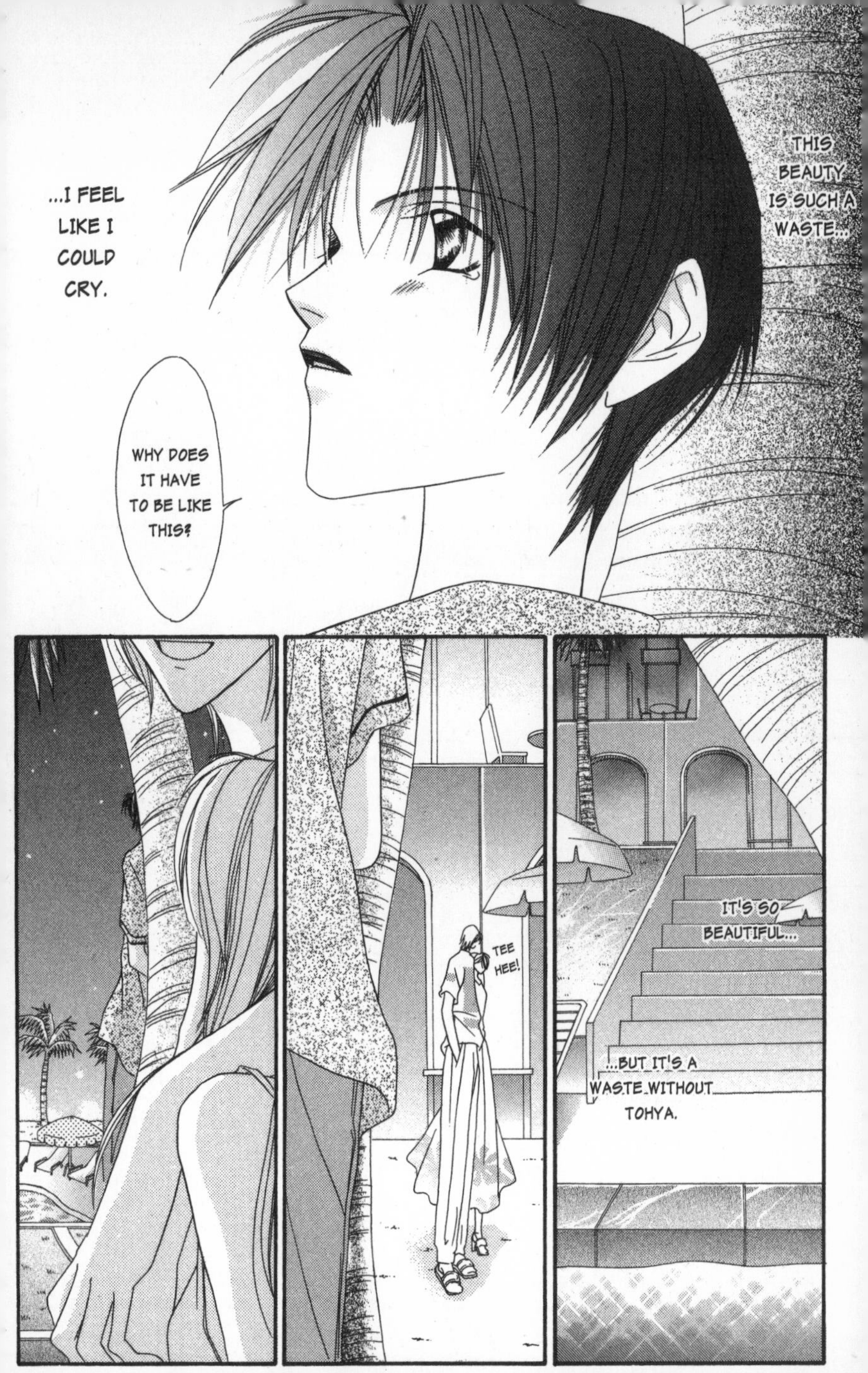
THIS BEAUTY IS SUCH A WASTE...
...I FEEL LIKE I COULD CRY.
WHY DOES IT HAVE TO BE LIKE THIS?
IT'S SO BEAUTIFUL...
...BUT IT'S A WASTE WITHOUT TOHYA.
TEE HEE!

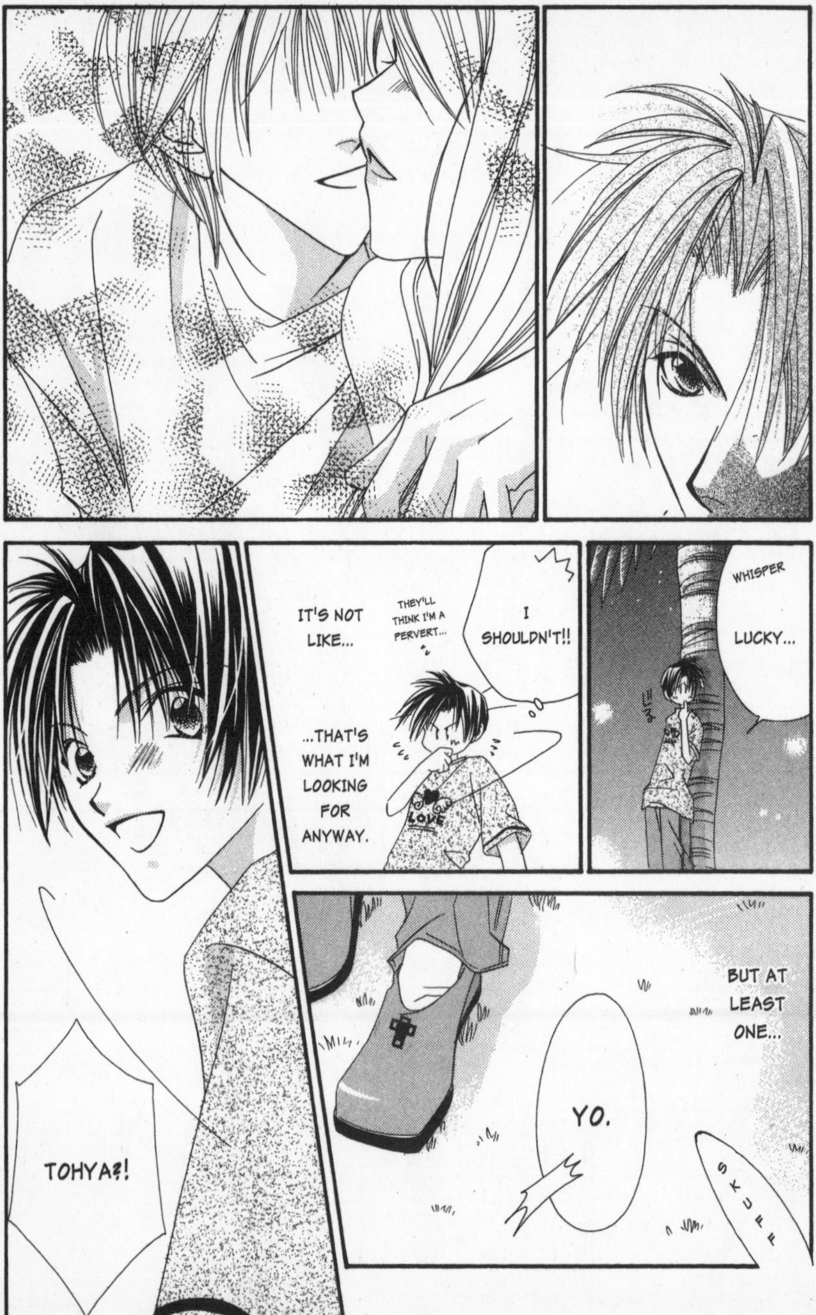
WHISPER
LUCKY...
I SHOULDN'T!!
THEY'LL THINK I'M A PERVERT...
IT'S NOT LIKE...
...THAT'S WHAT I'M LOOKING FOR ANYWAY.
LOVE
BUT AT LEAST ONE...
SKUFF
YO.
TOHYA?!

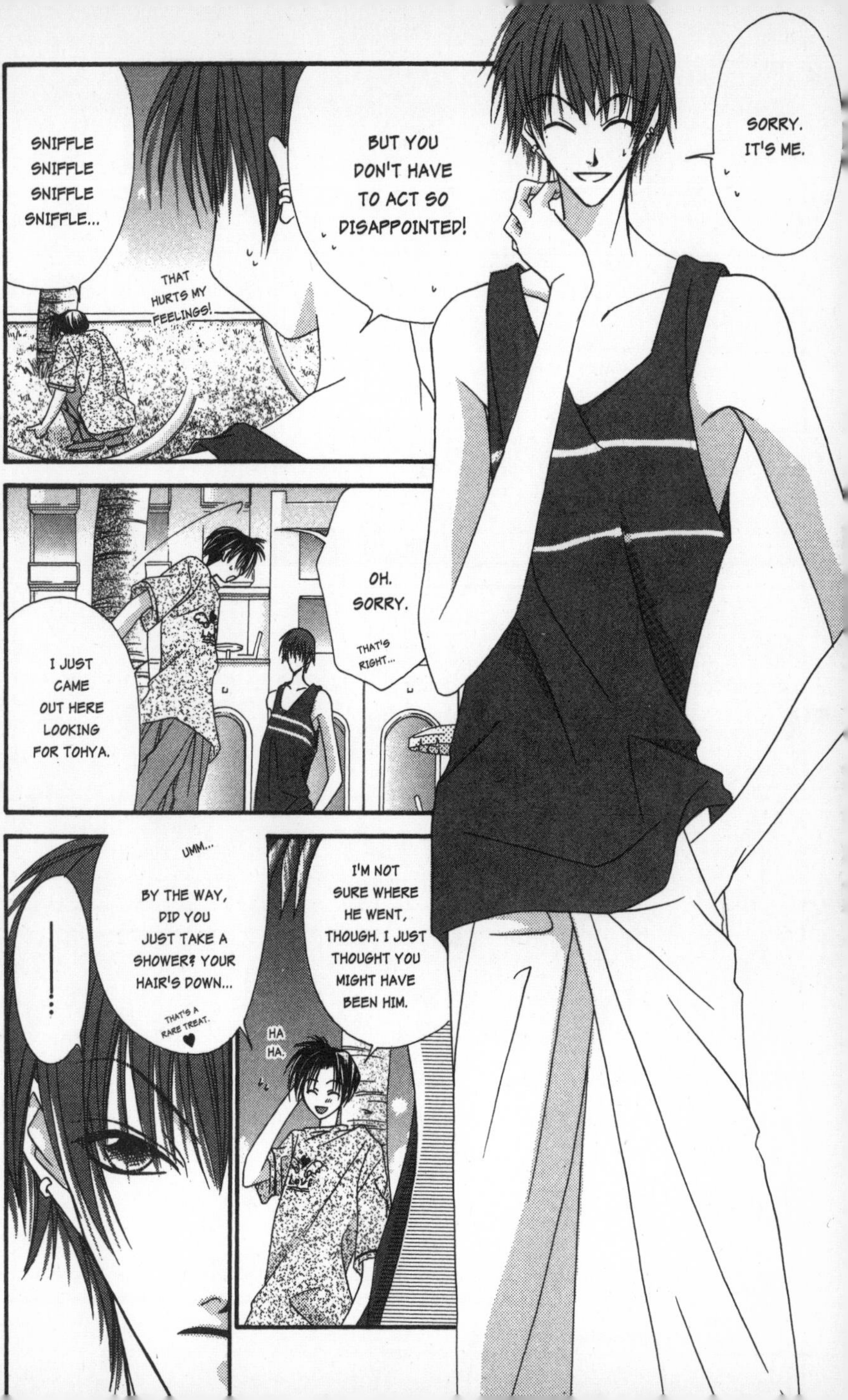
SORRY. IT'S ME.
BUT YOU DON'T HAVE TO ACT SO DISAPPOINTED!
THAT HURTS MY FEELINGS!
SNIFFLE SNIFFLE SNIFFLE SNIFFLE...
OH. SORRY.
THAT'S RIGHT...
I JUST CAME OUT HERE LOOKING FOR TOHYA.
I'M NOT SURE WHERE HE WENT, THOUGH. I JUST THOUGHT YOU MIGHT HAVE BEEN HIM.
HA HA.
UMM...
BY THE WAY, DID YOU JUST TAKE A SHOWER? YOUR HAIR'S DOWN...
THAT'S A RARE TREAT. ♥

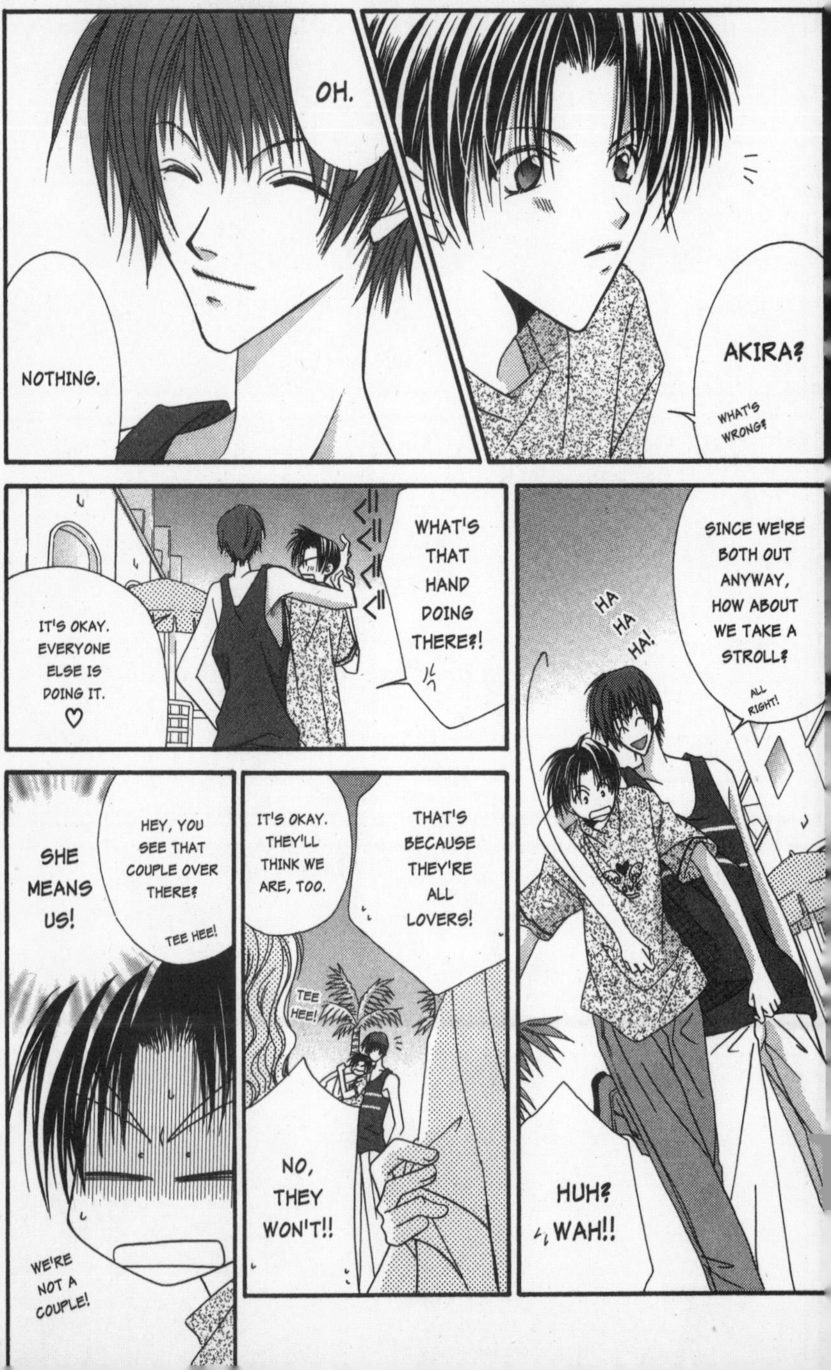
AKIRA?
WHAT'S WRONG?
OH.
NOTHING.
SINCE WE'RE BOTH OUT ANYWAY, HOW ABOUT WE TAKE A STROLL?
ALL RIGHT!
HA HA HA!
HUH? WAH!!
WHAT'S THAT HAND DOING THERE?!
IT'S OKAY. EVERYONE ELSE IS DOING IT. ♡
THAT'S BECAUSE THEY'RE ALL LOVERS!
IT'S OKAY. THEY'LL THINK WE ARE, TOO.
TEE HEE!
NO, THEY WON'T!!
HEY, YOU SEE THAT COUPLE OVER THERE?
TEE HEE!
SHE MEANS US!
WE'RE NOT A COUPLE!

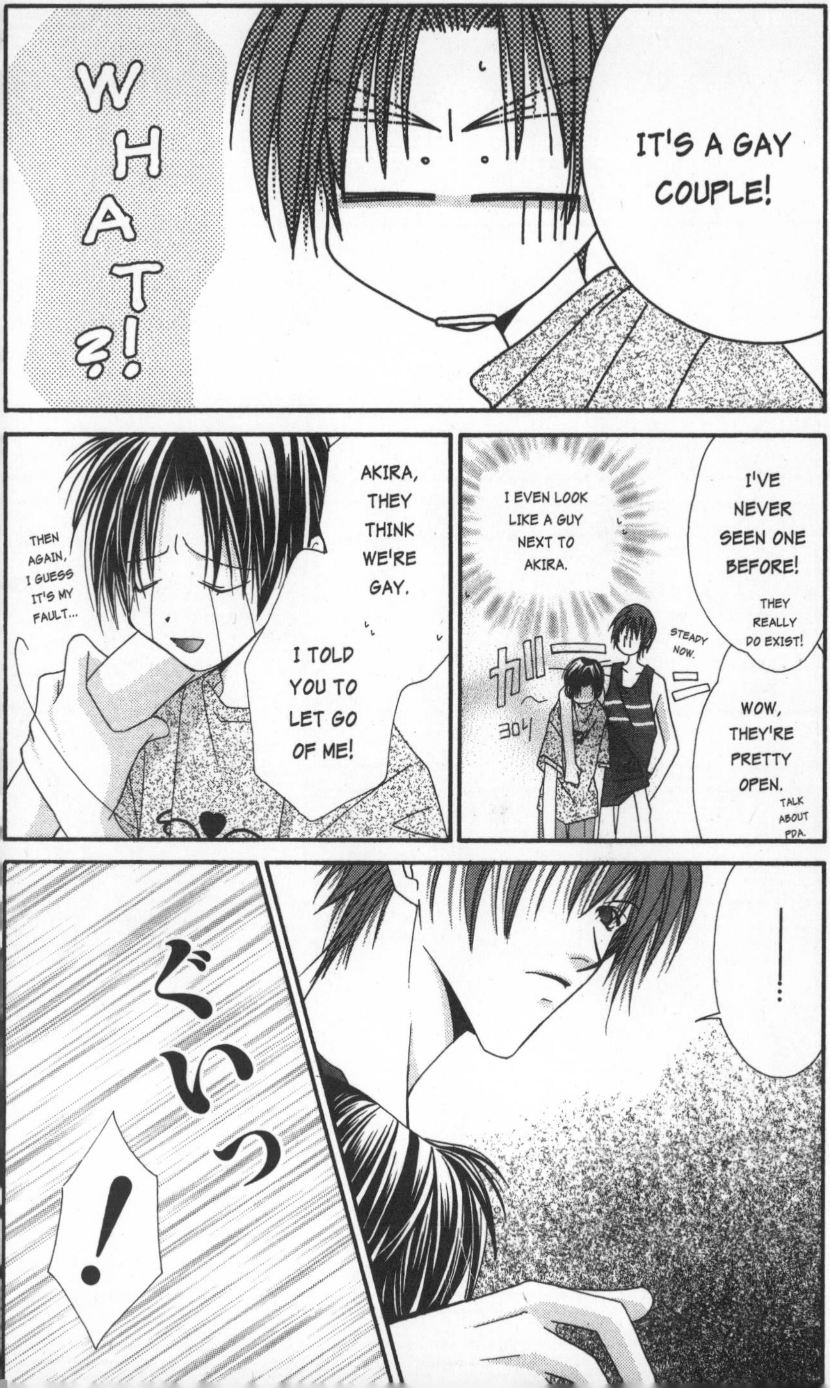
IT'S A GAY COUPLE!
WHAT?!
I'VE NEVER SEEN ONE BEFORE!
THEY REALLY DO EXIST!
WOW, THEY'RE PRETTY OPEN.
TALK ABOUT PDA.
STEADY NOW.
I EVEN LOOK LIKE A GUY NEXT TO AKIRA.
カリー
ヨロ
AKIRA, THEY THINK WE'RE GAY.
I TOLD YOU TO LET GO OF ME!
THEN AGAIN, I GUESS IT'S MY FAULT...
—...
ぐいっ
!

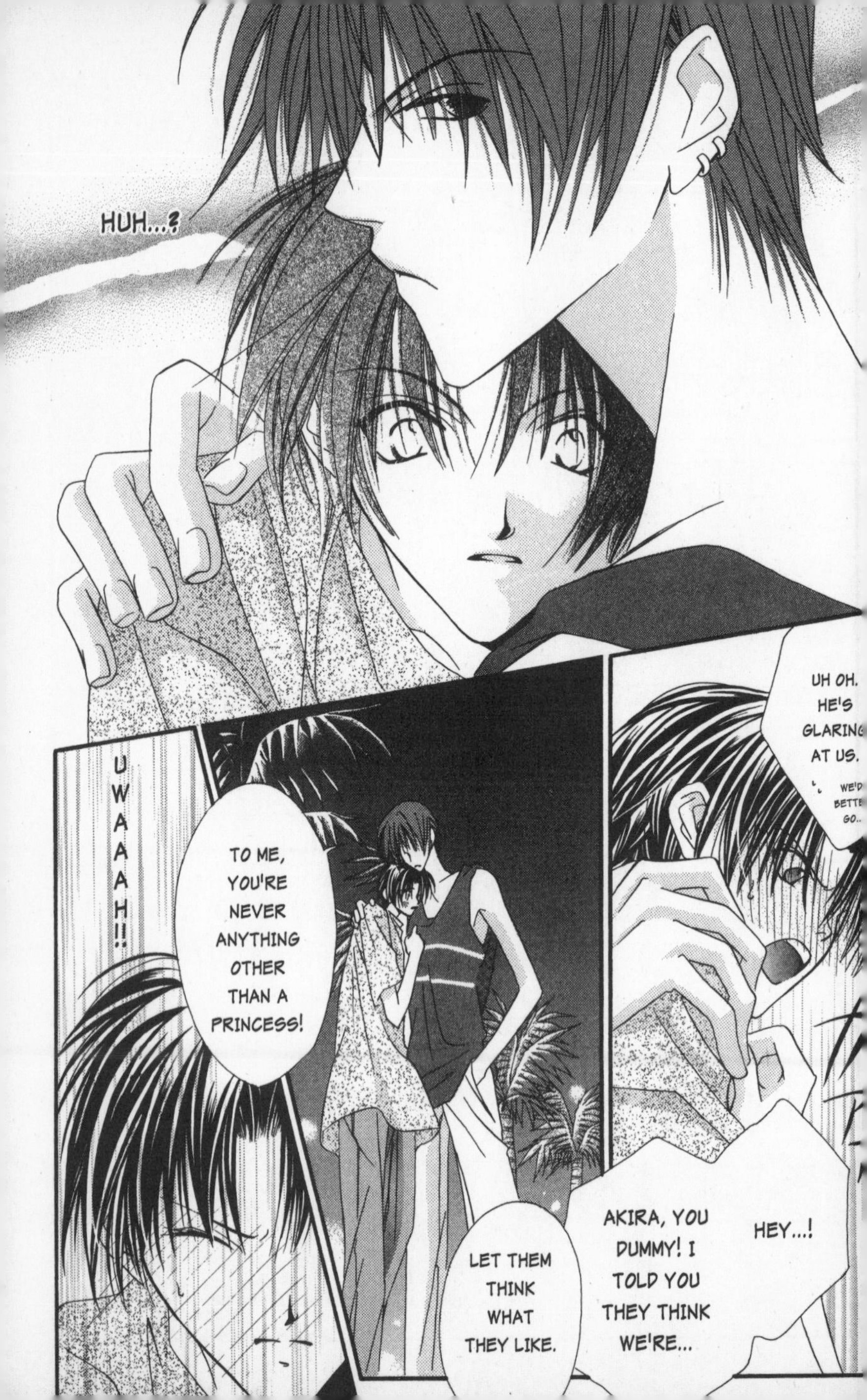
HUH...?
UH OH. HE'S GLARING AT US.
WE'D BETTE GO..
TO ME, YOU'RE NEVER ANYTHING OTHER THAN A PRINCESS!
UWAAAAAH!!
HEY...!
AKIRA, YOU DUMMY! I TOLD YOU THEY THINK WE'RE...
LET THEM THINK WHAT THEY LIKE.

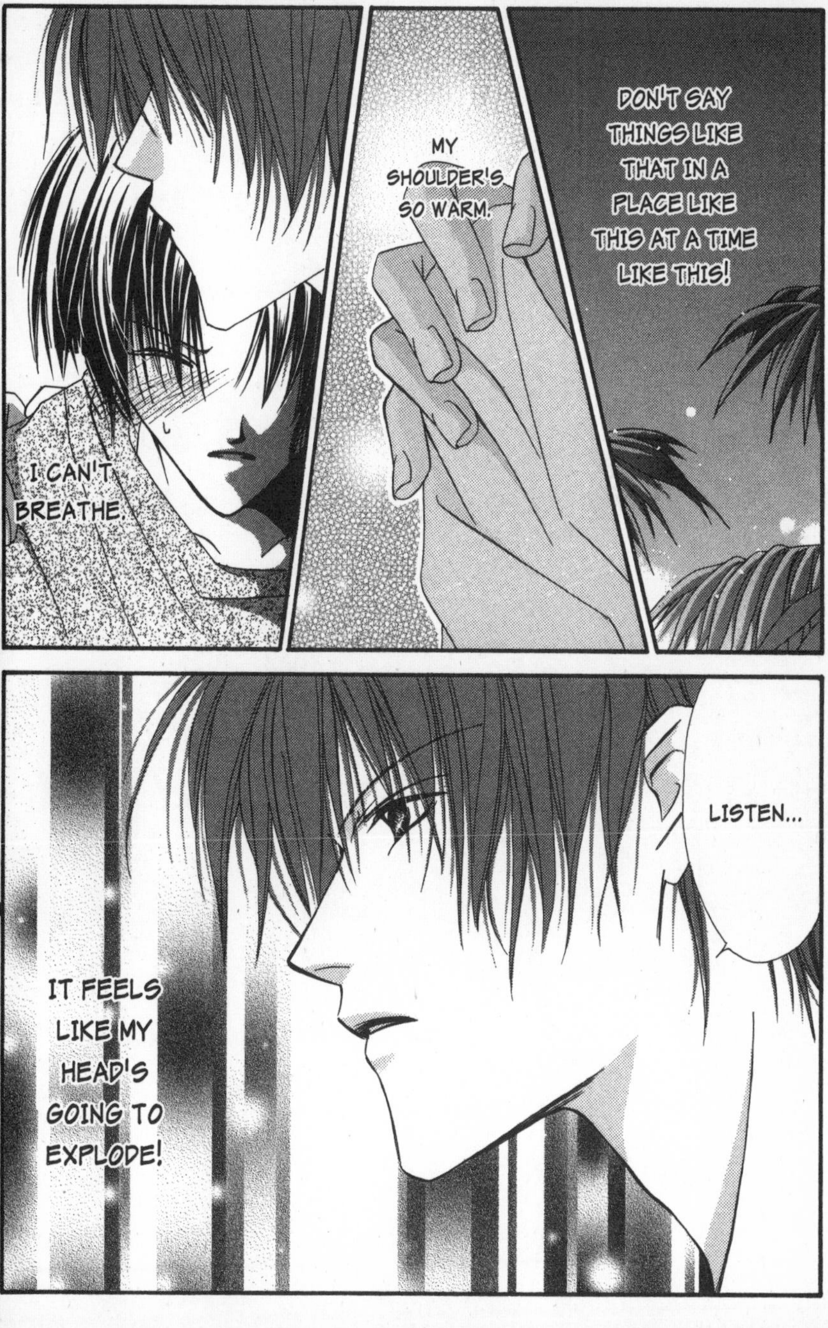
DON'T SAY THINGS LIKE THAT IN A PLACE LIKE THIS AT A TIME LIKE THIS!
MY SHOULDER'S SO WARM.
I CAN'T BREATHE.
LISTEN...
IT FEELS LIKE MY HEAD'S GOING TO EXPLODE!

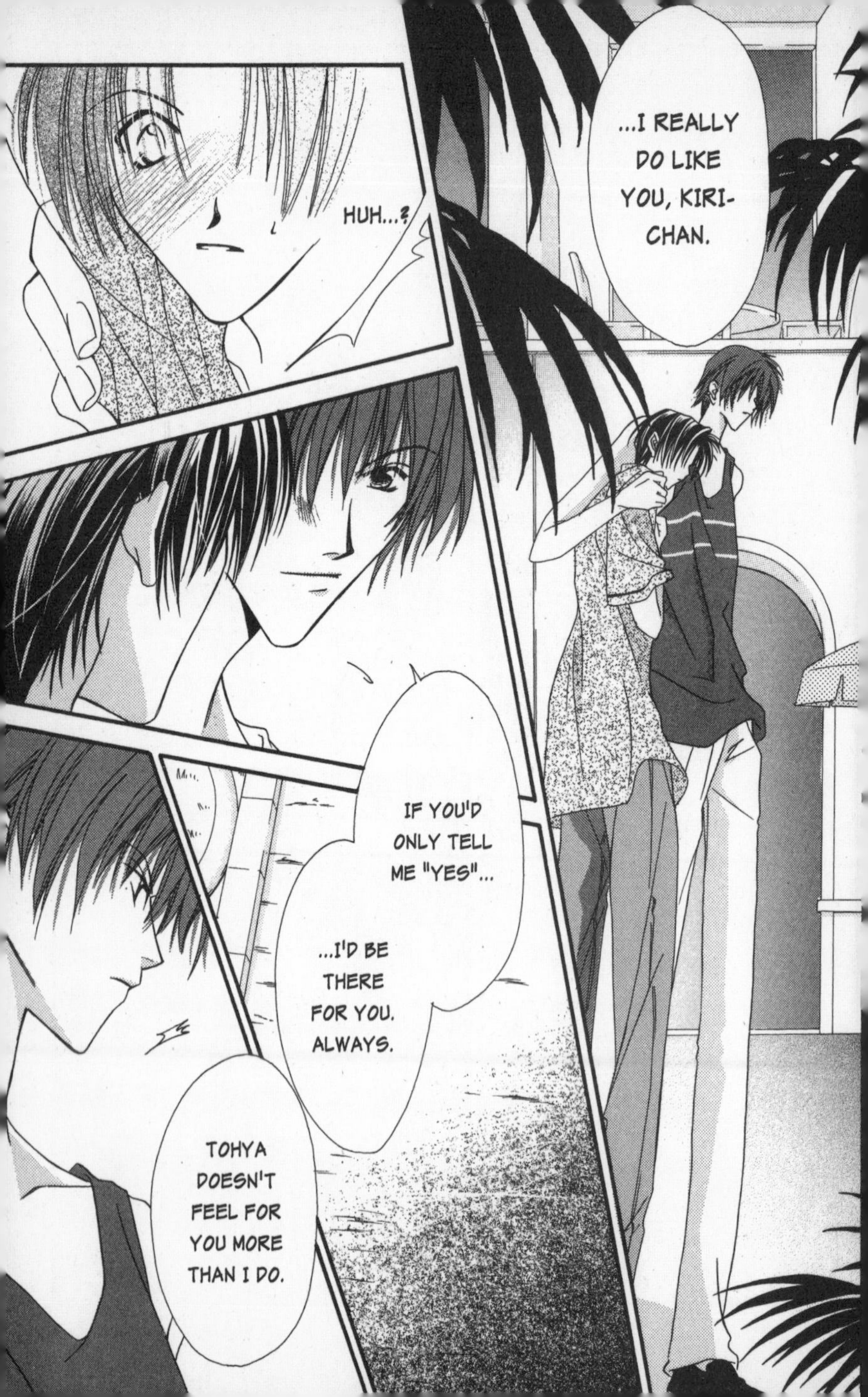
...I REALLY DO LIKE YOU, KIRI-CHAN.
HUH...?
IF YOU'D ONLY TELL ME "YES"...
...I'D BE THERE FOR YOU. ALWAYS.
TOHYA DOESN'T FEEL FOR YOU MORE THAN I DO.

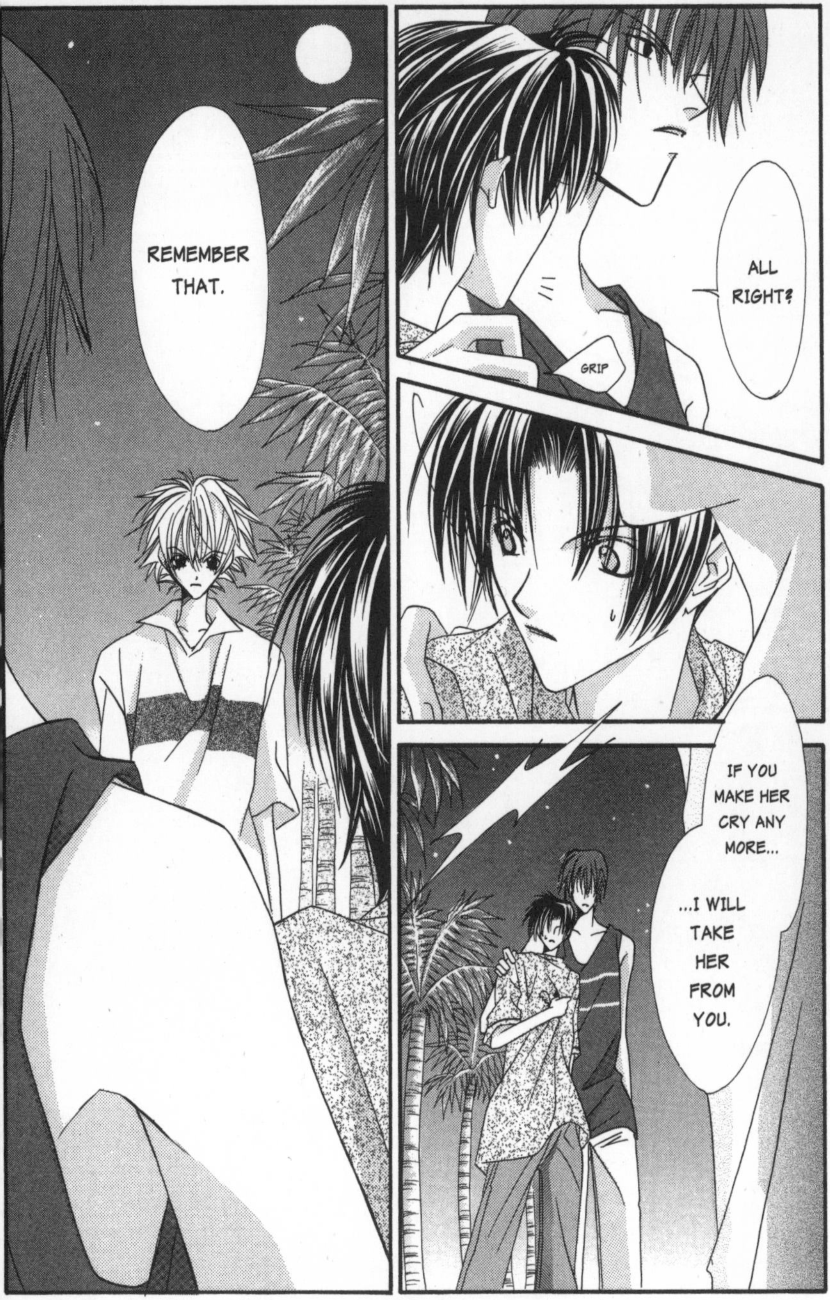
ALL RIGHT?
GRIP
IF YOU MAKE HER CRY ANY MORE...
...I WILL TAKE HER FROM YOU.
REMEMBER THAT.

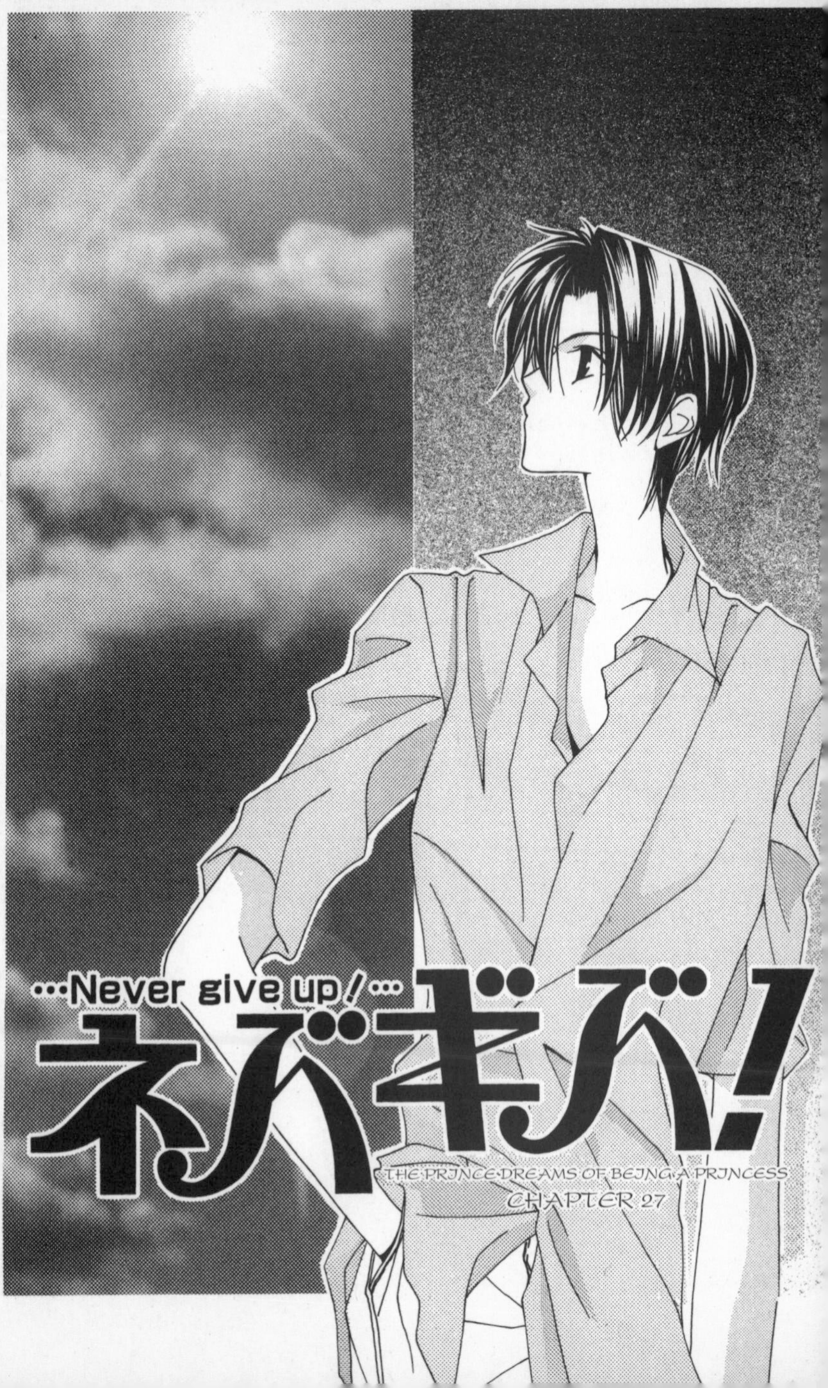

...Never give up!...
ネバギバ!
THE PRINCE DREAMS OF BEING A PRINCESS
CHAPTER 27

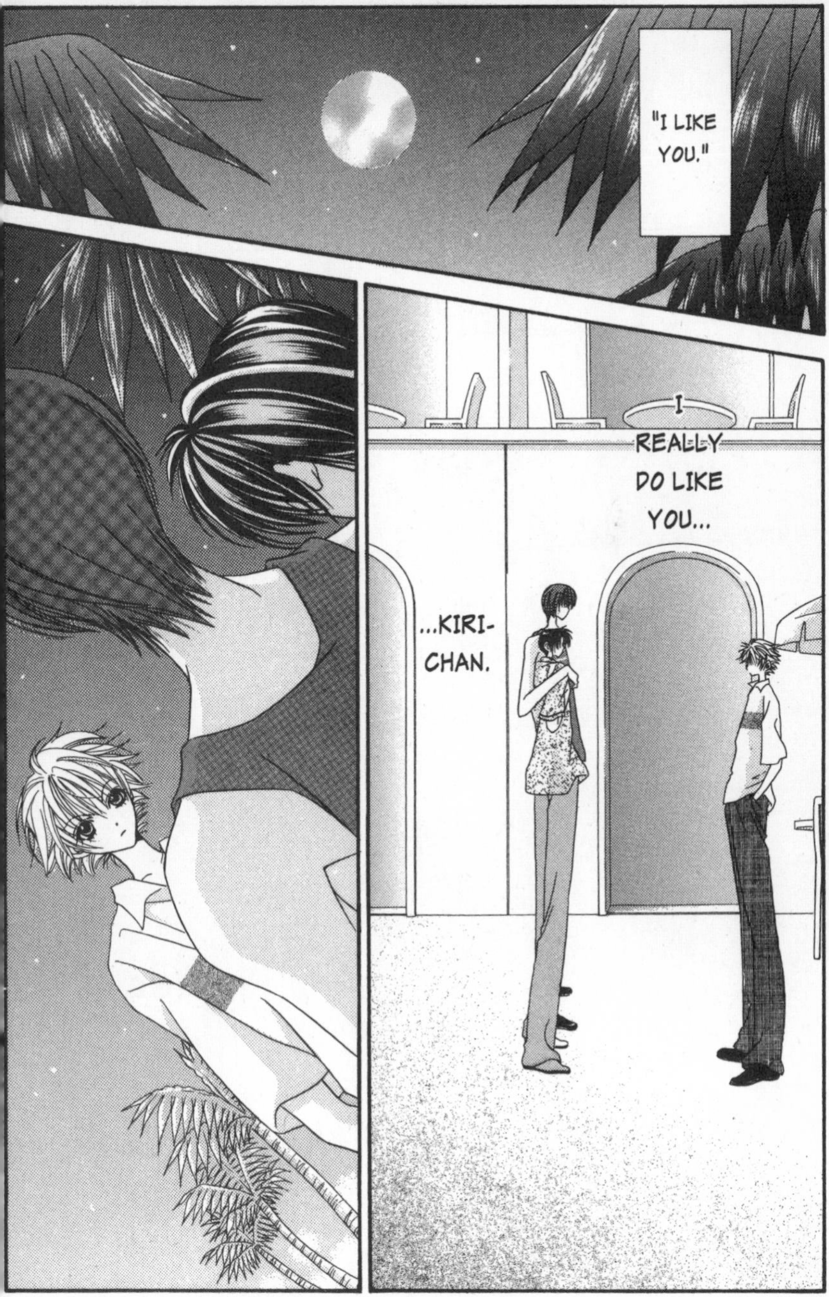
"I LIKE YOU."
I REALLY DO LIKE YOU...
...KIRI-CHAN.

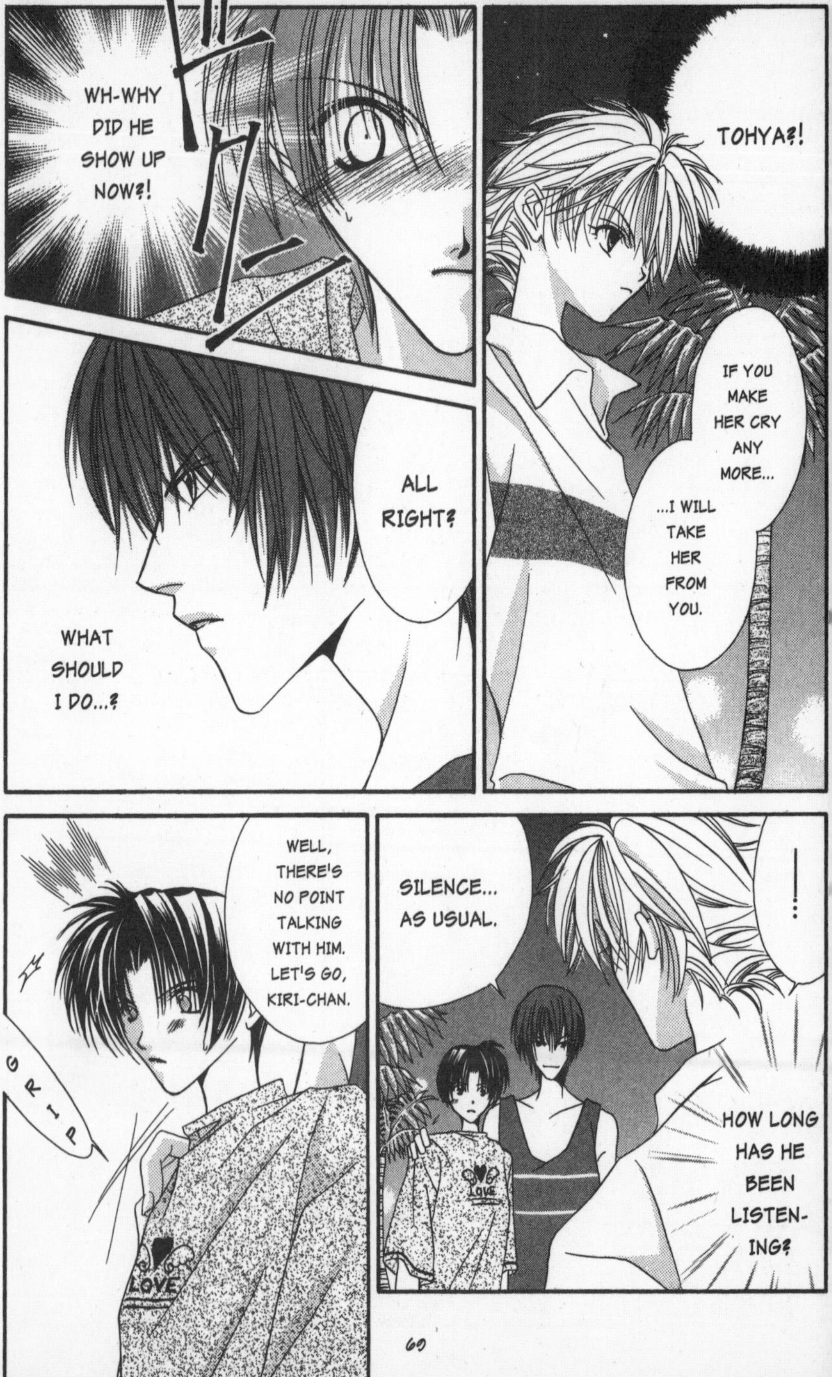

TOHYA?!
IF YOU MAKE HER CRY ANY MORE...
...I WILL TAKE HER FROM YOU.
WH-WHY DID HE SHOW UP NOW?!
ALL RIGHT?
WHAT SHOULD I DO...?
SILENCE... AS USUAL.
HOW LONG HAS HE BEEN LISTENING?
WELL, THERE'S NO POINT TALKING WITH HIM. LET'S GO, KIRI-CHAN.
GRIP
LOVE
LOVE

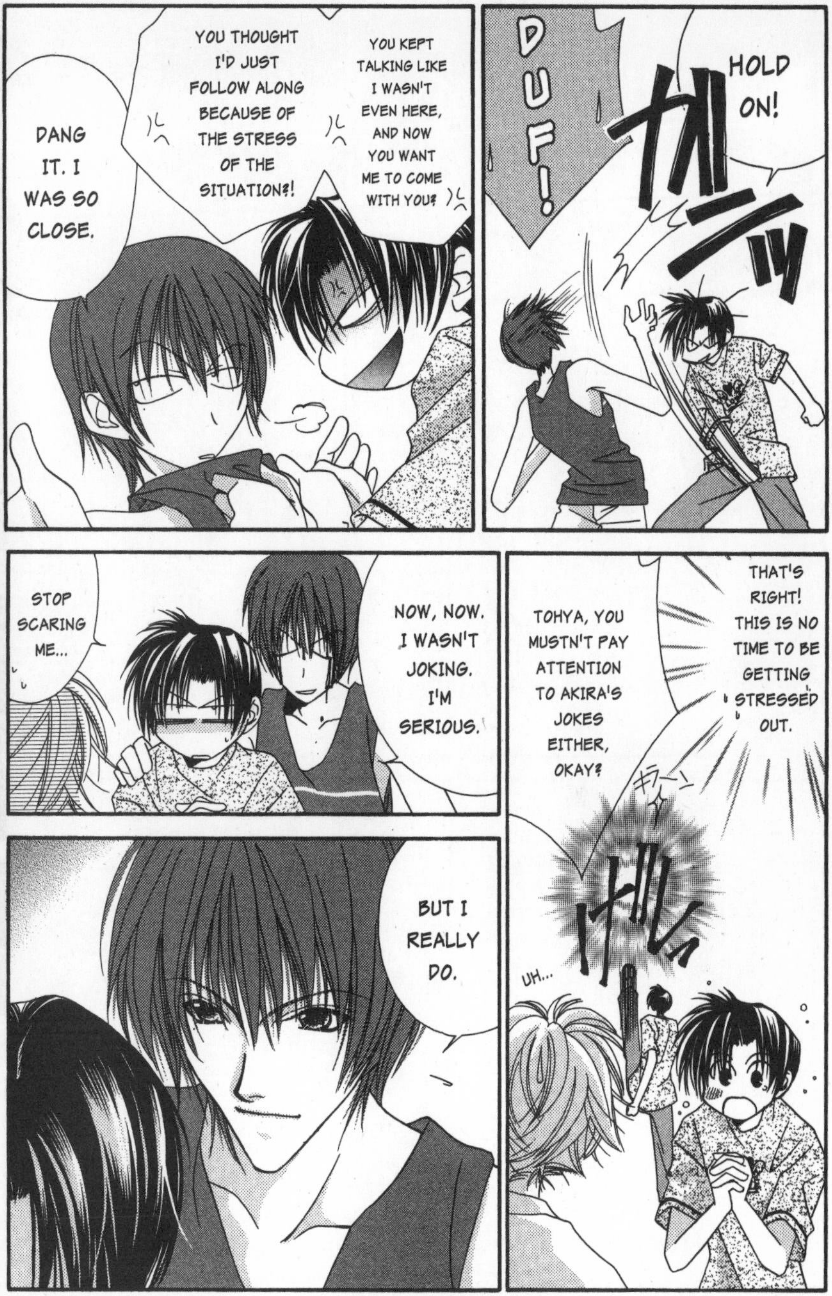
DUF!
HOLD ON!
YOU KEPT TALKING LIKE I WASN'T EVEN HERE, AND NOW YOU WANT ME TO COME WITH YOU?
YOU THOUGHT I'D JUST FOLLOW ALONG BECAUSE OF THE STRESS OF THE SITUATION?!
DANG IT. I WAS SO CLOSE.
THAT'S RIGHT! THIS IS NO TIME TO BE GETTING STRESSED OUT.
TOHYA, YOU MUSTN'T PAY ATTENTION TO AKIRA'S JOKES EITHER, OKAY?
UH...
NOW, NOW. I WASN'T JOKING. I'M SERIOUS.
STOP SCARING ME...
BUT I REALLY DO.

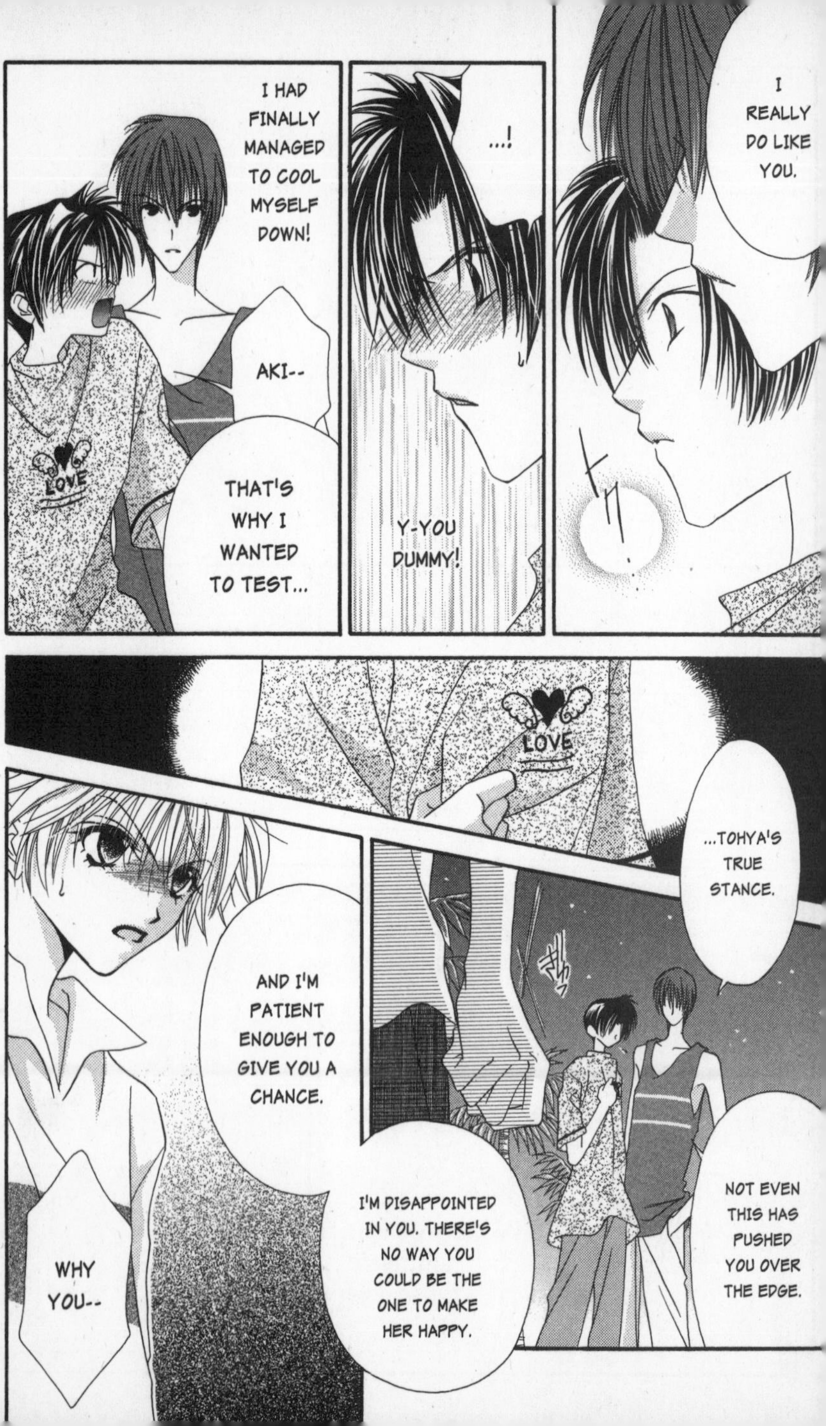
I REALLY DO LIKE YOU.
...!
Y-YOU DUMMY!
I HAD FINALLY MANAGED TO COOL MYSELF DOWN!
AKI--
THAT'S WHY I WANTED TO TEST...
...TOHYA'S TRUE STANCE.
NOT EVEN THIS HAS PUSHED YOU OVER THE EDGE.
I'M DISAPPOINTED IN YOU. THERE'S NO WAY YOU COULD BE THE ONE TO MAKE HER HAPPY.
AND I'M PATIENT ENOUGH TO GIVE YOU A CHANCE.
WHY YOU--

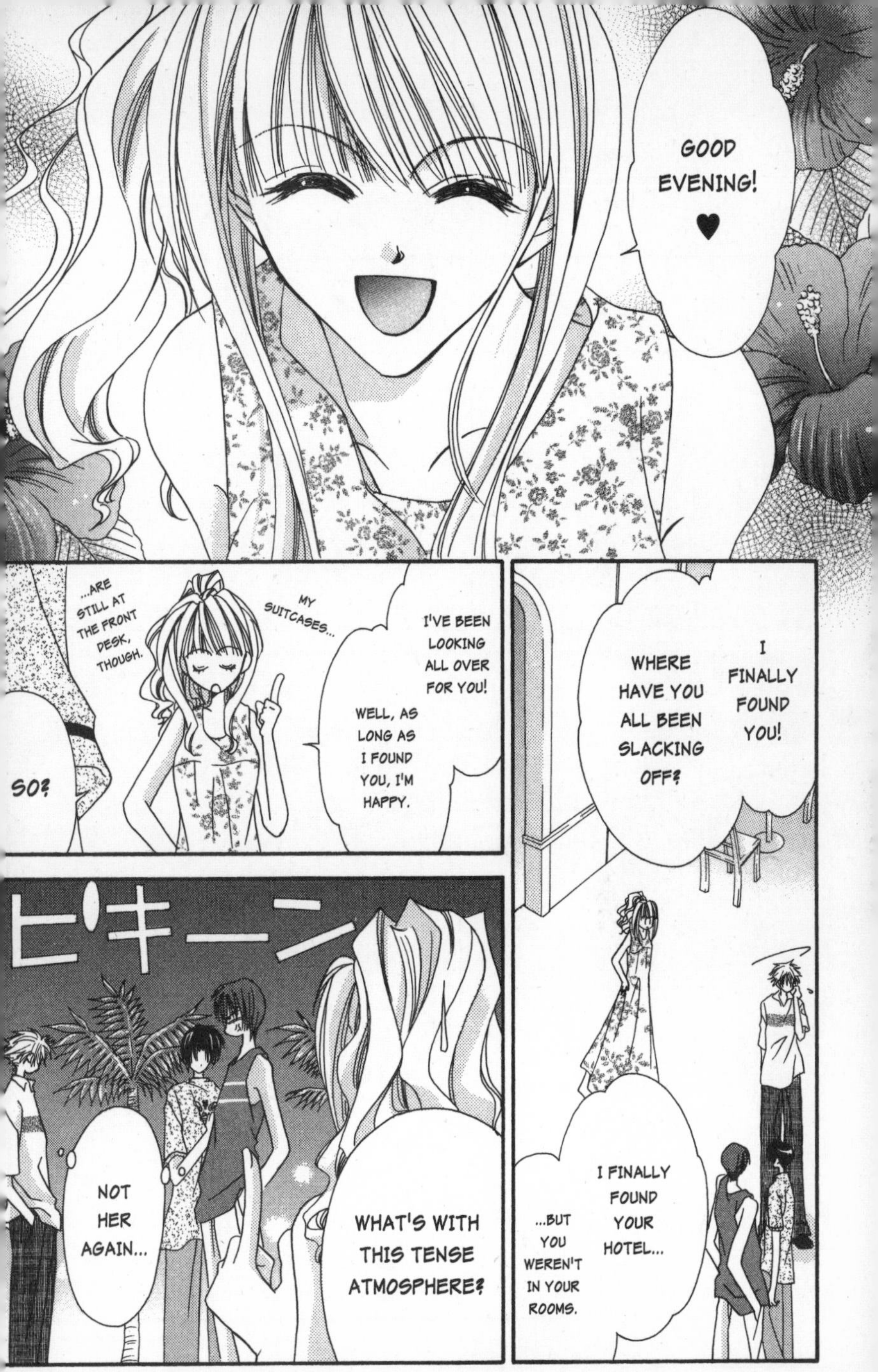
GOOD EVENING! ♥
I FINALLY FOUND YOU!
WHERE HAVE YOU ALL BEEN SLACKING OFF?
I FINALLY FOUND YOUR HOTEL...
...BUT YOU WEREN'T IN YOUR ROOMS.
I'VE BEEN LOOKING ALL OVER FOR YOU!
WELL, AS LONG AS I FOUND YOU, I'M HAPPY.
MY SUITCASES...
...ARE STILL AT THE FRONT DESK, THOUGH.
SO?
ピキーン
WHAT'S WITH THIS TENSE ATMOSPHERE?
NOT HER AGAIN...

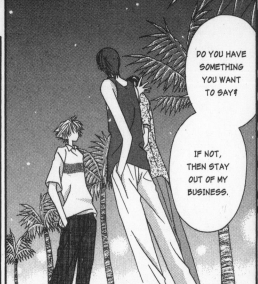

DO YOU HAVE SOMETHING YOU WANT TO SAY?

IF NOT, THEN STAY OUT OF MY BUSINESS.

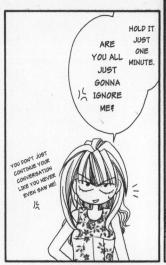

HOLD IT JUST ONE MINUTE.

ARE YOU ALL JUST GONNA IGNORE ME?

YOU DON'T JUST CONTINUE YOUR CONVERSATION LIKE YOU NEVER EVEN SAW ME!

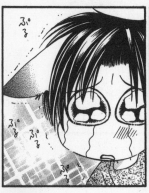

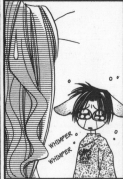

WHIMPER WHIMPER

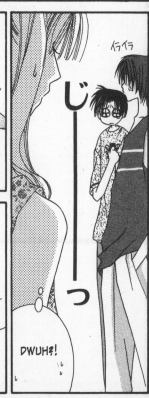

イライラ

じ

っ

DWUH?!

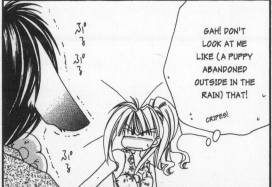

GAH! DON'T LOOK AT ME LIKE (A PUPPY ABANDONED OUTSIDE IN THE RAIN) THAT!

CRIPES!

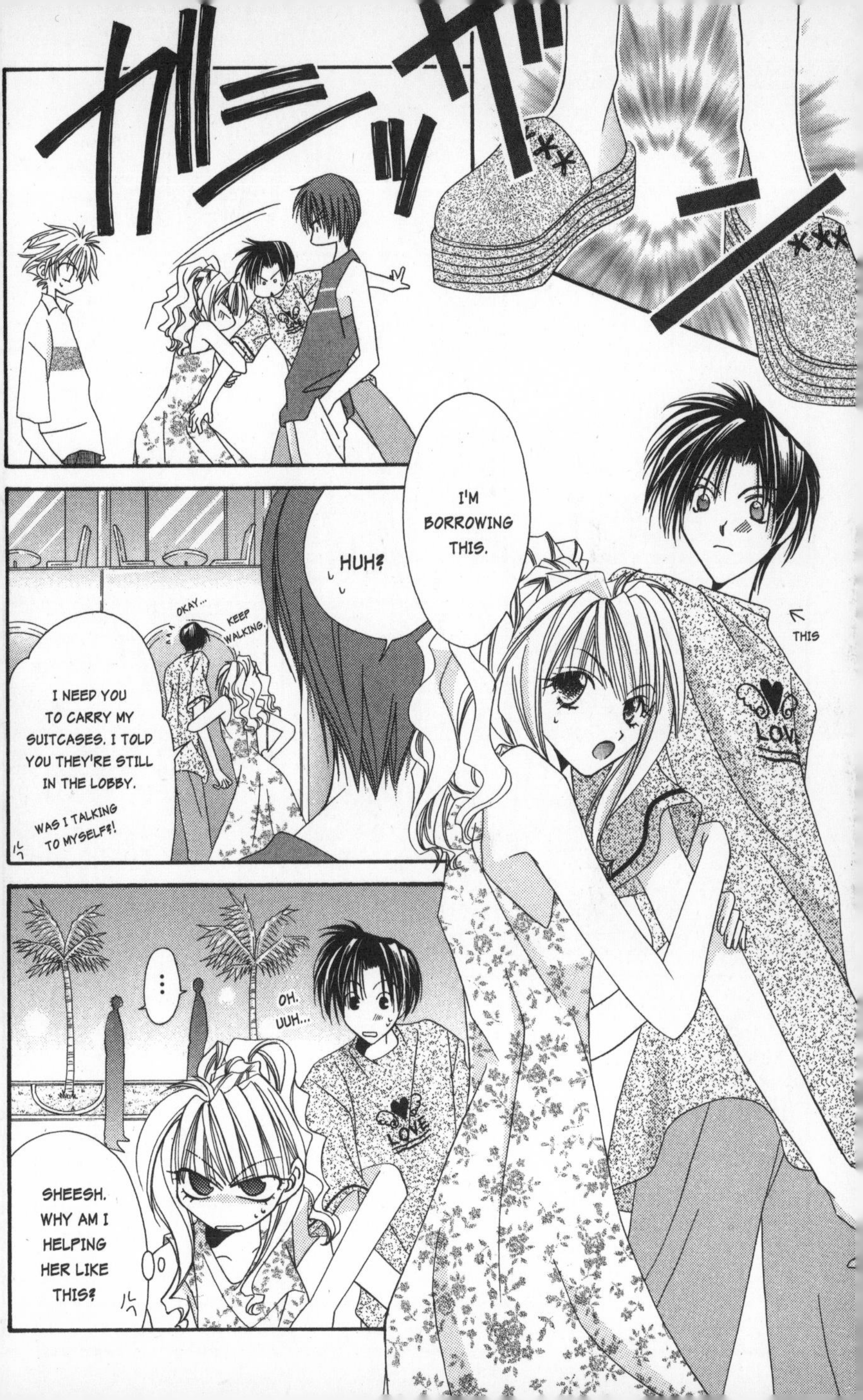
I'M BORROWING THIS.
THIS
HUH?
OKAY...
KEEP WALKING.
I NEED YOU TO CARRY MY SUITCASES. I TOLD YOU THEY'RE STILL IN THE LOBBY.
WAS I TALKING TO MYSELF?!
OH. UUH...
...
SHEESH. WHY AM I HELPING HER LIKE THIS?

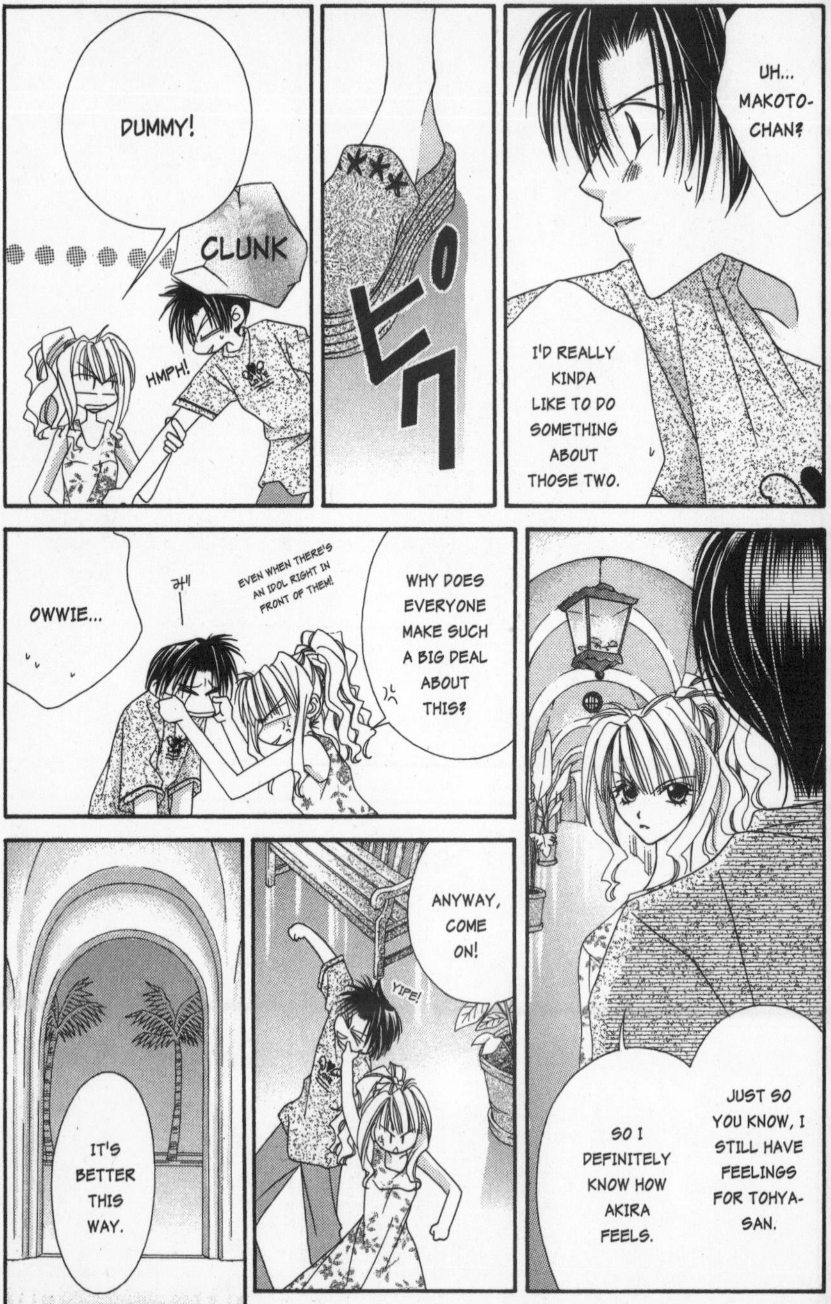
UH... MAKOTO-CHAN?
I'D REALLY KINDA LIKE TO DO SOMETHING ABOUT THOSE TWO.
ピク
DUMMY!
CLUNK
HMPH!
JUST SO YOU KNOW, I STILL HAVE FEELINGS FOR TOHYA-SAN.
SO I DEFINITELY KNOW HOW AKIRA FEELS.
WHY DOES EVERYONE MAKE SUCH A BIG DEAL ABOUT THIS?
EVEN WHEN THERE'S AN IDOL RIGHT IN FRONT OF THEM!
OWWIE...
ANYWAY, COME ON!
YIPE!
IT'S BETTER THIS WAY.

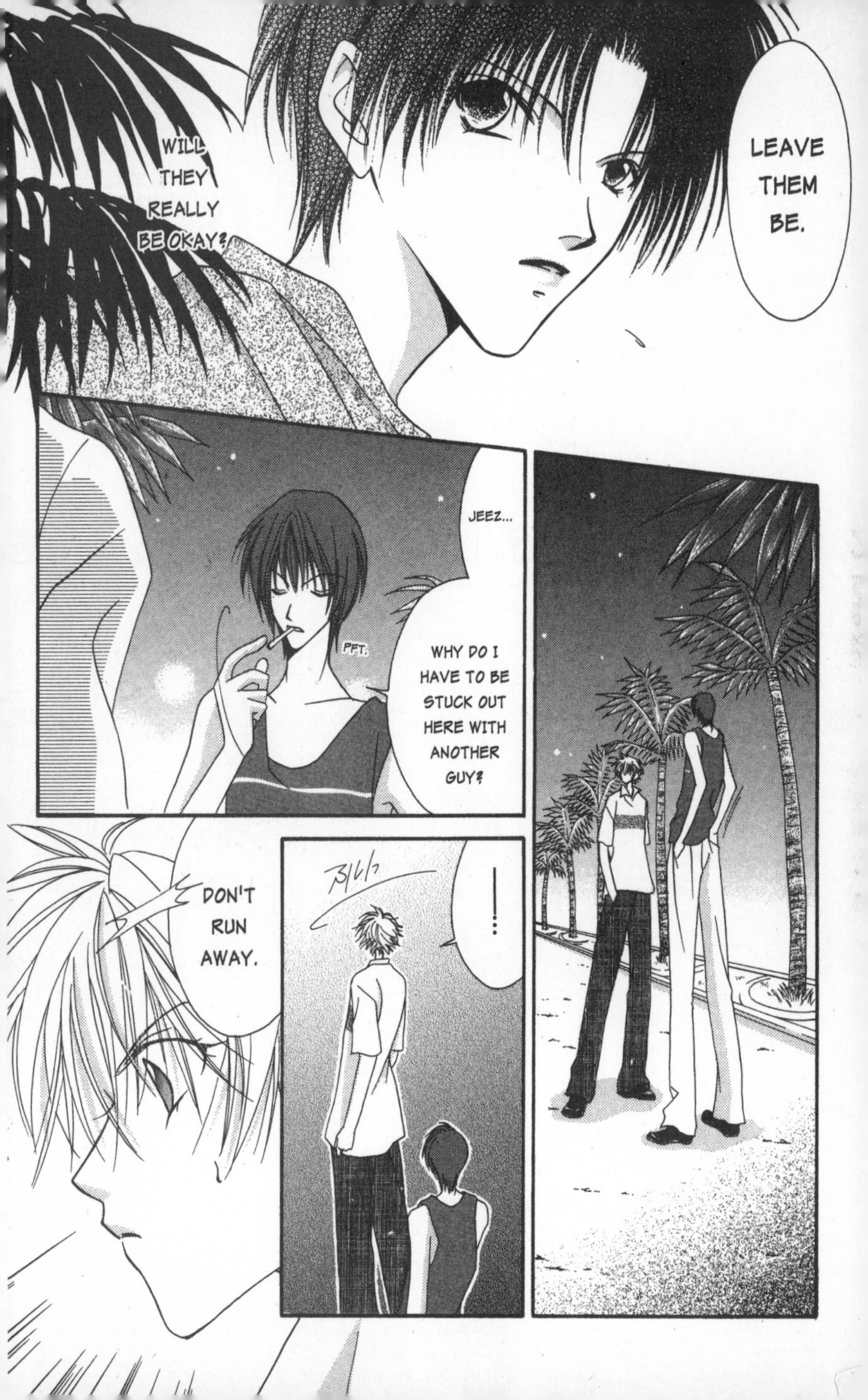
LEAVE THEM BE.
WILL THEY REALLY BE OKAY?
JEEZ...
WHY DO I HAVE TO BE STUCK OUT HERE WITH ANOTHER GUY?
PFT.
...!
DON'T RUN AWAY.

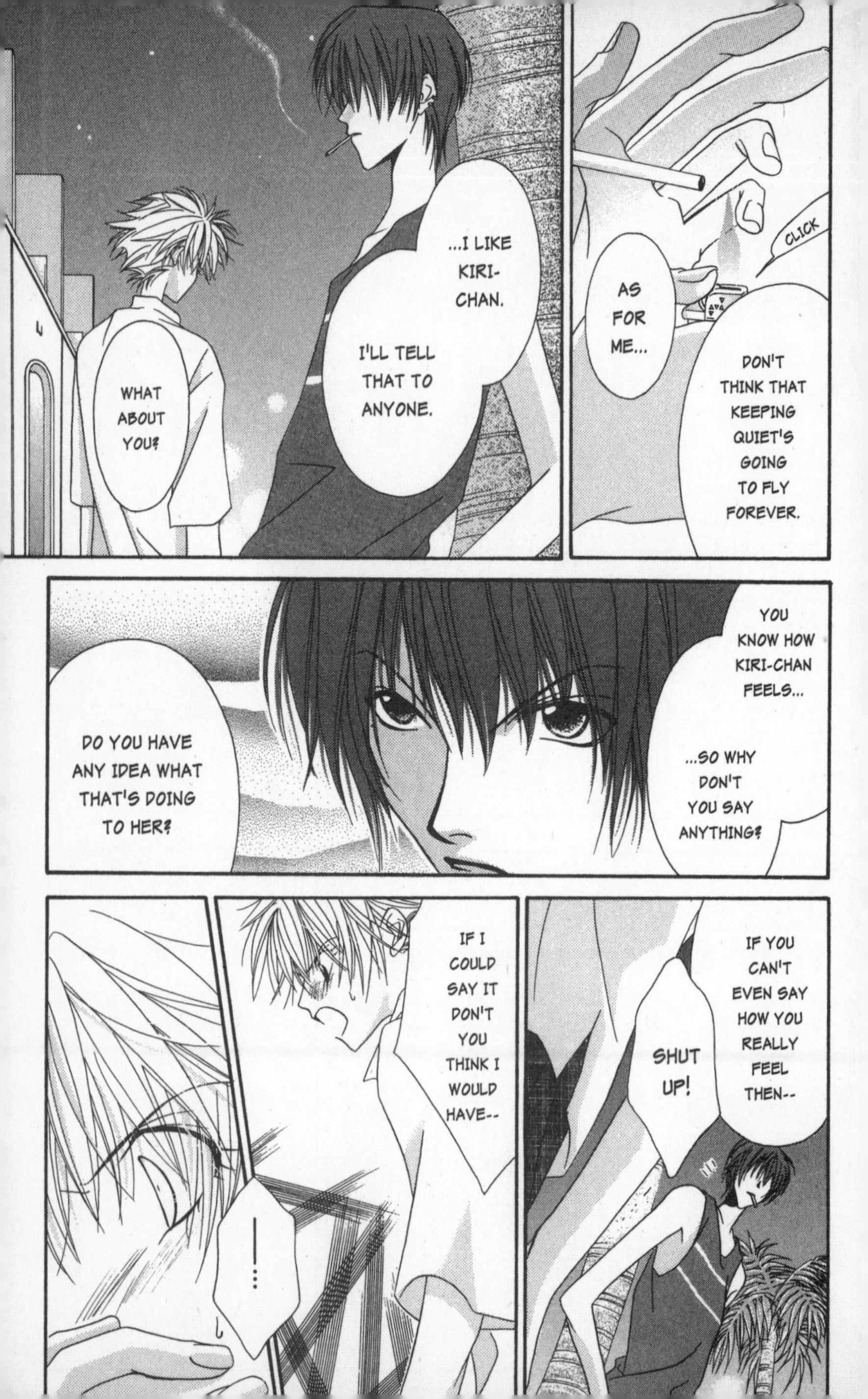
CLICK
AS FOR ME...
DON'T THINK THAT KEEPING QUIET'S GOING TO FLY FOREVER.
...I LIKE KIRI-CHAN.
I'LL TELL THAT TO ANYONE.
WHAT ABOUT YOU?
YOU KNOW HOW KIRI-CHAN FEELS...
...SO WHY DON'T YOU SAY ANYTHING?
DO YOU HAVE ANY IDEA WHAT THAT'S DOING TO HER?
IF YOU CAN'T EVEN SAY HOW YOU REALLY FEEL THEN--
SHUT UP!
IF I COULD SAY IT DON'T YOU THINK I WOULD HAVE--
......

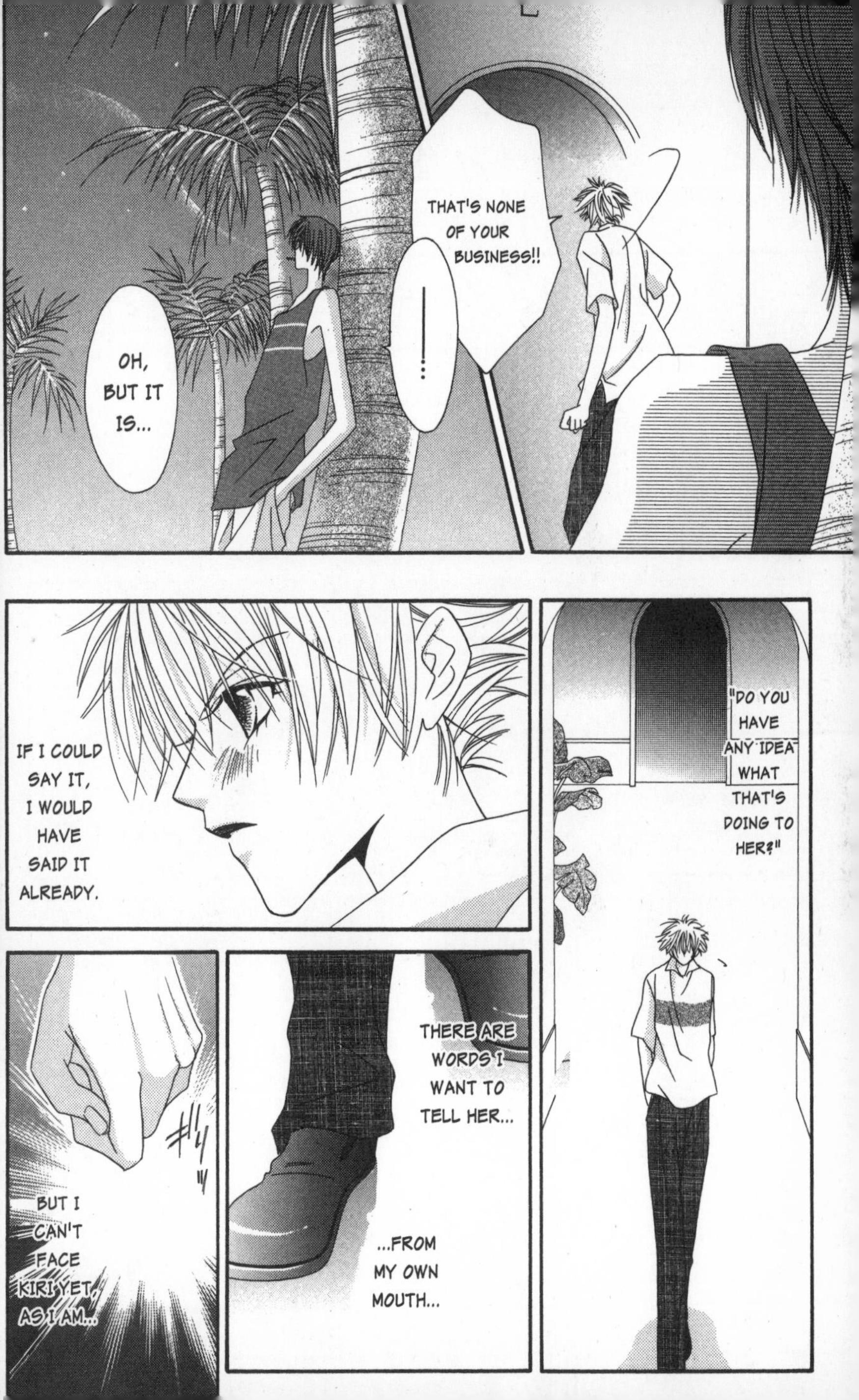
THAT'S NONE OF YOUR BUSINESS!!
OH, BUT IT IS...
—!
"DO YOU HAVE ANY IDEA WHAT THAT'S DOING TO HER?"
IF I COULD SAY IT, I WOULD HAVE SAID IT ALREADY.
THERE ARE WORDS I WANT TO TELL HER...
...FROM MY OWN MOUTH...
BUT I CAN'T FACE KIRI YET, AS I AM...

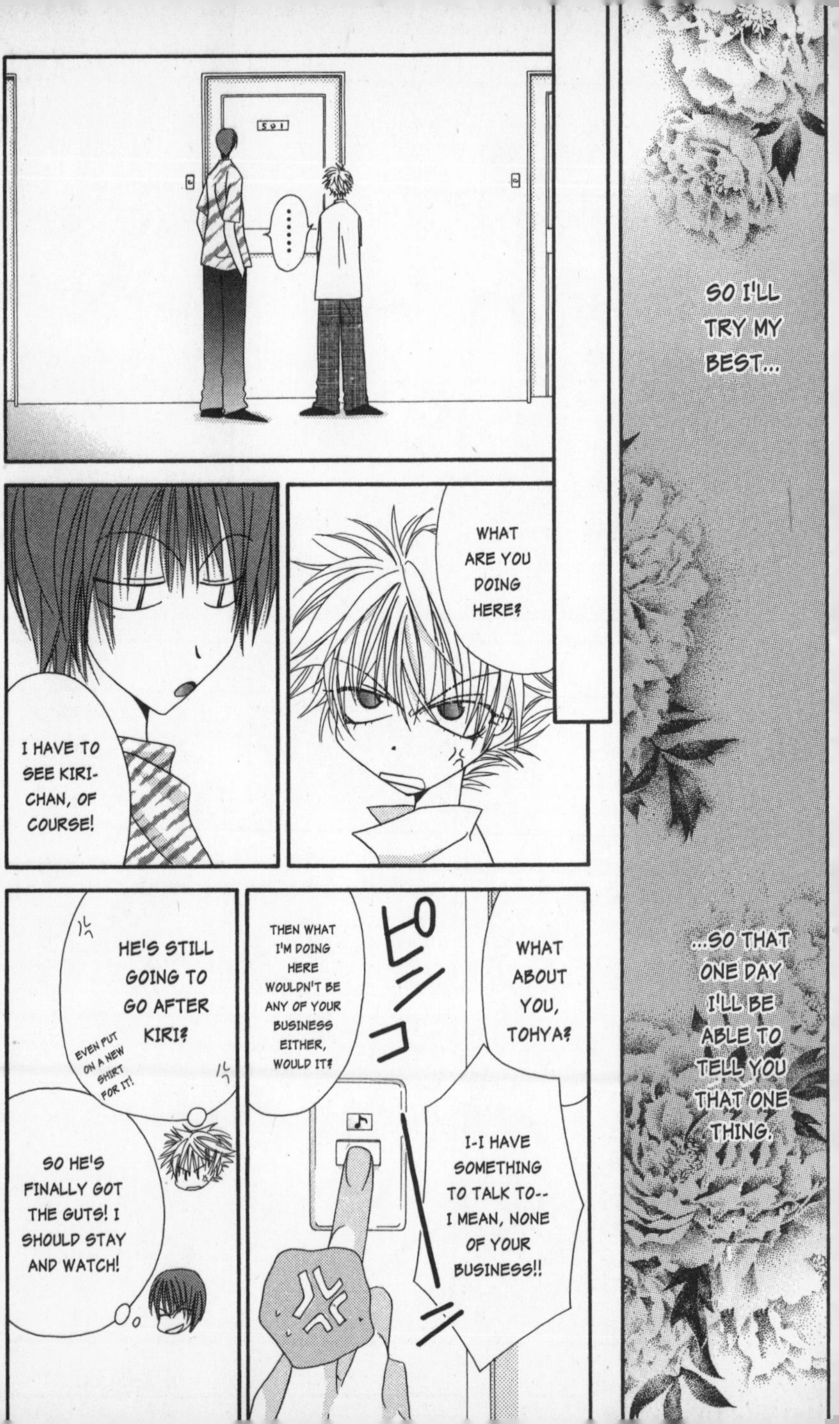
SO I'LL TRY MY BEST...
...SO THAT ONE DAY I'LL BE ABLE TO TELL YOU THAT ONE THING.
......
WHAT ARE YOU DOING HERE?
I HAVE TO SEE KIRI-CHAN, OF COURSE!
WHAT ABOUT YOU, TOHYA?
I-I HAVE SOMETHING TO TALK TO-- I MEAN, NONE OF YOUR BUSINESS!!
ピンコ
THEN WHAT I'M DOING HERE WOULDN'T BE ANY OF YOUR BUSINESS EITHER, WOULD IT?
HE'S STILL GOING TO GO AFTER KIRI?
EVEN PUT ON A NEW SHIRT FOR IT!
SO HE'S FINALLY GOT THE GUTS! I SHOULD STAY AND WATCH!

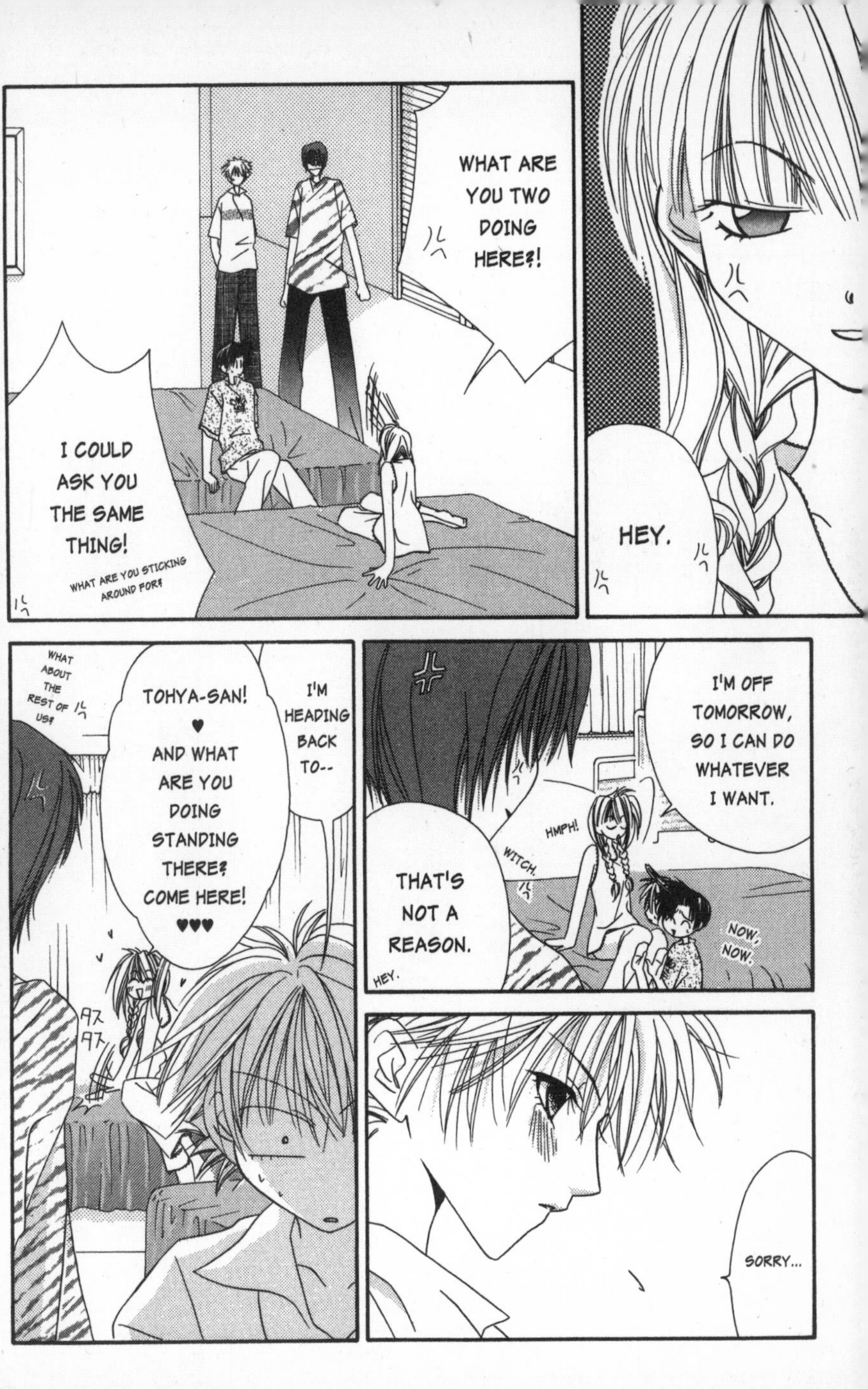
HEY.
WHAT ARE YOU TWO DOING HERE?!
I COULD ASK YOU THE SAME THING!
WHAT ARE YOU STICKING AROUND FOR?
I'M OFF TOMORROW, SO I CAN DO WHATEVER I WANT.
HMPH!
WITCH.
THAT'S NOT A REASON.
NOW, NOW.
HEY.
SORRY...
I'M HEADING BACK TO--
TOHYA-SAN! ♥ AND WHAT ARE YOU DOING STANDING THERE? COME HERE! ♥♥♥
WHAT ABOUT THE REST OF US?

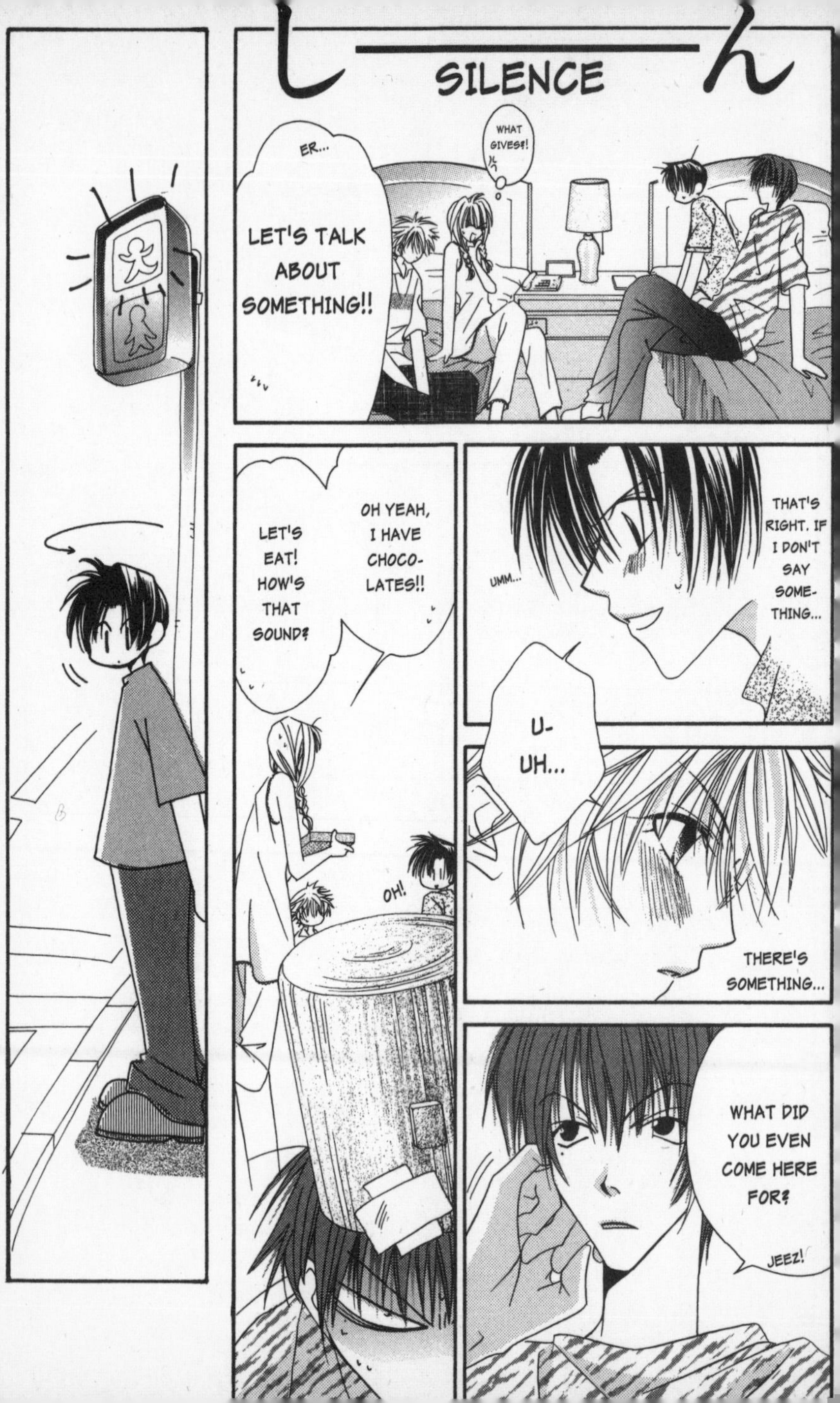
しーーん
SILENCE
WHAT GIVES?!
ER... LET'S TALK ABOUT SOMETHING!!
THAT'S RIGHT. IF I DON'T SAY SOMETHING...
UMM...
OH YEAH, I HAVE CHOCOLATES!!
LET'S EAT! HOW'S THAT SOUND?
U-UH...
THERE'S SOMETHING...
OH!
WHAT DID YOU EVEN COME HERE FOR?
JEEZ!

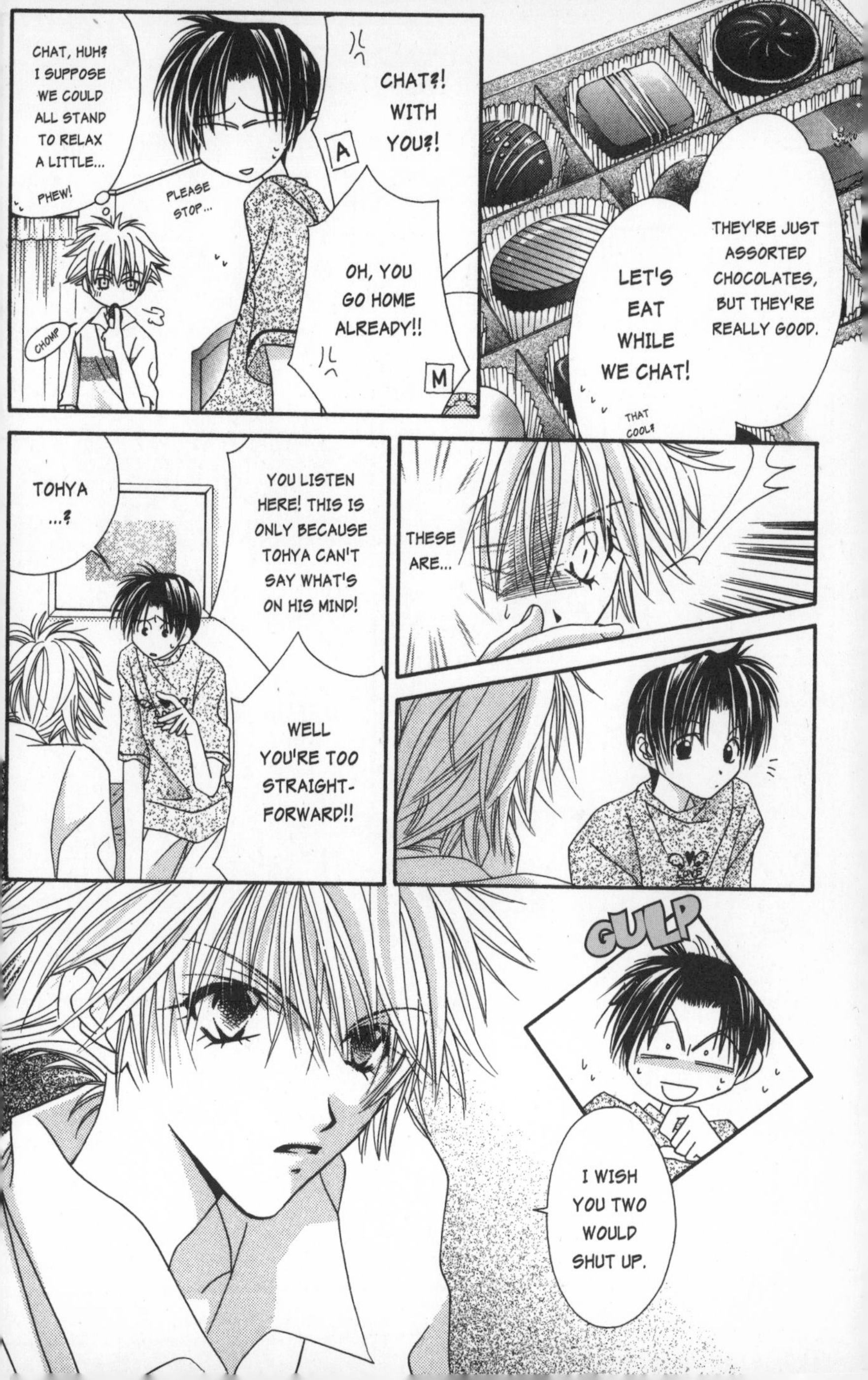
THEY'RE JUST ASSORTED CHOCOLATES, BUT THEY'RE REALLY GOOD.
LET'S EAT WHILE WE CHAT!
THAT COOL?
CHAT?! WITH YOU?!
A
OH, YOU GO HOME ALREADY!!
M
PLEASE STOP...
CHAT, HUH? I SUPPOSE WE COULD ALL STAND TO RELAX A LITTLE...
PHEW!
CHOMP
THESE ARE...
YOU LISTEN HERE! THIS IS ONLY BECAUSE TOHYA CAN'T SAY WHAT'S ON HIS MIND!
TOHYA ...?
WELL YOU'RE TOO STRAIGHT-FORWARD!!
GULP
I WISH YOU TWO WOULD SHUT UP.

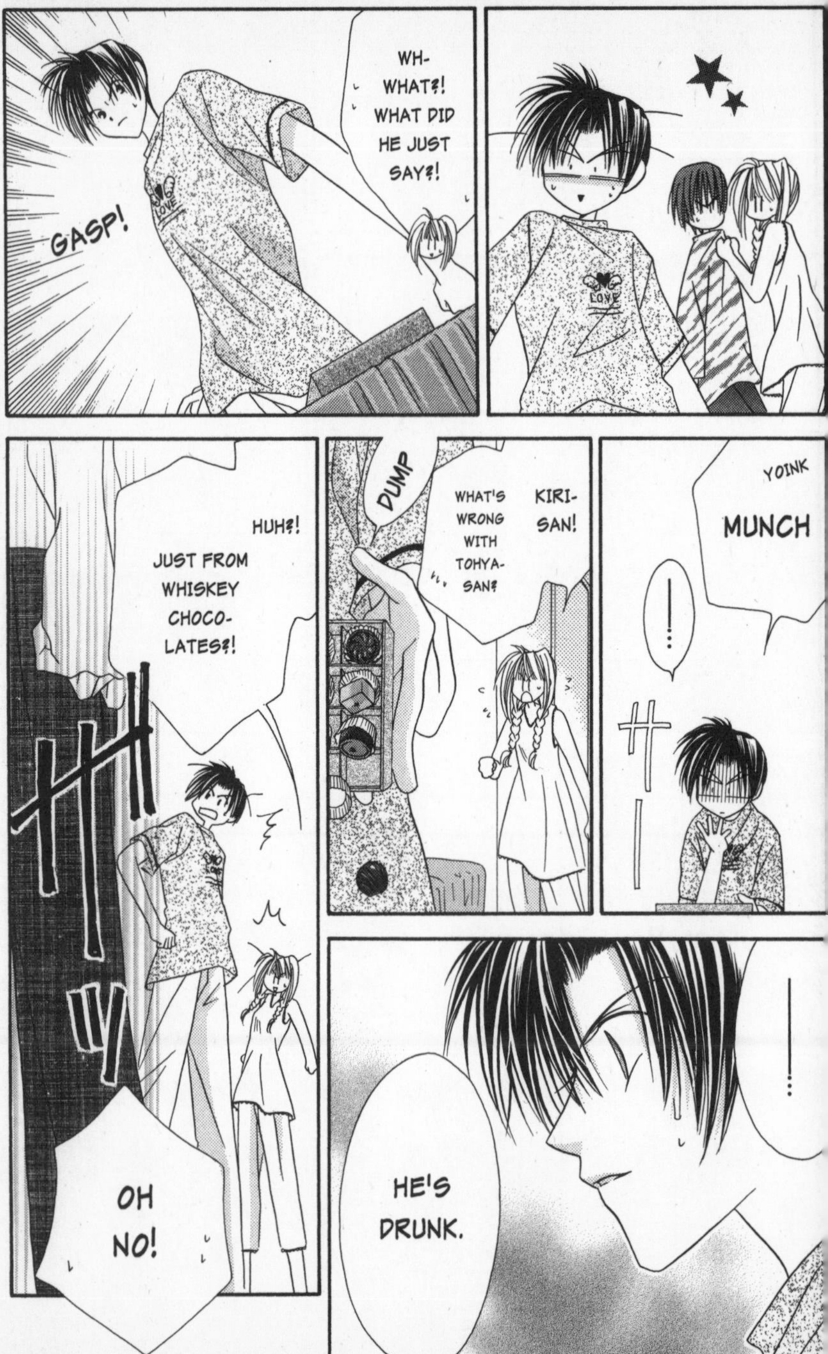
WH- WHAT?! WHAT DID HE JUST SAY?!
GASP!
YOINK
MUNCH
!...
DUMP
KIRI-SAN!
WHAT'S WRONG WITH TOHYA-SAN?
...
HE'S DRUNK.
HUH?!
JUST FROM WHISKEY CHOCO-LATES?!
OH NO!

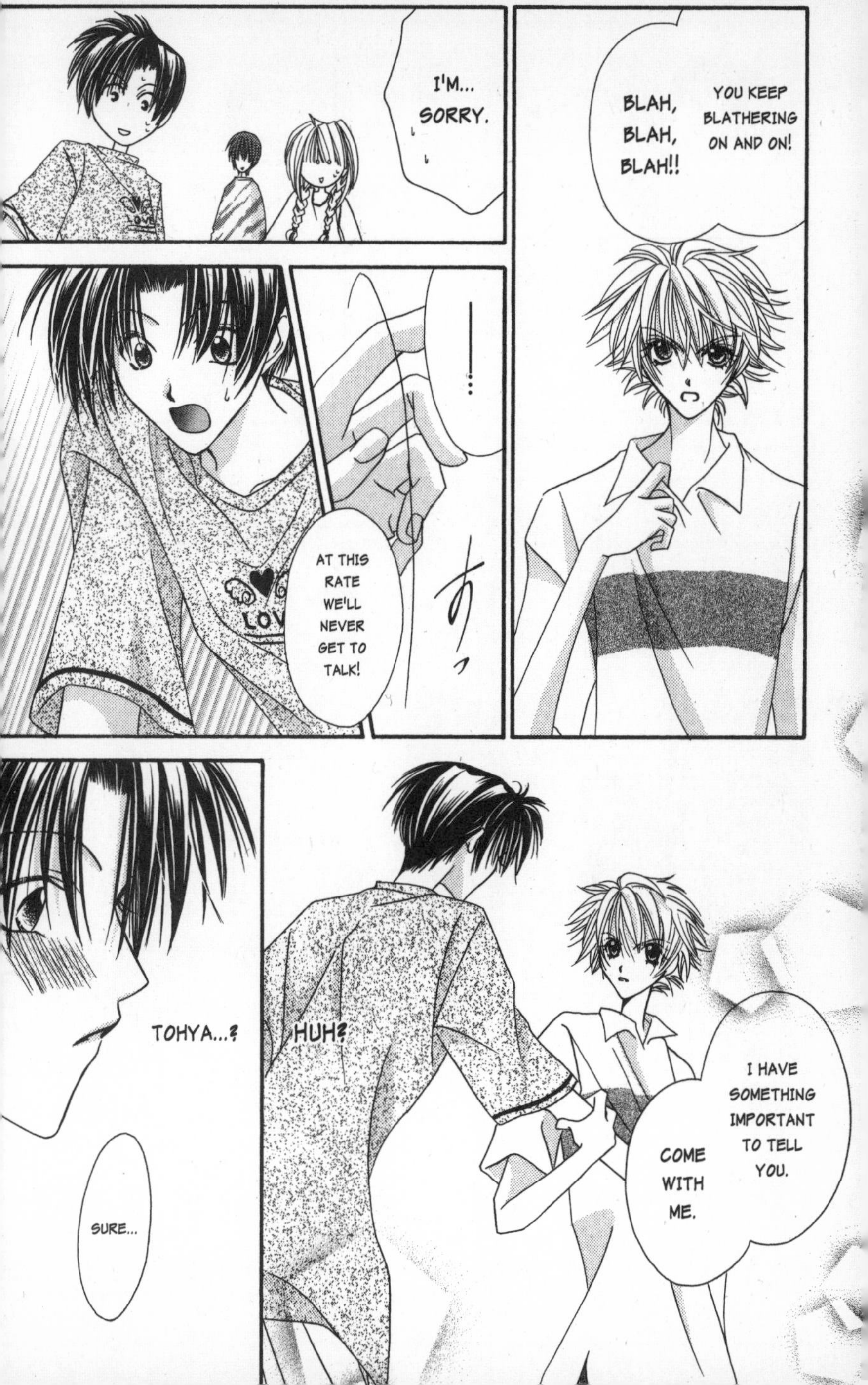
YOU KEEP BLATHERING ON AND ON!
BLAH, BLAH, BLAH!!
I'M... SORRY.
...!!
あっ
AT THIS RATE WE'LL NEVER GET TO TALK!
I HAVE SOMETHING IMPORTANT TO TELL YOU.
COME WITH ME.
HUH?
TOHYA...?
SURE...

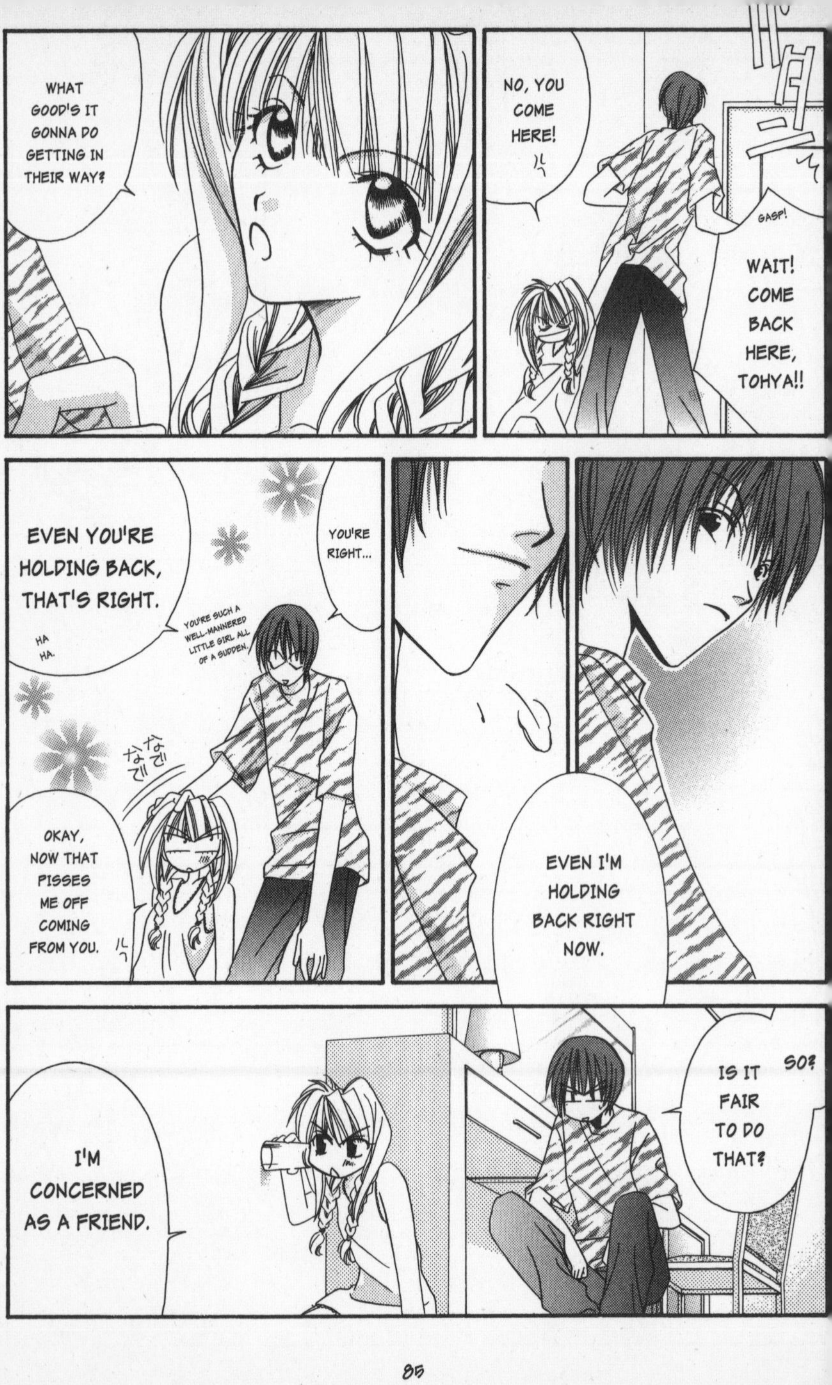
NO, YOU COME HERE!
GASP!
WAIT! COME BACK HERE, TOHYA!!
WHAT GOOD'S IT GONNA DO GETTING IN THEIR WAY?
EVEN I'M HOLDING BACK RIGHT NOW.
YOU'RE RIGHT...
EVEN YOU'RE HOLDING BACK, THAT'S RIGHT.
HA HA.
YOU'RE SUCH A WELL-MANNERED LITTLE GIRL ALL OF A SUDDEN.
なでなで
OKAY, NOW THAT PISSES ME OFF COMING FROM YOU.
SO?
IS IT FAIR TO DO THAT?
I'M CONCERNED AS A FRIEND.

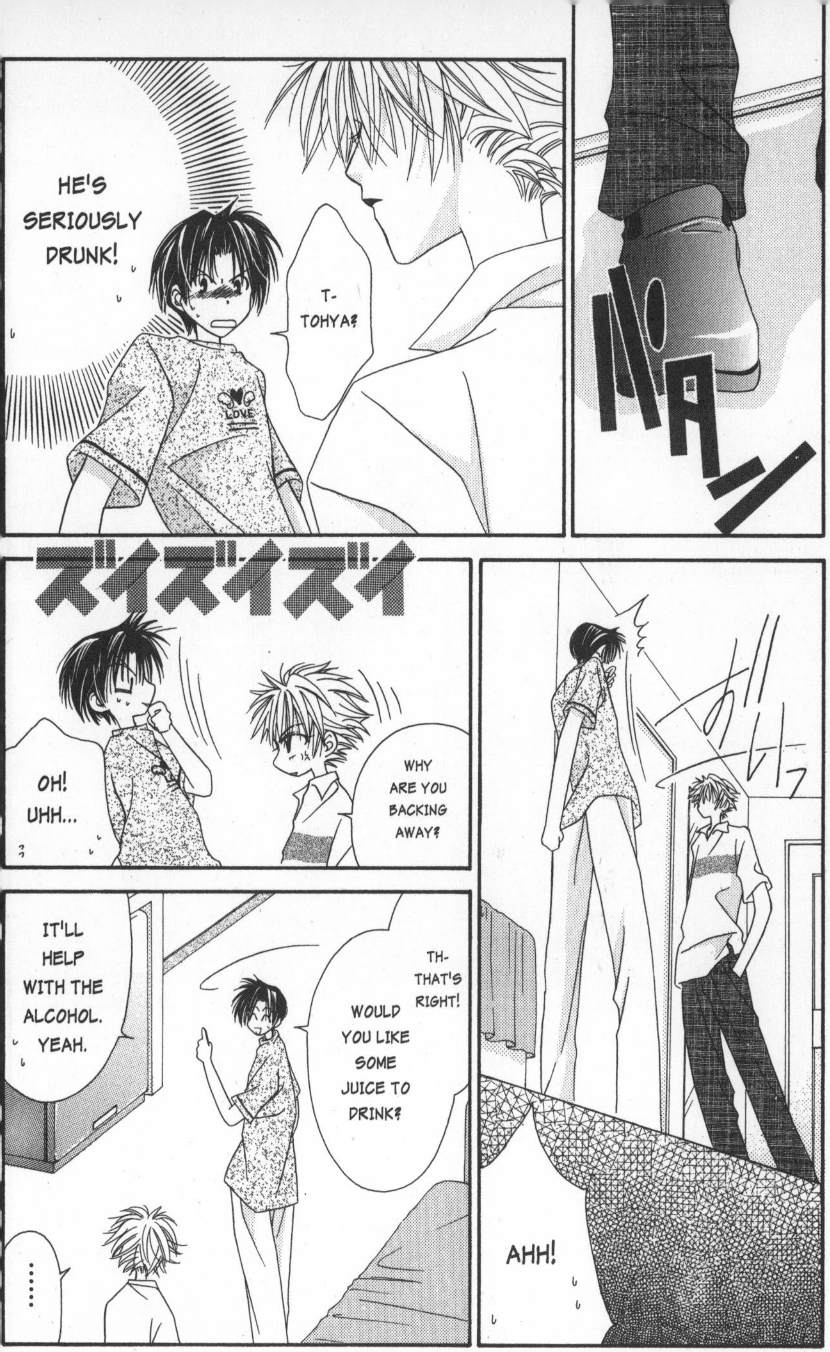
バタン
T-TOHYA?
HE'S SERIOUSLY DRUNK!
AHH!
ズイズイズイ
WHY ARE YOU BACKING AWAY?
OH! UHH...
TH-THAT'S RIGHT!
WOULD YOU LIKE SOME JUICE TO DRINK?
IT'LL HELP WITH THE ALCOHOL. YEAH.
......

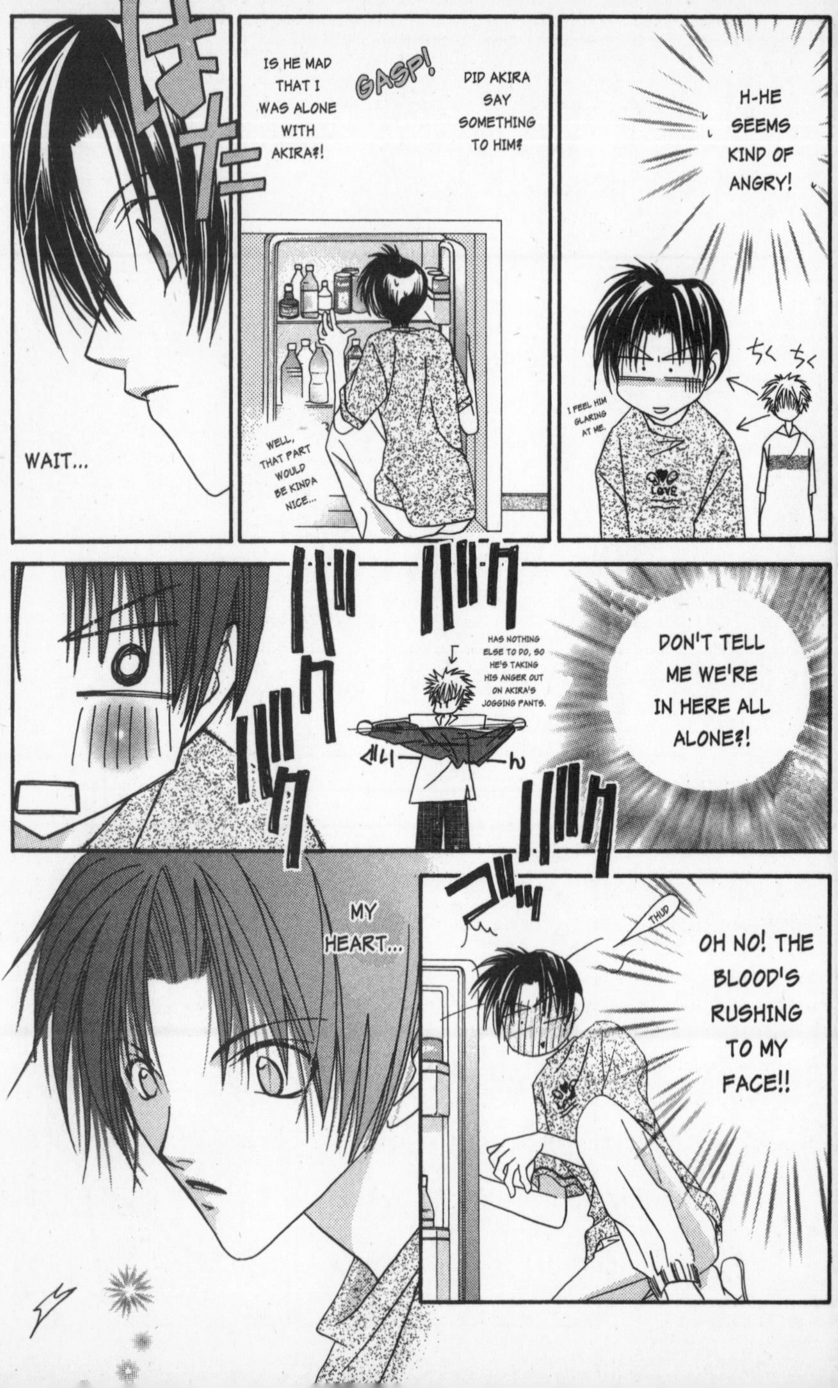
H-HE SEEMS KIND OF ANGRY!
ちく ちく
I FEEL HIM GLARING AT ME.
DID AKIRA SAY SOMETHING TO HIM?
GASP!
IS HE MAD THAT I WAS ALONE WITH AKIRA?!
WELL, THAT PART WOULD BE KINDA NICE...
WAIT...
DON'T TELL ME WE'RE IN HERE ALL ALONE?!
HAS NOTHING ELSE TO DO, SO HE'S TAKING HIS ANGER OUT ON AKIRA'S JOGGING PANTS.
OH NO! THE BLOOD'S RUSHING TO MY FACE!!
THUD
MY HEART...

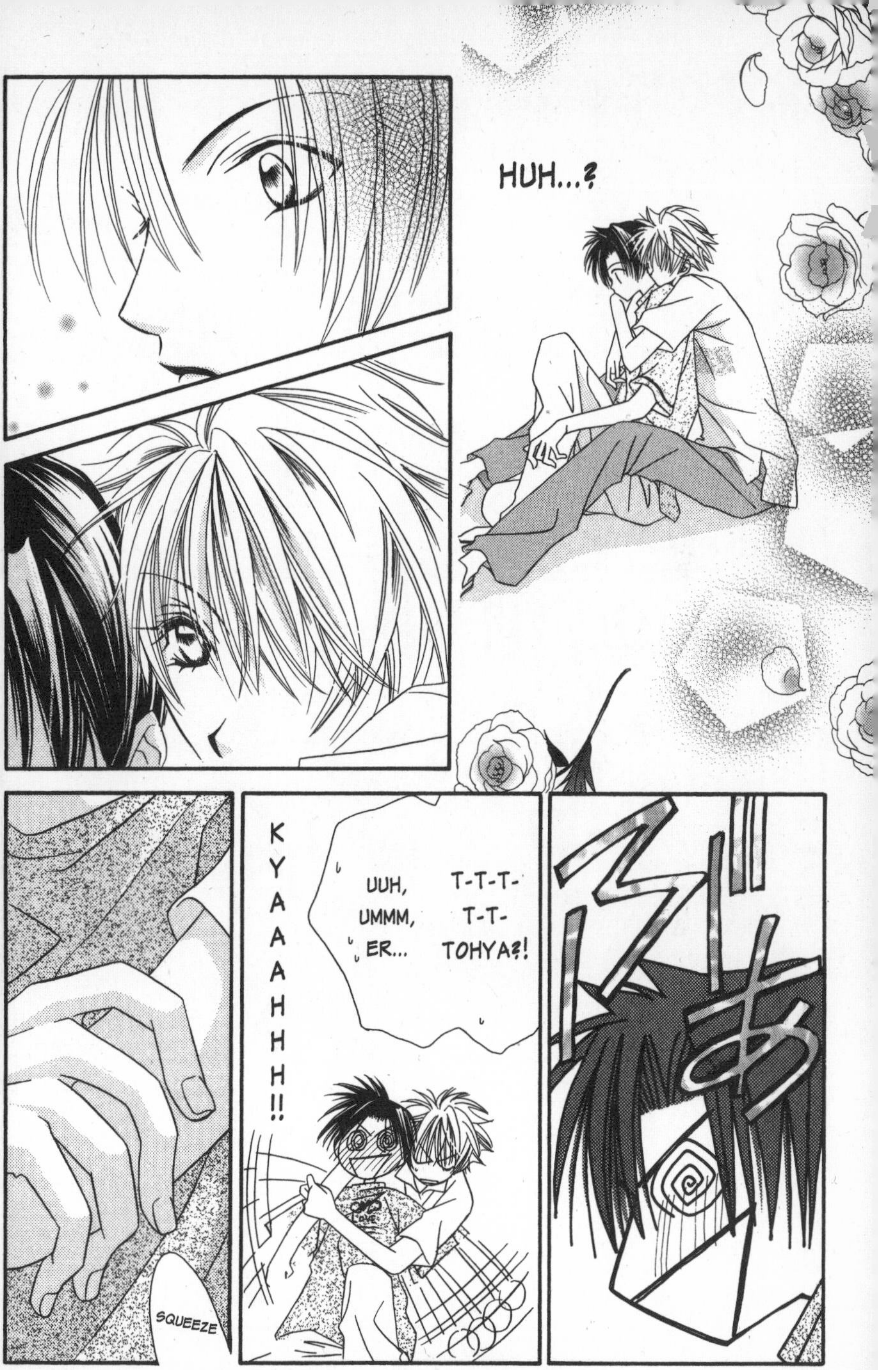
HUH...?
T-T-T-T-T-TOHYA?!
UUH, UMMM, ER...
KYAAAAHHH!!
SQUEEZE

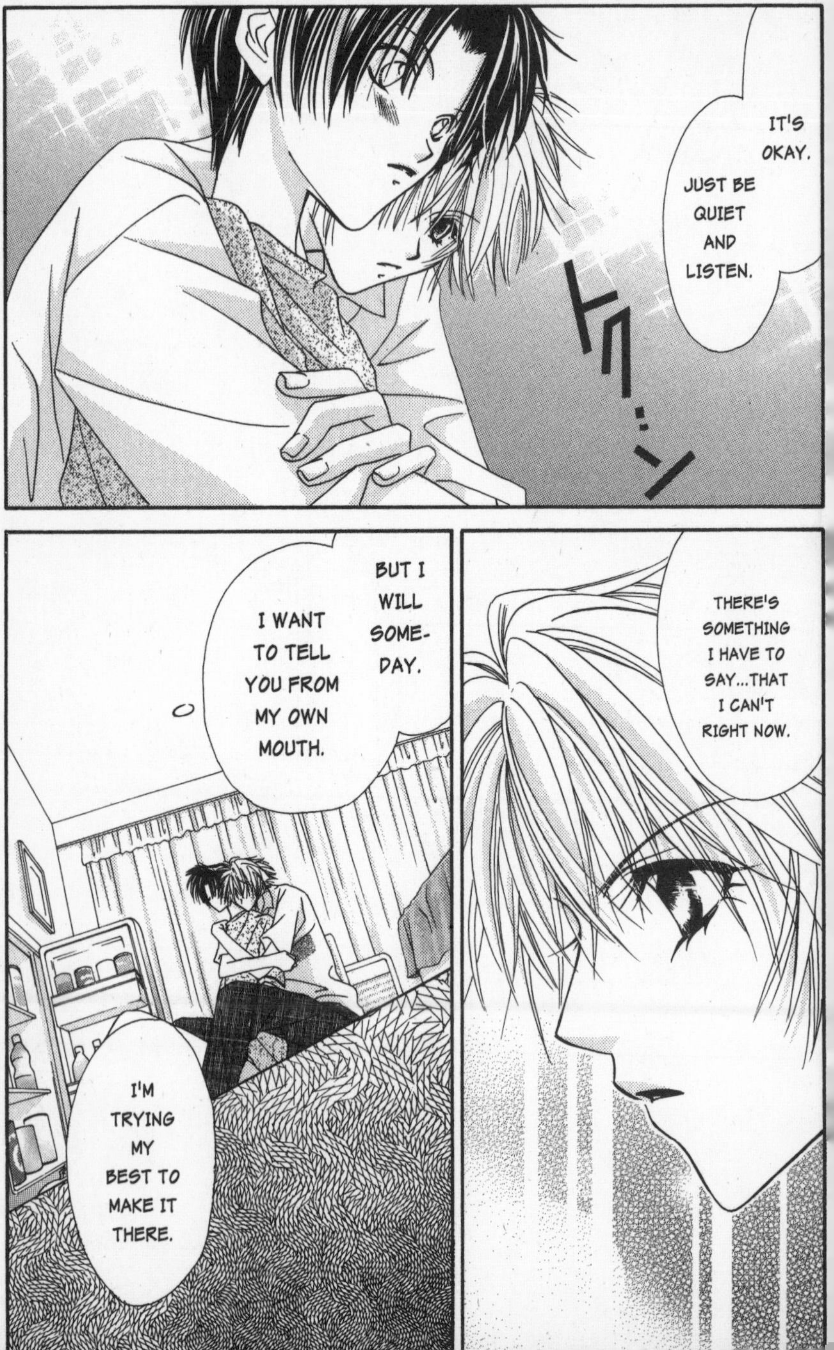
IT'S OKAY.
JUST BE QUIET AND LISTEN.
トク…ン
THERE'S SOMETHING I HAVE TO SAY...THAT I CAN'T RIGHT NOW.
BUT I WILL SOME-DAY.
I WANT TO TELL YOU FROM MY OWN MOUTH.
I'M TRYING MY BEST TO MAKE IT THERE.

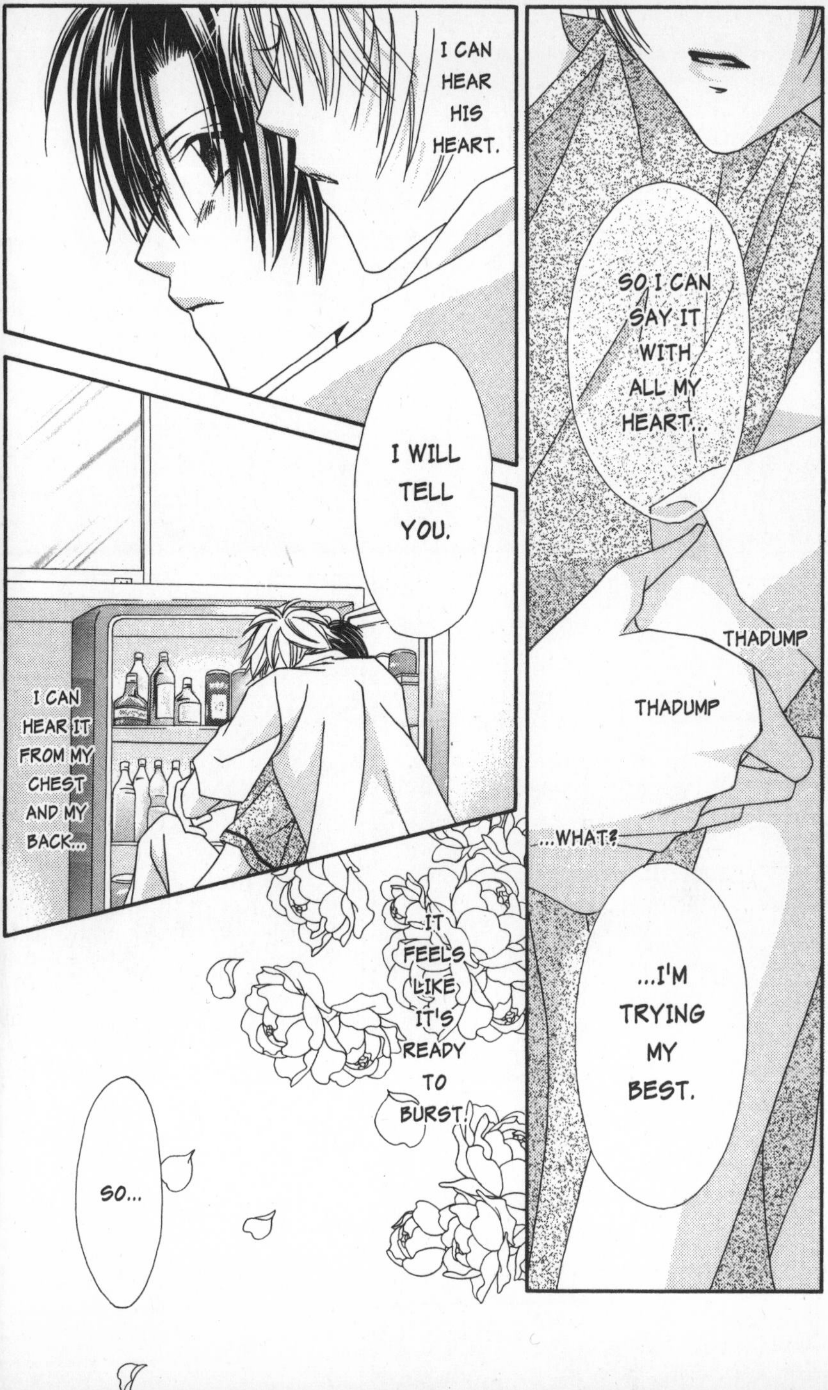

SO I CAN SAY IT WITH ALL MY HEART...
THADUMP
THADUMP
...WHAT?
...I'M TRYING MY BEST.
I CAN HEAR HIS HEART.
I WILL TELL YOU.
I CAN HEAR IT FROM MY CHEST AND MY BACK...
IT FEELS LIKE IT'S READY TO BURST!
SO...

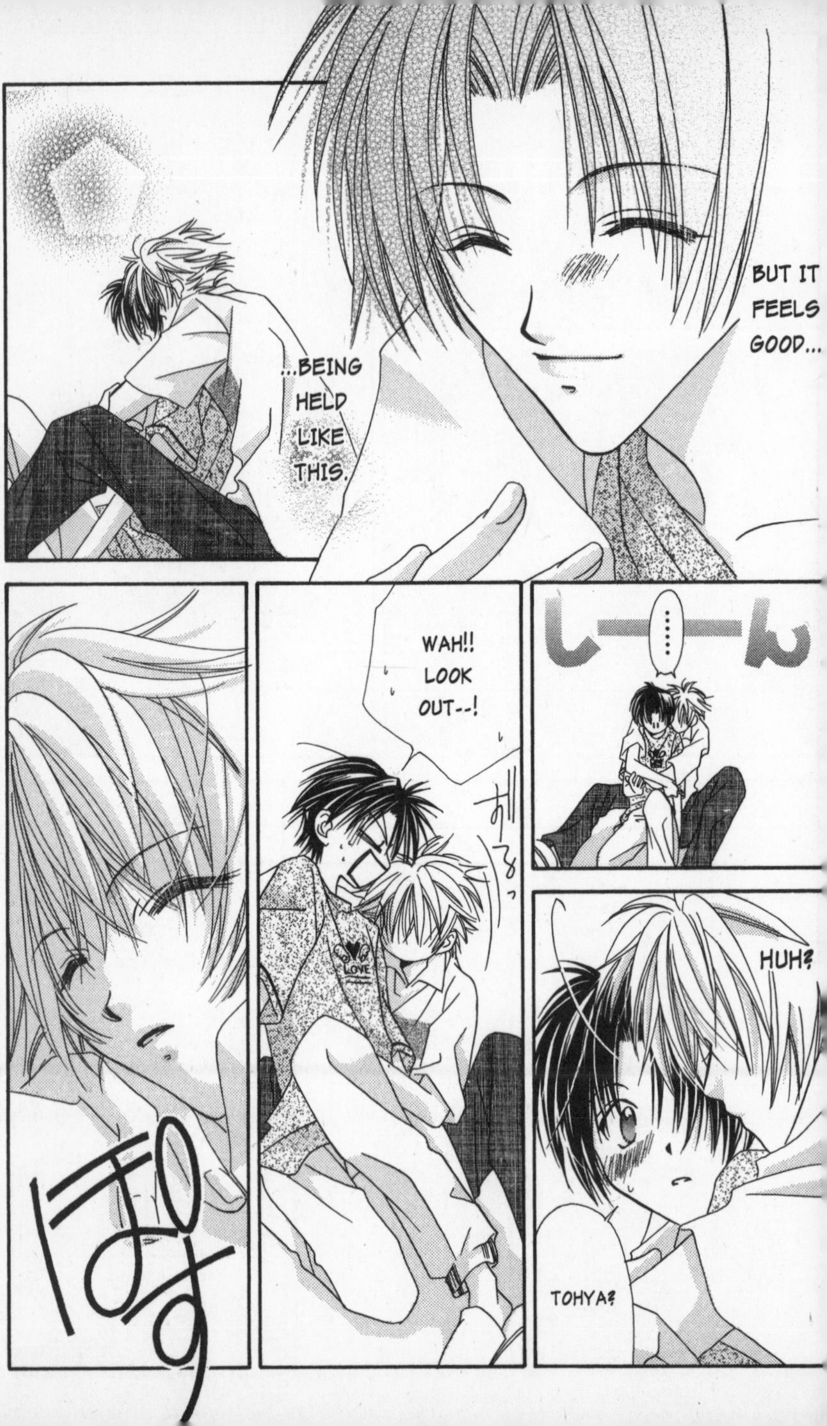
BUT IT FEELS GOOD...
...BEING HELD LIKE THIS.
しーん
......
HUH?
TOHYA?
WAH!! LOOK OUT--!
ぽす

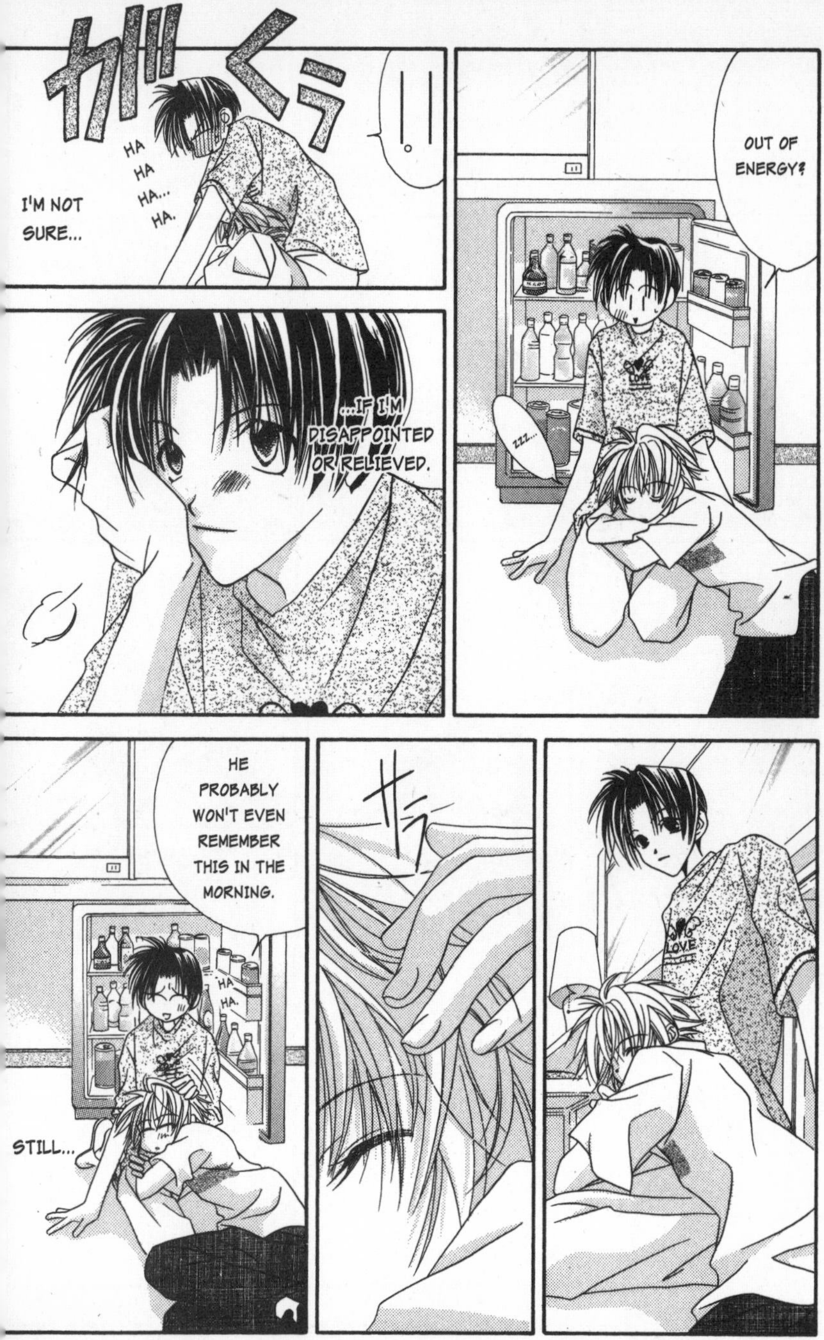
OUT OF ENERGY?
ZZZ...
!!
HA HA HA... HA.
I'M NOT SURE...
...IF I'M DISAPPOINTED OR RELIEVED.
サラ
HE PROBABLY WON'T EVEN REMEMBER THIS IN THE MORNING.
HA HA.
STILL...

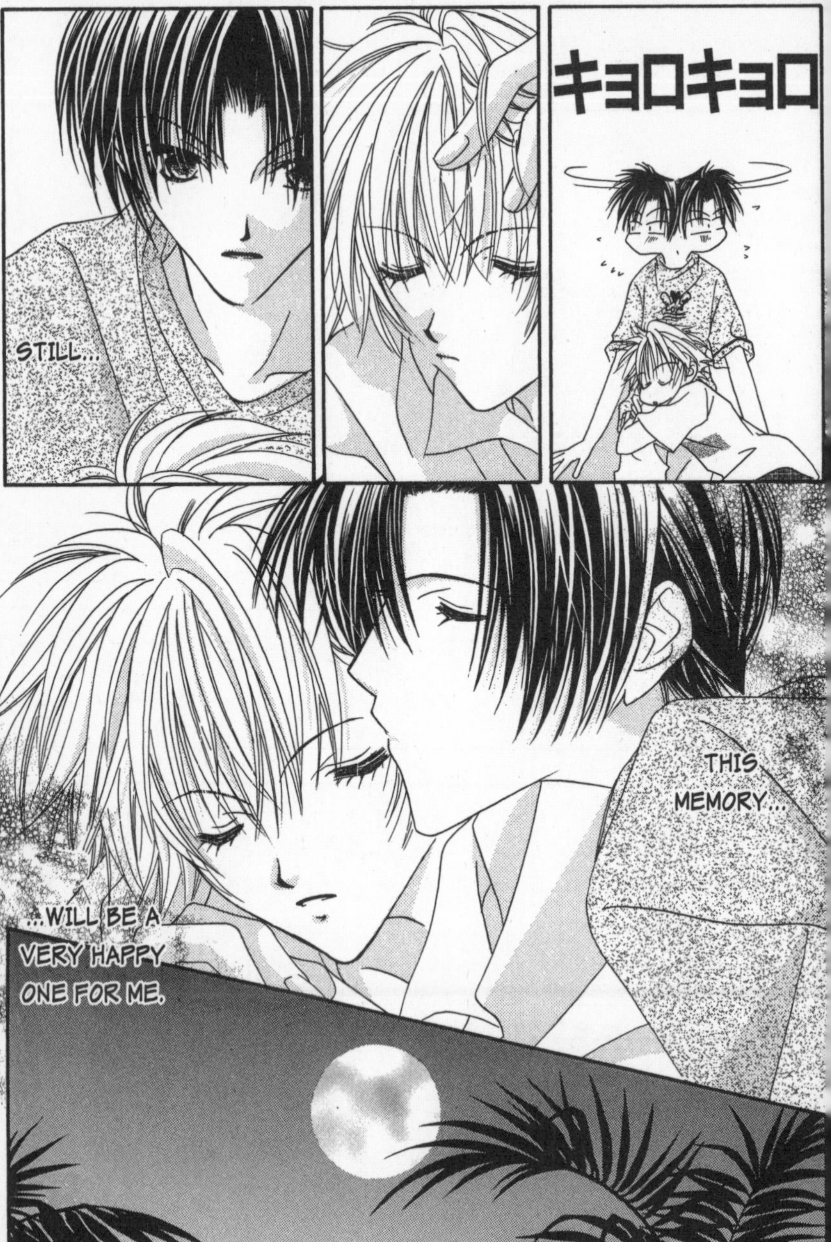
キョロキョロ
STILL...
THIS MEMORY...
...WILL BE A VERY HAPPY ONE FOR ME.

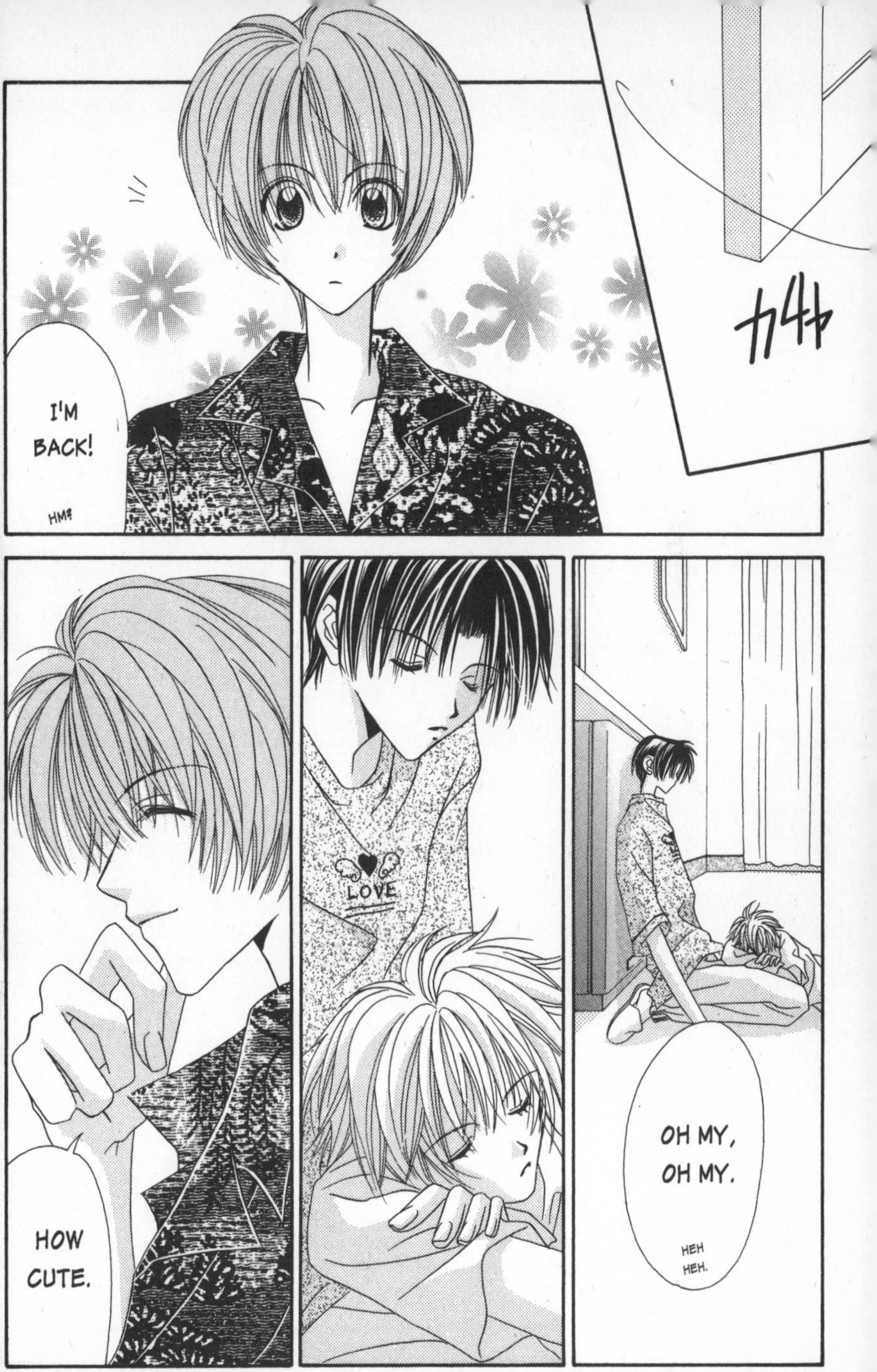
カチャ
I'M BACK!
HM?
OH MY, OH MY.
HEH HEH.
HOW CUTE.

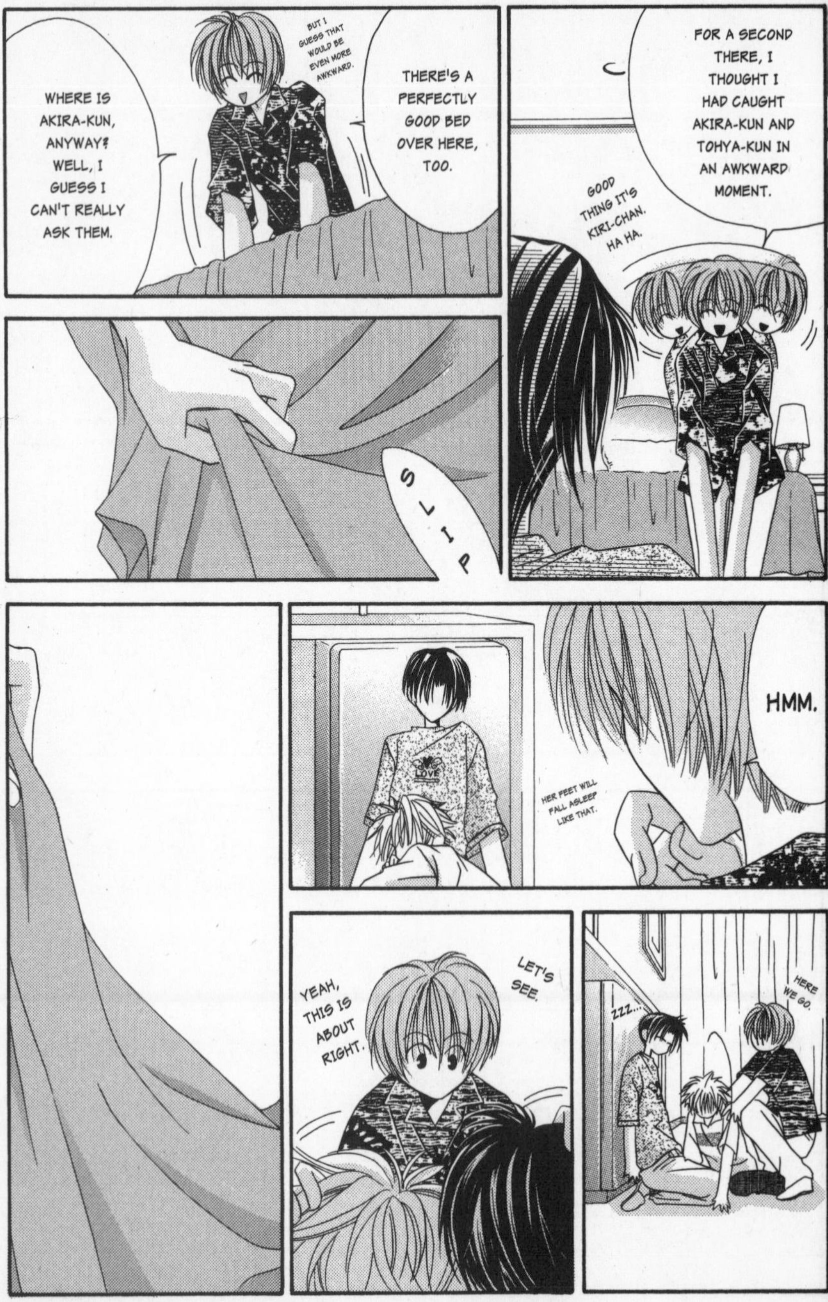
FOR A SECOND THERE, I THOUGHT I HAD CAUGHT AKIRA-KUN AND TOHYA-KUN IN AN AWKWARD MOMENT.
GOOD THING IT'S KIRI-CHAN. HA HA.
THERE'S A PERFECTLY GOOD BED OVER HERE, TOO.
BUT I GUESS THAT WOULD BE EVEN MORE AWKWARD.
WHERE IS AKIRA-KUN, ANYWAY? WELL, I GUESS I CAN'T REALLY ASK THEM.
SLIP
HMM.
HER FEET WILL FALL ASLEEP LIKE THAT.
HERE WE GO.
ZZZ...
LET'S SEE.
YEAH, THIS IS ABOUT RIGHT.

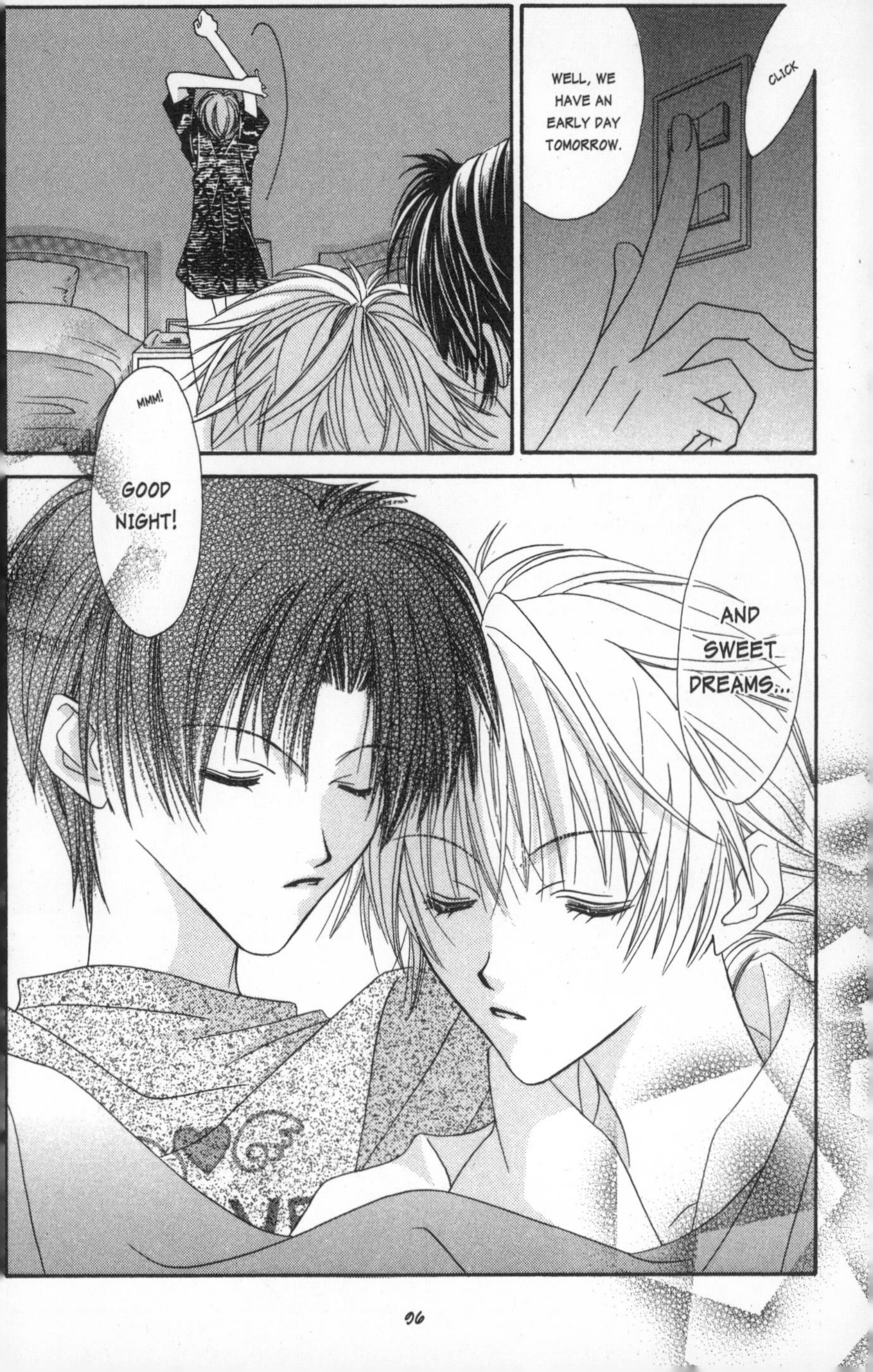
WELL, WE HAVE AN EARLY DAY TOMORROW.
CLICK
MMM!
GOOD NIGHT!
AND SWEET DREAMS...

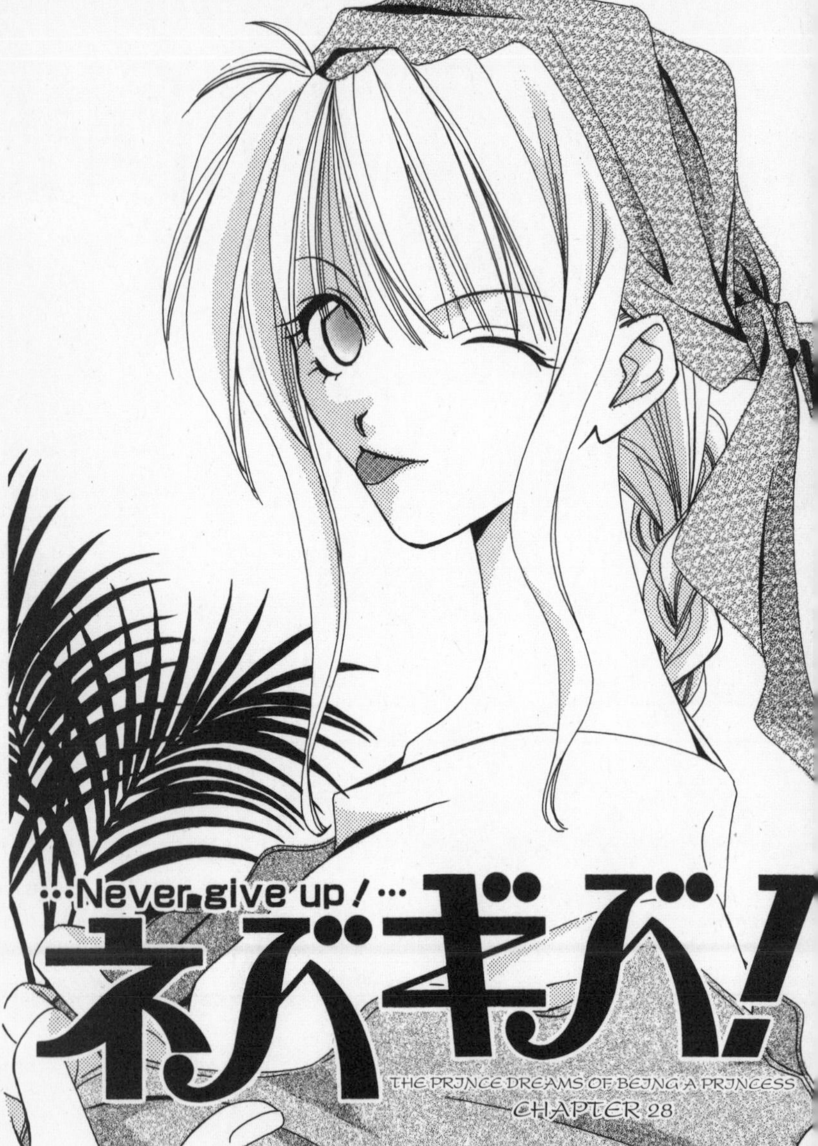
...Never give up!...
ネバギバ!
THE PRINCE DREAMS OF BEING A PRINCESS
CHAPTER 28

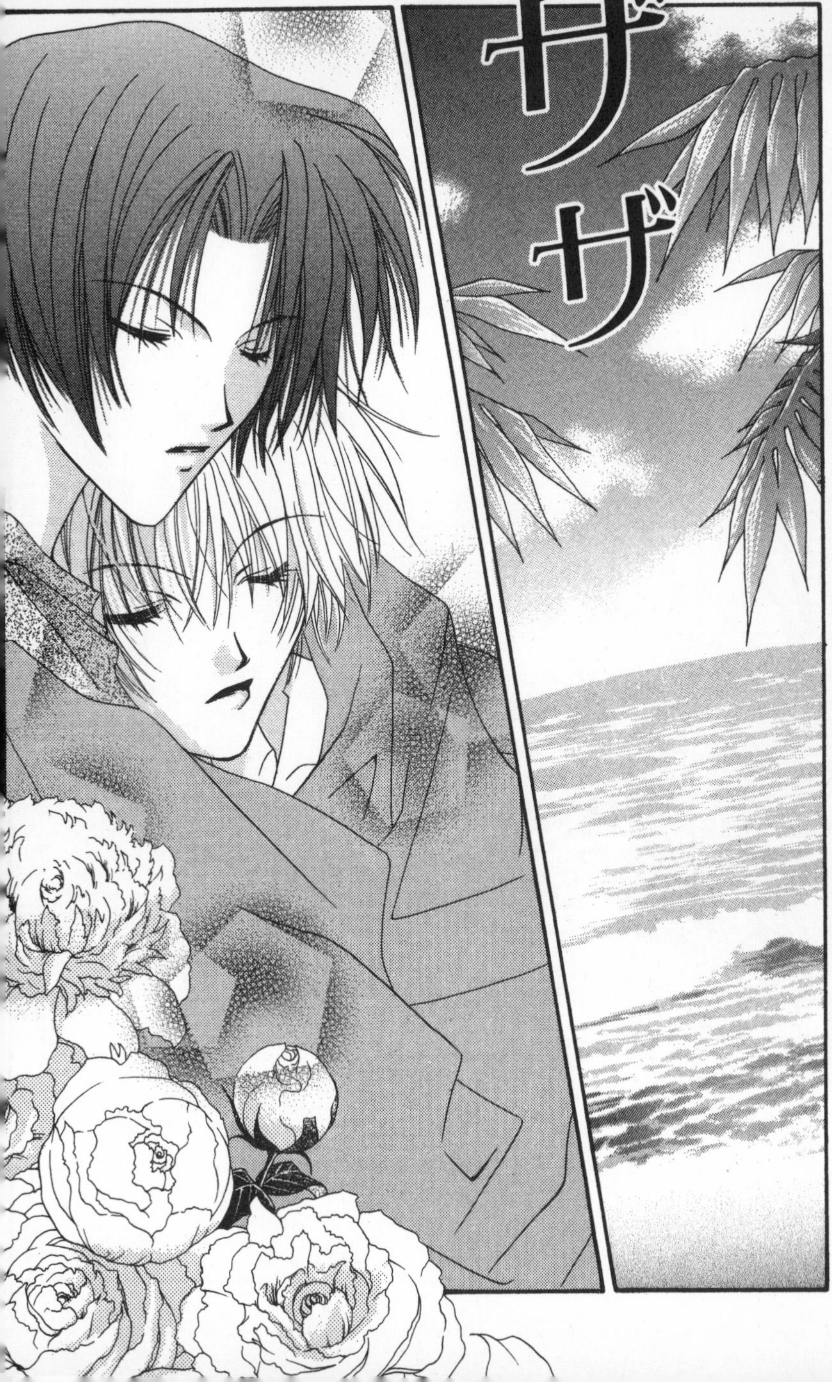
ザザ

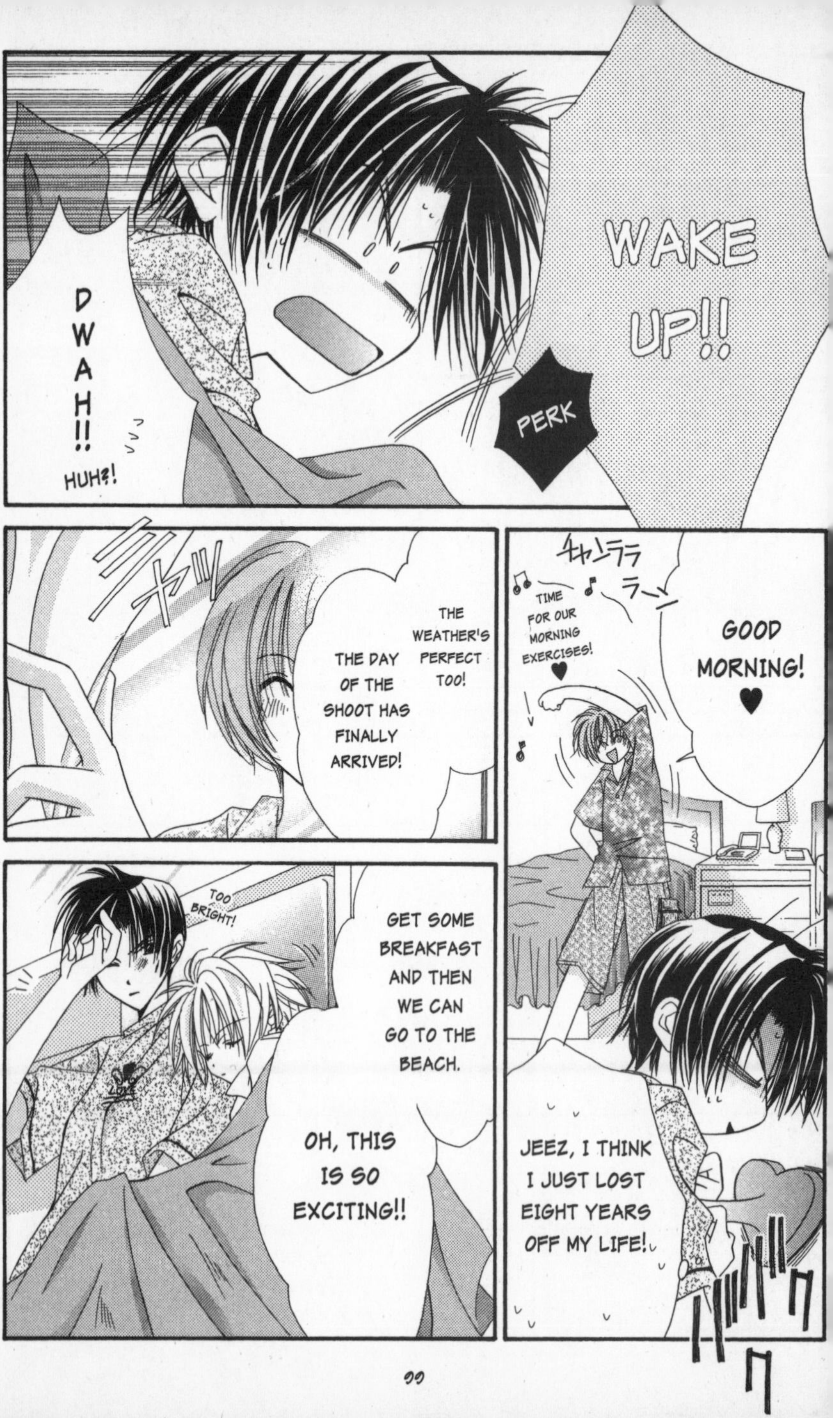
WAKE UP!!
PERK
DWAH!!
HUH?!
GOOD MORNING! ♥
チャンララ ラーン
TIME FOR OUR MORNING EXERCISES! ♥
JEEZ, I THINK I JUST LOST EIGHT YEARS OFF MY LIFE!
THE WEATHER'S PERFECT TOO!
THE DAY OF THE SHOOT HAS FINALLY ARRIVED!
TOO BRIGHT!
GET SOME BREAKFAST AND THEN WE CAN GO TO THE BEACH.
OH, THIS IS SO EXCITING!!

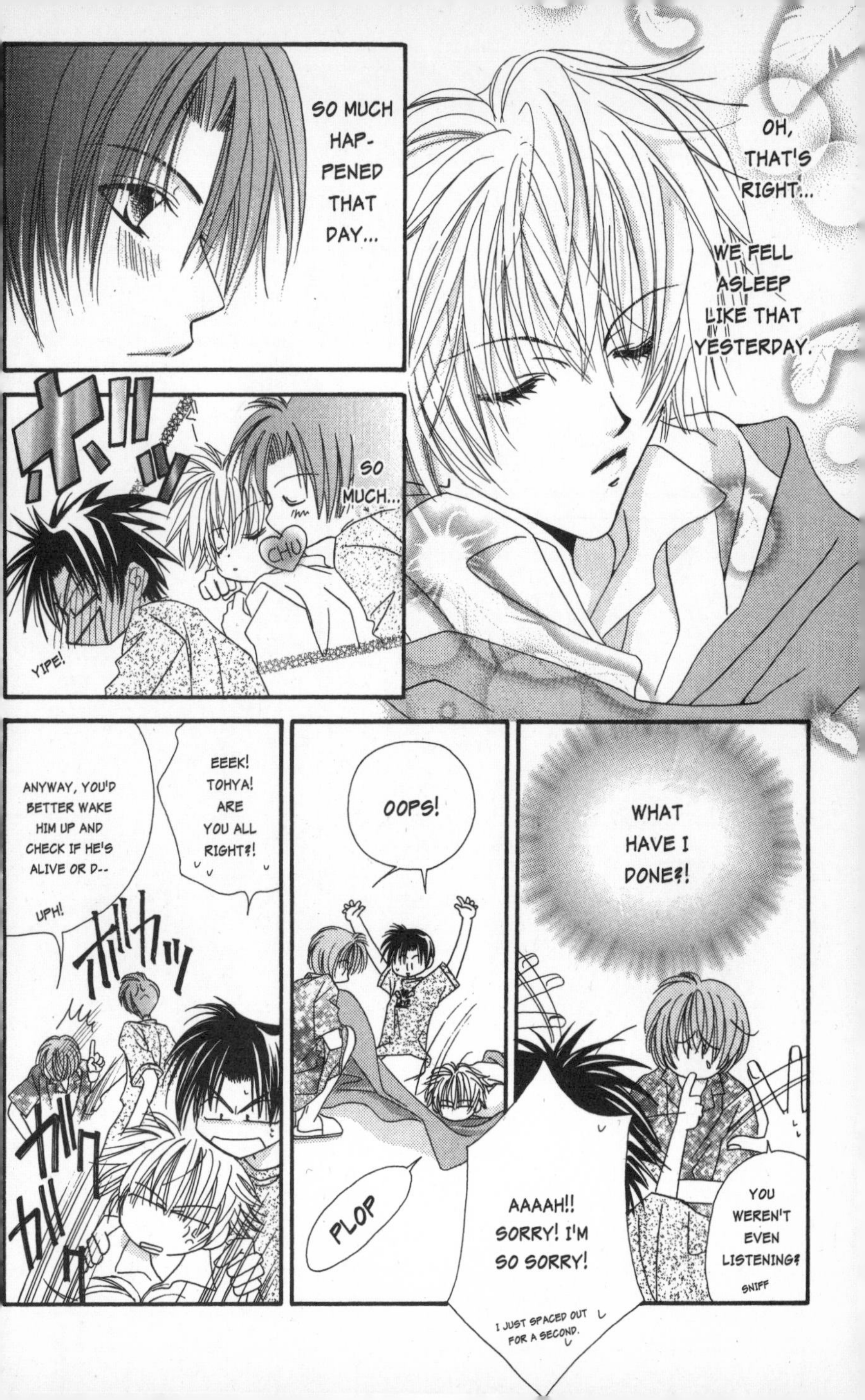
OH, THAT'S RIGHT...
WE FELL ASLEEP LIKE THAT YESTERDAY.
SO MUCH HAP-PENED THAT DAY...
SO MUCH...
CHU
YIPE!
WHAT HAVE I DONE?!
YOU WEREN'T EVEN LISTENING?
SNIFF
AAAAH!! SORRY! I'M SO SORRY!
I JUST SPACED OUT FOR A SECOND.
OOPS!
PLOP
EEEK! TOHYA! ARE YOU ALL RIGHT?!
ANYWAY, YOU'D BETTER WAKE HIM UP AND CHECK IF HE'S ALIVE OR D--
UPH!

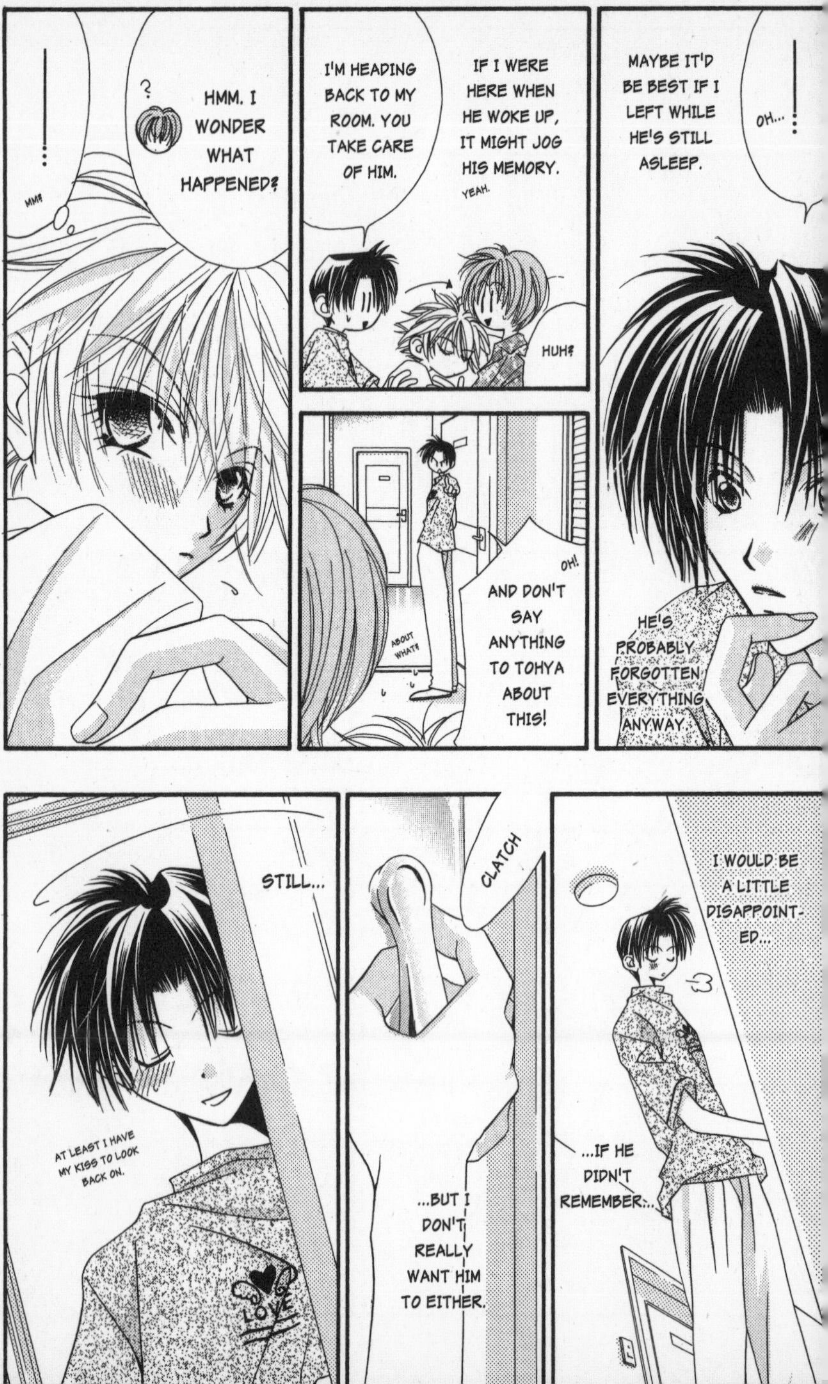
OH...
MAYBE IT'D BE BEST IF I LEFT WHILE HE'S STILL ASLEEP.
HE'S PROBABLY FORGOTTEN EVERYTHING ANYWAY.
IF I WERE HERE WHEN HE WOKE UP, IT MIGHT JOG HIS MEMORY.
YEAH.
I'M HEADING BACK TO MY ROOM. YOU TAKE CARE OF HIM.
HUH?
OH!
AND DON'T SAY ANYTHING TO TOHYA ABOUT THIS!
ABOUT WHAT?
HMM. I WONDER WHAT HAPPENED?
MM?
I WOULD BE A LITTLE DISAPPOINTED...
...IF HE DIDN'T REMEMBER...
CLATCH
...BUT I DON'T REALLY WANT HIM TO EITHER.
STILL...
AT LEAST I HAVE MY KISS TO LOOK BACK ON.
LOVE

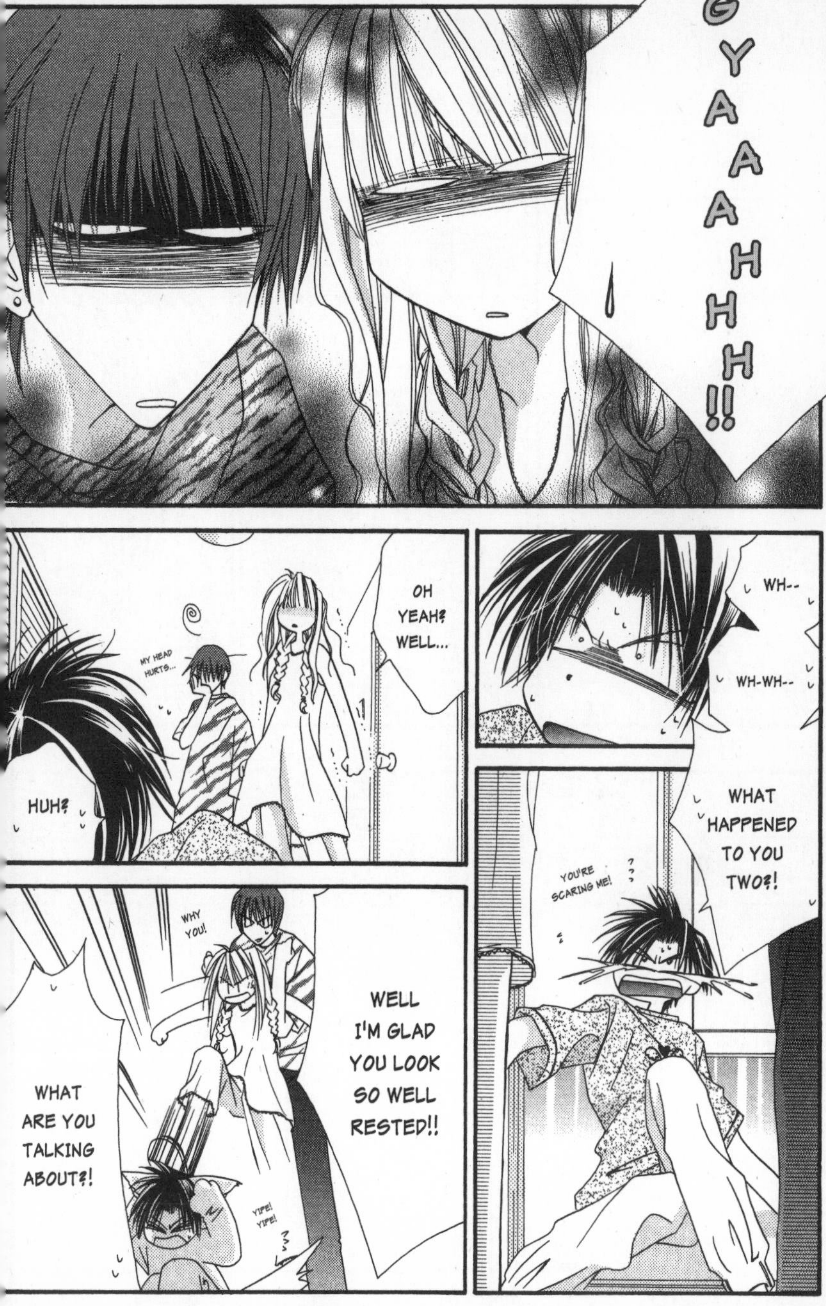
GYAAAHHH!!
WH--
WH-WH--
WHAT HAPPENED TO YOU TWO?!
YOU'RE SCARING ME!
OH YEAH? WELL...
MY HEAD HURTS...
HUH?
WELL I'M GLAD YOU LOOK SO WELL RESTED!!
WHY YOU!
YIPE! YIPE!
WHAT ARE YOU TALKING ABOUT?!

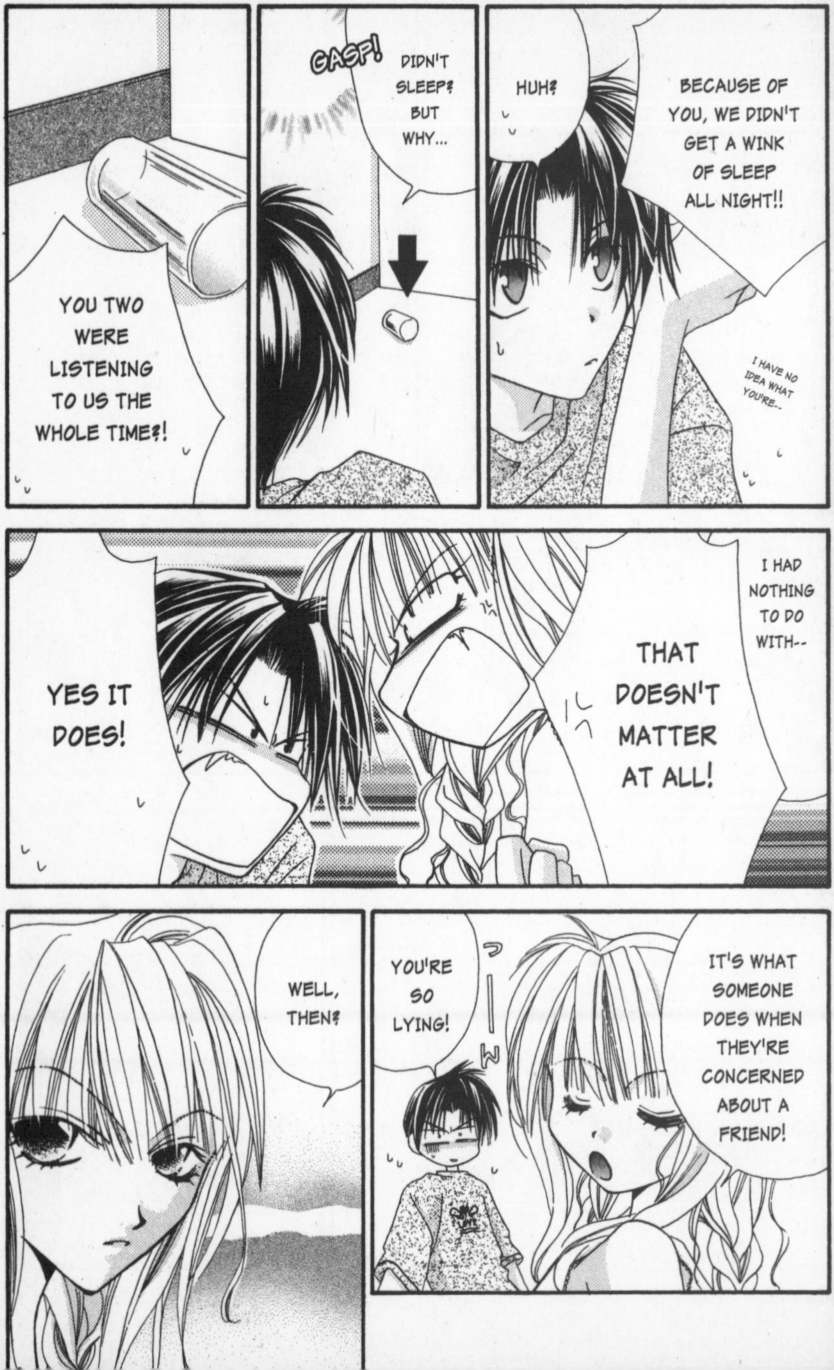
BECAUSE OF YOU, WE DIDN'T GET A WINK OF SLEEP ALL NIGHT!!
HUH?
I HAVE NO IDEA WHAT YOU'RE--
DIDN'T SLEEP? BUT WHY...
GASP!
YOU TWO WERE LISTENING TO US THE WHOLE TIME?!
I HAD NOTHING TO DO WITH--
THAT DOESN'T MATTER AT ALL!
YES IT DOES!
IT'S WHAT SOMEONE DOES WHEN THEY'RE CONCERNED ABOUT A FRIEND!
YOU'RE SO LYING!
WELL, THEN?

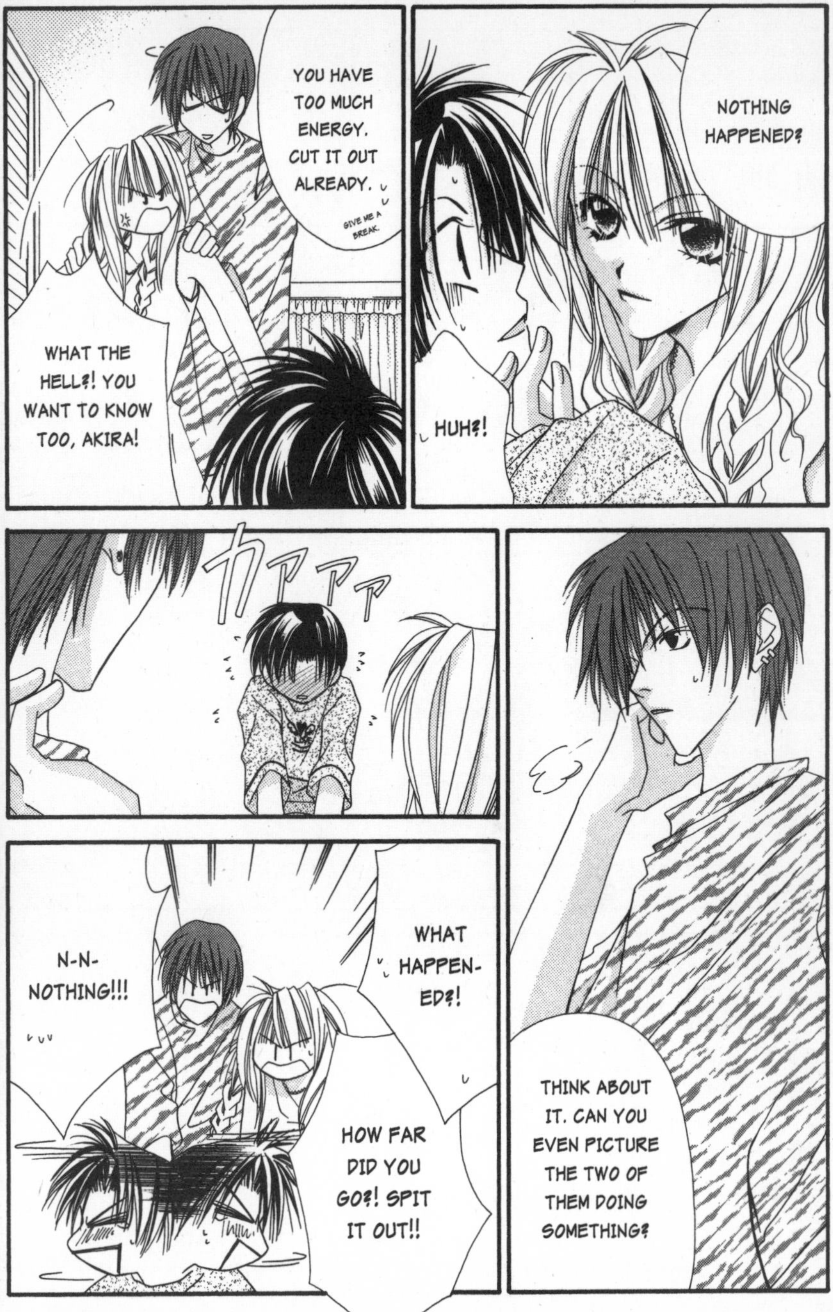
NOTHING HAPPENED?
HUH?!
YOU HAVE TOO MUCH ENERGY. CUT IT OUT ALREADY.
GIVE ME A BREAK.
WHAT THE HELL?! YOU WANT TO KNOW TOO, AKIRA!
THINK ABOUT IT. CAN YOU EVEN PICTURE THE TWO OF THEM DOING SOMETHING?
カァァァ
WHAT HAPPEN-ED?!
HOW FAR DID YOU GO?! SPIT IT OUT!!
N-N-NOTHING!!!

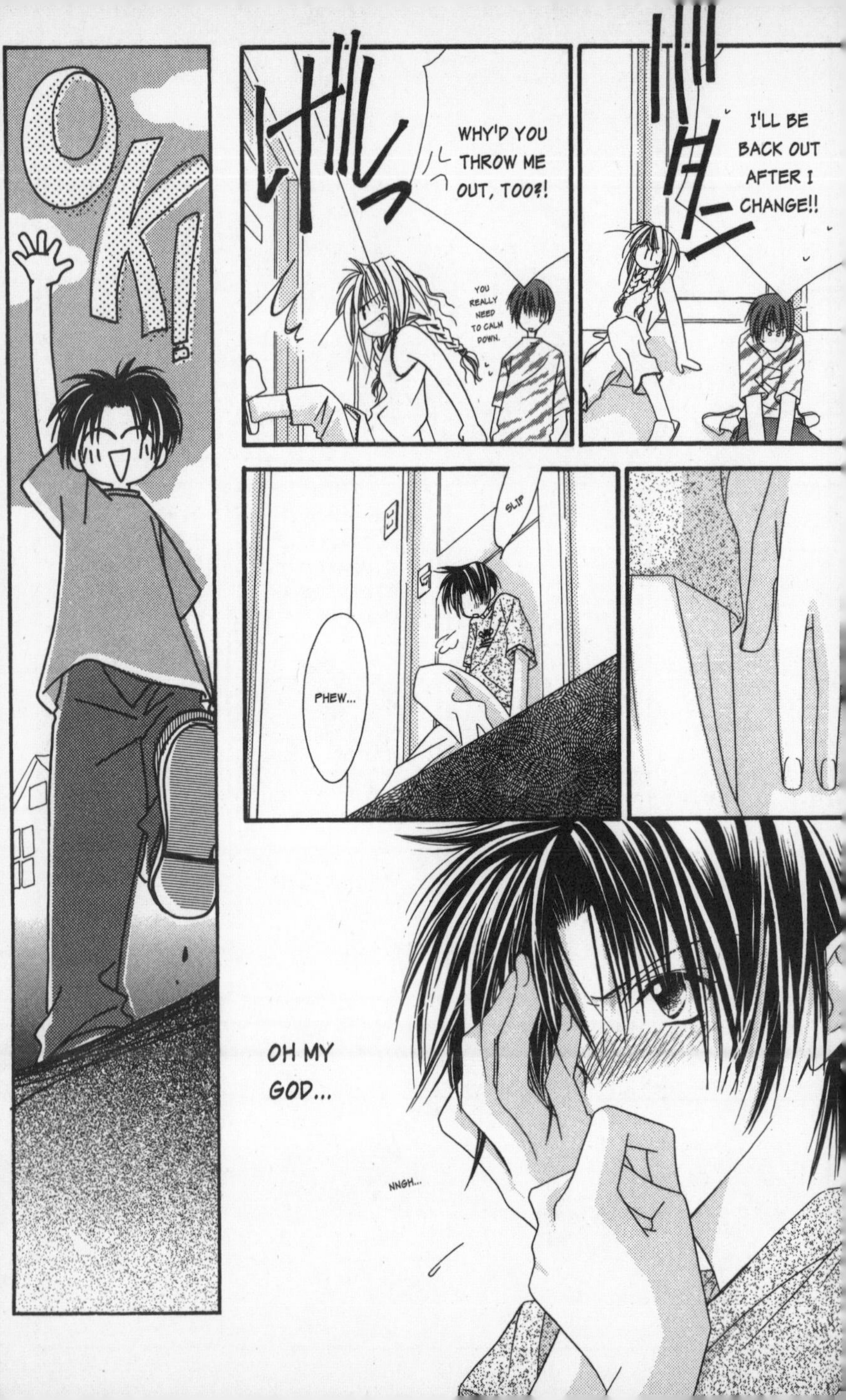
I'LL BE BACK OUT AFTER I CHANGE!!
WHY'D YOU THROW ME OUT, TOO?!
YOU REALLY NEED TO CALM DOWN.
SLIP
PHEW...
OH MY GOD...
NNGH...
OK!

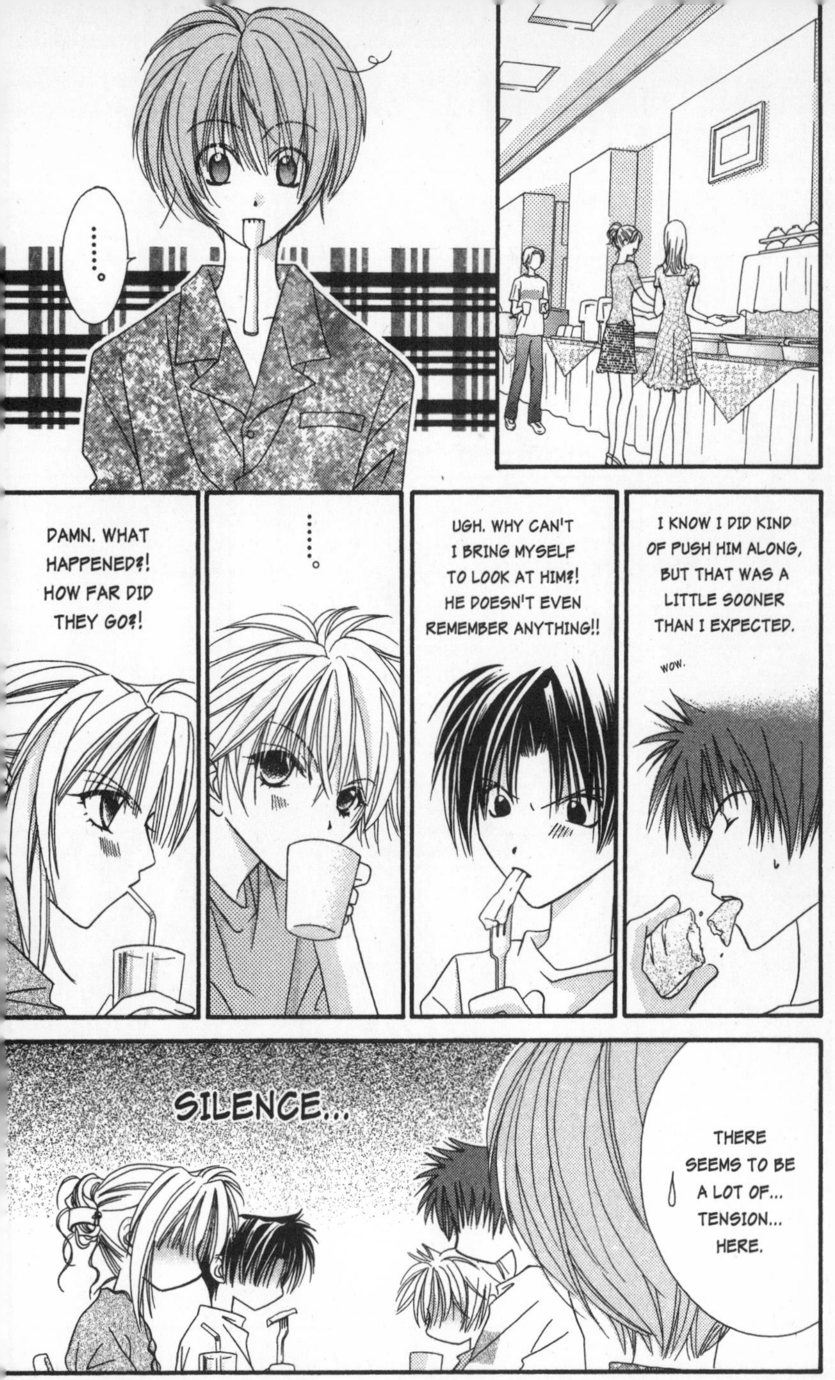
……。
I KNOW I DID KIND OF PUSH HIM ALONG, BUT THAT WAS A LITTLE SOONER THAN I EXPECTED.
WOW.
UGH. WHY CAN'T I BRING MYSELF TO LOOK AT HIM?! HE DOESN'T EVEN REMEMBER ANYTHING!!
……。
DAMN. WHAT HAPPENED?! HOW FAR DID THEY GO?!
THERE SEEMS TO BE A LOT OF... TENSION... HERE.
SILENCE...

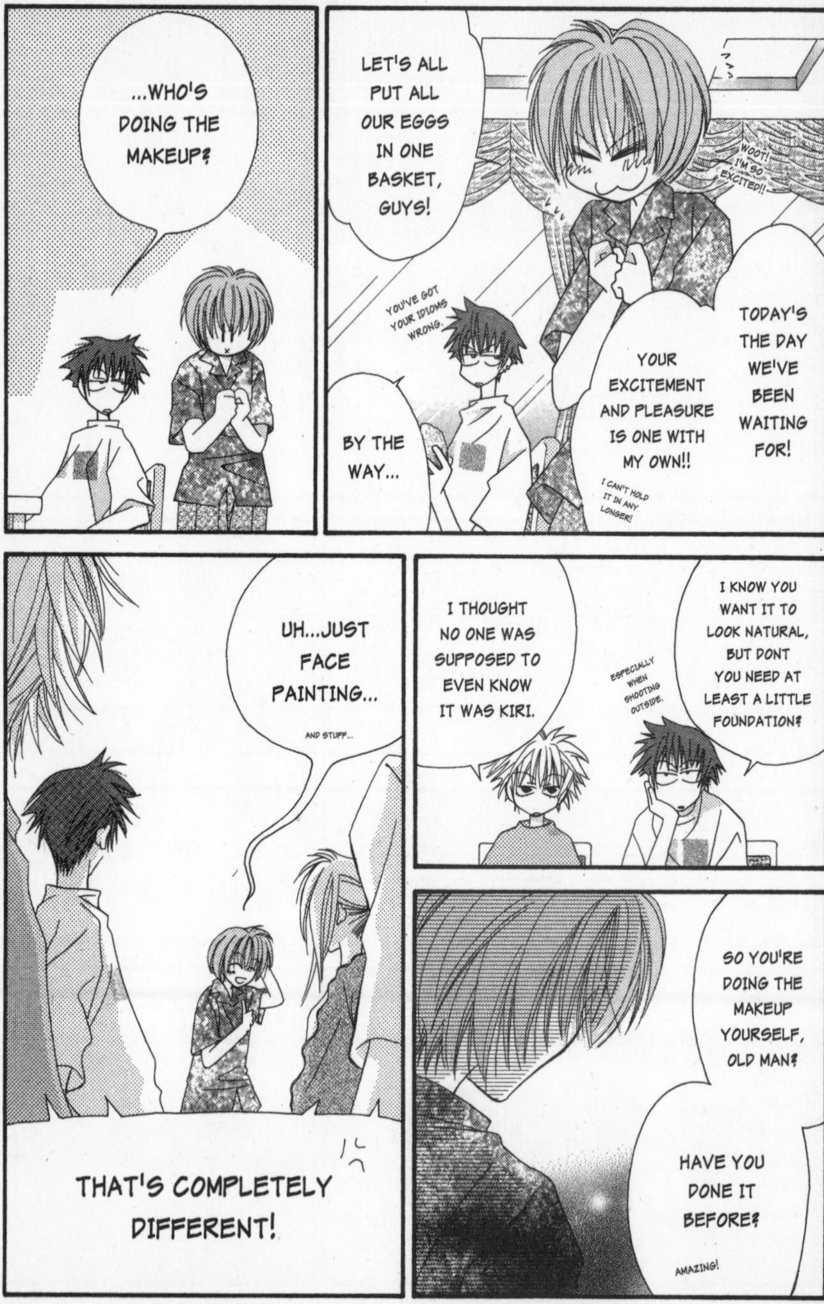
WOOT! I'M SO EXCITED!!
LET'S ALL PUT ALL OUR EGGS IN ONE BASKET, GUYS!
TODAY'S THE DAY WE'VE BEEN WAITING FOR!
YOUR EXCITEMENT AND PLEASURE IS ONE WITH MY OWN!!
I CAN'T HOLD IT IN ANY LONGER!
YOU'VE GOT YOUR IDIOMS WRONG.
BY THE WAY...
...WHO'S DOING THE MAKEUP?
I KNOW YOU WANT IT TO LOOK NATURAL, BUT DONT YOU NEED AT LEAST A LITTLE FOUNDATION?
ESPECIALLY WHEN SHOOTING OUTSIDE.
I THOUGHT NO ONE WAS SUPPOSED TO EVEN KNOW IT WAS KIRI.
SO YOU'RE DOING THE MAKEUP YOURSELF, OLD MAN?
HAVE YOU DONE IT BEFORE?
AMAZING!
UH...JUST FACE PAINTING...
AND STUFF...
THAT'S COMPLETELY DIFFERENT!

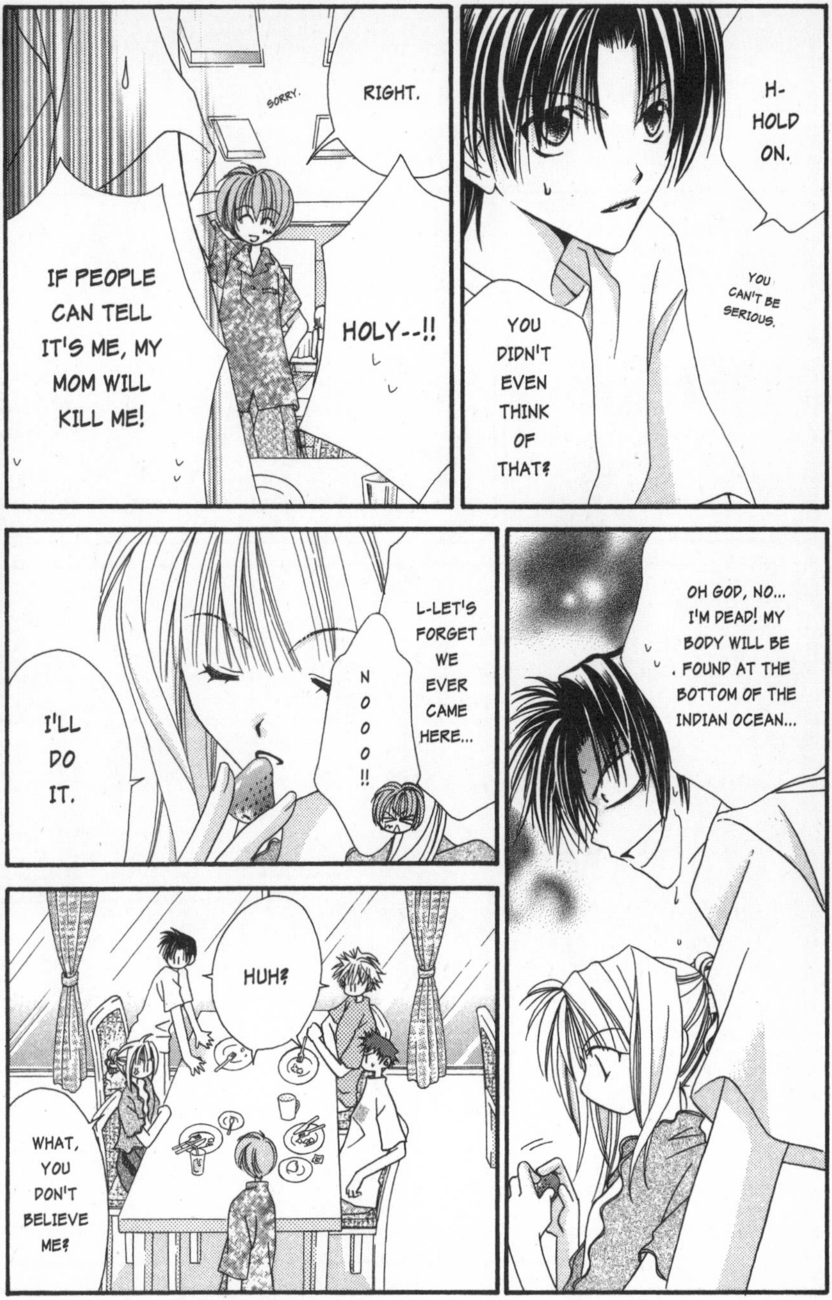
H-HOLD ON.
YOU CAN'T BE SERIOUS.
YOU DIDN'T EVEN THINK OF THAT?
RIGHT.
SORRY.
IF PEOPLE CAN TELL IT'S ME, MY MOM WILL KILL ME!
HOLY--!!
OH GOD, NO... I'M DEAD! MY BODY WILL BE FOUND AT THE BOTTOM OF THE INDIAN OCEAN...
L-LET'S FORGET WE EVER CAME HERE...
NOOOO!!
I'LL DO IT.
HUH?
WHAT, YOU DON'T BELIEVE ME?

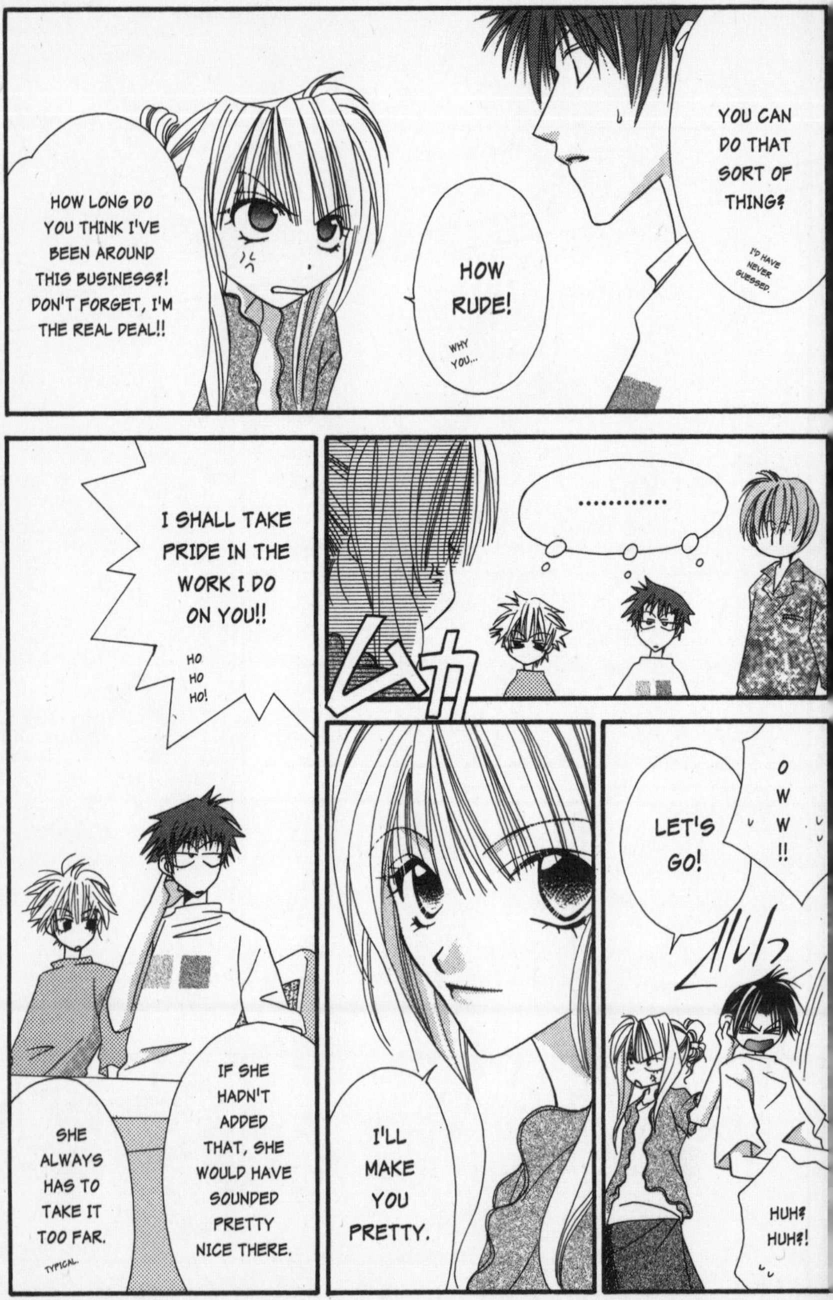
YOU CAN DO THAT SORT OF THING?
I'D HAVE NEVER GUESSED.
HOW RUDE!
WHY YOU...
HOW LONG DO YOU THINK I'VE BEEN AROUND THIS BUSINESS?! DON'T FORGET, I'M THE REAL DEAL!!
....
ムカ
OWW!!
LET'S GO!
HUH? HUH?!
I'LL MAKE YOU PRETTY.
I SHALL TAKE PRIDE IN THE WORK I DO ON YOU!!
HO HO HO!
IF SHE HADN'T ADDED THAT, SHE WOULD HAVE SOUNDED PRETTY NICE THERE.
SHE ALWAYS HAS TO TAKE IT TOO FAR.
TYPICAL.

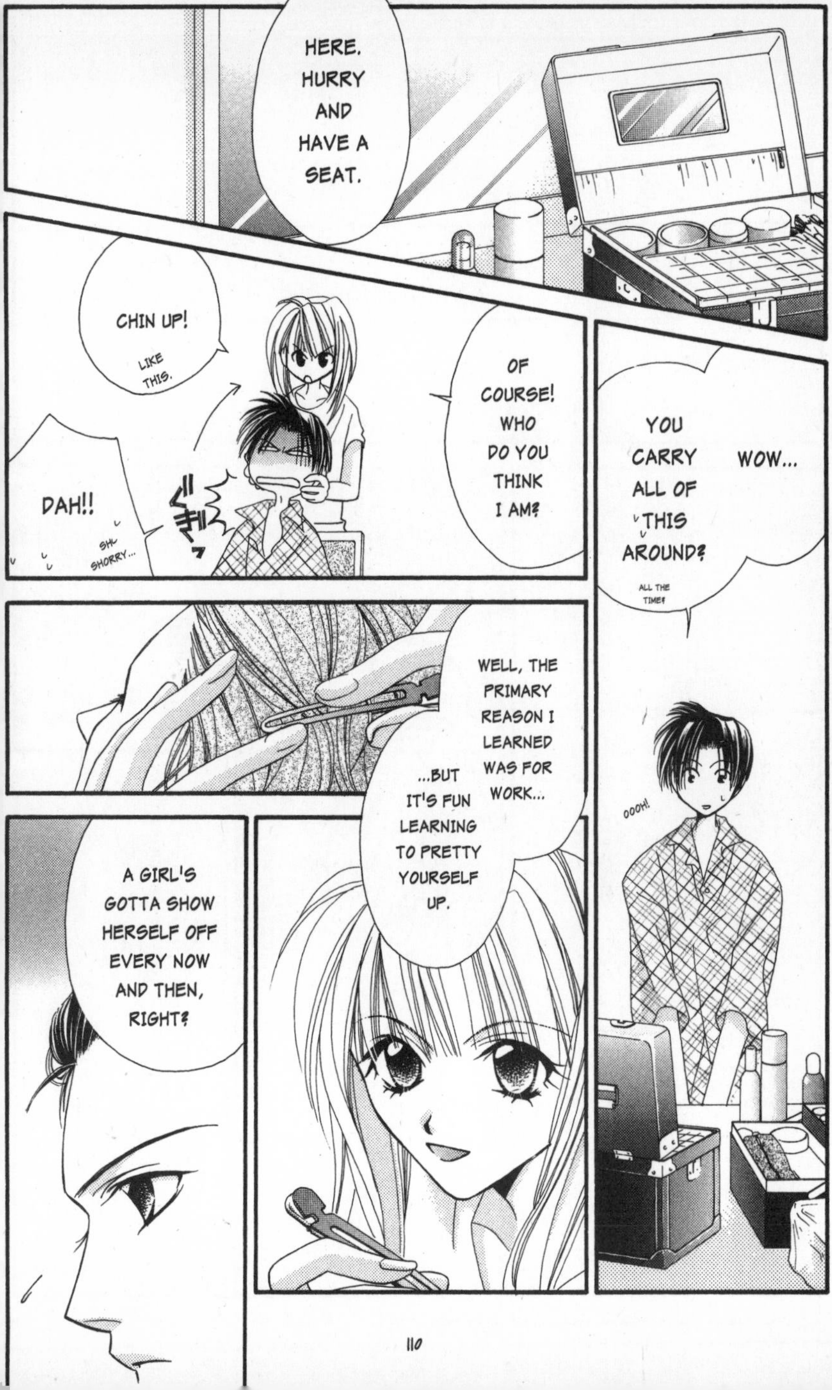
HERE. HURRY AND HAVE A SEAT.
WOW...
YOU CARRY ALL OF THIS AROUND?
ALL THE TIME?
OOOH!
OF COURSE! WHO DO YOU THINK I AM?
CHIN UP!
LIKE THIS.
DAH!!
SH- SHORRY...
WELL, THE PRIMARY REASON I LEARNED WAS FOR WORK...
...BUT IT'S FUN LEARNING TO PRETTY YOURSELF UP.
A GIRL'S GOTTA SHOW HERSELF OFF EVERY NOW AND THEN, RIGHT?

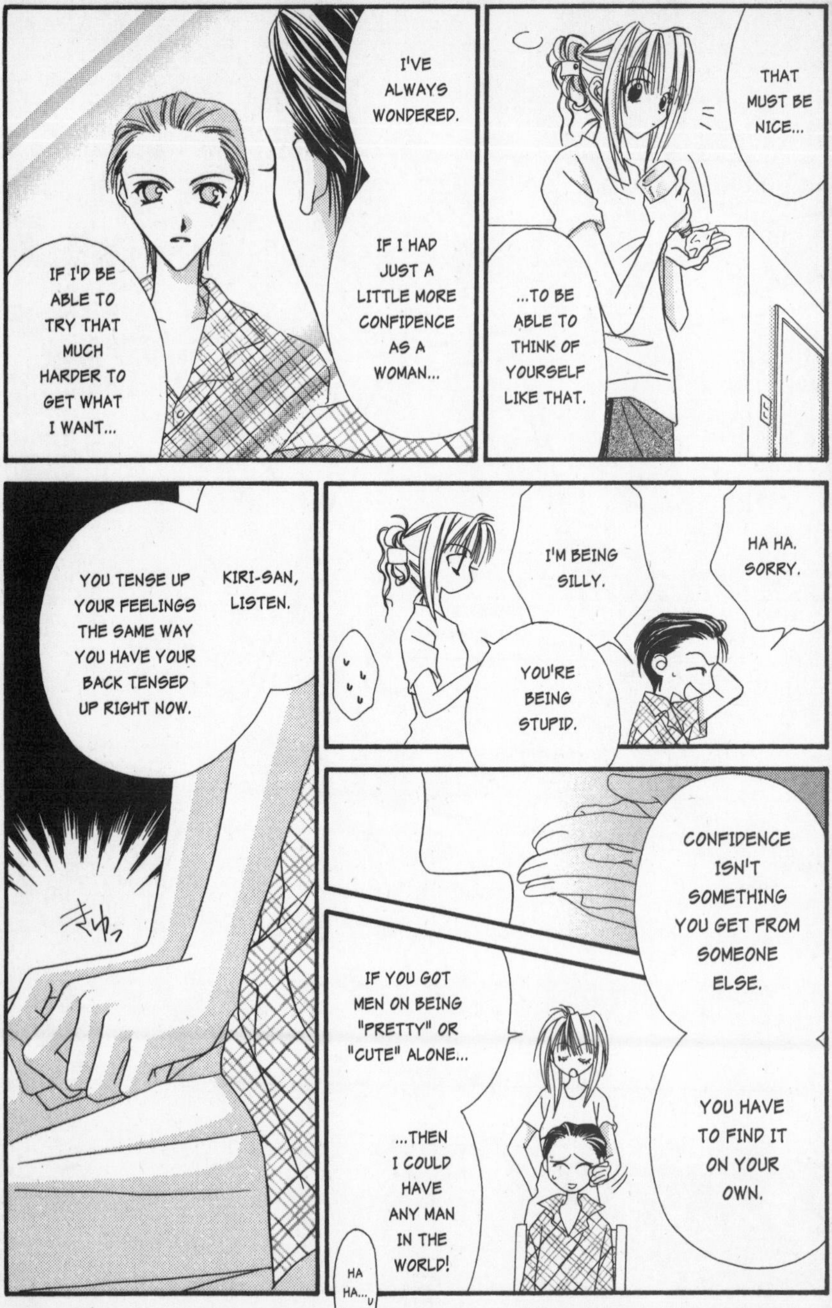
THAT MUST BE NICE...
...TO BE ABLE TO THINK OF YOURSELF LIKE THAT.
I'VE ALWAYS WONDERED.
IF I HAD JUST A LITTLE MORE CONFIDENCE AS A WOMAN...
IF I'D BE ABLE TO TRY THAT MUCH HARDER TO GET WHAT I WANT...
HA HA. SORRY.
I'M BEING SILLY.
YOU'RE BEING STUPID.
CONFIDENCE ISN'T SOMETHING YOU GET FROM SOMEONE ELSE.
YOU HAVE TO FIND IT ON YOUR OWN.
IF YOU GOT MEN ON BEING "PRETTY" OR "CUTE" ALONE...
...THEN I COULD HAVE ANY MAN IN THE WORLD!
HA HA...
KIRI-SAN, LISTEN.
YOU TENSE UP YOUR FEELINGS THE SAME WAY YOU HAVE YOUR BACK TENSED UP RIGHT NOW.
きゅっ

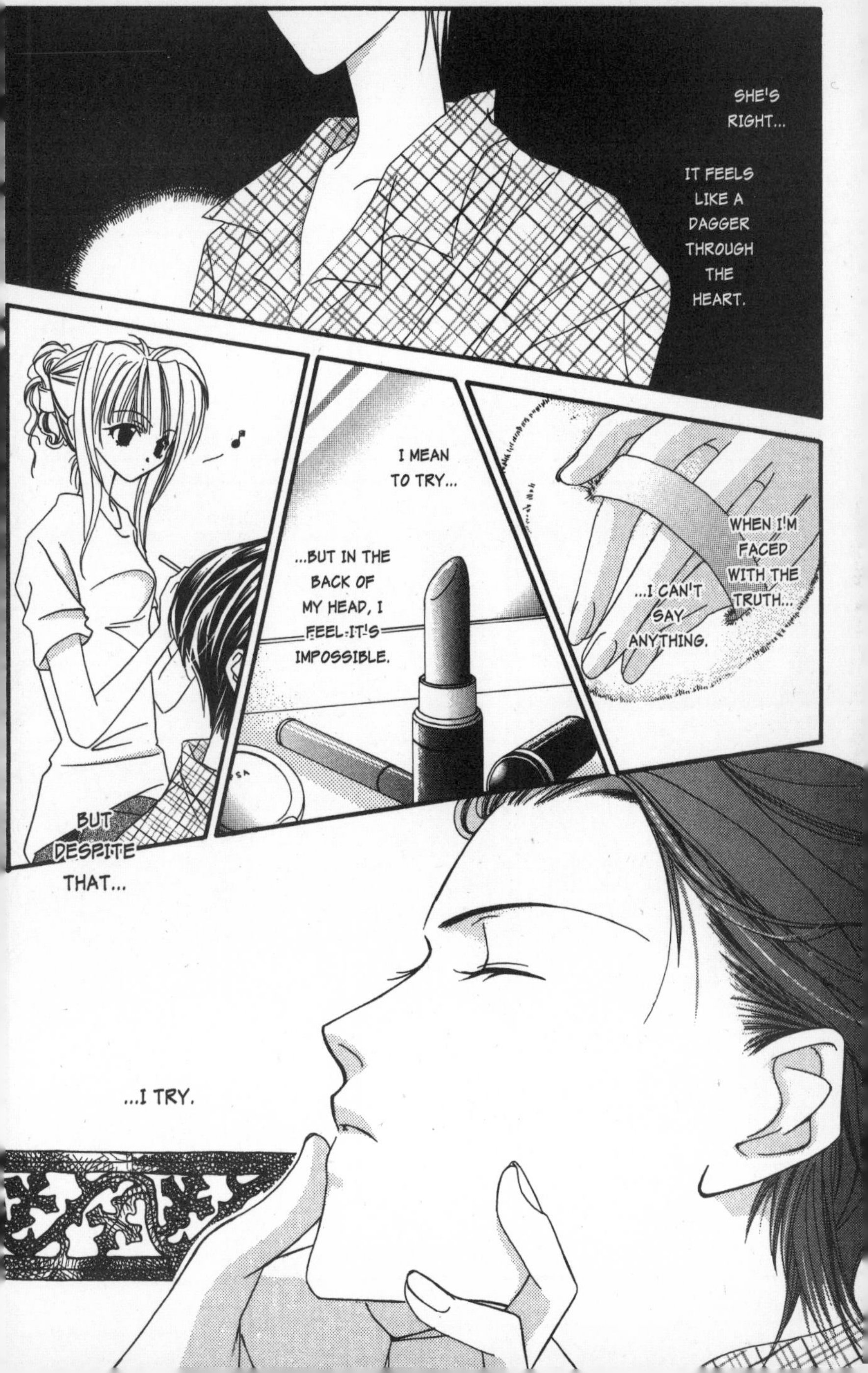
SHE'S RIGHT...
IT FEELS LIKE A DAGGER THROUGH THE HEART.
WHEN I'M FACED WITH THE TRUTH...
...I CAN'T SAY ANYTHING.
I MEAN TO TRY...
...BUT IN THE BACK OF MY HEAD, I FEEL IT'S IMPOSSIBLE.
BUT DESPITE THAT...
...I TRY.

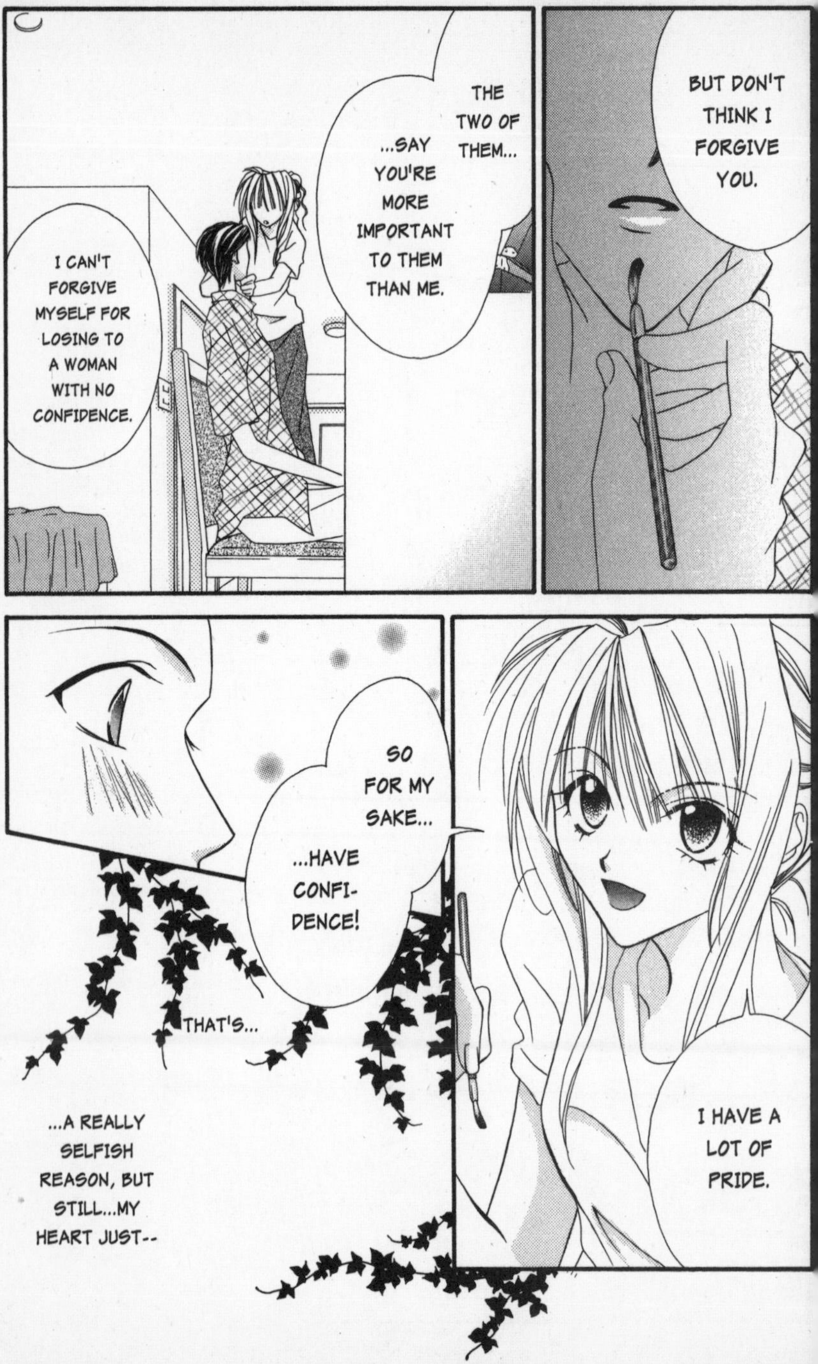
BUT DON'T THINK I FORGIVE YOU.
THE TWO OF THEM...
...SAY YOU'RE MORE IMPORTANT TO THEM THAN ME.
I CAN'T FORGIVE MYSELF FOR LOSING TO A WOMAN WITH NO CONFIDENCE.
I HAVE A LOT OF PRIDE.
SO FOR MY SAKE...
...HAVE CONFIDENCE!
THAT'S...
...A REALLY SELFISH REASON, BUT STILL...MY HEART JUST--

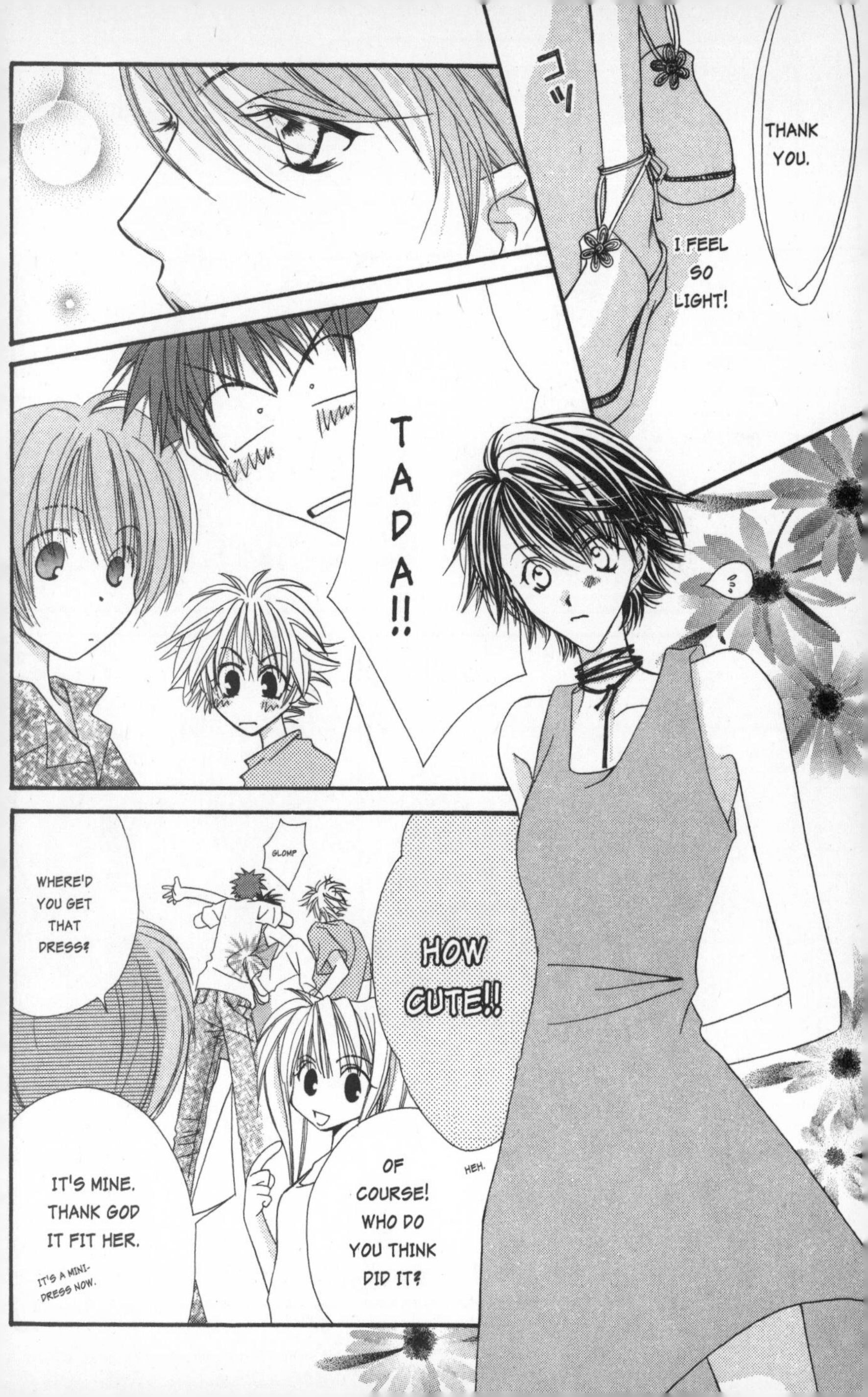
コッ
THANK YOU.
I FEEL SO LIGHT!
TADA!!
HOW CUTE!!
OF COURSE! WHO DO YOU THINK DID IT?
HEH.
GLOMP
WHERE'D YOU GET THAT DRESS?
IT'S MINE. THANK GOD IT FIT HER.
IT'S A MINI-DRESS NOW.

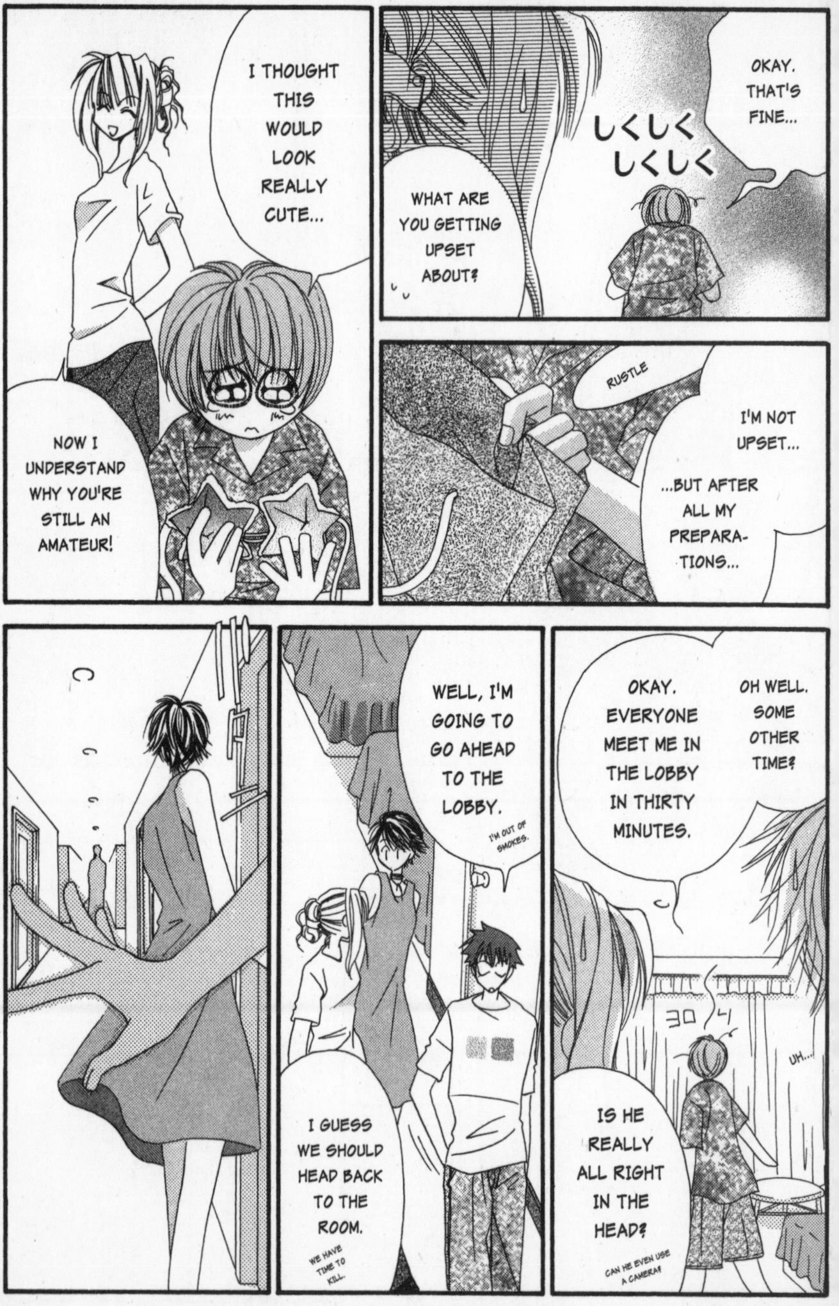
OKAY. THAT'S FINE...
しくしく しくしく
WHAT ARE YOU GETTING UPSET ABOUT?
RUSTLE
I'M NOT UPSET...
...BUT AFTER ALL MY PREPARATIONS...
I THOUGHT THIS WOULD LOOK REALLY CUTE...
NOW I UNDERSTAND WHY YOU'RE STILL AN AMATEUR!
OH WELL. SOME OTHER TIME?
OKAY. EVERYONE MEET ME IN THE LOBBY IN THIRTY MINUTES.
UH...
ヨロ
IS HE REALLY ALL RIGHT IN THE HEAD?
CAN HE EVEN USE A CAMERA?
WELL, I'M GOING TO GO AHEAD TO THE LOBBY.
I'M OUT OF SMOKES.
I GUESS WE SHOULD HEAD BACK TO THE ROOM.
WE HAVE TIME TO KILL.

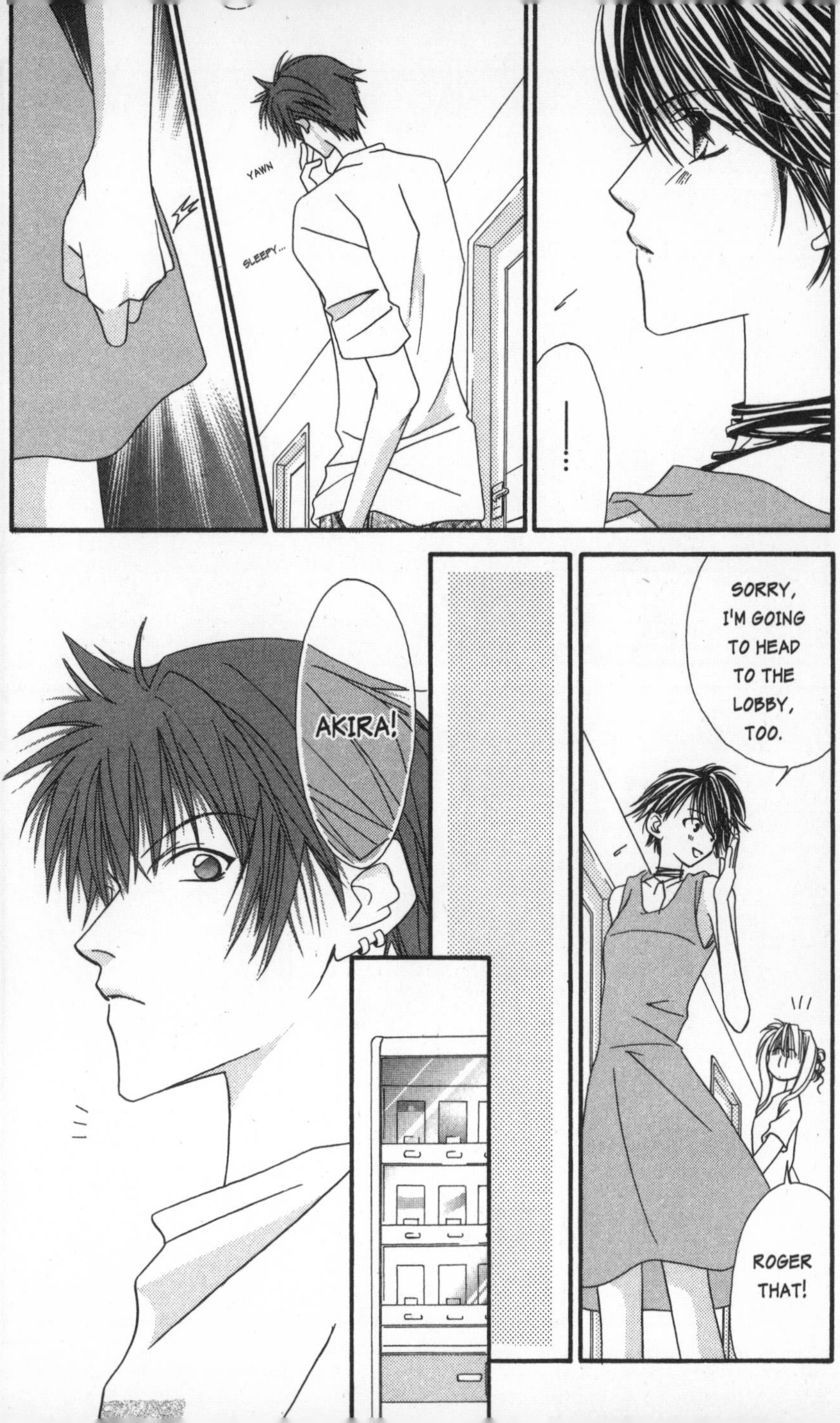
...
YAWN
SLEEPY...
SORRY, I'M GOING TO HEAD TO THE LOBBY, TOO.
ROGER THAT!
AKIRA!

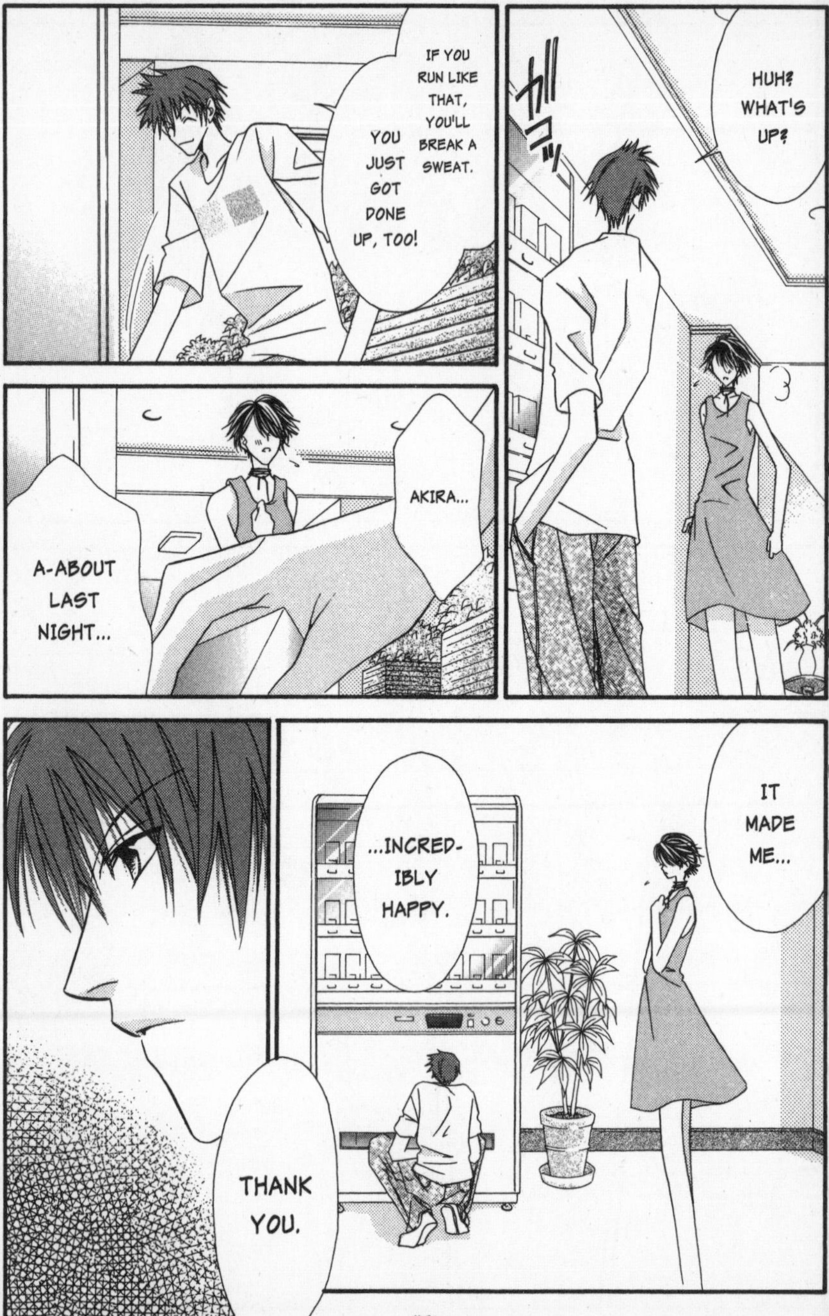
HUH? WHAT'S UP?
IF YOU RUN LIKE THAT, YOU'LL BREAK A SWEAT.
YOU JUST GOT DONE UP, TOO!
AKIRA...
A-ABOUT LAST NIGHT...
IT MADE ME...
...INCRED-IBLY HAPPY.
THANK YOU.

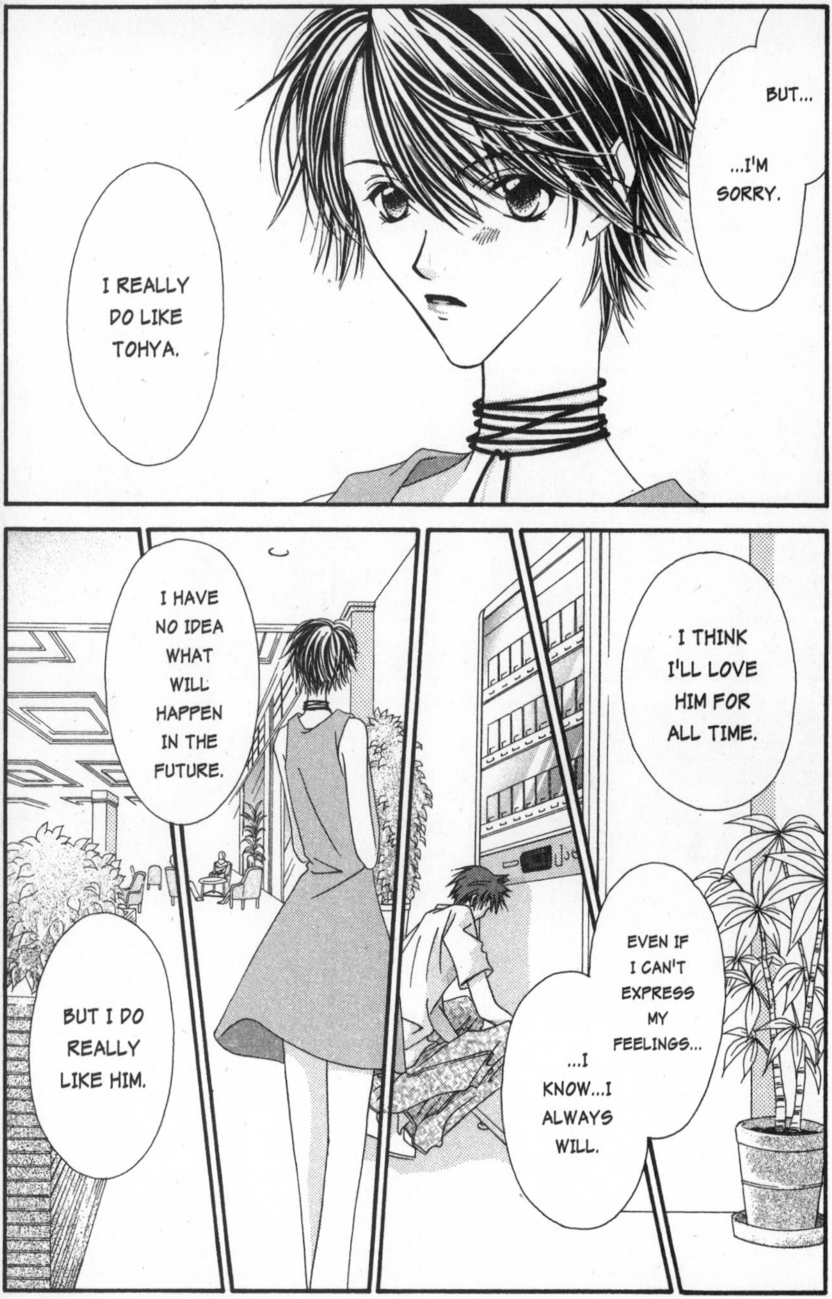
BUT...
...I'M SORRY.
I REALLY DO LIKE TOHYA.
I THINK I'LL LOVE HIM FOR ALL TIME.
EVEN IF I CAN'T EXPRESS MY FEELINGS...
...I KNOW...I ALWAYS WILL.
I HAVE NO IDEA WHAT WILL HAPPEN IN THE FUTURE.
BUT I DO REALLY LIKE HIM.

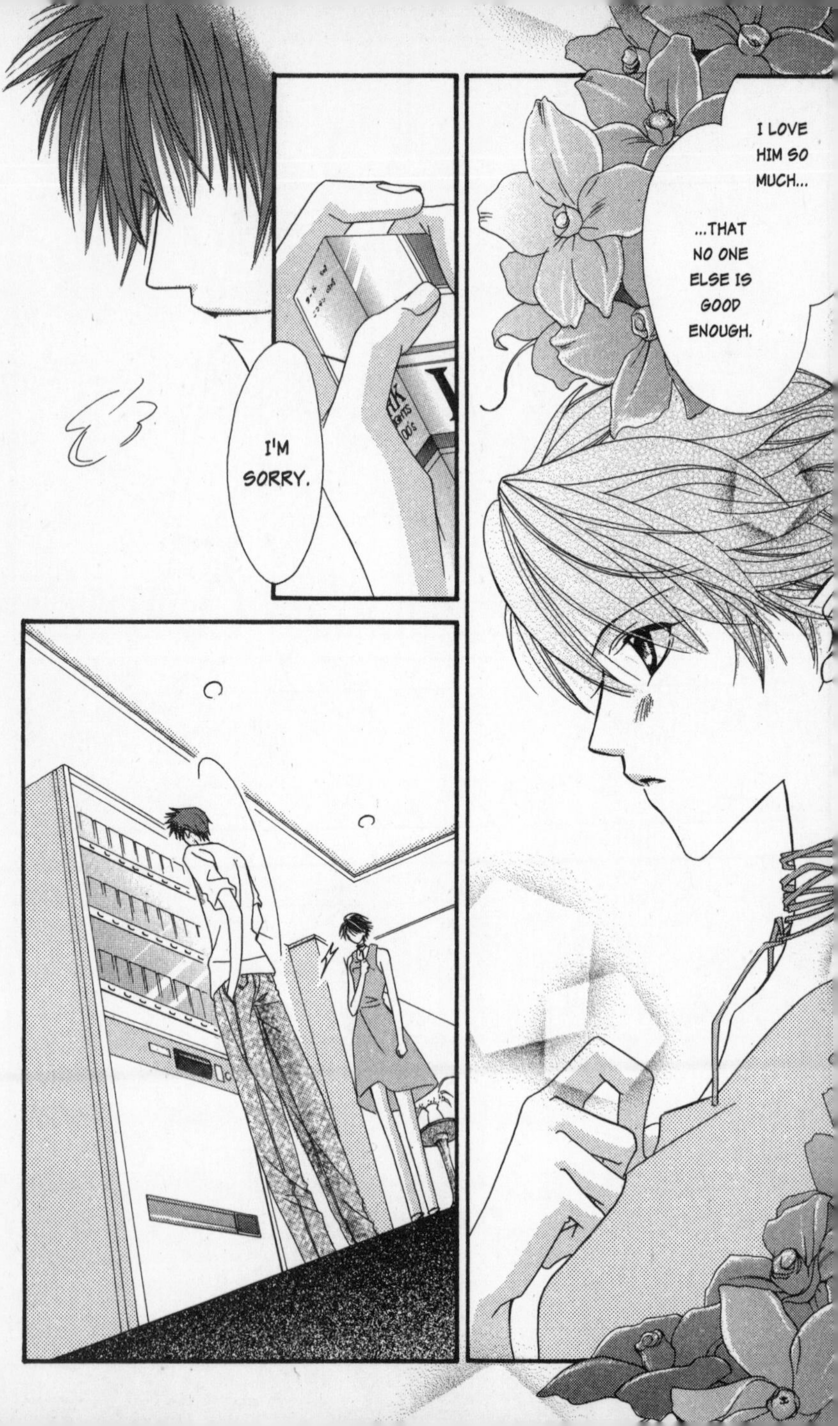
I LOVE HIM SO MUCH...
...THAT NO ONE ELSE IS GOOD ENOUGH.
I'M SORRY.

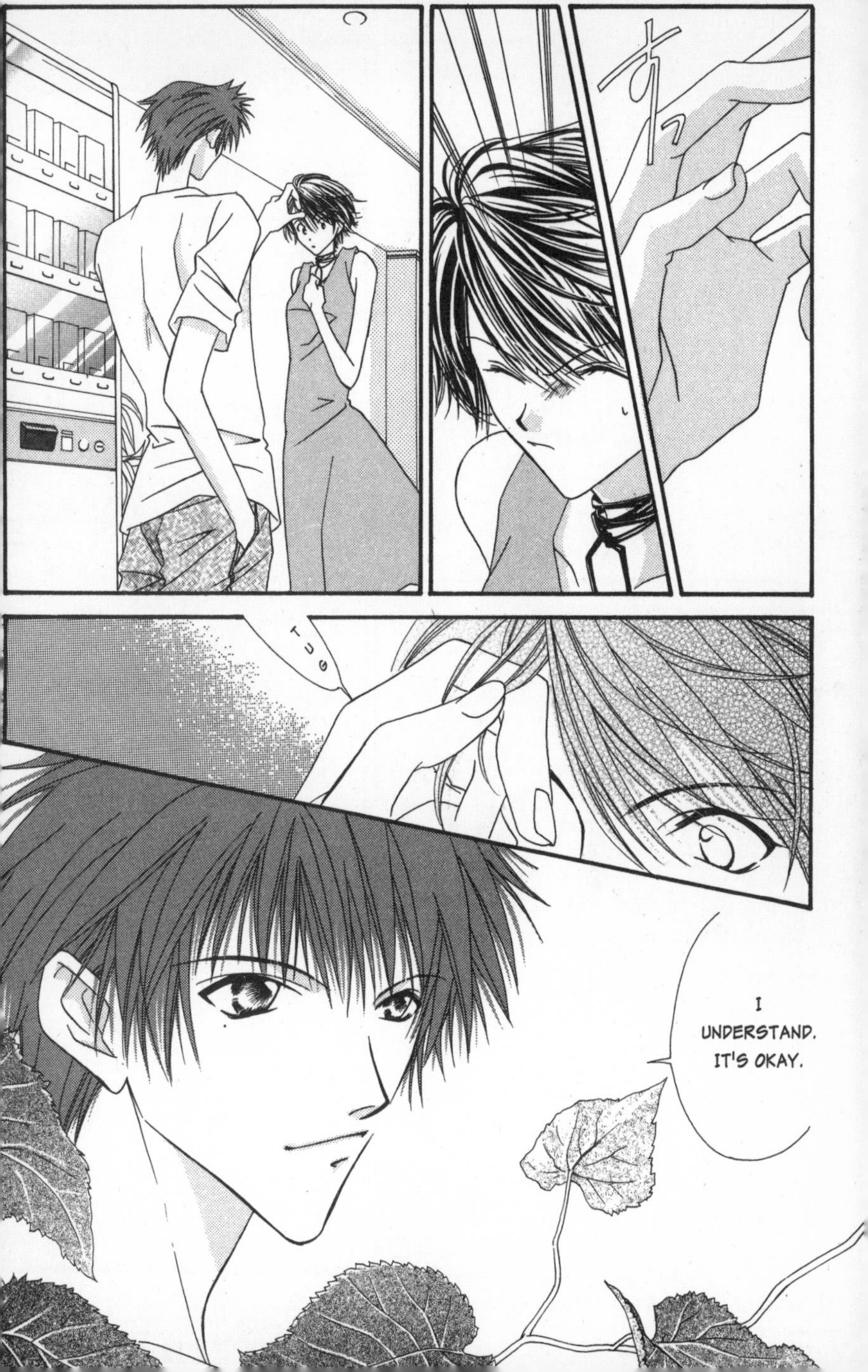
すっ
TUG
I UNDERSTAND. IT'S OKAY.

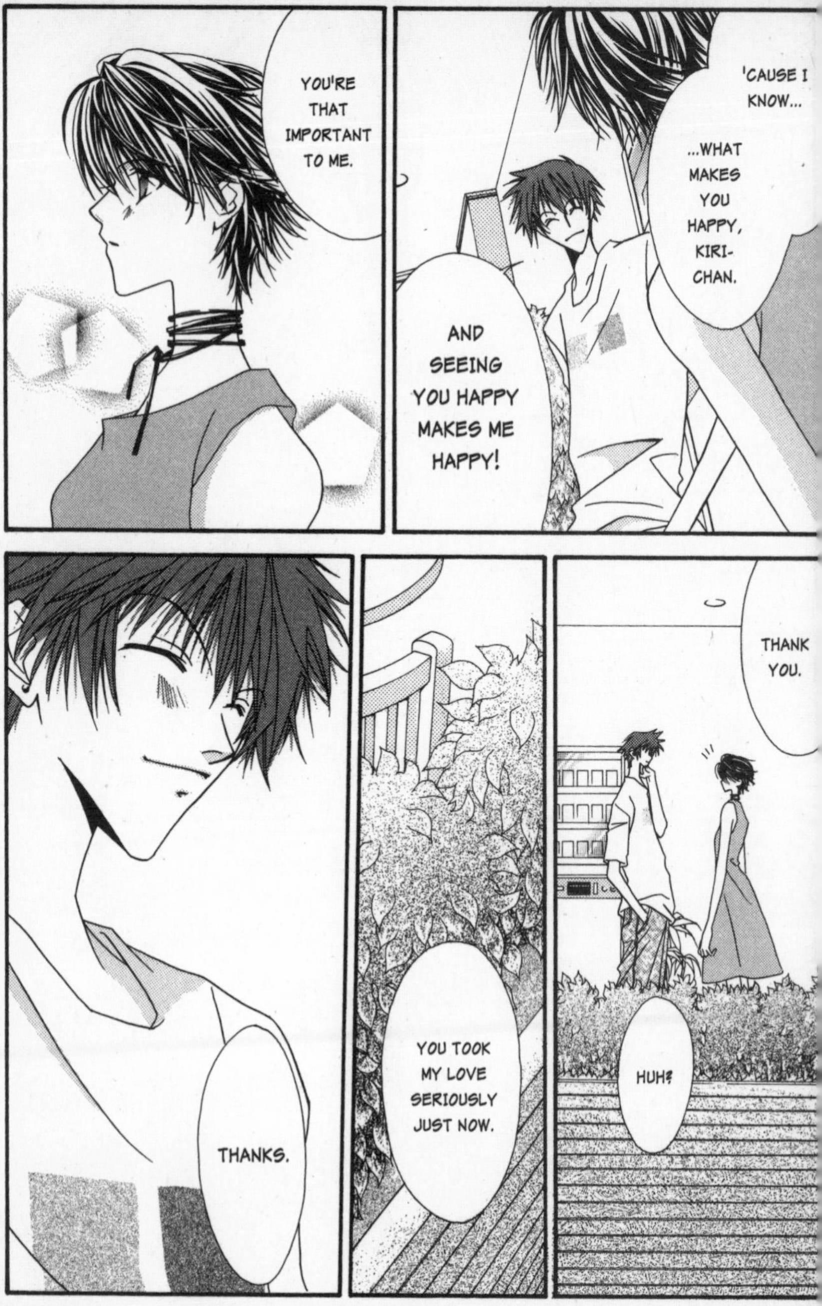
'CAUSE I KNOW...
...WHAT MAKES YOU HAPPY, KIRI-CHAN.
AND SEEING YOU HAPPY MAKES ME HAPPY!
YOU'RE THAT IMPORTANT TO ME.
THANK YOU.
HUH?
YOU TOOK MY LOVE SERIOUSLY JUST NOW.
THANKS.

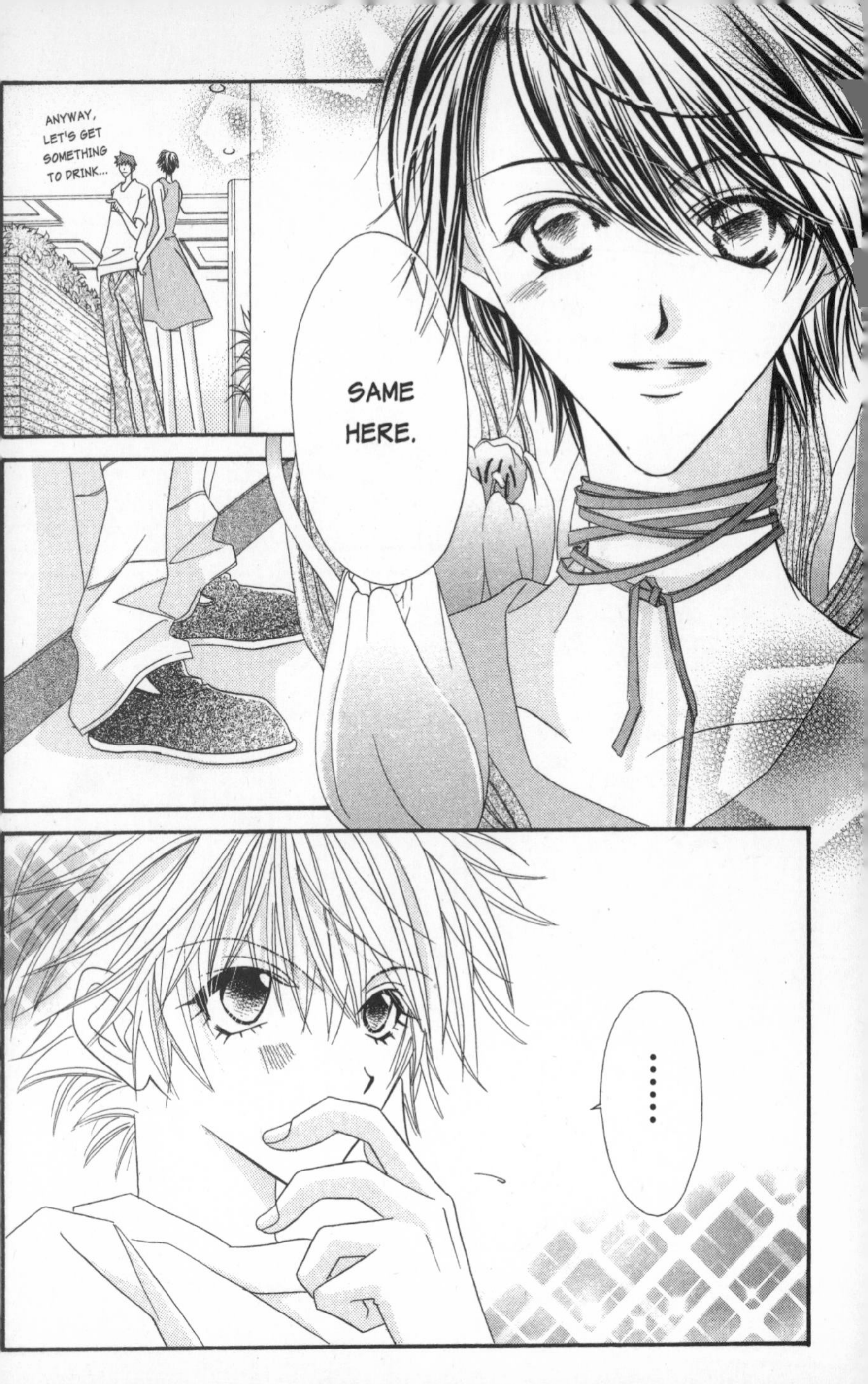
SAME HERE.
ANYWAY, LET'S GET SOMETHING TO DRINK...
......

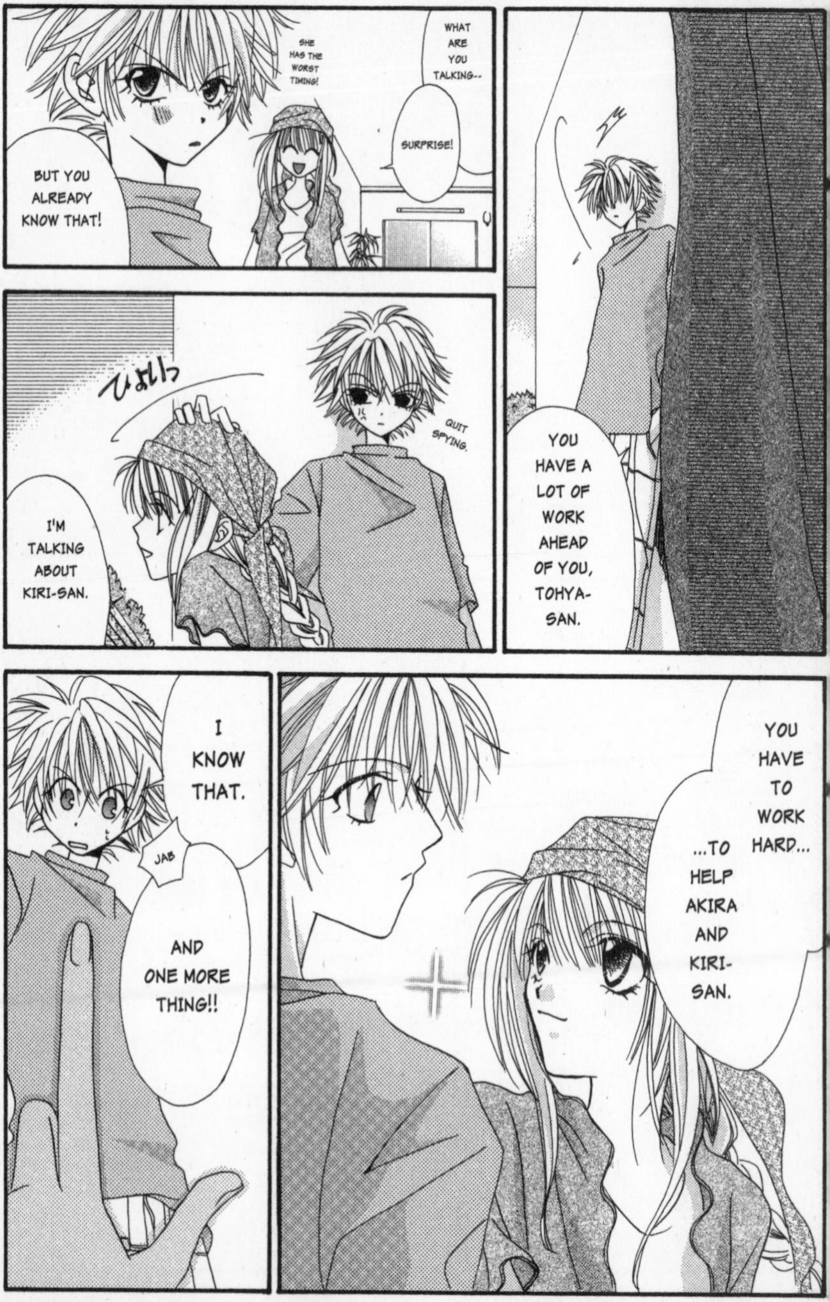
YOU HAVE A LOT OF WORK AHEAD OF YOU, TOHYA-SAN.
WHAT ARE YOU TALKING--
SURPRISE!
SHE HAS THE WORST TIMING!
BUT YOU ALREADY KNOW THAT!
ひょいっ
QUIT SPYING.
I'M TALKING ABOUT KIRI-SAN.
YOU HAVE TO WORK HARD...
...TO HELP AKIRA AND KIRI-SAN.
I KNOW THAT.
JAB
AND ONE MORE THING!!

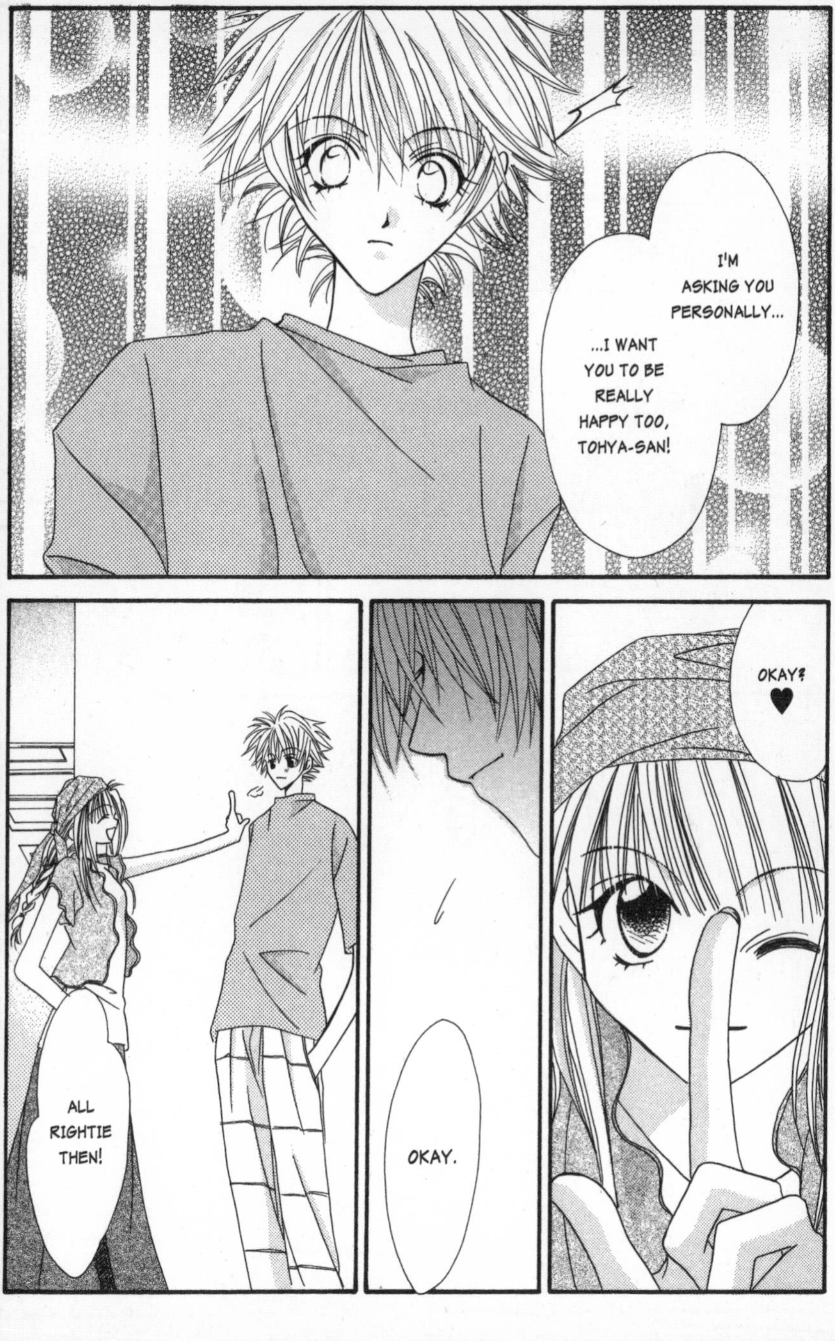
I'M ASKING YOU PERSONALLY...
...I WANT YOU TO BE REALLY HAPPY TOO, TOHYA-SAN!
OKAY? ♥
OKAY.
ALL RIGHTIE THEN!

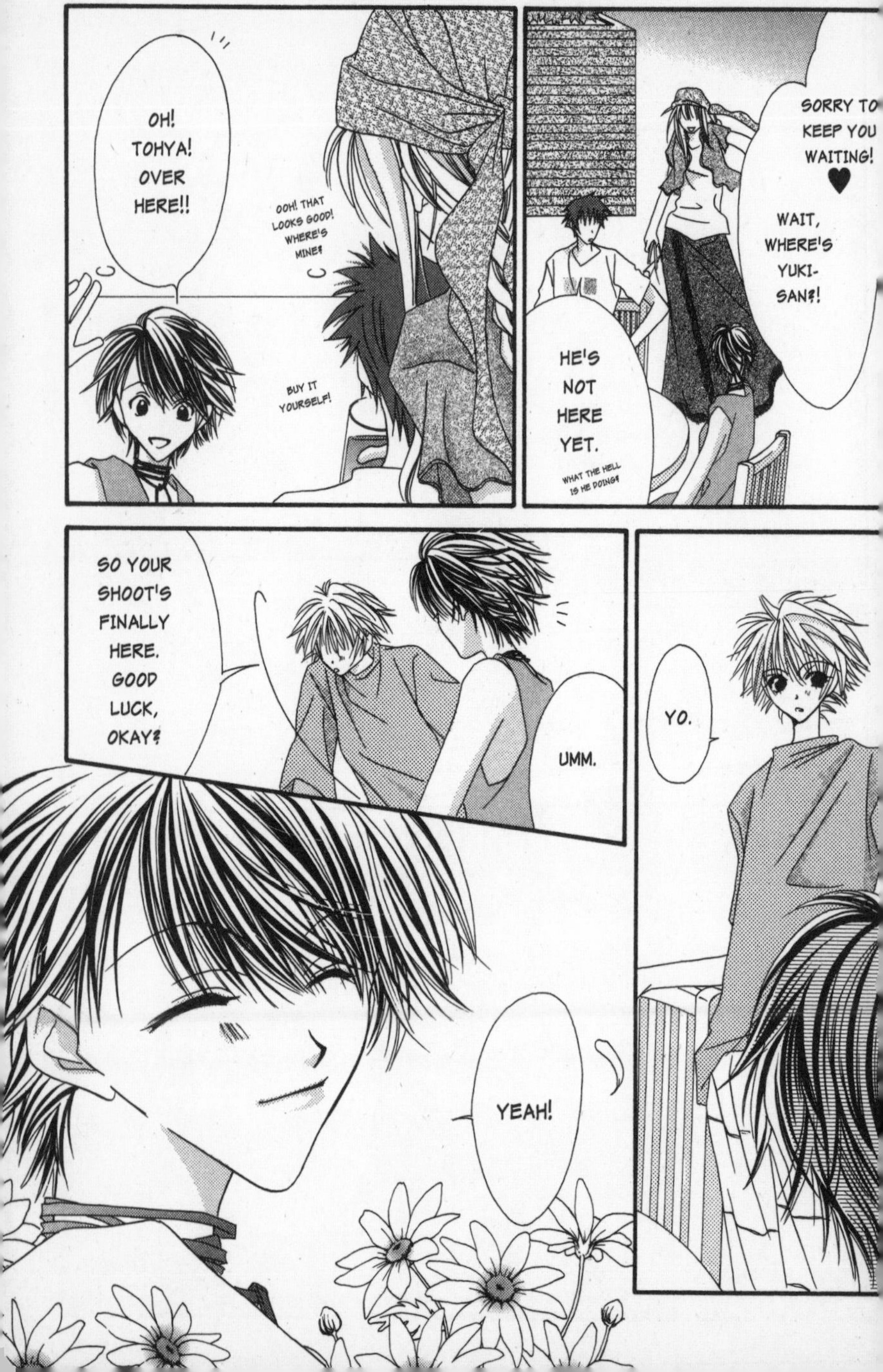
SORRY TO KEEP YOU WAITING! ♥
WAIT, WHERE'S YUKI-SAN?!
HE'S NOT HERE YET.
WHAT THE HELL IS HE DOING?
OH! TOHYA! OVER HERE!!
OOH! THAT LOOKS GOOD! WHERE'S MINE?
BUY IT YOURSELF!
YO.
UMM.
SO YOUR SHOOT'S FINALLY HERE. GOOD LUCK, OKAY?
YEAH!

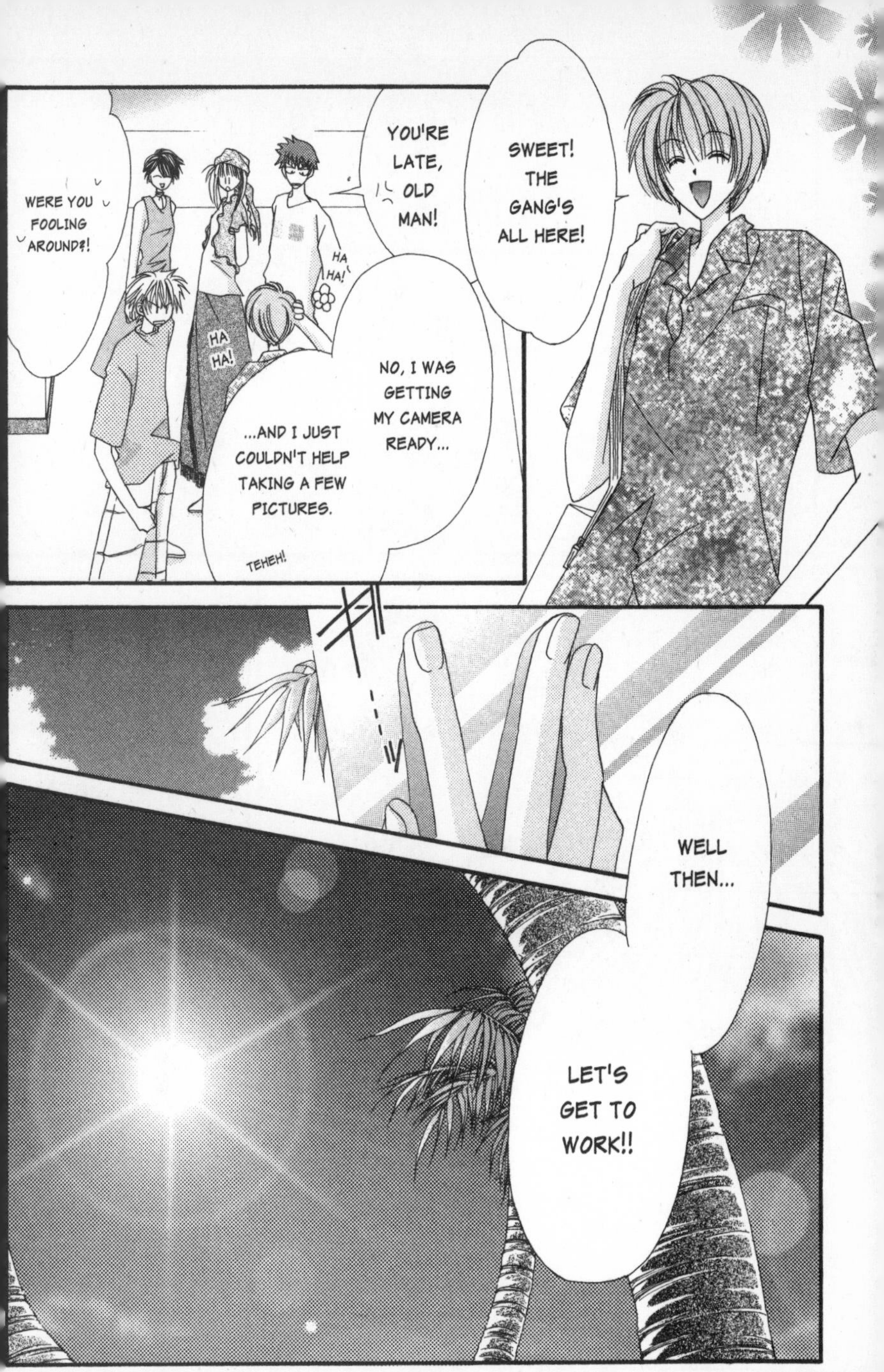
SWEET! THE GANG'S ALL HERE!
YOU'RE LATE, OLD MAN!
WERE YOU FOOLING AROUND?!
HA HA!
HA HA!
NO, I WAS GETTING MY CAMERA READY...
...AND I JUST COULDN'T HELP TAKING A FEW PICTURES.
TEHEH!
WELL THEN...
LET'S GET TO WORK!!

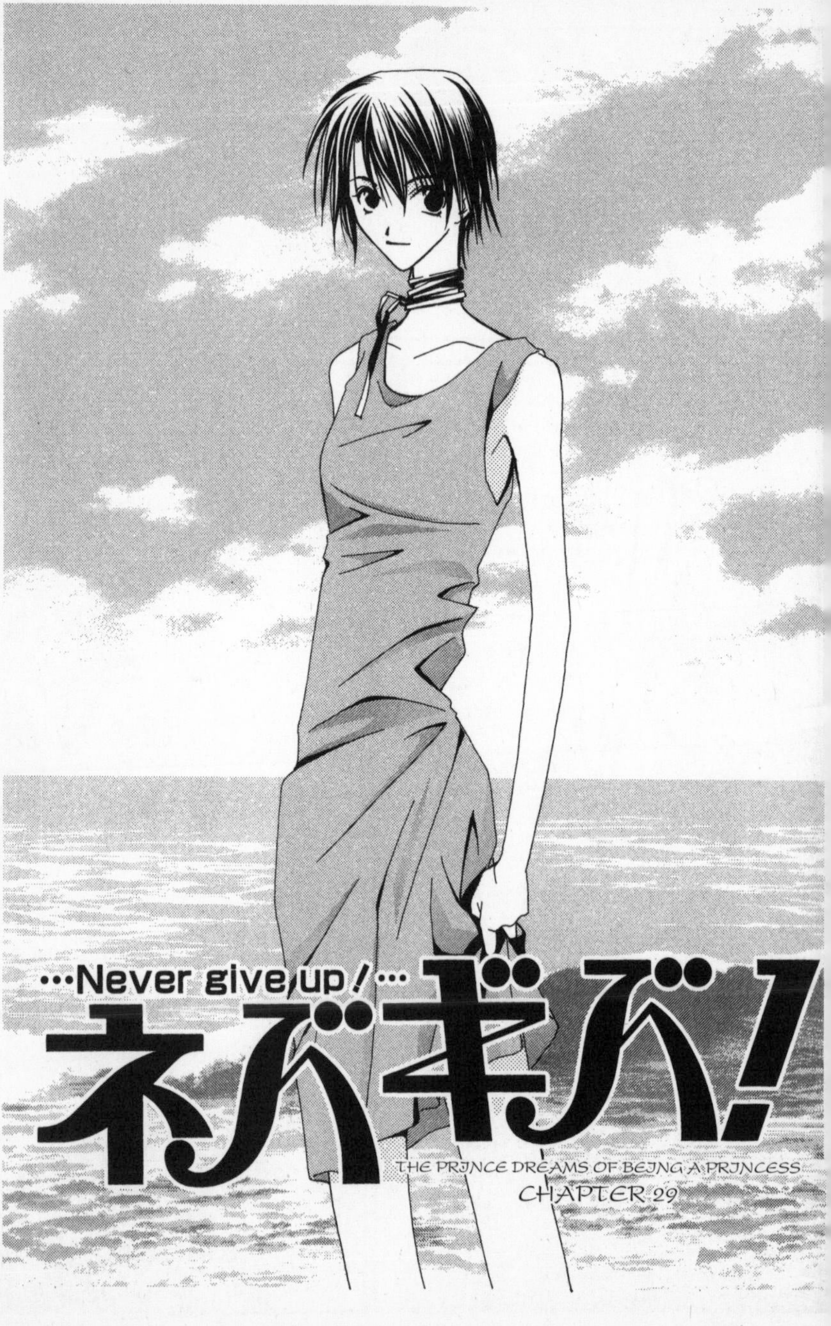

…Never give up!…
ネバギバ!
THE PRINCE DREAMS OF BEING A PRINCESS
CHAPTER 29

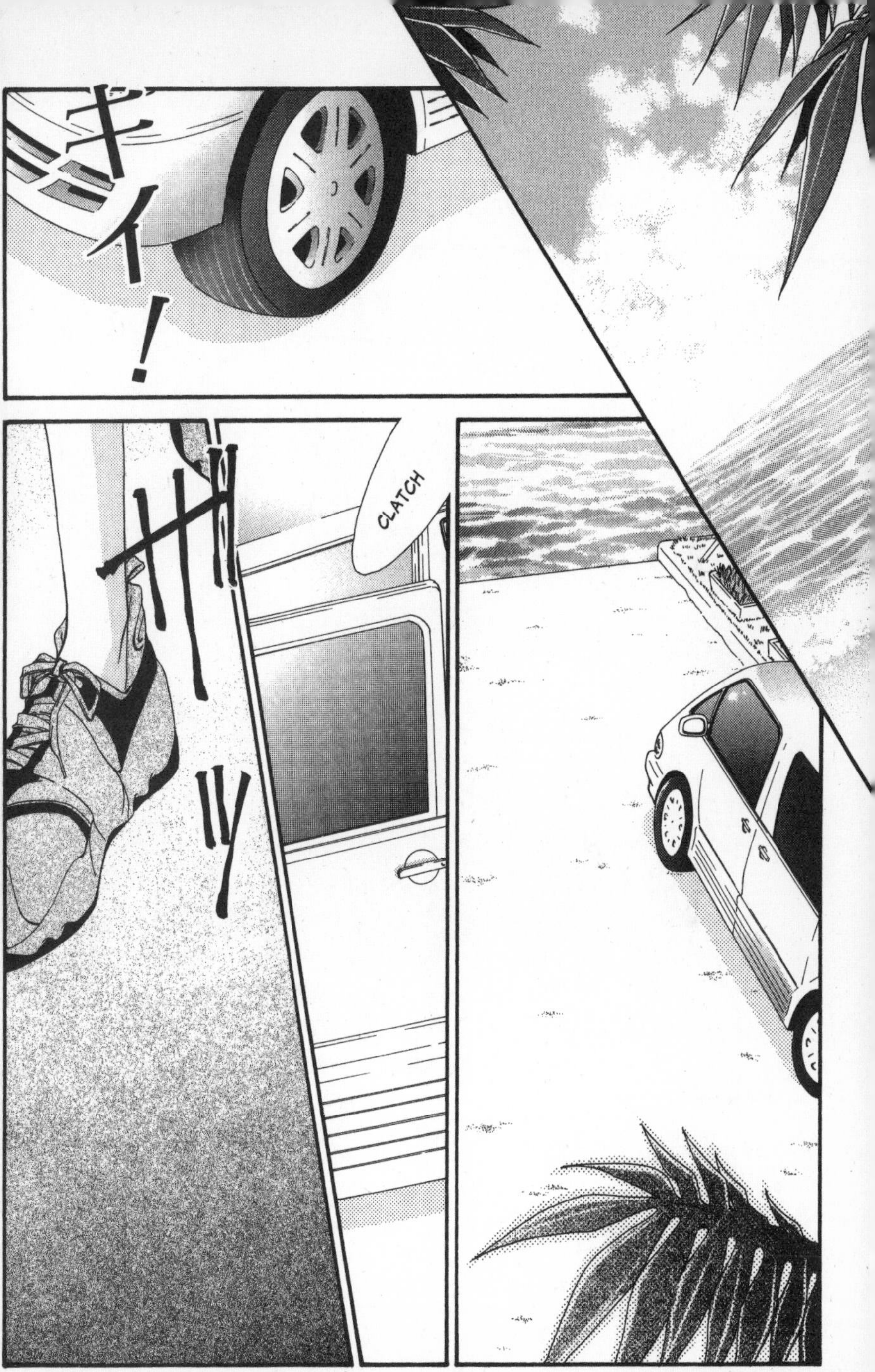
キィ!
CLATCH
ザッ

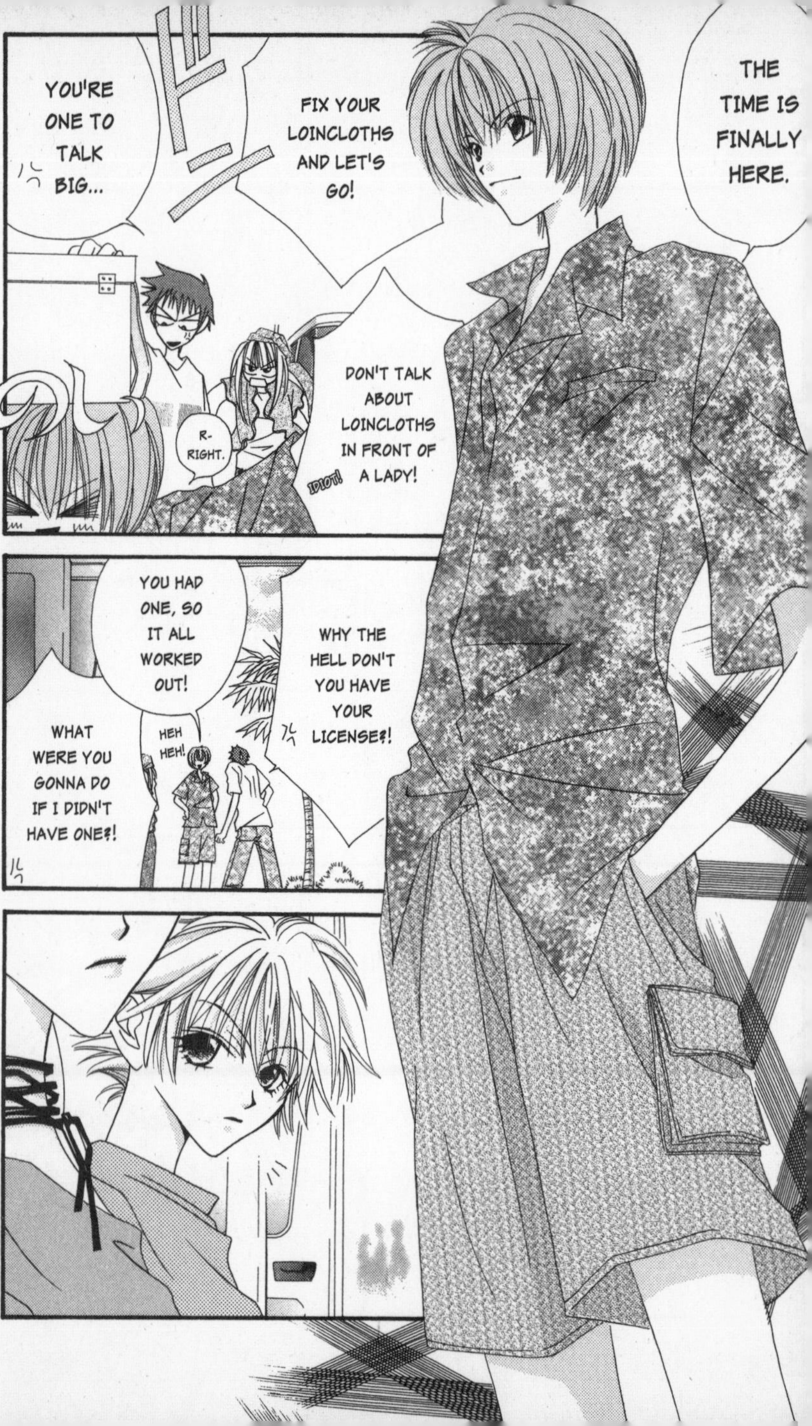
THE TIME IS FINALLY HERE.
FIX YOUR LOINCLOTHS AND LET'S GO!
YOU'RE ONE TO TALK BIG...
DON'T TALK ABOUT LOINCLOTHS IN FRONT OF A LADY!
IDIOT!
R-RIGHT.
WHY THE HELL DON'T YOU HAVE YOUR LICENSE?!
YOU HAD ONE, SO IT ALL WORKED OUT!
HEH HEH!
WHAT WERE YOU GONNA DO IF I DIDN'T HAVE ONE?!

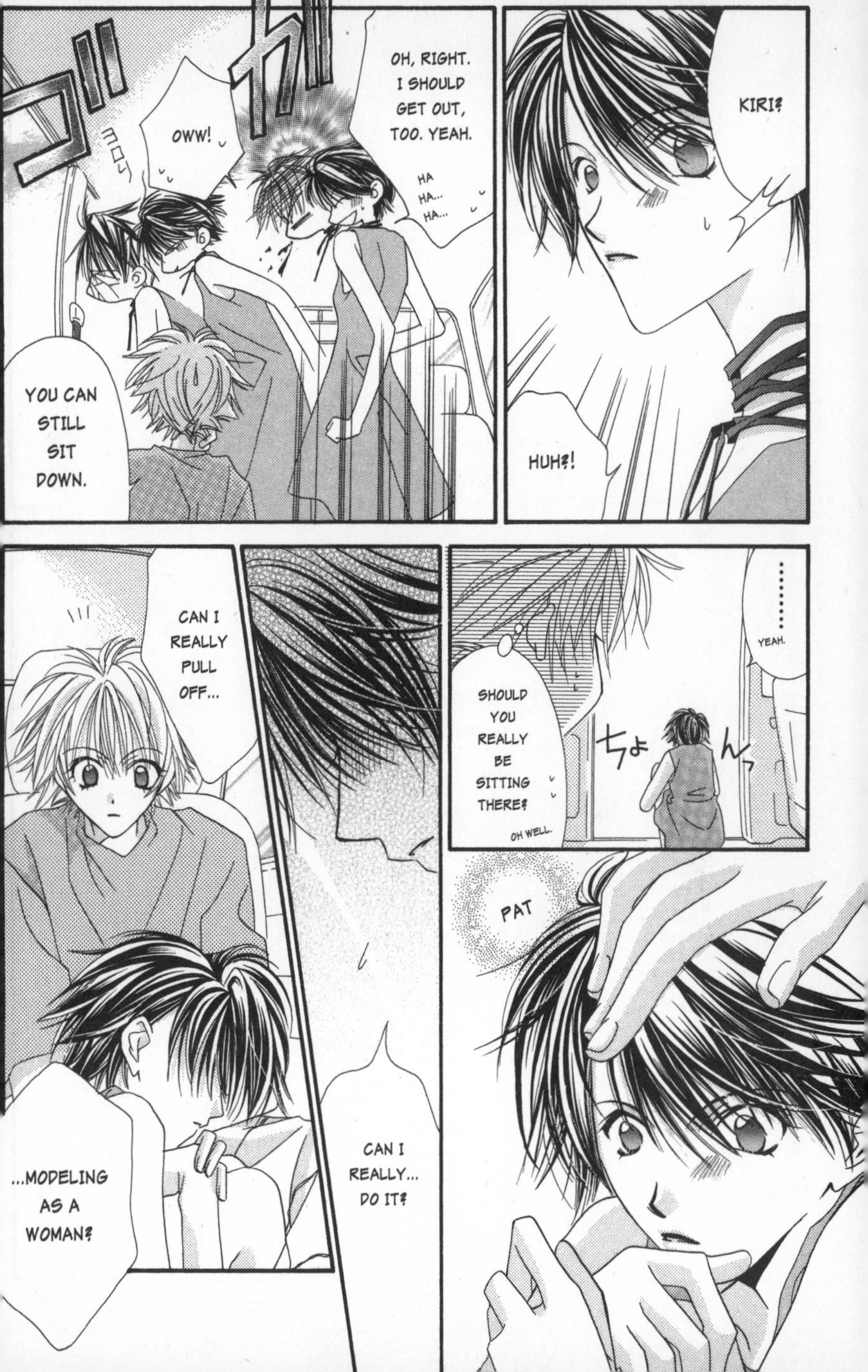

KIRI?
HUH?!
OH, RIGHT. I SHOULD GET OUT, TOO. YEAH.
HA HA... HA...
OWW!
YOU CAN STILL SIT DOWN.
......
YEAH.
SHOULD YOU REALLY BE SITTING THERE?
OH WELL.
PAT
CAN I REALLY... DO IT?
CAN I REALLY PULL OFF...
...MODELING AS A WOMAN?

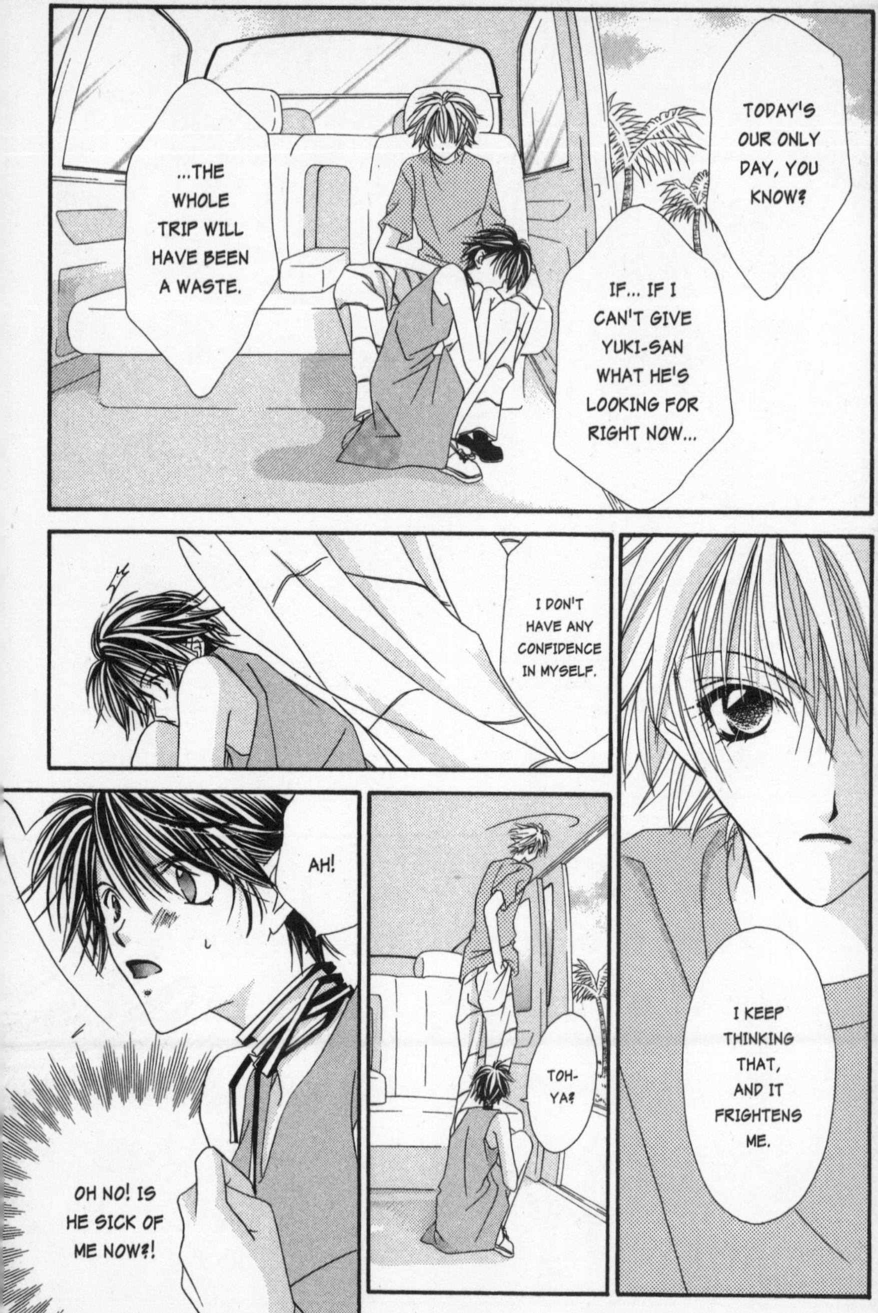
TODAY'S OUR ONLY DAY, YOU KNOW?
IF... IF I CAN'T GIVE YUKI-SAN WHAT HE'S LOOKING FOR RIGHT NOW...
...THE WHOLE TRIP WILL HAVE BEEN A WASTE.
I DON'T HAVE ANY CONFIDENCE IN MYSELF.
I KEEP THINKING THAT, AND IT FRIGHTENS ME.
TOH-YA?
AH!
OH NO! IS HE SICK OF ME NOW?!

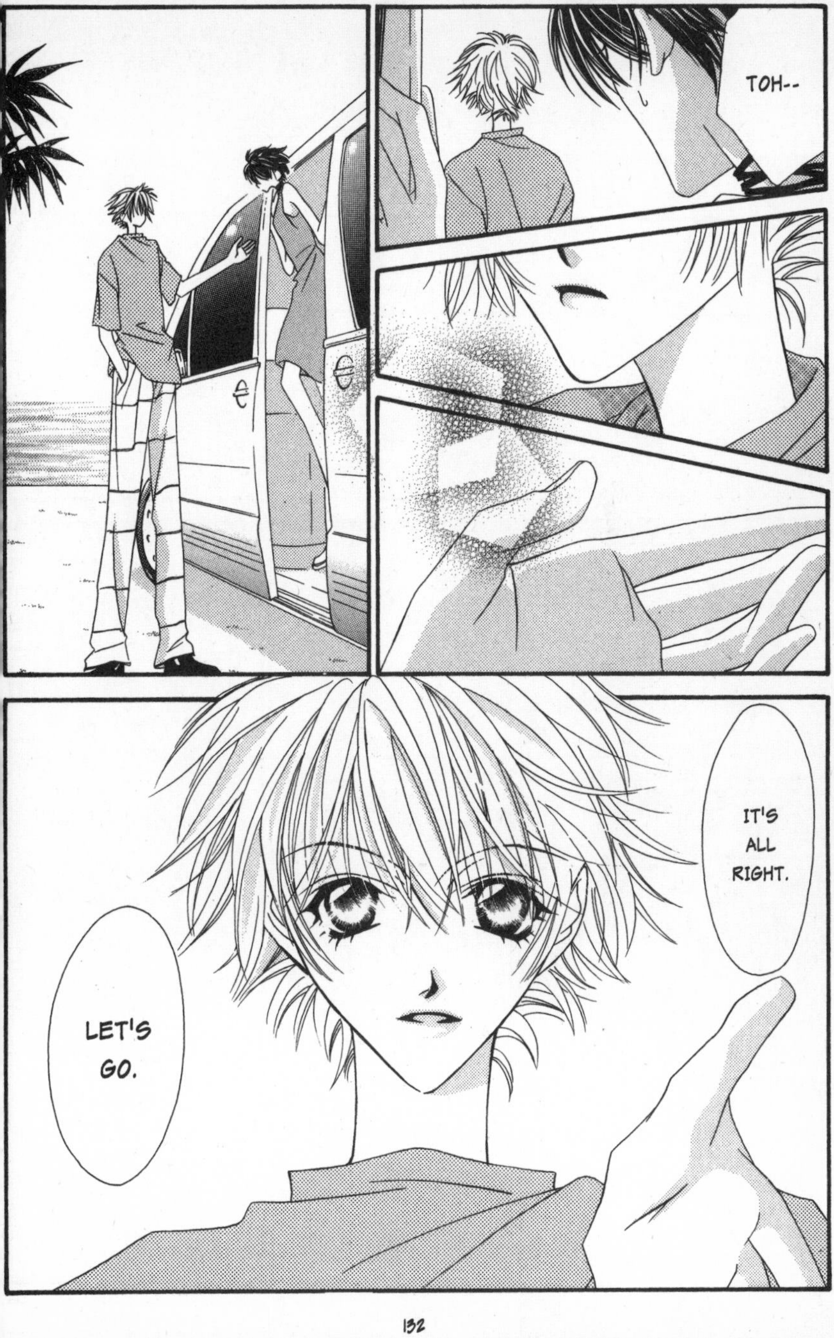
TOH--
IT'S ALL RIGHT.
LET'S GO.

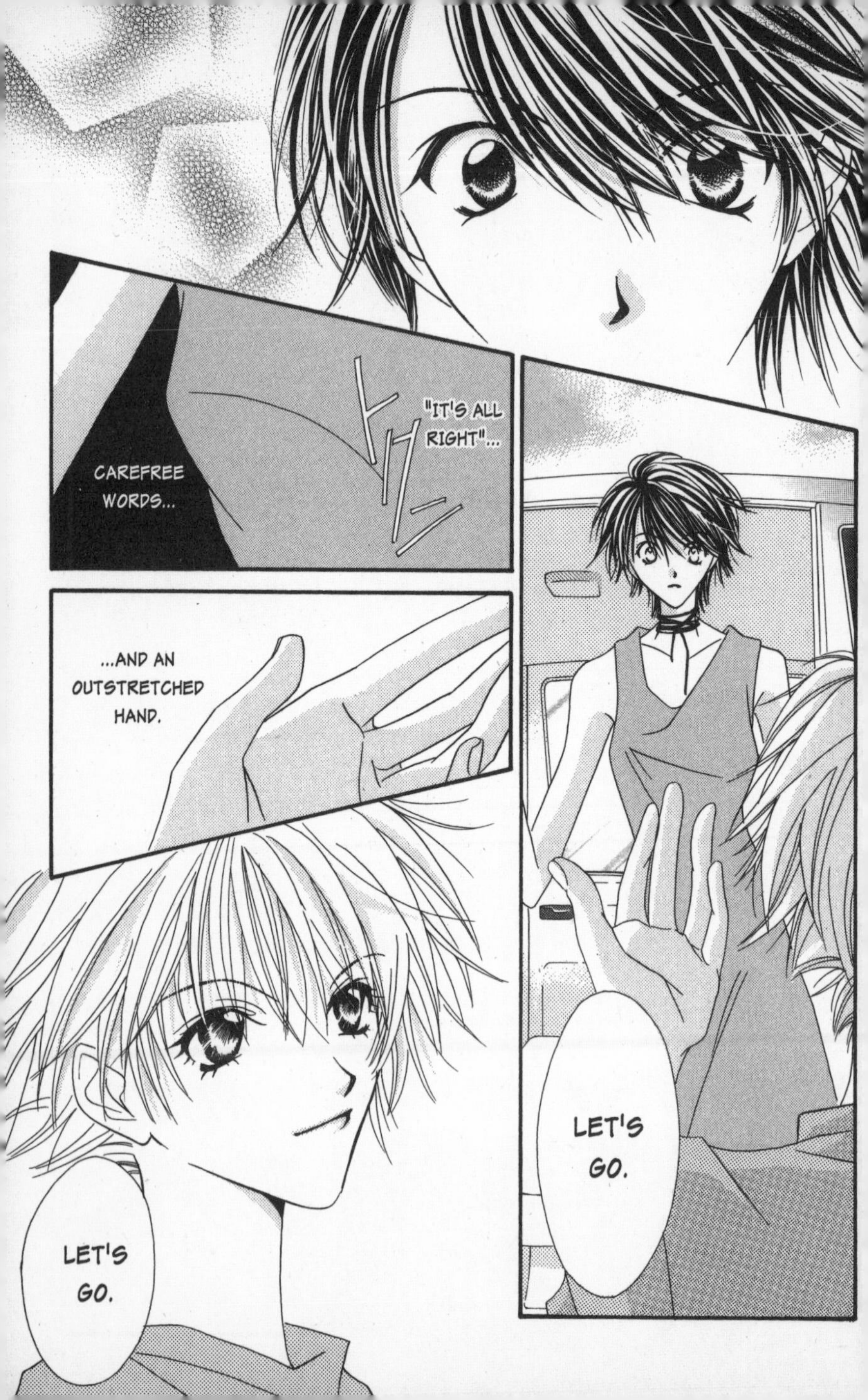
"IT'S ALL RIGHT"...
CAREFREE WORDS...
...AND AN OUTSTRETCHED HAND.
LET'S GO.
LET'S GO.

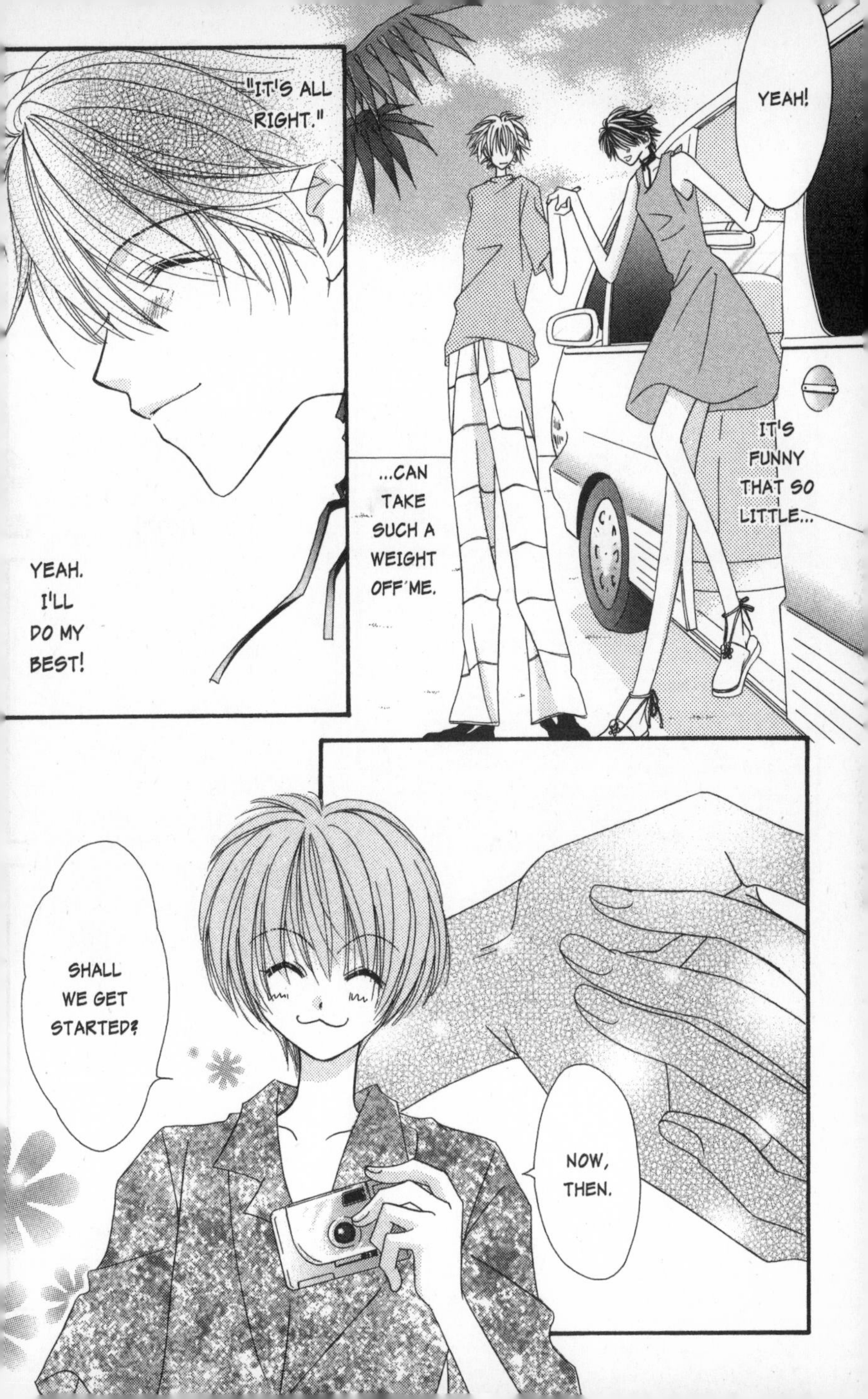
YEAH!
IT'S FUNNY THAT SO LITTLE...
...CAN TAKE SUCH A WEIGHT OFF ME.
"IT'S ALL RIGHT."
YEAH. I'LL DO MY BEST!
NOW, THEN.
SHALL WE GET STARTED?

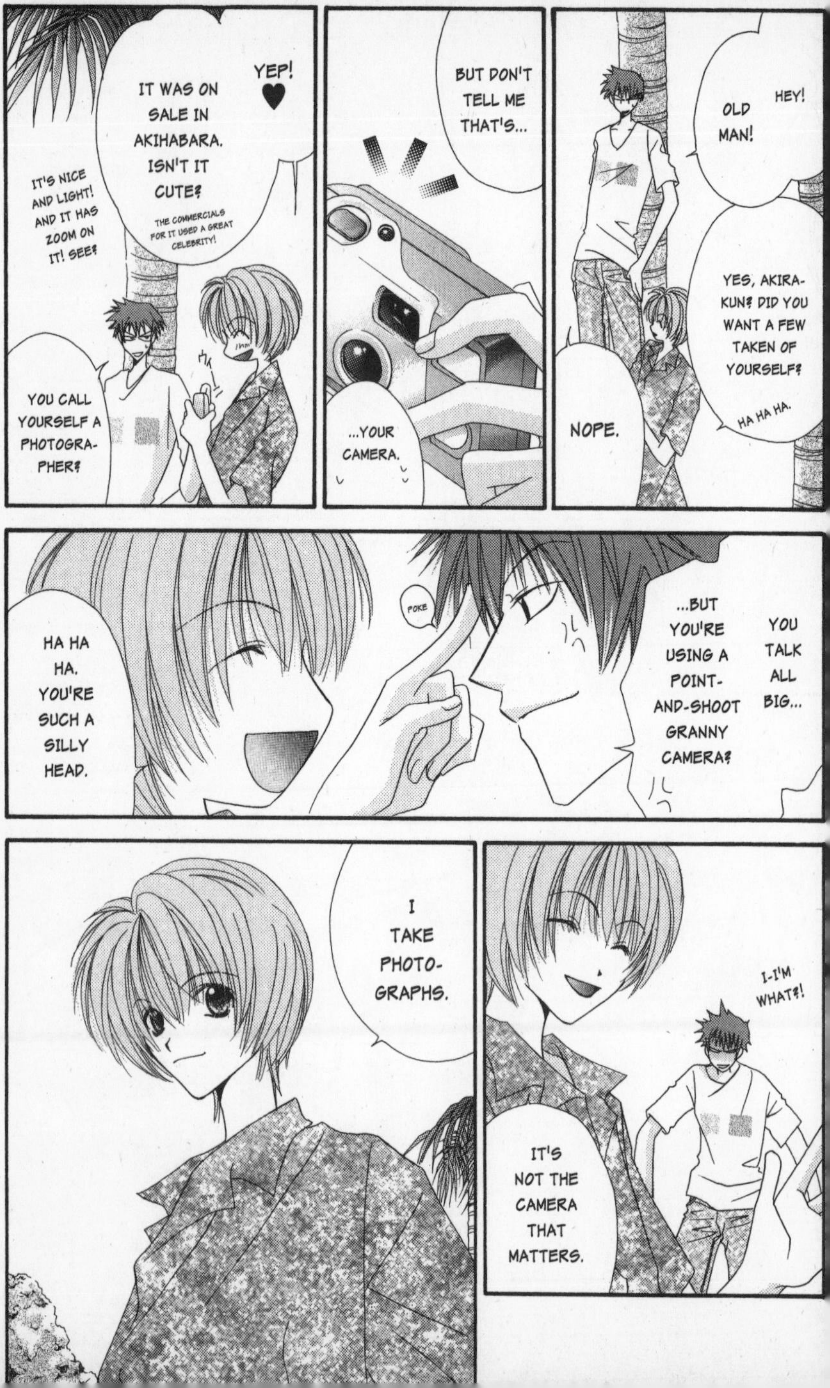
HEY!
OLD MAN!
YES, AKIRA-KUN? DID YOU WANT A FEW TAKEN OF YOURSELF?
HA HA HA.
NOPE.
BUT DON'T TELL ME THAT'S...
...YOUR CAMERA.
YEP! ♥
IT WAS ON SALE IN AKIHABARA. ISN'T IT CUTE?
THE COMMERCIALS FOR IT USED A GREAT CELEBRITY!
IT'S NICE AND LIGHT! AND IT HAS ZOOM ON IT! SEE?
YOU CALL YOURSELF A PHOTOGRA-PHER?
YOU TALK ALL BIG...
...BUT YOU'RE USING A POINT-AND-SHOOT GRANNY CAMERA?
POKE
HA HA HA. YOU'RE SUCH A SILLY HEAD.
I-I'M WHAT?!
IT'S NOT THE CAMERA THAT MATTERS.
I TAKE PHOTO-GRAPHS.

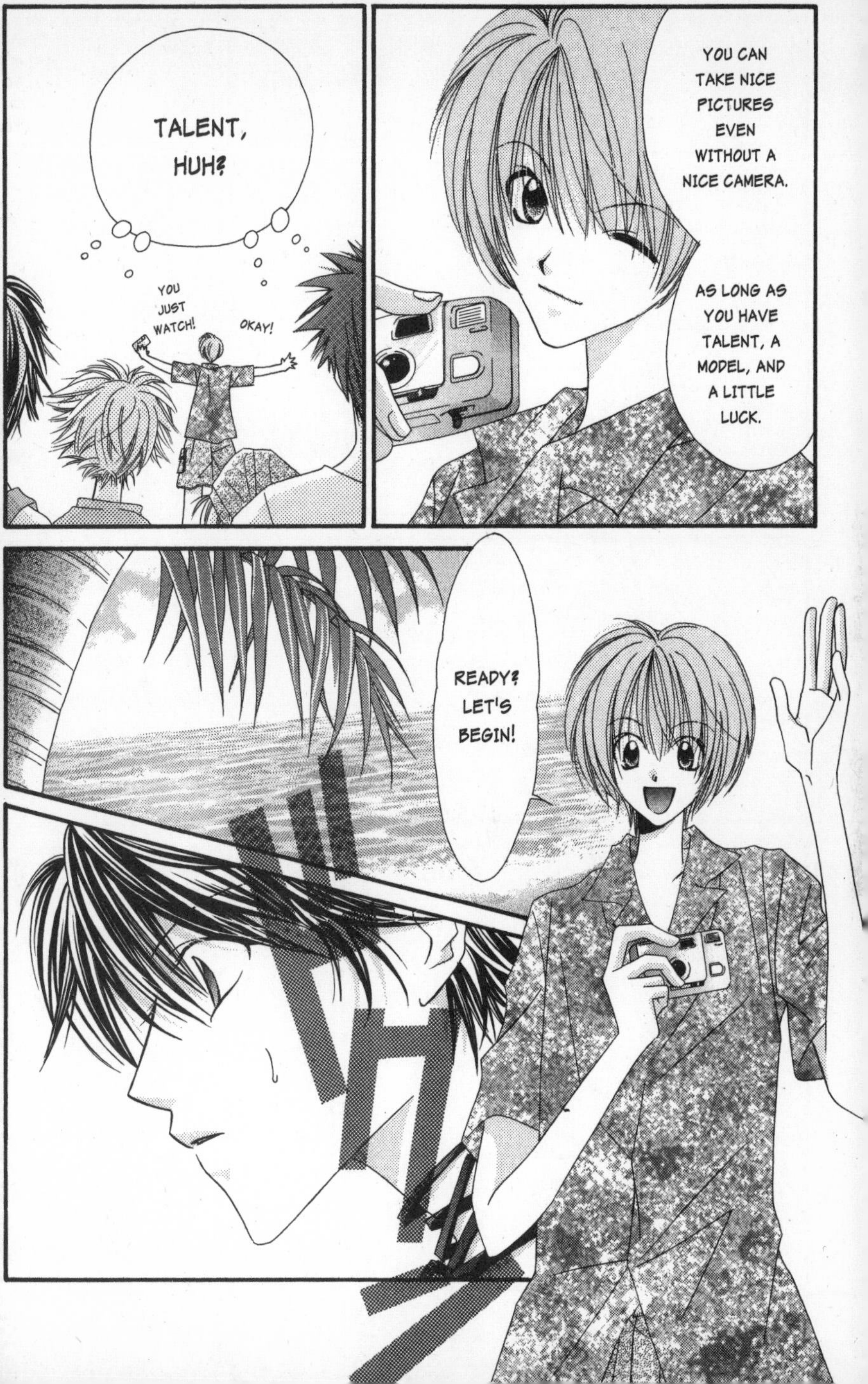
YOU CAN TAKE NICE PICTURES EVEN WITHOUT A NICE CAMERA.
AS LONG AS YOU HAVE TALENT, A MODEL, AND A LITTLE LUCK.
TALENT, HUH?
YOU JUST WATCH!
OKAY!
READY? LET'S BEGIN!

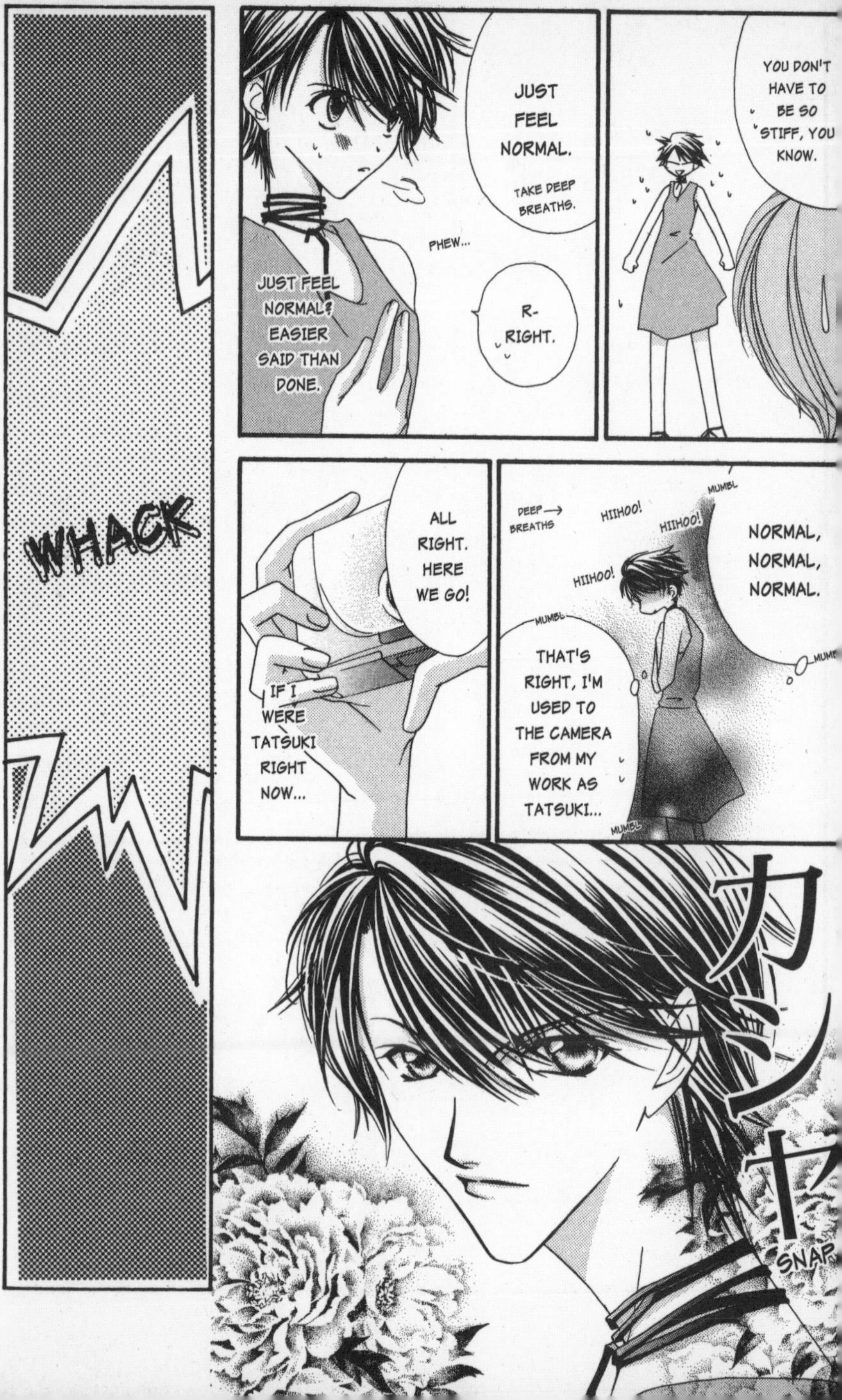
YOU DON'T HAVE TO BE SO STIFF, YOU KNOW.
JUST FEEL NORMAL.
TAKE DEEP BREATHS.
PHEW...
R- RIGHT.
JUST FEEL NORMAL? EASIER SAID THAN DONE.
MUMBL
NORMAL, NORMAL, NORMAL.
HIIHOO!
HIIHOO!
DEEP → BREATHS
HIIHOO!
MUMBL
THAT'S RIGHT, I'M USED TO THE CAMERA FROM MY WORK AS TATSUKI...
MUMBL
MUMBL
ALL RIGHT. HERE WE GO!
IF I WERE TATSUKI RIGHT NOW...
カシャ
SNAP
WHACK

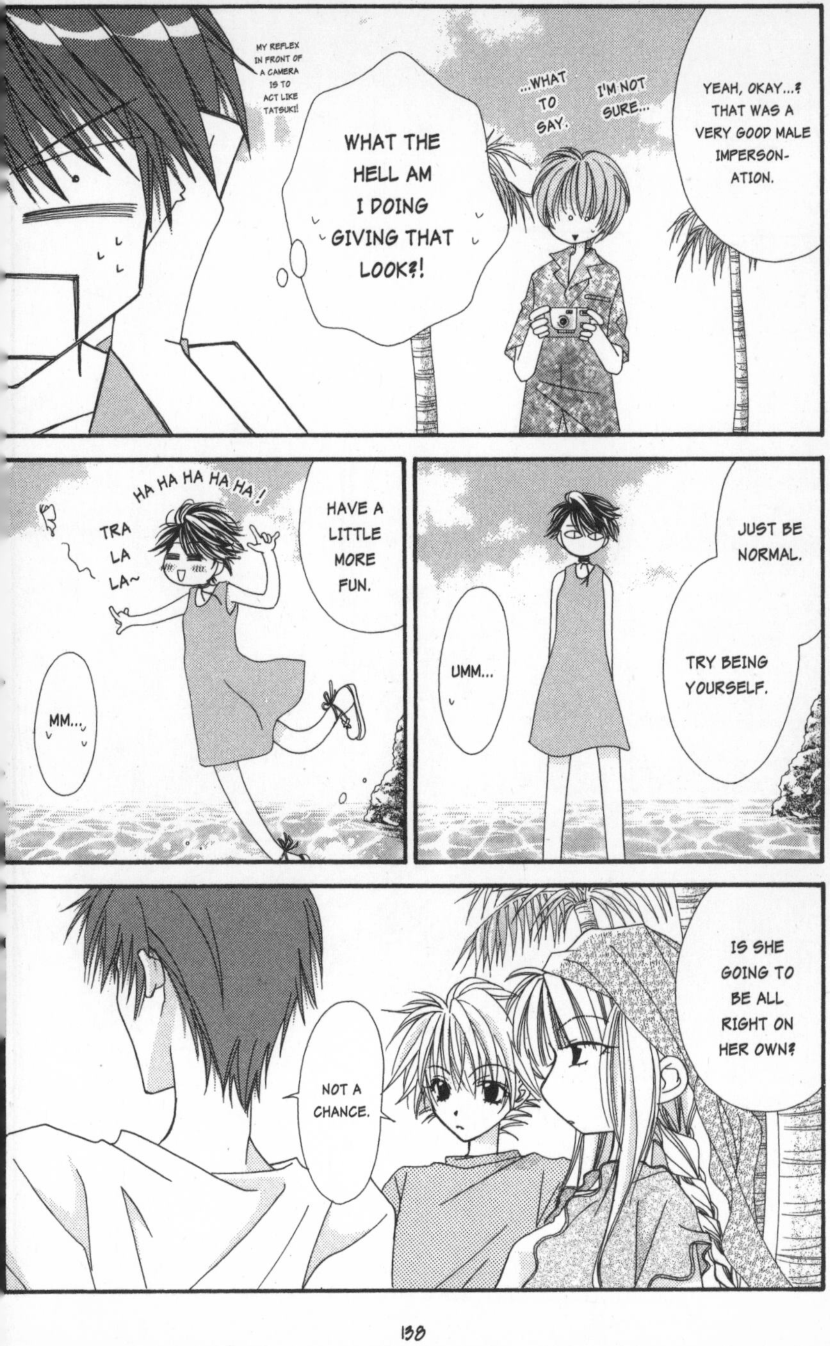
YEAH, OKAY...? THAT WAS A VERY GOOD MALE IMPERSON-ATION.
I'M NOT SURE...
...WHAT TO SAY.
WHAT THE HELL AM I DOING GIVING THAT LOOK?!
MY REFLEX IN FRONT OF A CAMERA IS TO ACT LIKE TATSUKI!
JUST BE NORMAL.
TRY BEING YOURSELF.
UMM...
HAVE A LITTLE MORE FUN.
HA HA HA HA HA!
TRA LA LA~
MM...
IS SHE GOING TO BE ALL RIGHT ON HER OWN?
NOT A CHANCE.

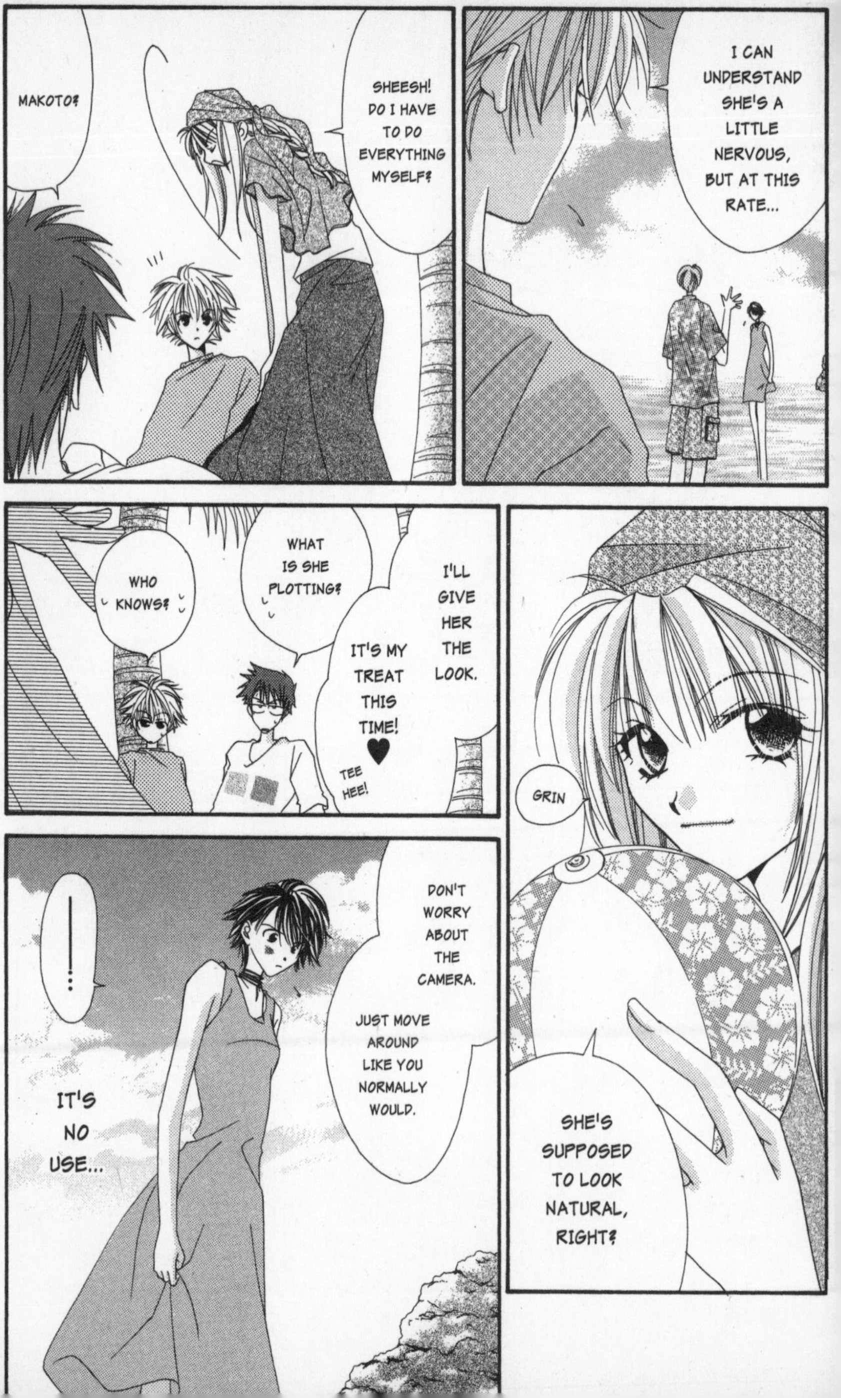
I CAN UNDERSTAND SHE'S A LITTLE NERVOUS, BUT AT THIS RATE...
SHEESH! DO I HAVE TO DO EVERYTHING MYSELF?
MAKOTO?
GRIN
SHE'S SUPPOSED TO LOOK NATURAL, RIGHT?
I'LL GIVE HER THE LOOK.
IT'S MY TREAT THIS TIME!
TEE HEE!
WHAT IS SHE PLOTTING?
WHO KNOWS?
DON'T WORRY ABOUT THE CAMERA.
JUST MOVE AROUND LIKE YOU NORMALLY WOULD.
!...
IT'S NO USE...

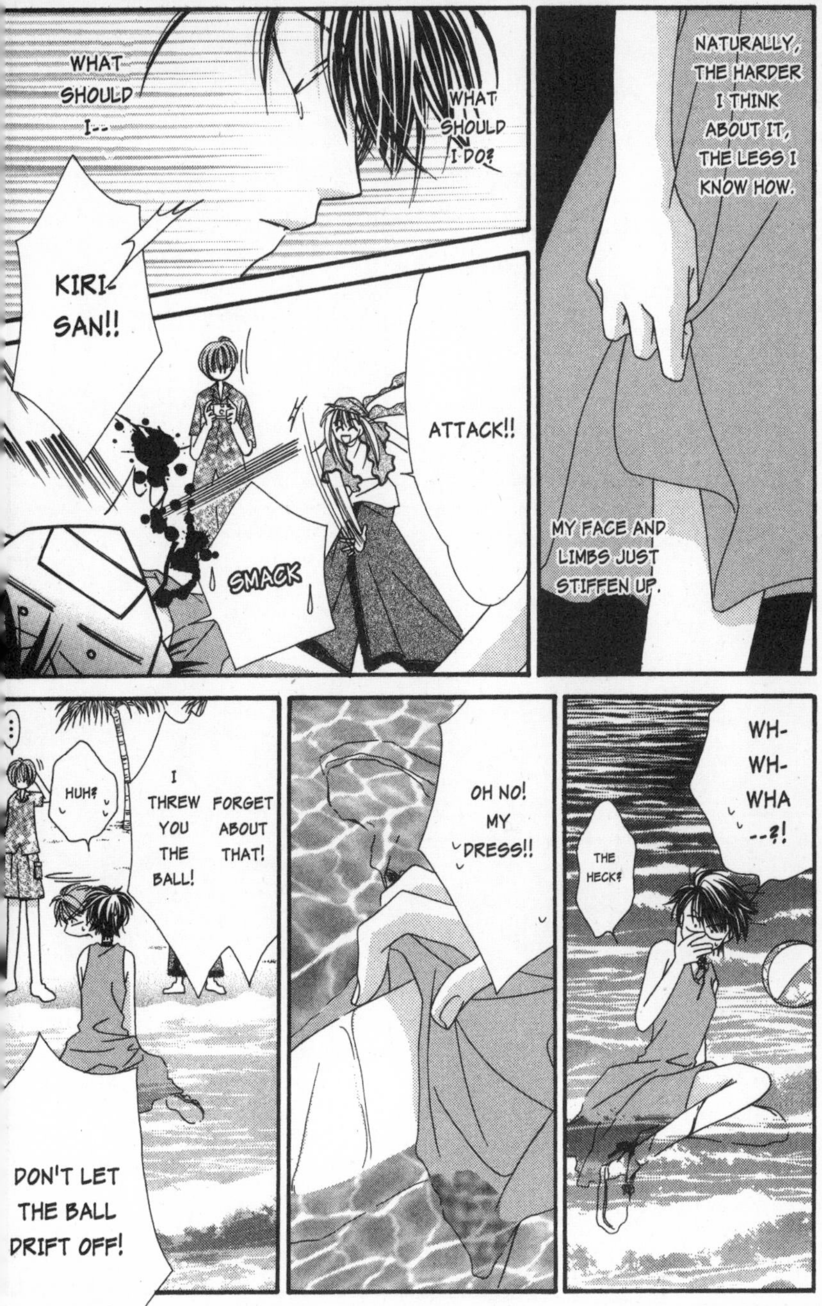
NATURALLY, THE HARDER I THINK ABOUT IT, THE LESS I KNOW HOW.
MY FACE AND LIMBS JUST STIFFEN UP.
WHAT SHOULD I DO?
WHAT SHOULD I--
KIRI-SAN!!
ATTACK!!
SMACK
WH-WH-WHA--?!
THE HECK?
OH NO! MY DRESS!!
FORGET ABOUT THAT!
I THREW YOU THE BALL!
HUH?
...
DON'T LET THE BALL DRIFT OFF!
HURRY!

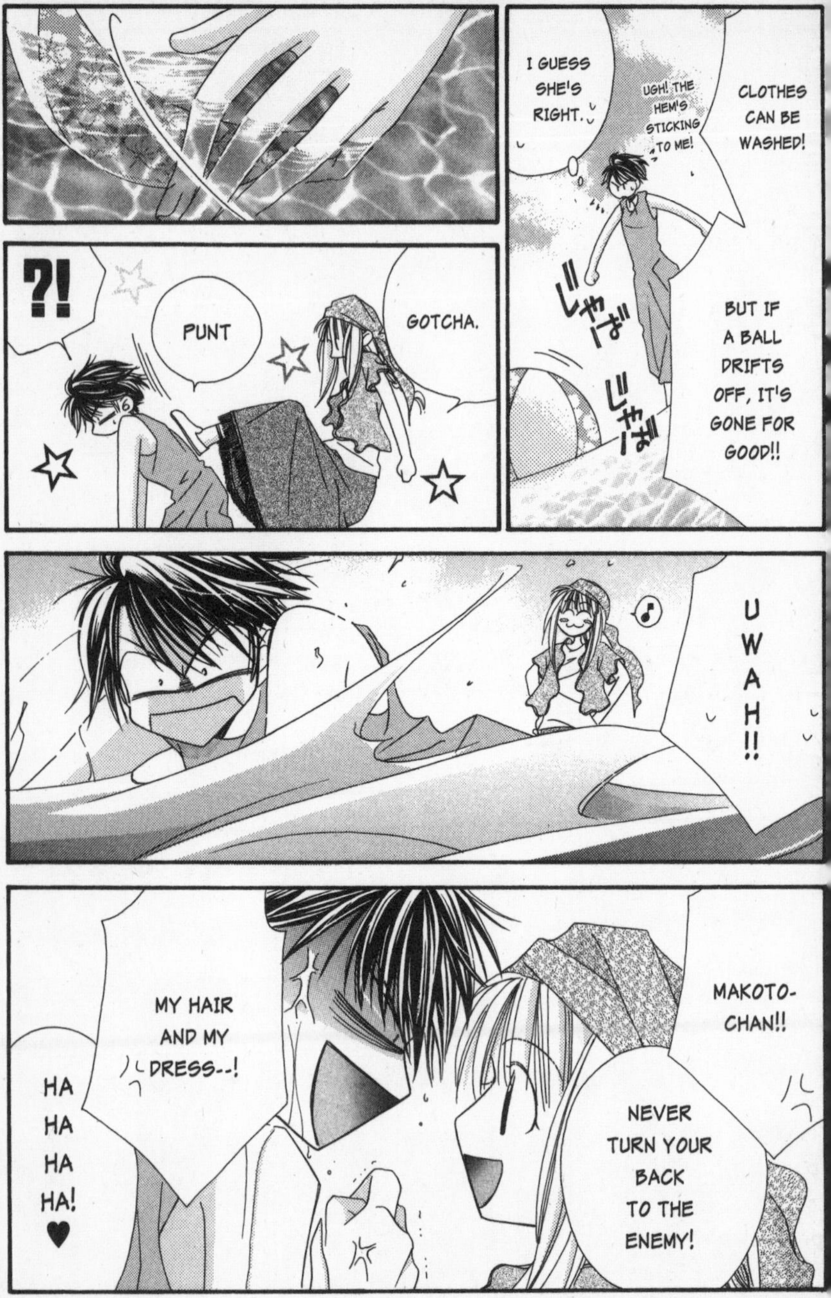
CLOTHES CAN BE WASHED!
UGH! THE HEM'S STICKING TO ME!
I GUESS SHE'S RIGHT.
BUT IF A BALL DRIFTS OFF, IT'S GONE FOR GOOD!!
じゃぼ
じゃぼ
GOTCHA.
PUNT
?!
UWAH!!
MAKOTO-CHAN!!
NEVER TURN YOUR BACK TO THE ENEMY!
MY HAIR AND MY DRESS--!
HA HA HA HA! ♥

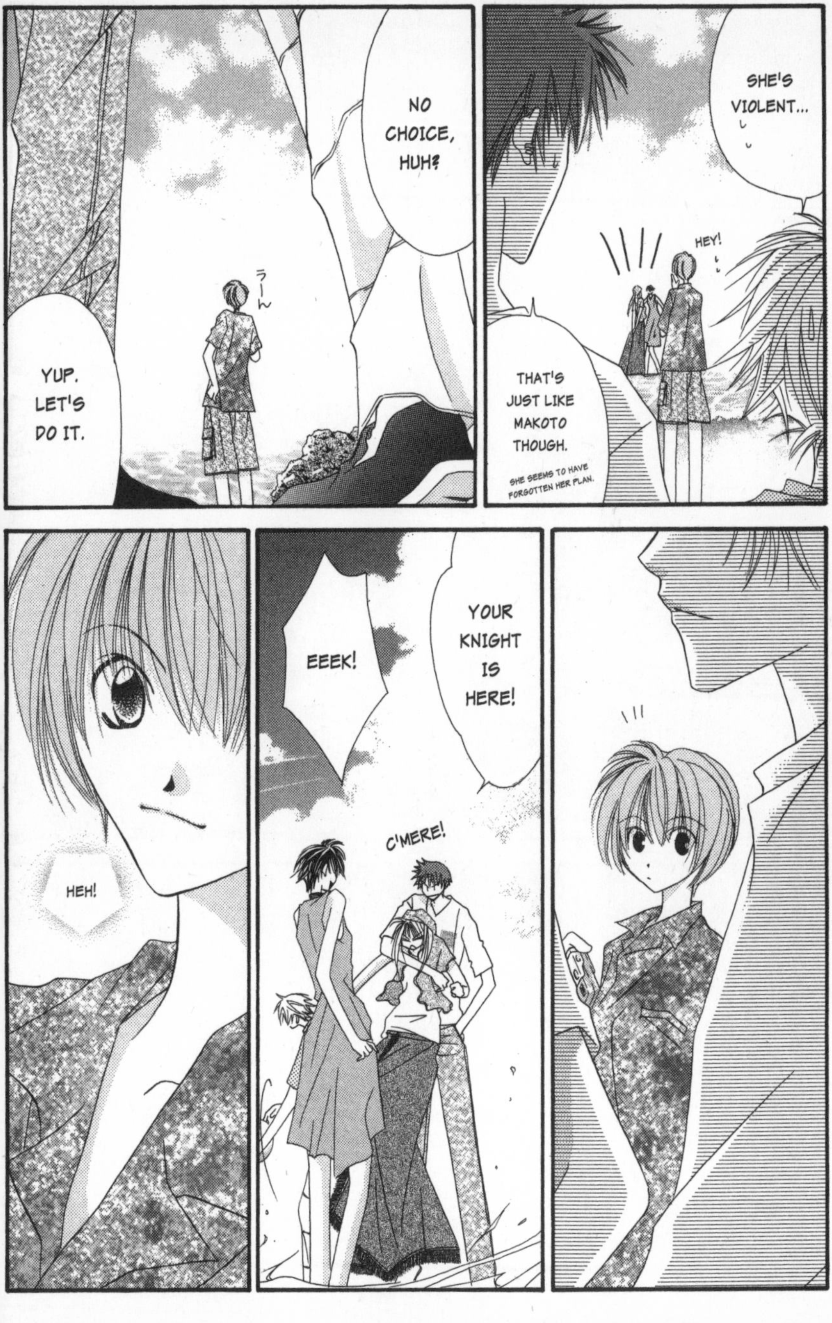
SHE'S VIOLENT...
HEY!
THAT'S JUST LIKE MAKOTO THOUGH.
SHE SEEMS TO HAVE FORGOTTEN HER PLAN.
NO CHOICE, HUH?
ラーん
YUP. LET'S DO IT.
YOUR KNIGHT IS HERE!
EEEK!
C'MERE!
HEH!

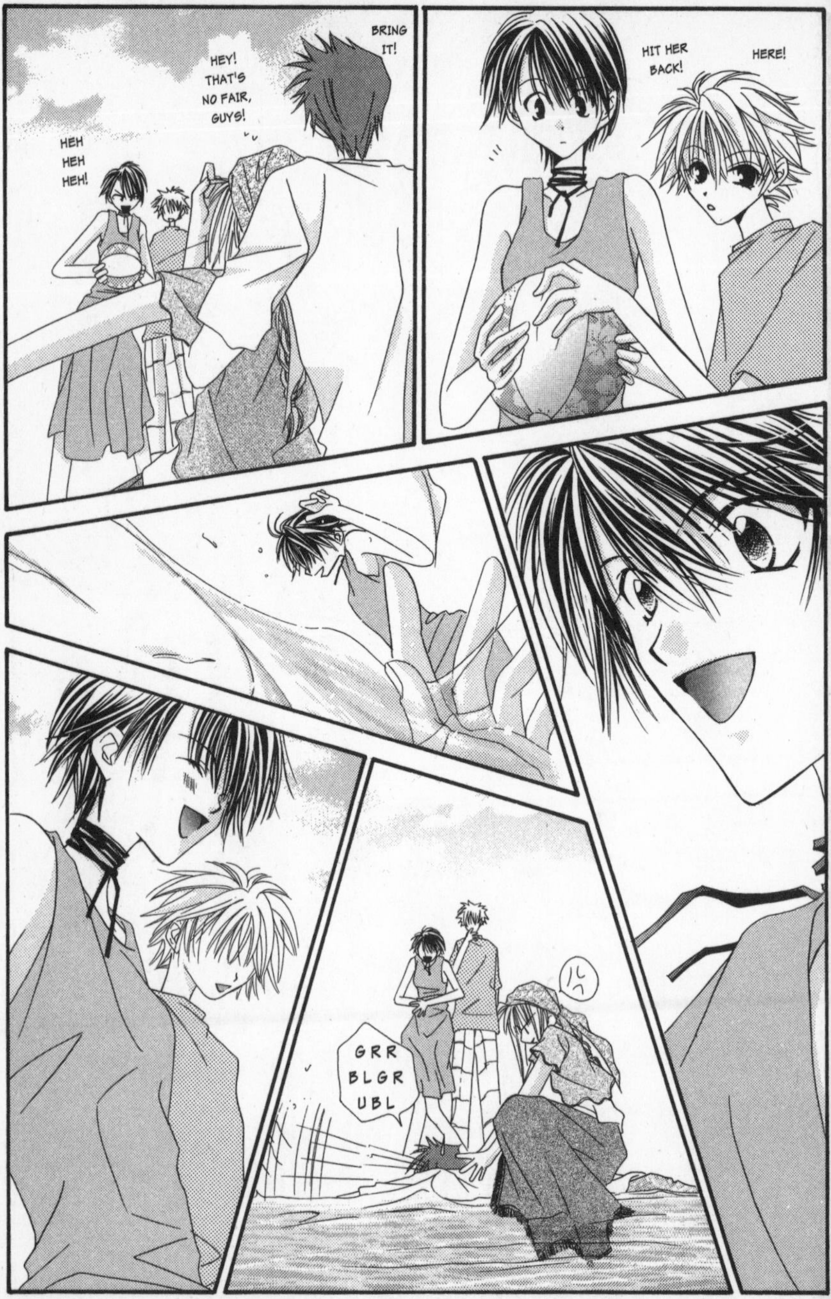
HERE!
HIT HER BACK!
BRING IT!
HEY! THAT'S NO FAIR, GUYS!
HEH HEH HEH!
GRR BLGR UBL

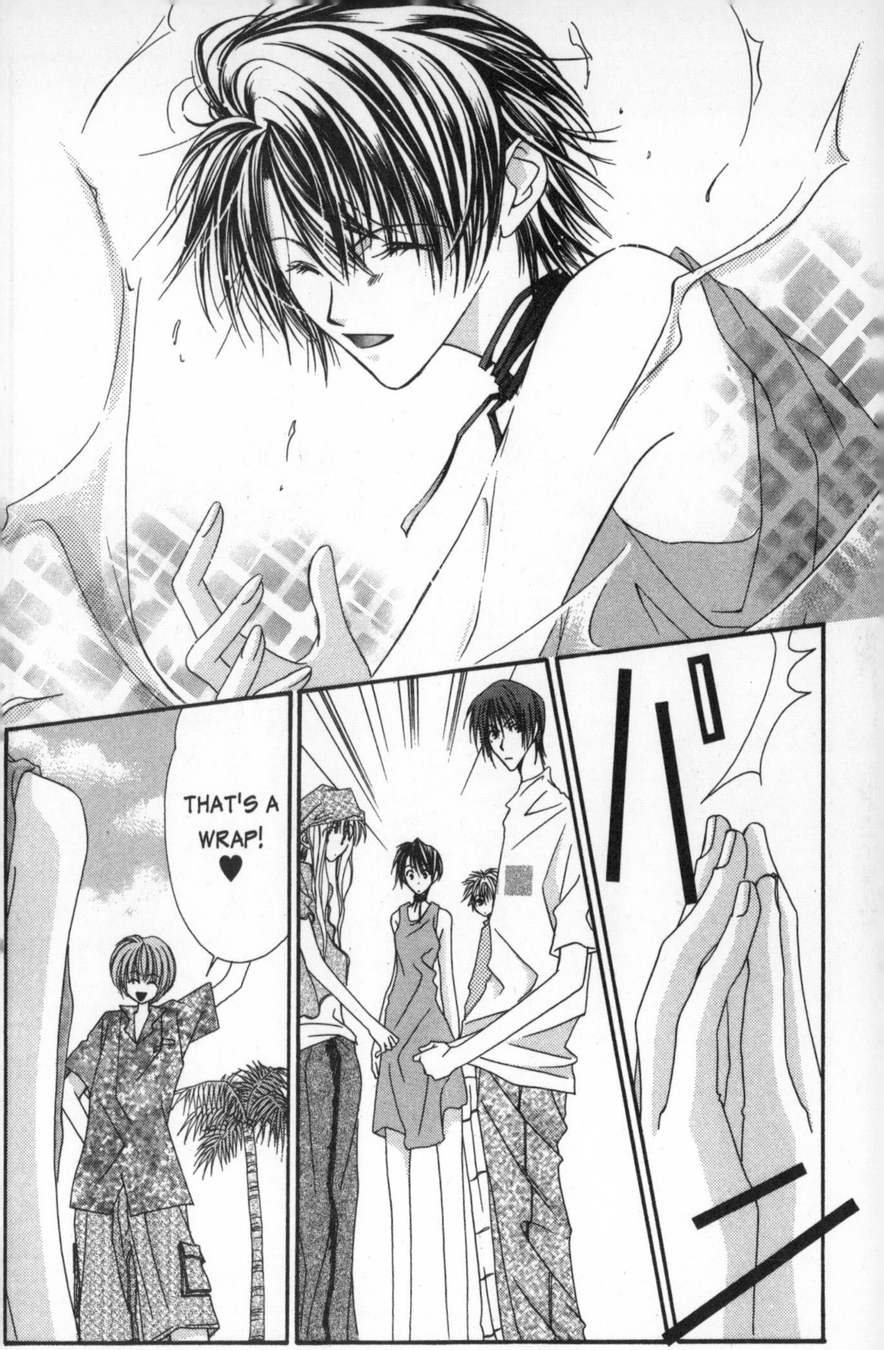
パ
THAT'S A WRAP! ♥

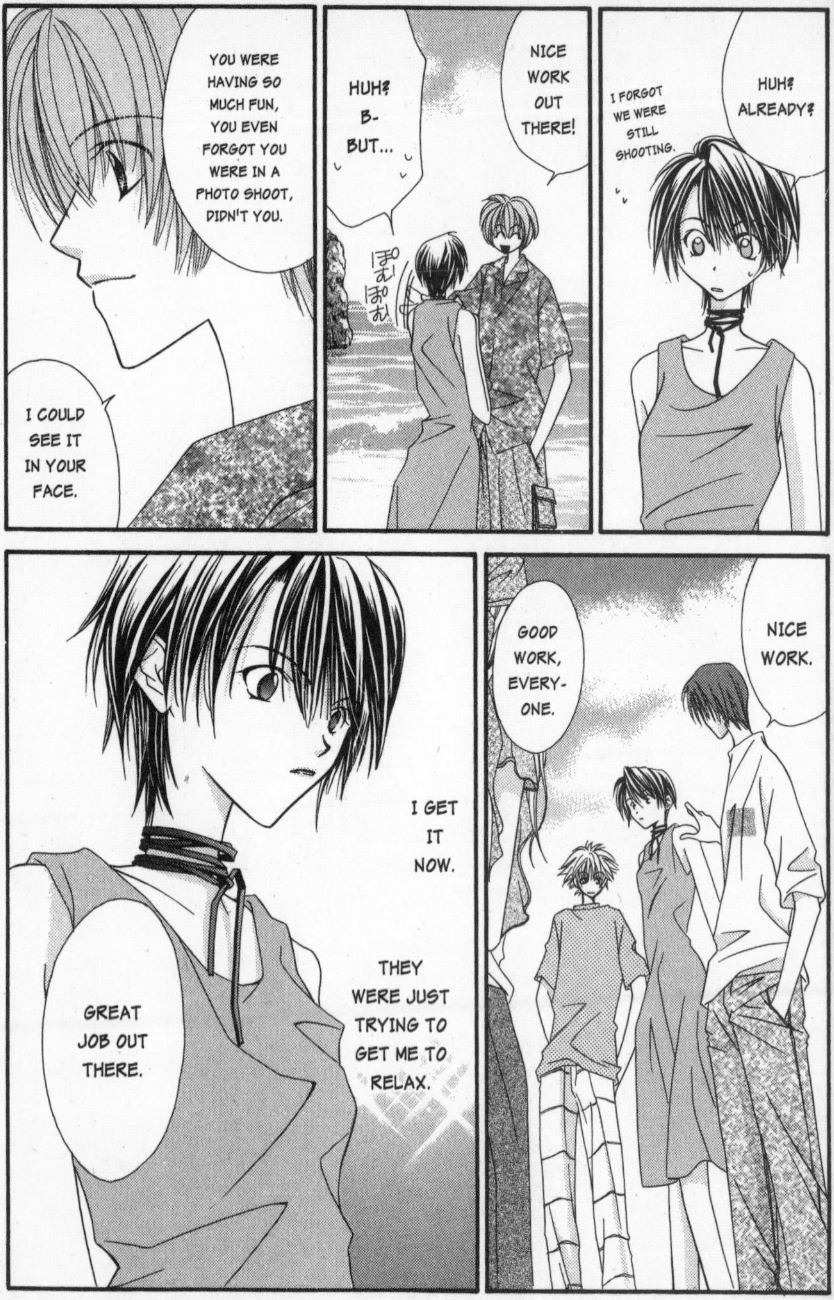
HUH? ALREADY?
I FORGOT WE WERE STILL SHOOTING.
NICE WORK OUT THERE!
HUH? B-BUT...
ぽむぽむ
YOU WERE HAVING SO MUCH FUN, YOU EVEN FORGOT YOU WERE IN A PHOTO SHOOT, DIDN'T YOU.
I COULD SEE IT IN YOUR FACE.
NICE WORK.
GOOD WORK, EVERY-ONE.
I GET IT NOW.
THEY WERE JUST TRYING TO GET ME TO RELAX.
GREAT JOB OUT THERE.

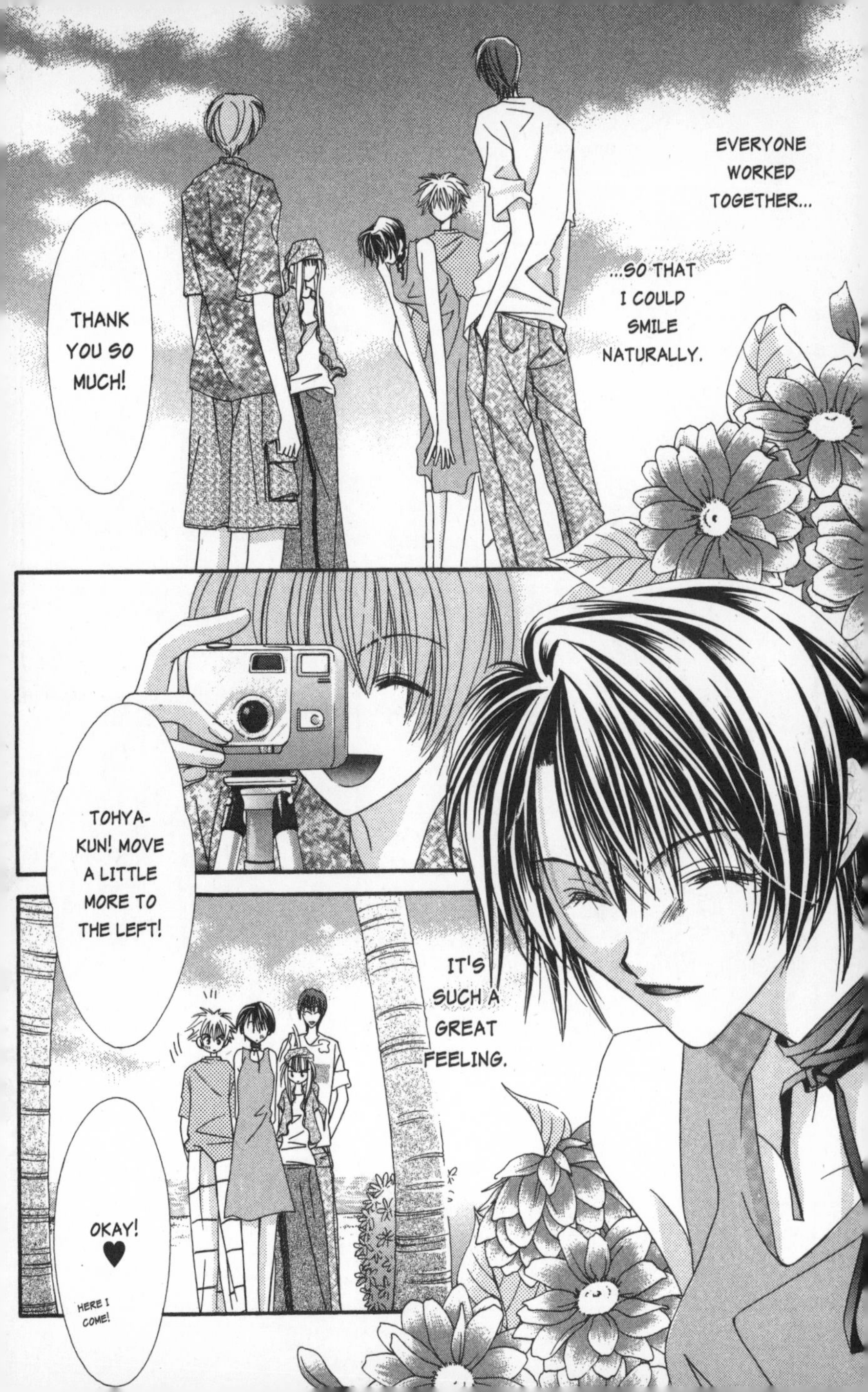
EVERYONE WORKED TOGETHER...
...SO THAT I COULD SMILE NATURALLY.
THANK YOU SO MUCH!
IT'S SUCH A GREAT FEELING.
TOHYA-KUN! MOVE A LITTLE MORE TO THE LEFT!
OKAY! ♥
HERE I COME!

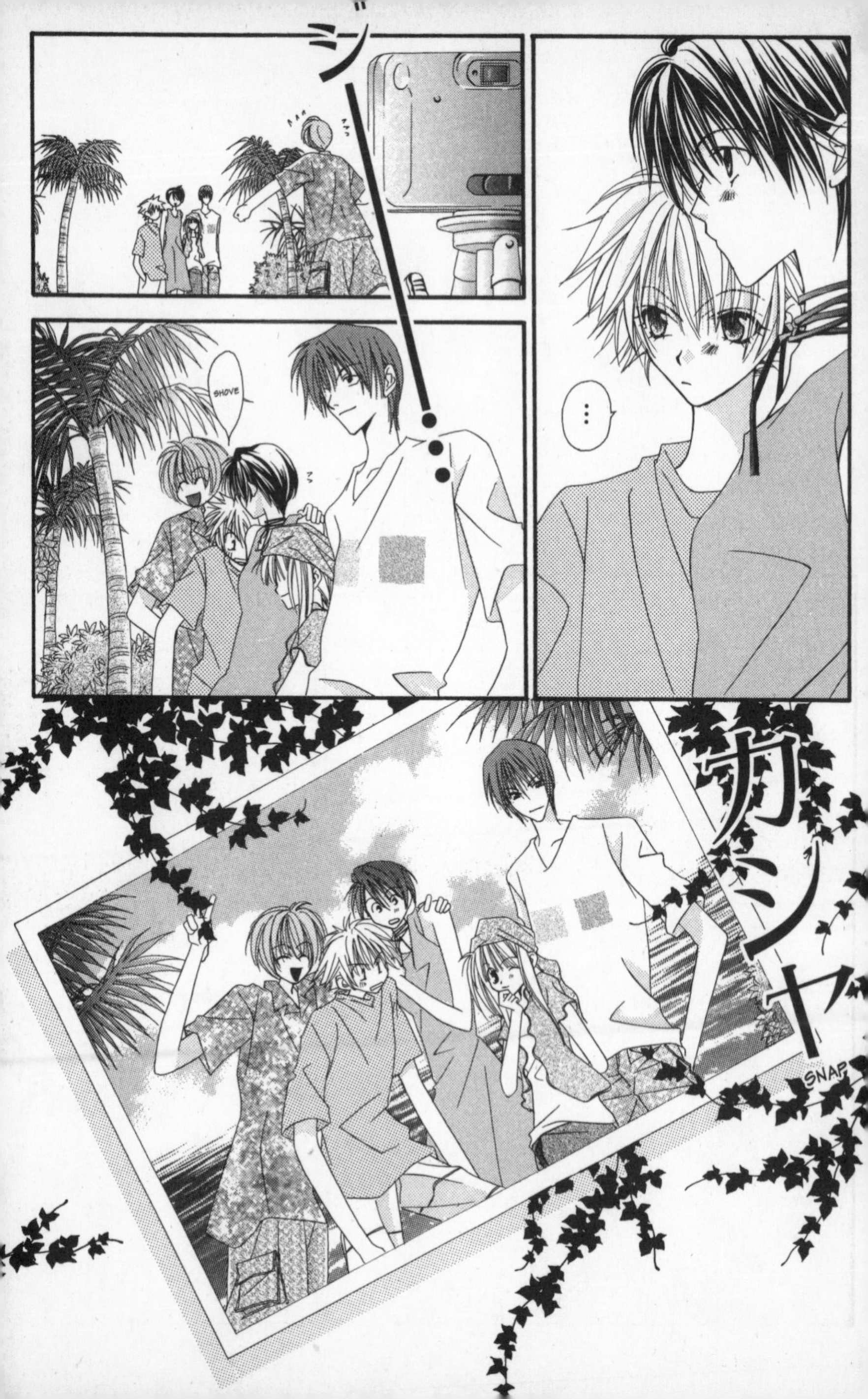
…
ジ
SHOVE
カシャ
SNAP

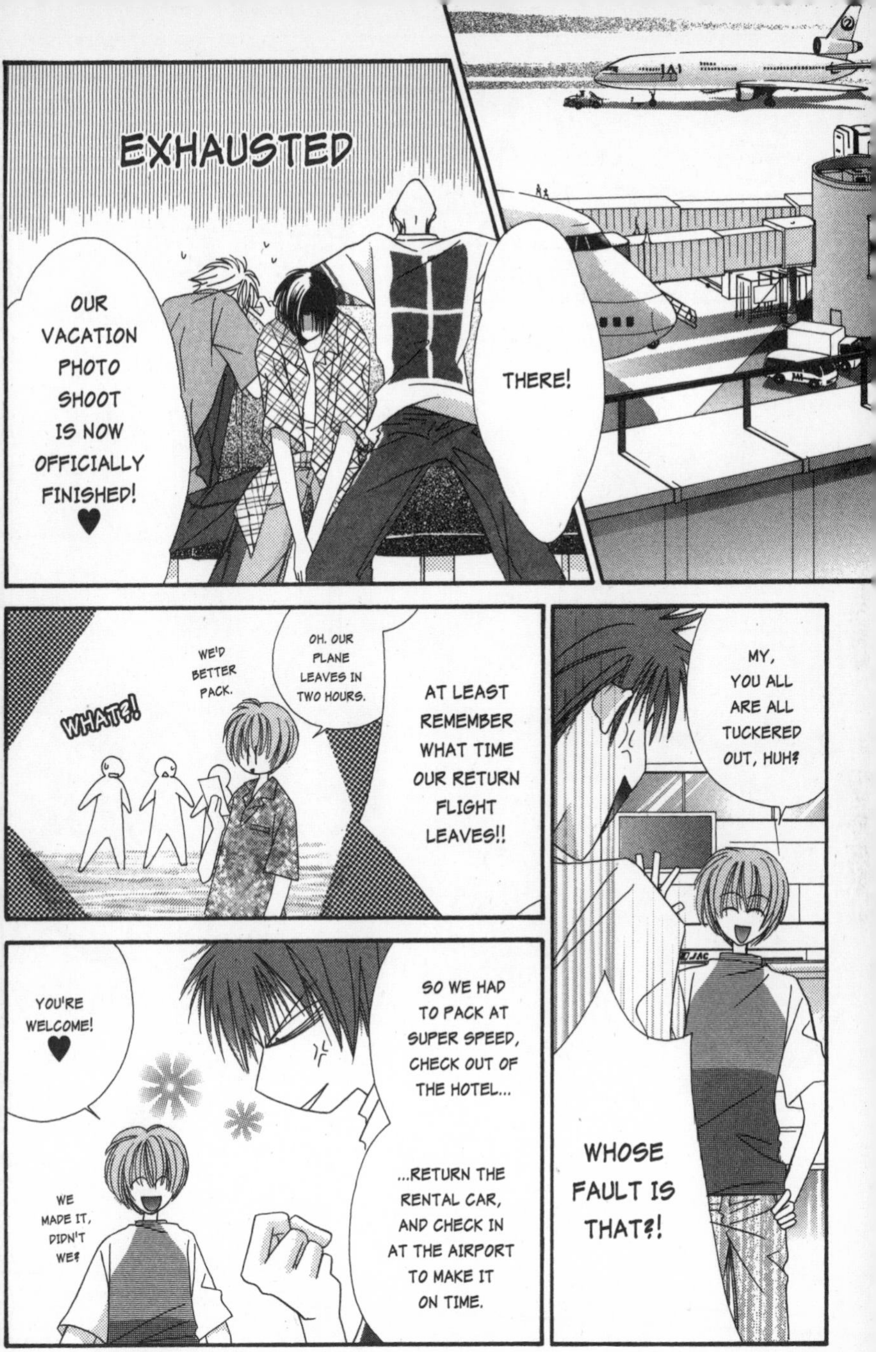
THERE!
EXHAUSTED
OUR VACATION PHOTO SHOOT IS NOW OFFICIALLY FINISHED! ♥
MY, YOU ALL ARE ALL TUCKERED OUT, HUH?
WHOSE FAULT IS THAT?!
AT LEAST REMEMBER WHAT TIME OUR RETURN FLIGHT LEAVES!!
OH. OUR PLANE LEAVES IN TWO HOURS.
WE'D BETTER PACK.
WHAT?!
SO WE HAD TO PACK AT SUPER SPEED, CHECK OUT OF THE HOTEL...
...RETURN THE RENTAL CAR, AND CHECK IN AT THE AIRPORT TO MAKE IT ON TIME.
YOU'RE WELCOME! ♥
WE MADE IT, DIDN'T WE?

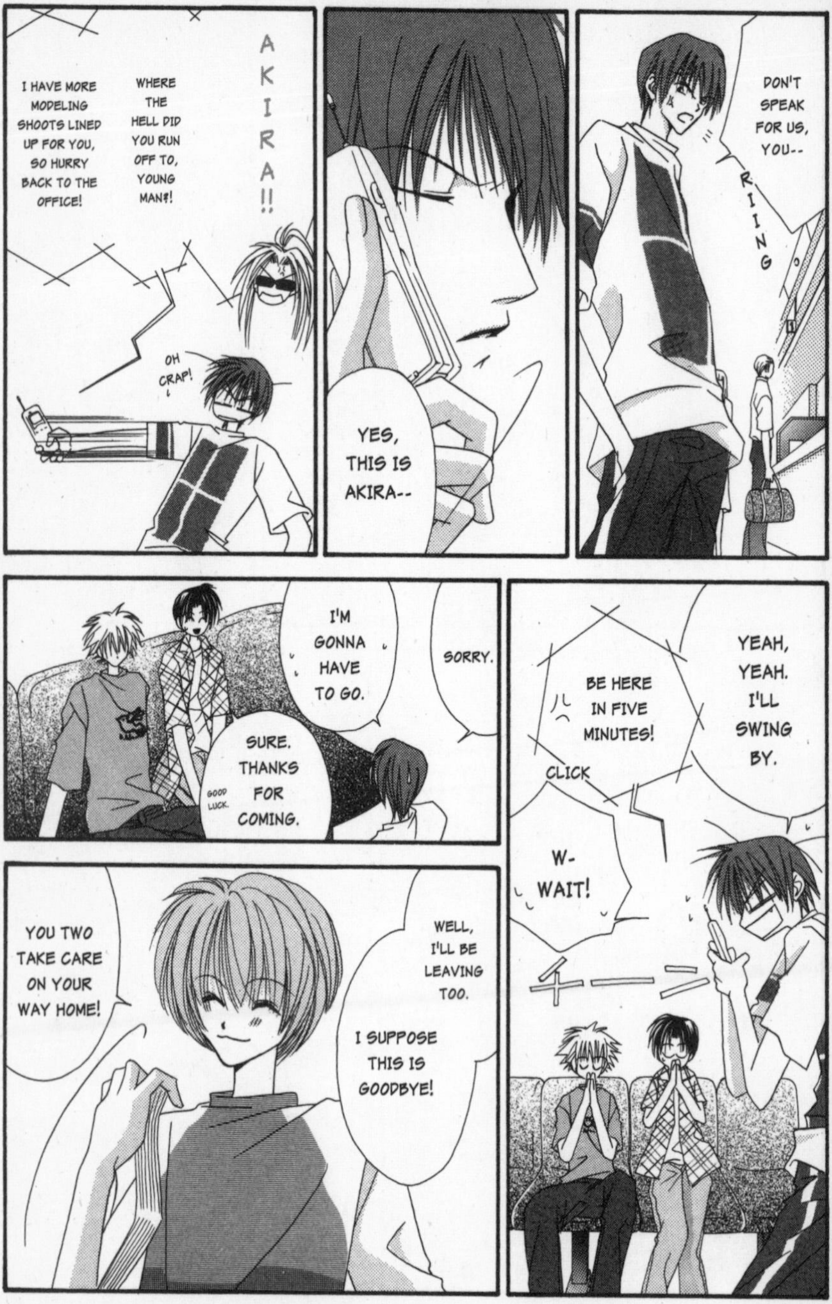
DON'T SPEAK FOR US, YOU--
RIING
YES, THIS IS AKIRA--
AKIRA!!
WHERE THE HELL DID YOU RUN OFF TO, YOUNG MAN?!
I HAVE MORE MODELING SHOOTS LINED UP FOR YOU, SO HURRY BACK TO THE OFFICE!
OH CRAP!
YEAH, YEAH. I'LL SWING BY.
BE HERE IN FIVE MINUTES!
CLICK
W- WAIT!
チーン
SORRY.
I'M GONNA HAVE TO GO.
SURE. THANKS FOR COMING.
GOOD LUCK.
WELL, I'LL BE LEAVING TOO.
I SUPPOSE THIS IS GOODBYE!
YOU TWO TAKE CARE ON YOUR WAY HOME!

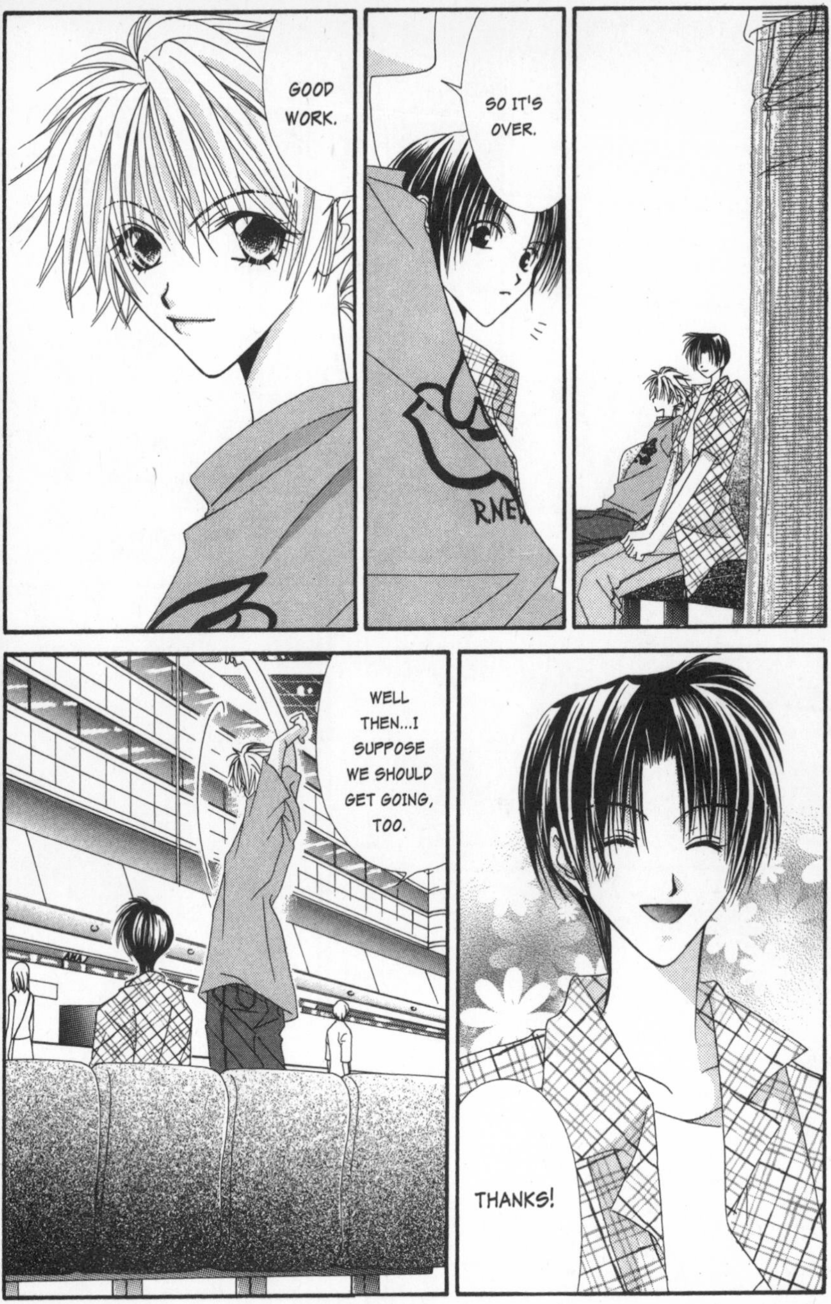
SO IT'S OVER.
GOOD WORK.
THANKS!
WELL THEN...I SUPPOSE WE SHOULD GET GOING, TOO.

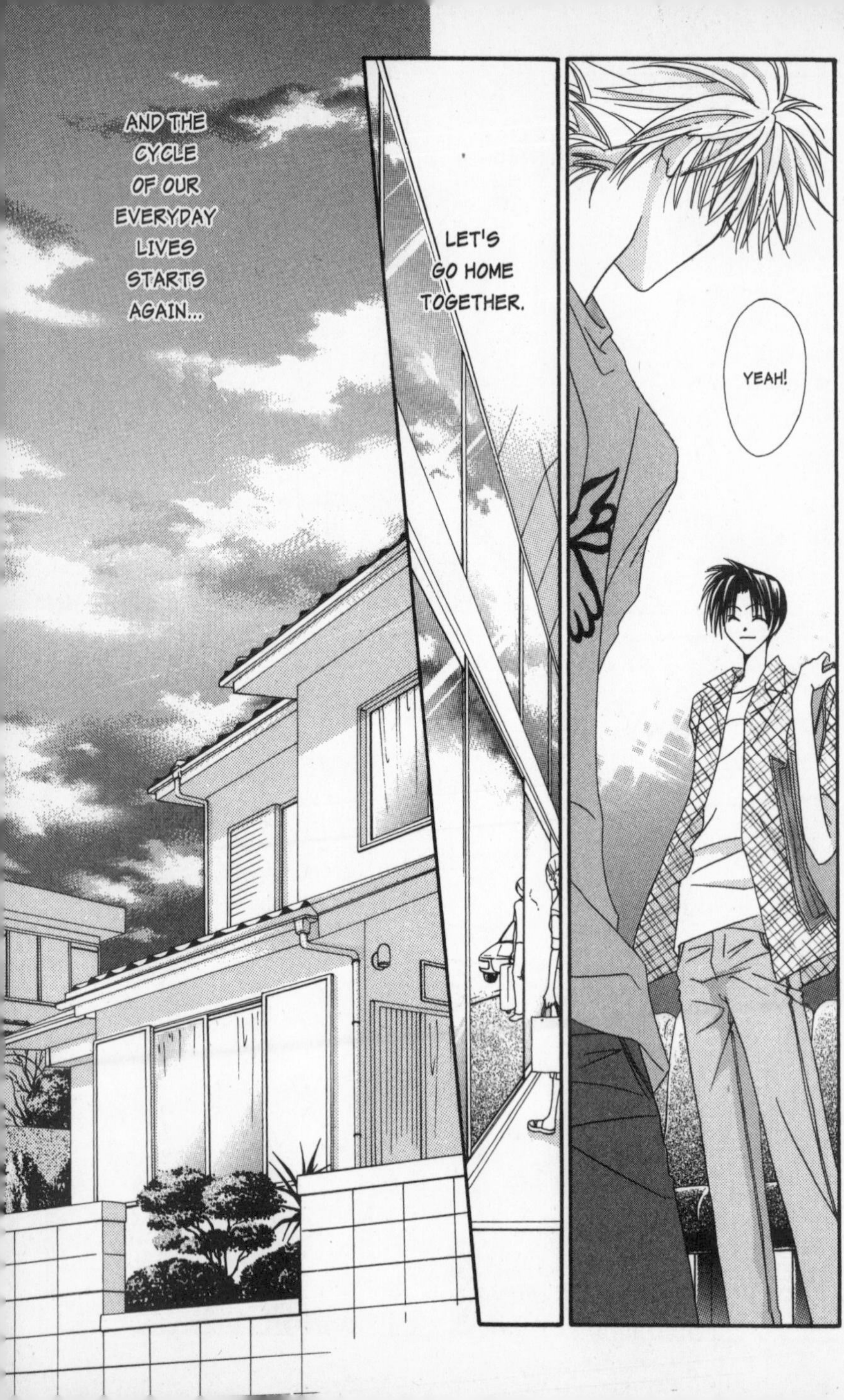
YEAH!
LET'S GO HOME TOGETHER.
AND THE CYCLE OF OUR EVERYDAY LIVES STARTS AGAIN...

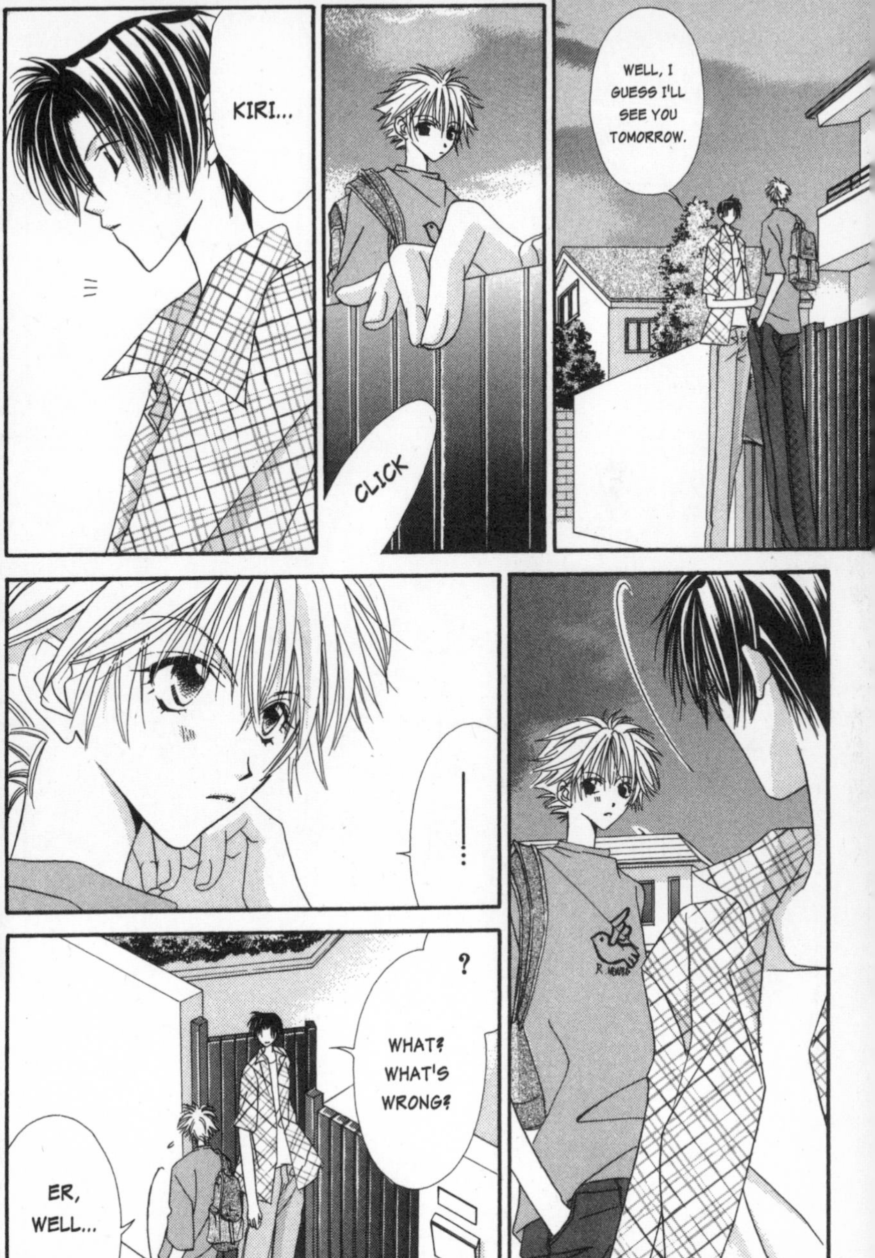
WELL, I GUESS I'LL SEE YOU TOMORROW.
CLICK
KIRI...
—...
?
WHAT? WHAT'S WRONG?
ER, WELL...

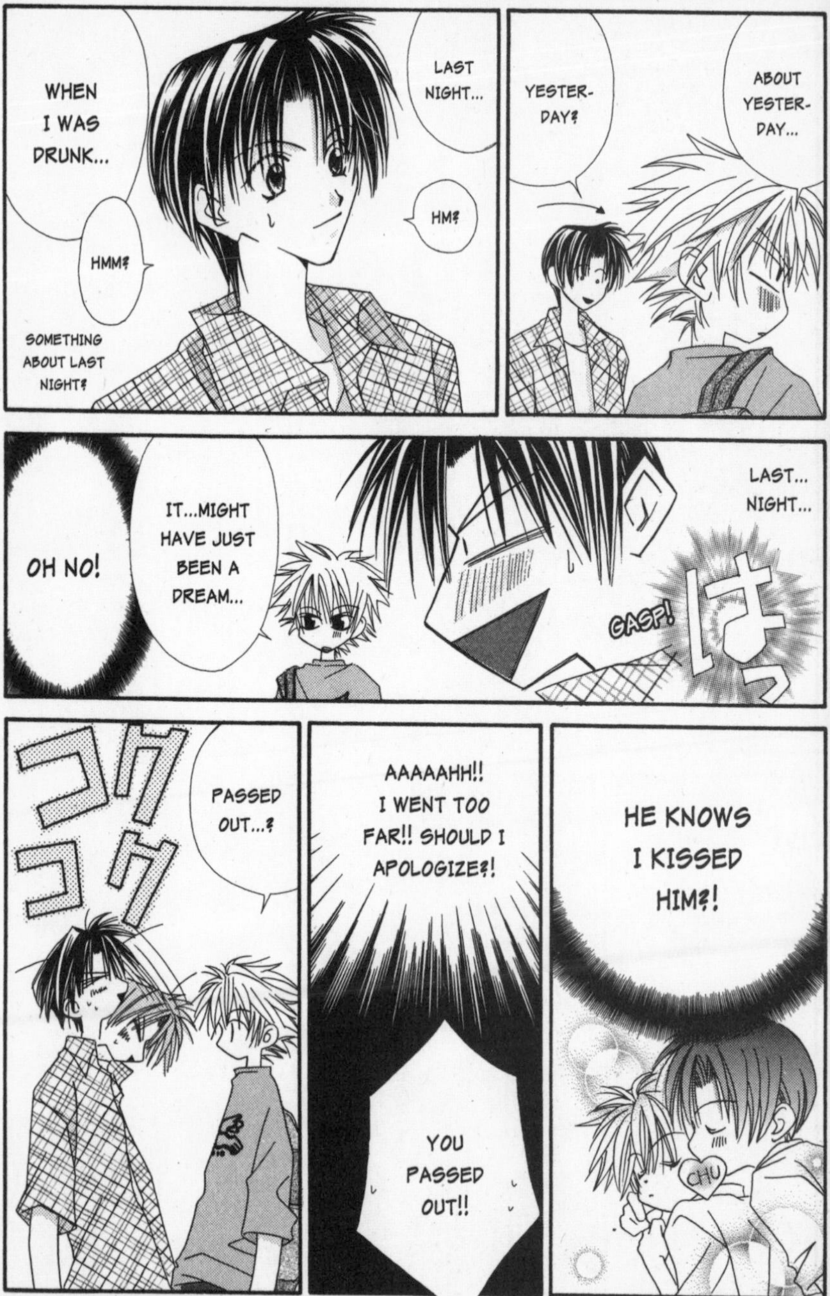
ABOUT YESTER-DAY...
YESTER-DAY?
LAST NIGHT...
HM?
WHEN I WAS DRUNK...
HMM?
SOMETHING ABOUT LAST NIGHT?
LAST... NIGHT...
はっ
GASP!
IT...MIGHT HAVE JUST BEEN A DREAM...
OH NO!
HE KNOWS I KISSED HIM?!
CHU
AAAAAHH!! I WENT TOO FAR!! SHOULD I APOLOGIZE?!
YOU PASSED OUT!!
PASSED OUT...?
コクコク

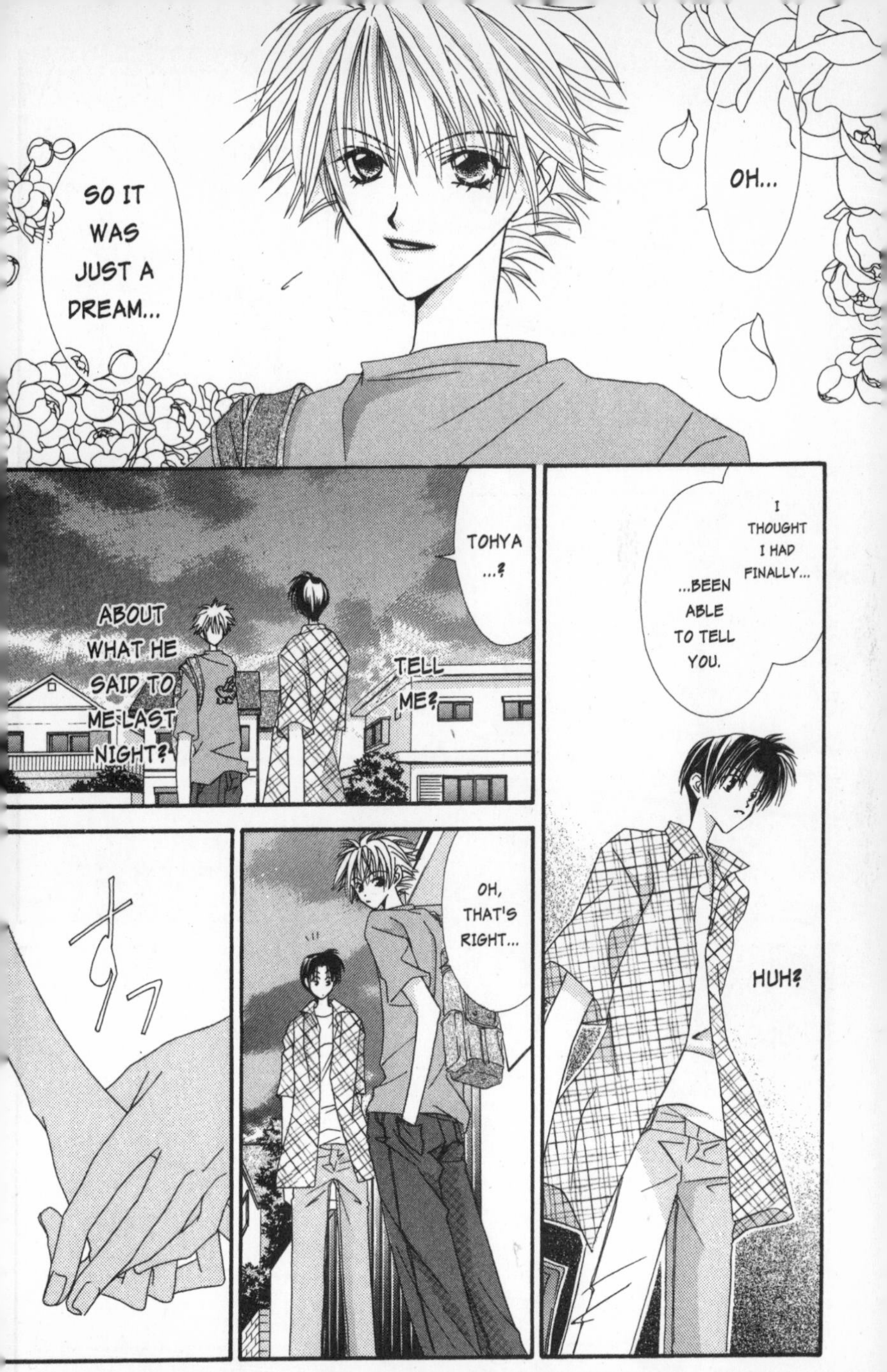

OH...
SO IT WAS JUST A DREAM...
I THOUGHT I HAD FINALLY...
...BEEN ABLE TO TELL YOU.
HUH?
TOHYA ...?
TELL ME?
ABOUT WHAT HE SAID TO ME LAST NIGHT?
OH, THAT'S RIGHT...

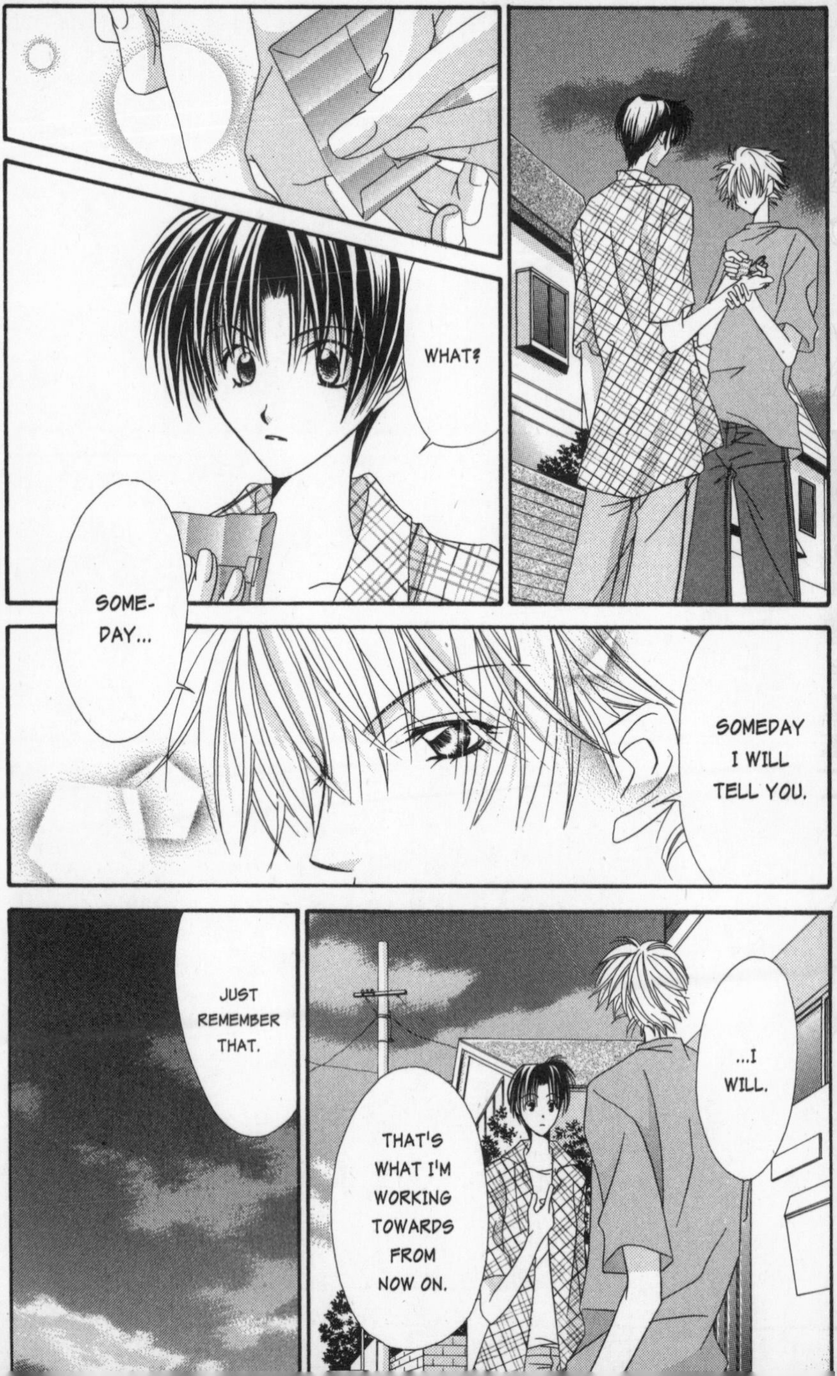
WHAT?
SOME-DAY...
SOMEDAY I WILL TELL YOU.
...I WILL.
THAT'S WHAT I'M WORKING TOWARDS FROM NOW ON.
JUST REMEMBER THAT.

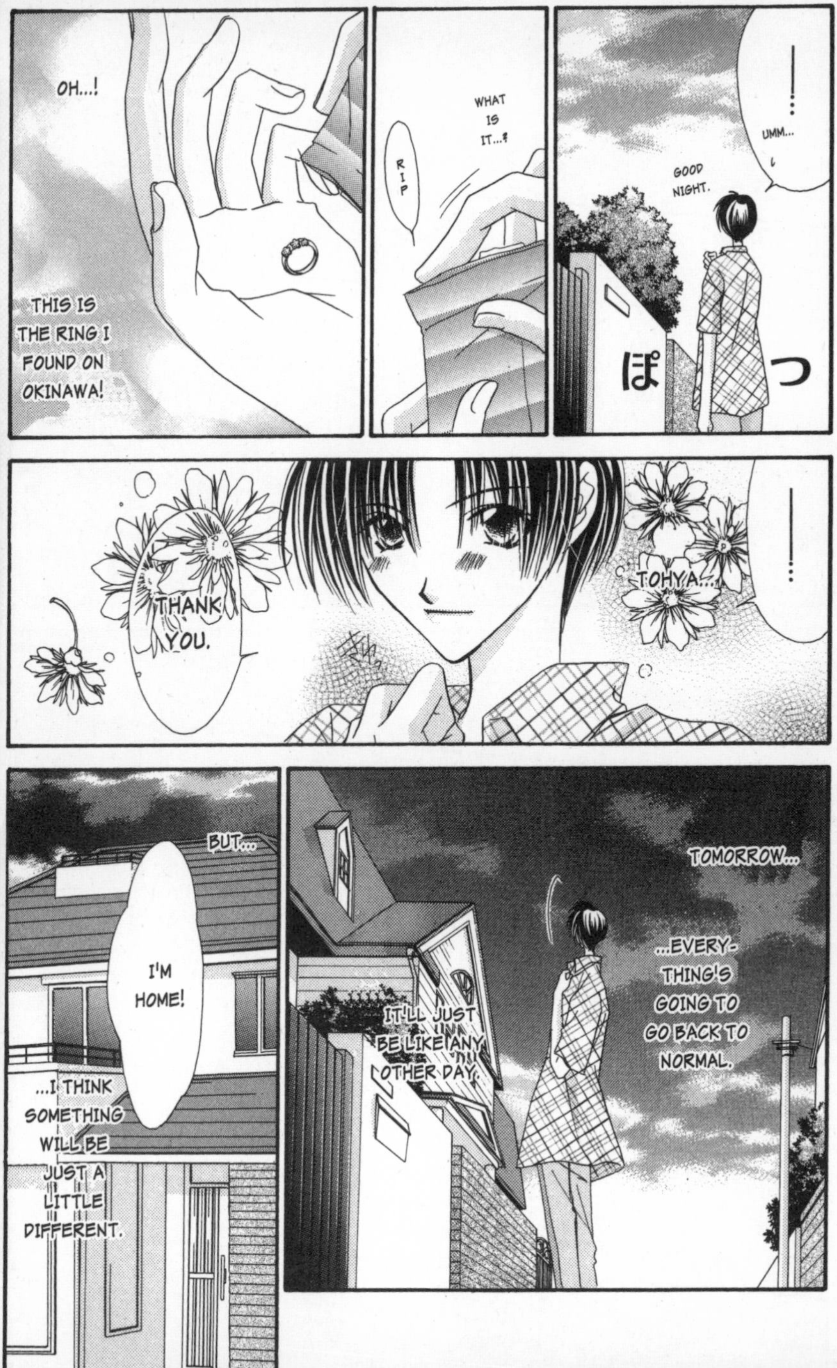

…UMM…!
GOOD NIGHT.
ぽっ
WHAT IS IT…?
RIP
OH…!
THIS IS THE RING I FOUND ON OKINAWA!
…!
TOHYA…
THANK YOU.
TOMORROW…
…EVERYTHING'S GOING TO GO BACK TO NORMAL.
IT'LL JUST BE LIKE ANY OTHER DAY.
BUT…
I'M HOME!
…I THINK SOMETHING WILL BE JUST A LITTLE DIFFERENT.

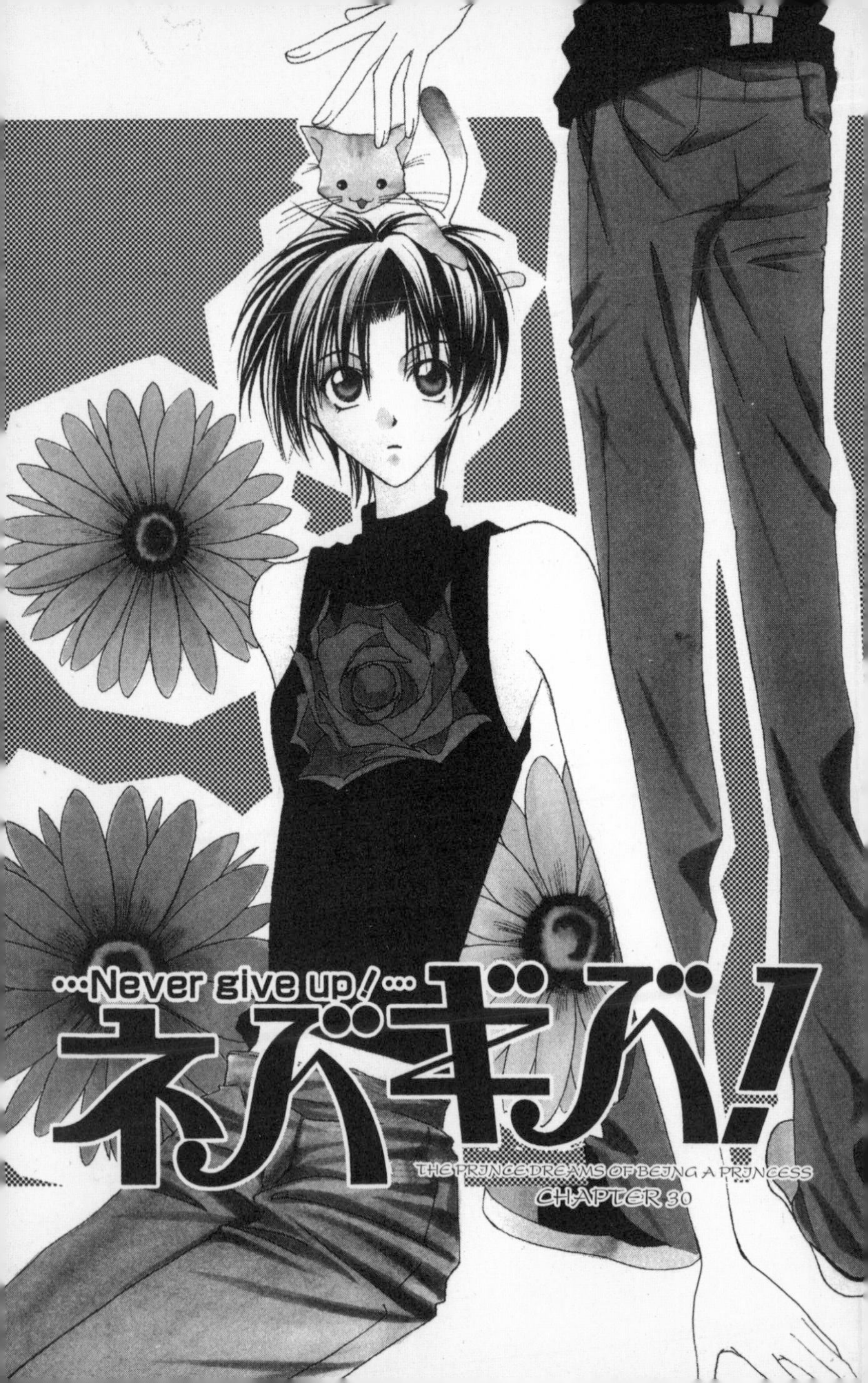

…Never give up!…
ネバギバ!
THE PRINCE DREAMS OF BEING A PRINCESS
CHAPTER 30

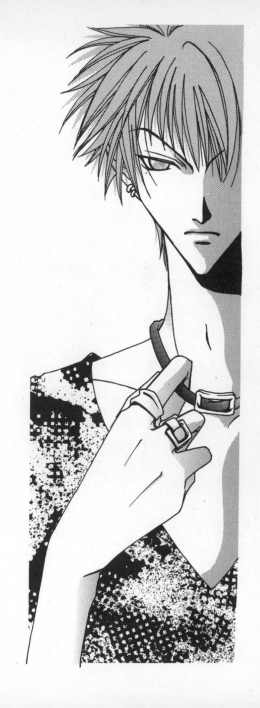

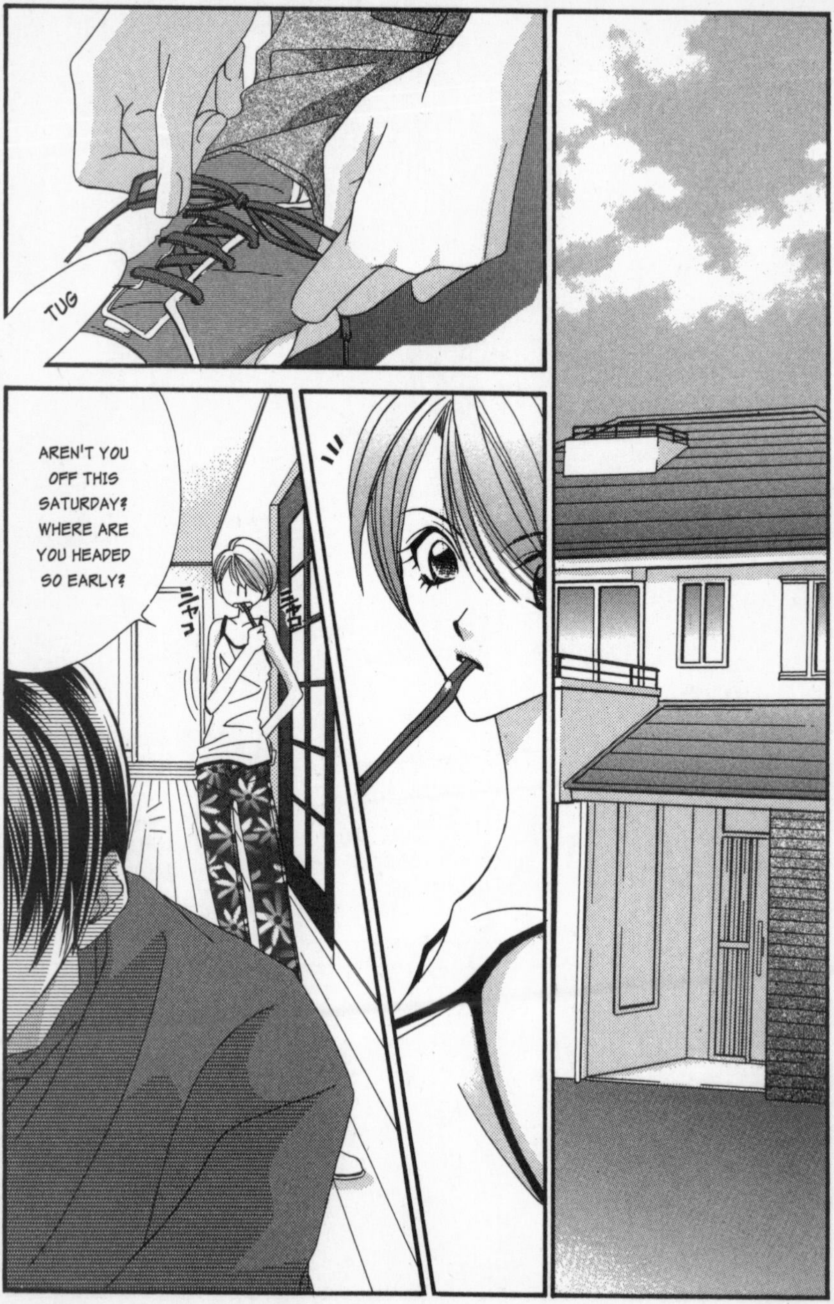
TUG
!!!
ニャコ
ニャコ
AREN'T YOU OFF THIS SATURDAY? WHERE ARE YOU HEADED SO EARLY?

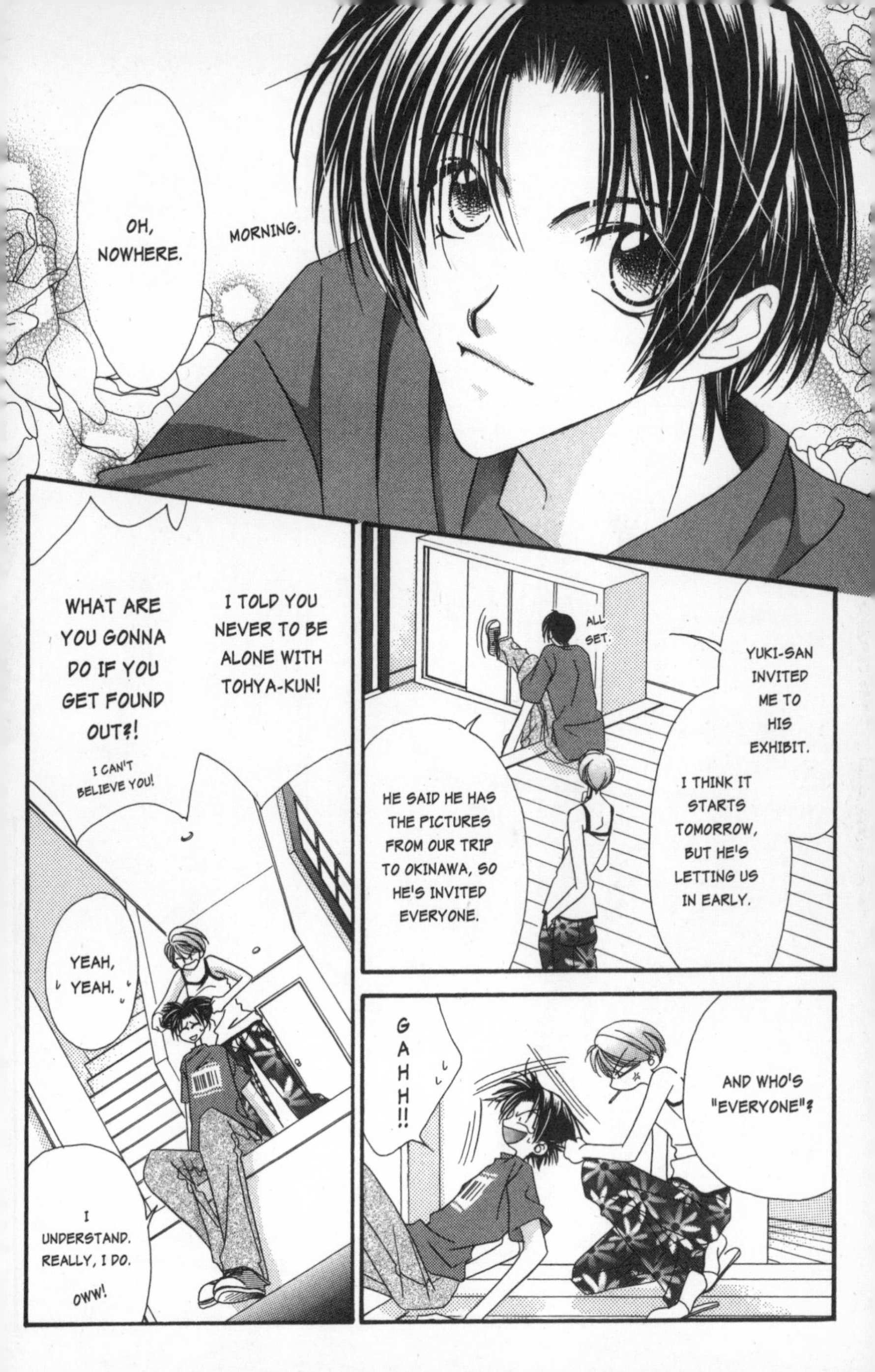
MORNING.
OH, NOWHERE.
ALL SET.
YUKI-SAN INVITED ME TO HIS EXHIBIT.
I THINK IT STARTS TOMORROW, BUT HE'S LETTING US IN EARLY.
HE SAID HE HAS THE PICTURES FROM OUR TRIP TO OKINAWA, SO HE'S INVITED EVERYONE.
AND WHO'S "EVERYONE"?
GAHH!!
I TOLD YOU NEVER TO BE ALONE WITH TOHYA-KUN!
WHAT ARE YOU GONNA DO IF YOU GET FOUND OUT?!
I CAN'T BELIEVE YOU!
YEAH, YEAH.
I UNDERSTAND. REALLY, I DO.
OWW!

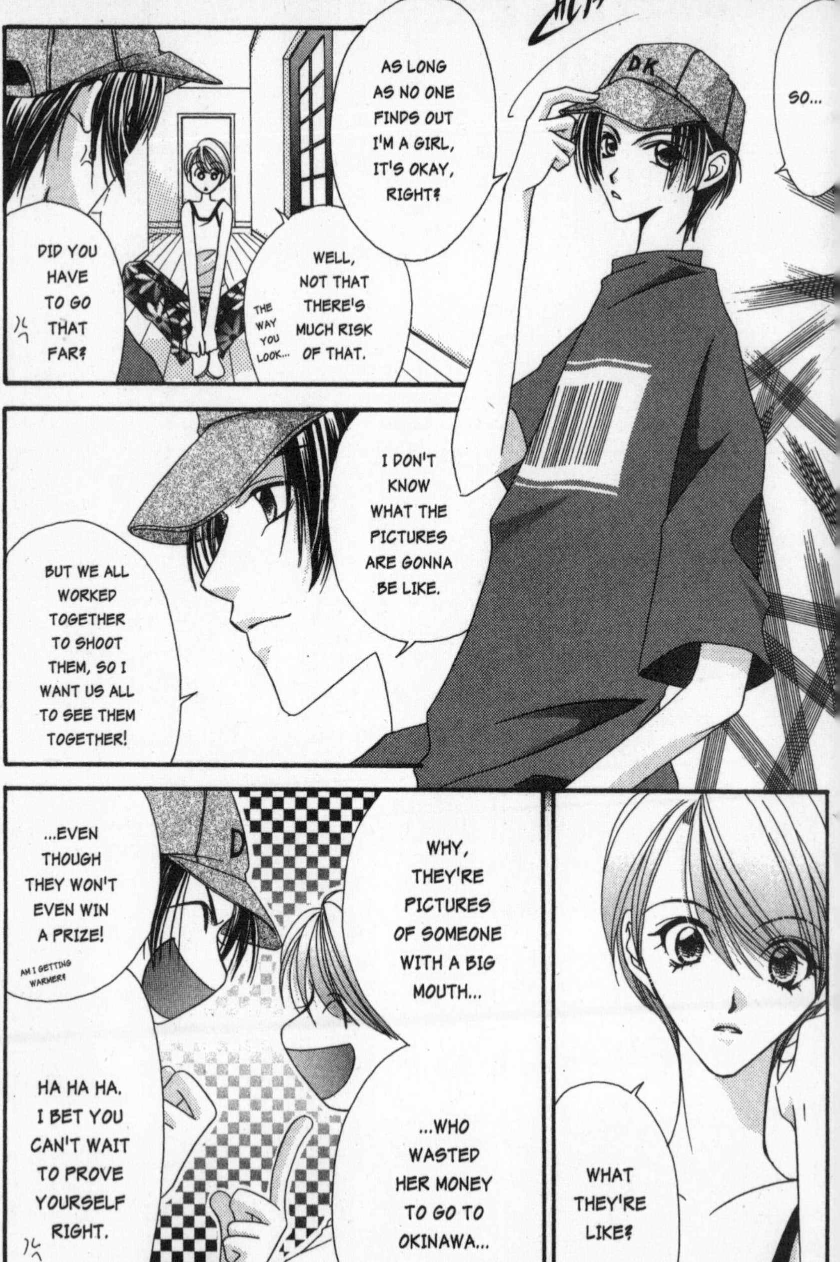
SO...
AS LONG AS NO ONE FINDS OUT I'M A GIRL, IT'S OKAY, RIGHT?
WELL, NOT THAT THERE'S MUCH RISK OF THAT.
THE WAY YOU LOOK...
DID YOU HAVE TO GO THAT FAR?
I DON'T KNOW WHAT THE PICTURES ARE GONNA BE LIKE.
BUT WE ALL WORKED TOGETHER TO SHOOT THEM, SO I WANT US ALL TO SEE THEM TOGETHER!
WHAT THEY'RE LIKE?
WHY, THEY'RE PICTURES OF SOMEONE WITH A BIG MOUTH...
...WHO WASTED HER MONEY TO GO TO OKINAWA...
...EVEN THOUGH THEY WON'T EVEN WIN A PRIZE!
AM I GETTING WARMER?
HA HA HA. I BET YOU CAN'T WAIT TO PROVE YOURSELF RIGHT.

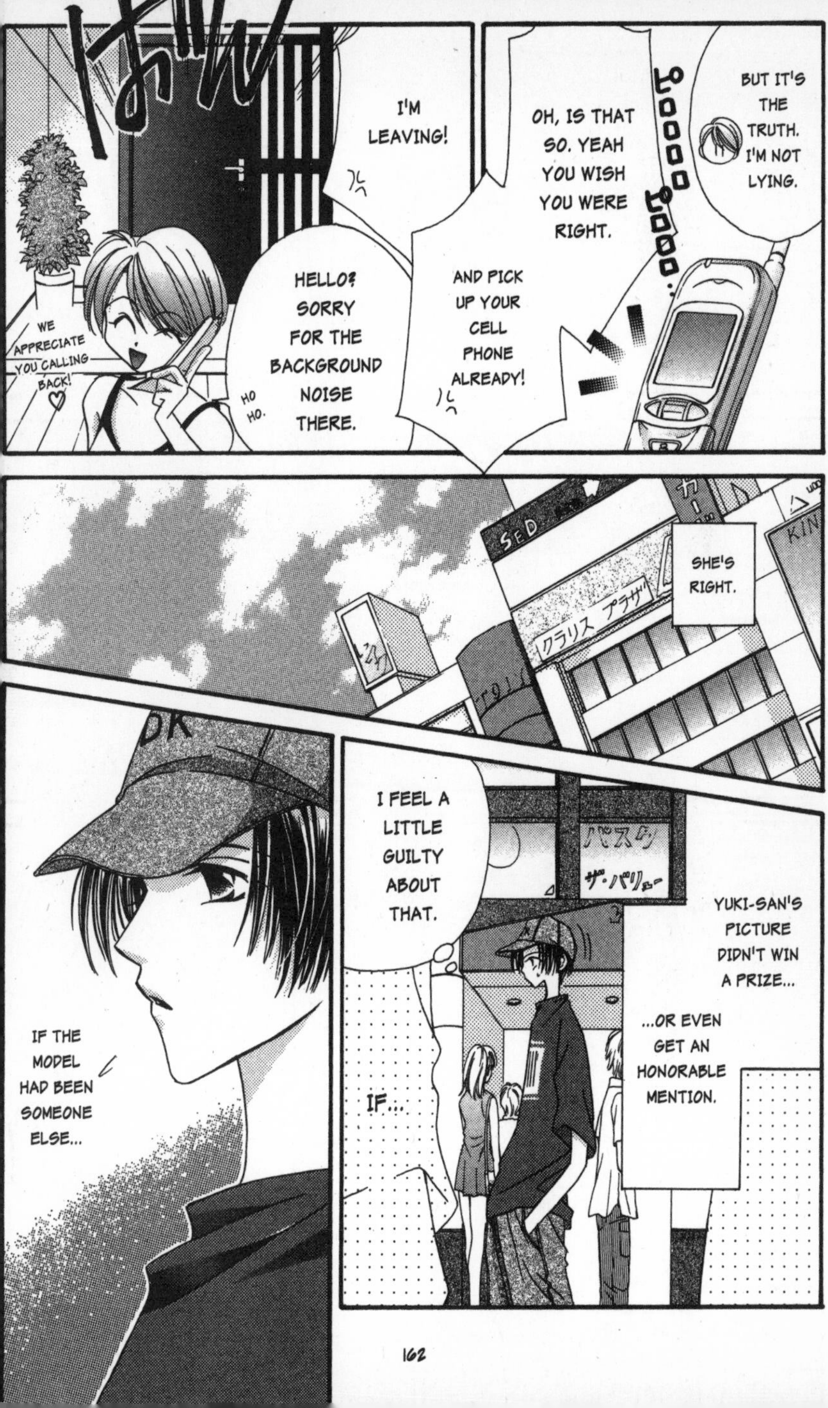
BUT IT'S THE TRUTH. I'M NOT LYING.
OH, IS THAT SO. YEAH YOU WISH YOU WERE RIGHT.
AND PICK UP YOUR CELL PHONE ALREADY!
I'M LEAVING!
HELLO? SORRY FOR THE BACKGROUND NOISE THERE.
HO HO.
WE APPRECIATE YOU CALLING BACK! ♡
SHE'S RIGHT.
クラリス プラザ
YUKI-SAN'S PICTURE DIDN'T WIN A PRIZE...
...OR EVEN GET AN HONORABLE MENTION.
I FEEL A LITTLE GUILTY ABOUT THAT.
IF...
IF THE MODEL HAD BEEN SOMEONE ELSE...

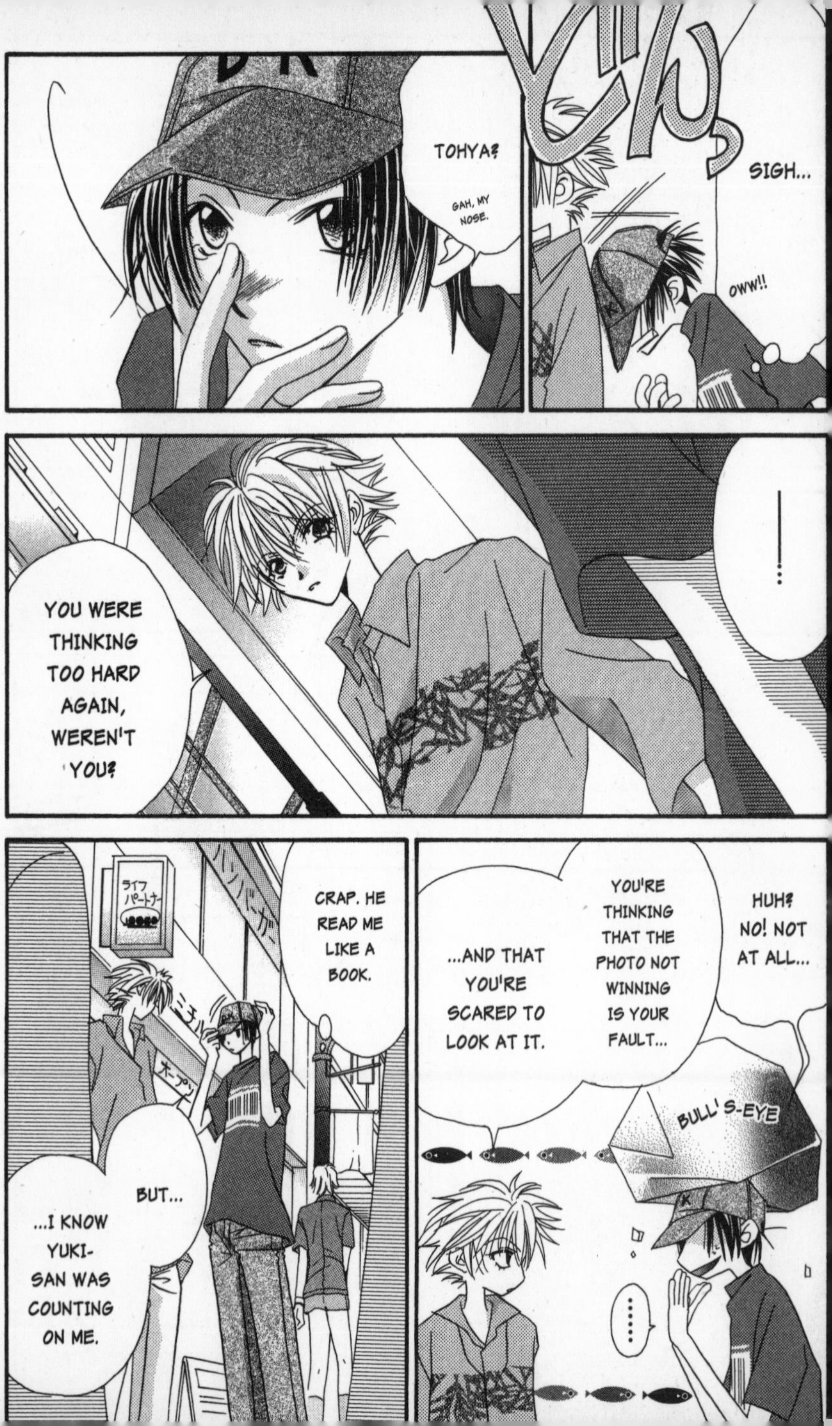
SIGH...
OWW!!
TOHYA?
GAH, MY NOSE.
—!
YOU WERE THINKING TOO HARD AGAIN, WEREN'T YOU?
HUH? NO! NOT AT ALL...
YOU'RE THINKING THAT THE PHOTO NOT WINNING IS YOUR FAULT...
...AND THAT YOU'RE SCARED TO LOOK AT IT.
BULL'S-EYE
......
CRAP. HE READ ME LIKE A BOOK.
BUT...
...I KNOW YUKI-SAN WAS COUNTING ON ME.

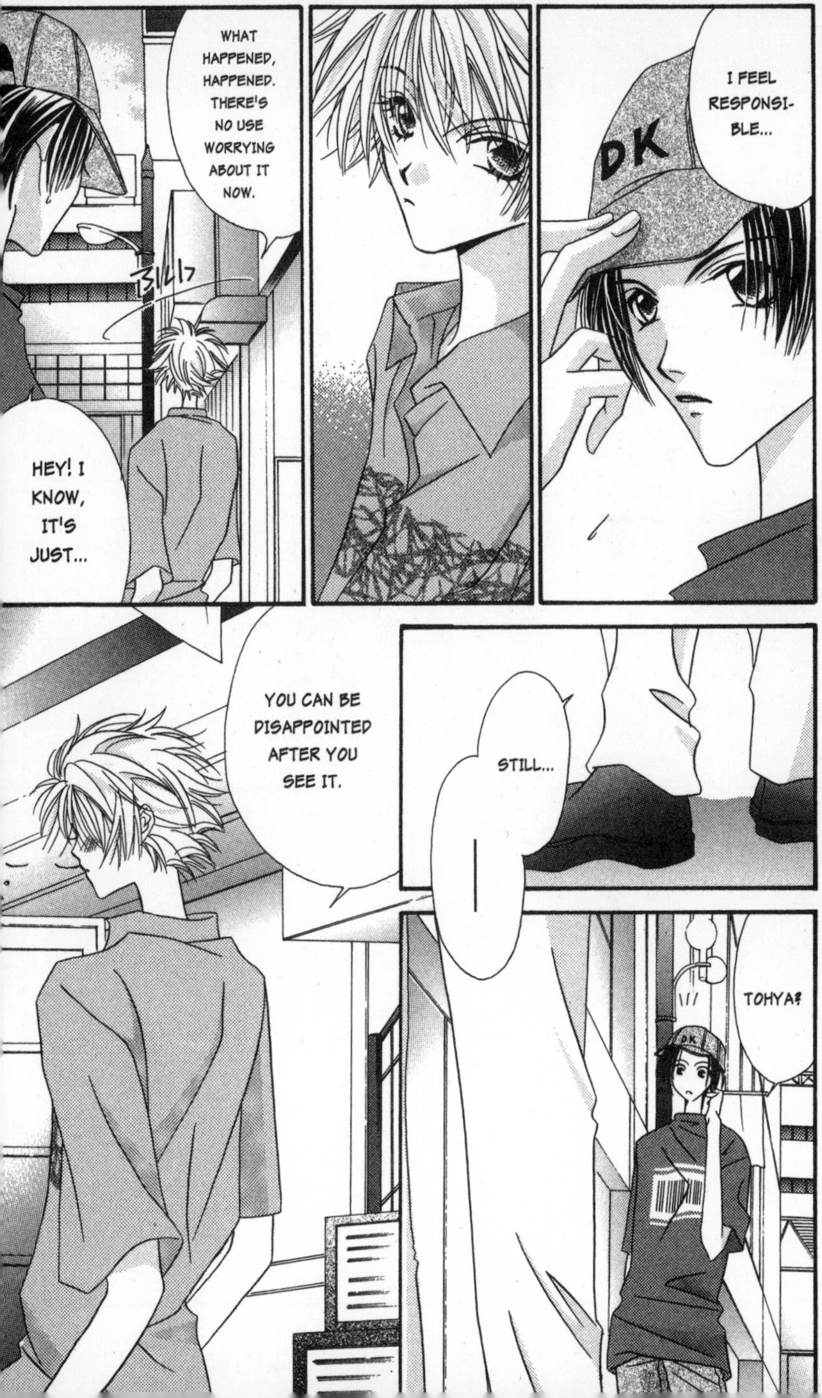
I FEEL RESPONSIBLE...
WHAT HAPPENED, HAPPENED. THERE'S NO USE WORRYING ABOUT IT NOW.
HEY! I KNOW, IT'S JUST...
STILL...
TOHYA?
YOU CAN BE DISAPPOINTED AFTER YOU SEE IT.

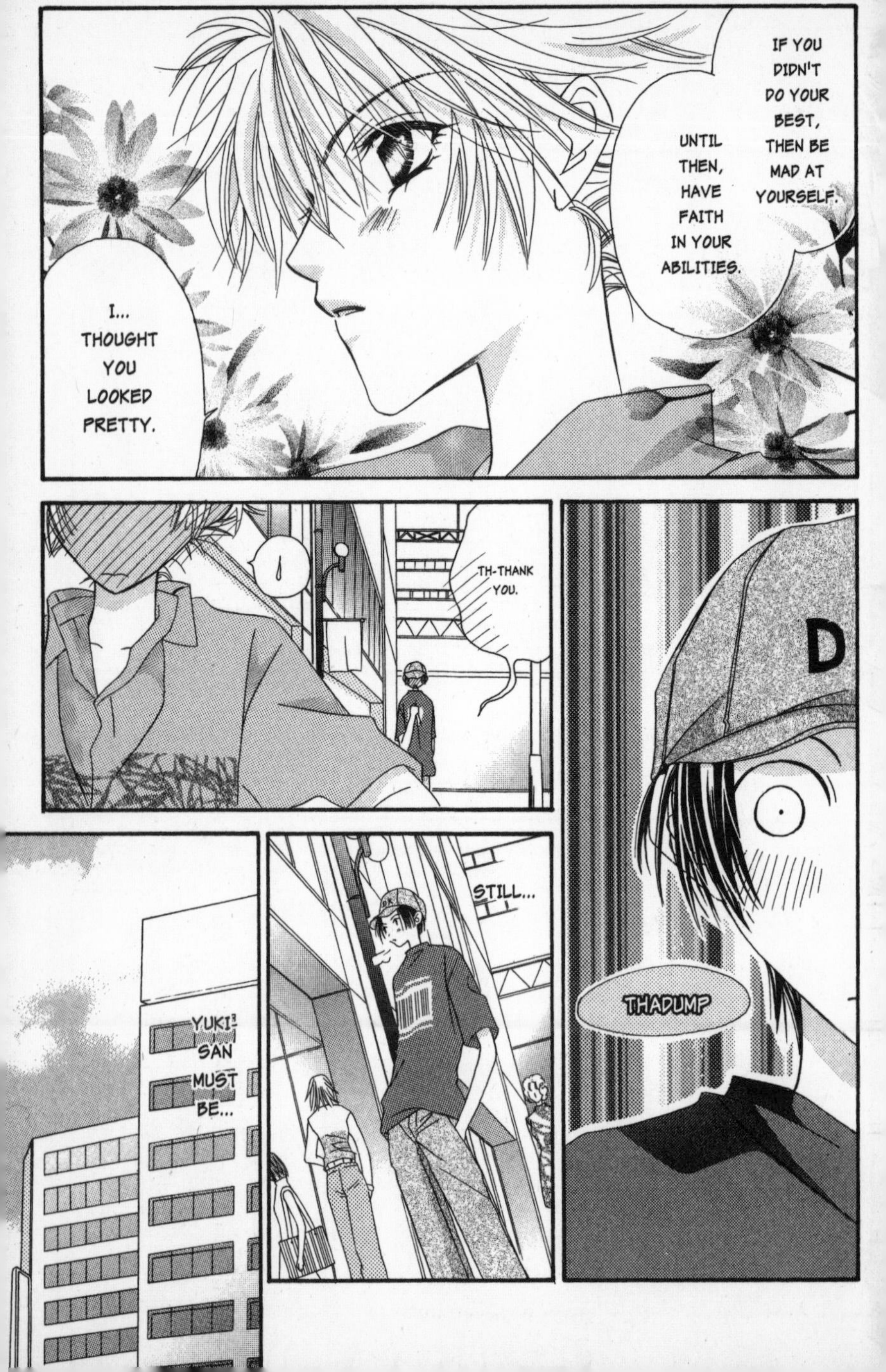
IF YOU DIDN'T DO YOUR BEST, THEN BE MAD AT YOURSELF.
UNTIL THEN, HAVE FAITH IN YOUR ABILITIES.
I... THOUGHT YOU LOOKED PRETTY.
THADUMP
!
TH-THANK YOU.
STILL...
YUKI-SAN MUST BE...

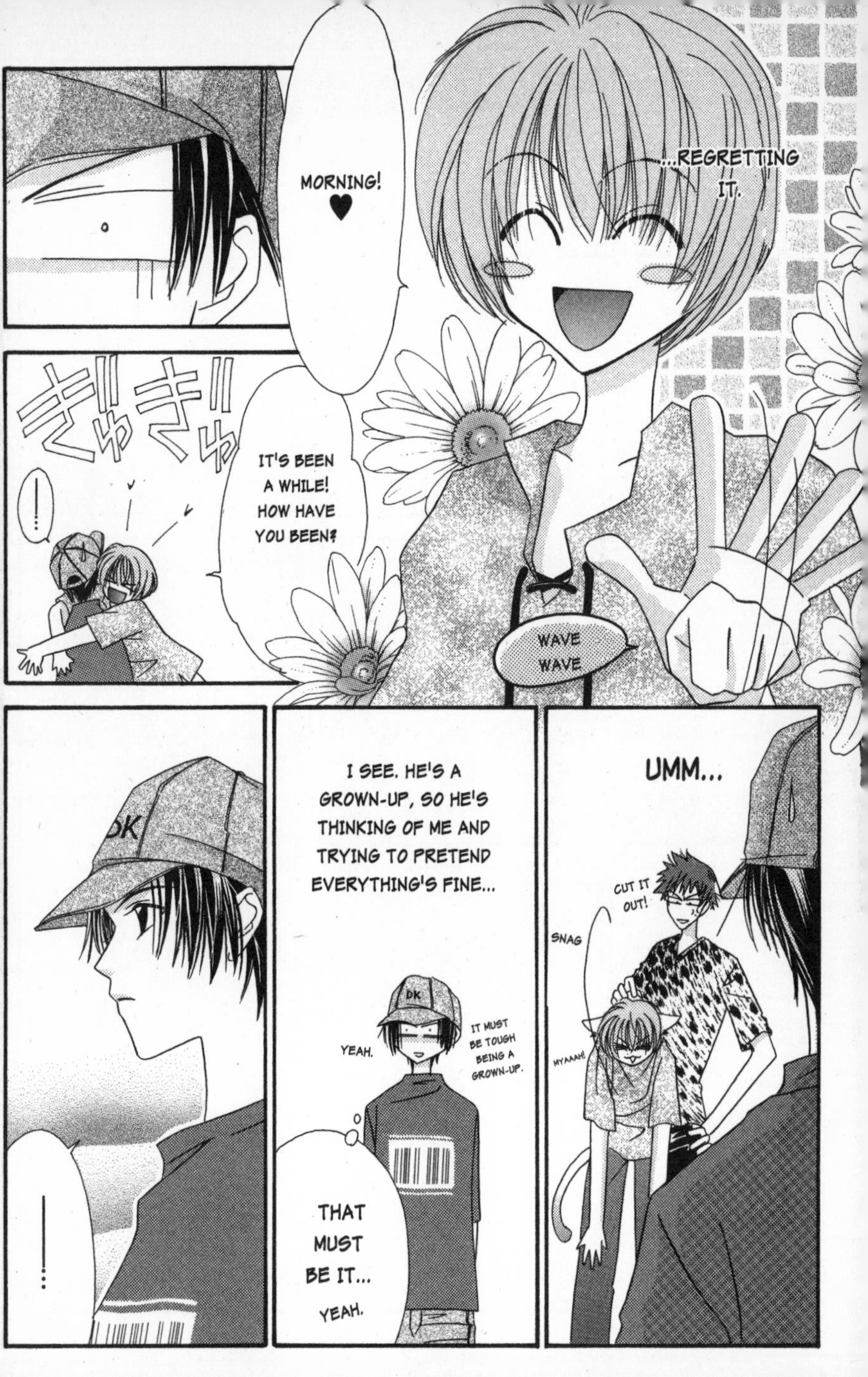
...REGRETTING IT.
MORNING! ♥
WAVE WAVE
ぎゅぎゅ
!
IT'S BEEN A WHILE! HOW HAVE YOU BEEN?
UMM...
CUT IT OUT!
SNAG
MYAAAH!
I SEE. HE'S A GROWN-UP, SO HE'S THINKING OF ME AND TRYING TO PRETEND EVERYTHING'S FINE...
IT MUST BE TOUGH BEING A GROWN-UP.
YEAH.
THAT MUST BE IT... YEAH.
......

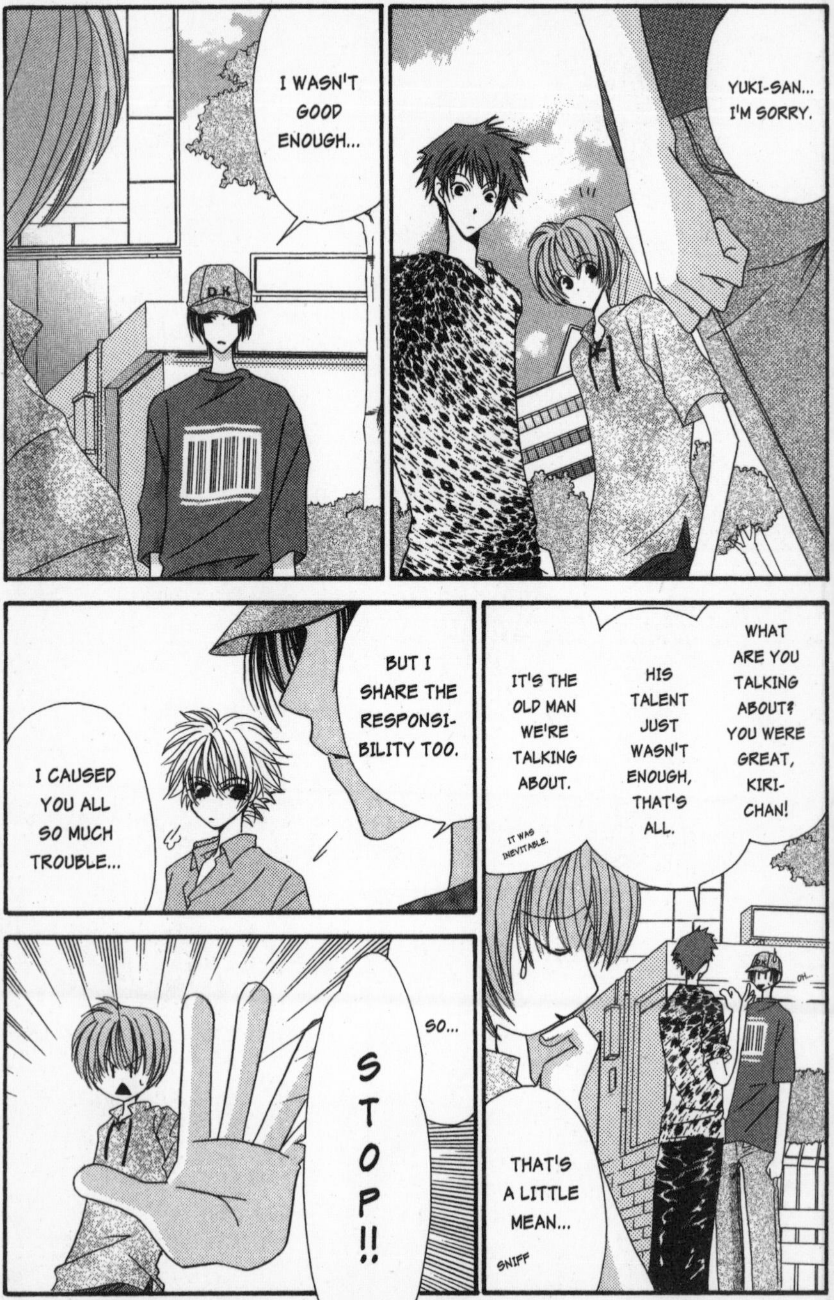
YUKI-SAN... I'M SORRY.
I WASN'T GOOD ENOUGH...
WHAT ARE YOU TALKING ABOUT? YOU WERE GREAT, KIRI-CHAN!
HIS TALENT JUST WASN'T ENOUGH, THAT'S ALL.
IT'S THE OLD MAN WE'RE TALKING ABOUT.
IT WAS INEVITABLE.
OH...
THAT'S A LITTLE MEAN...
SNIFF
BUT I SHARE THE RESPONSIBILITY TOO.
I CAUSED YOU ALL SO MUCH TROUBLE...
SO...
STOP!!

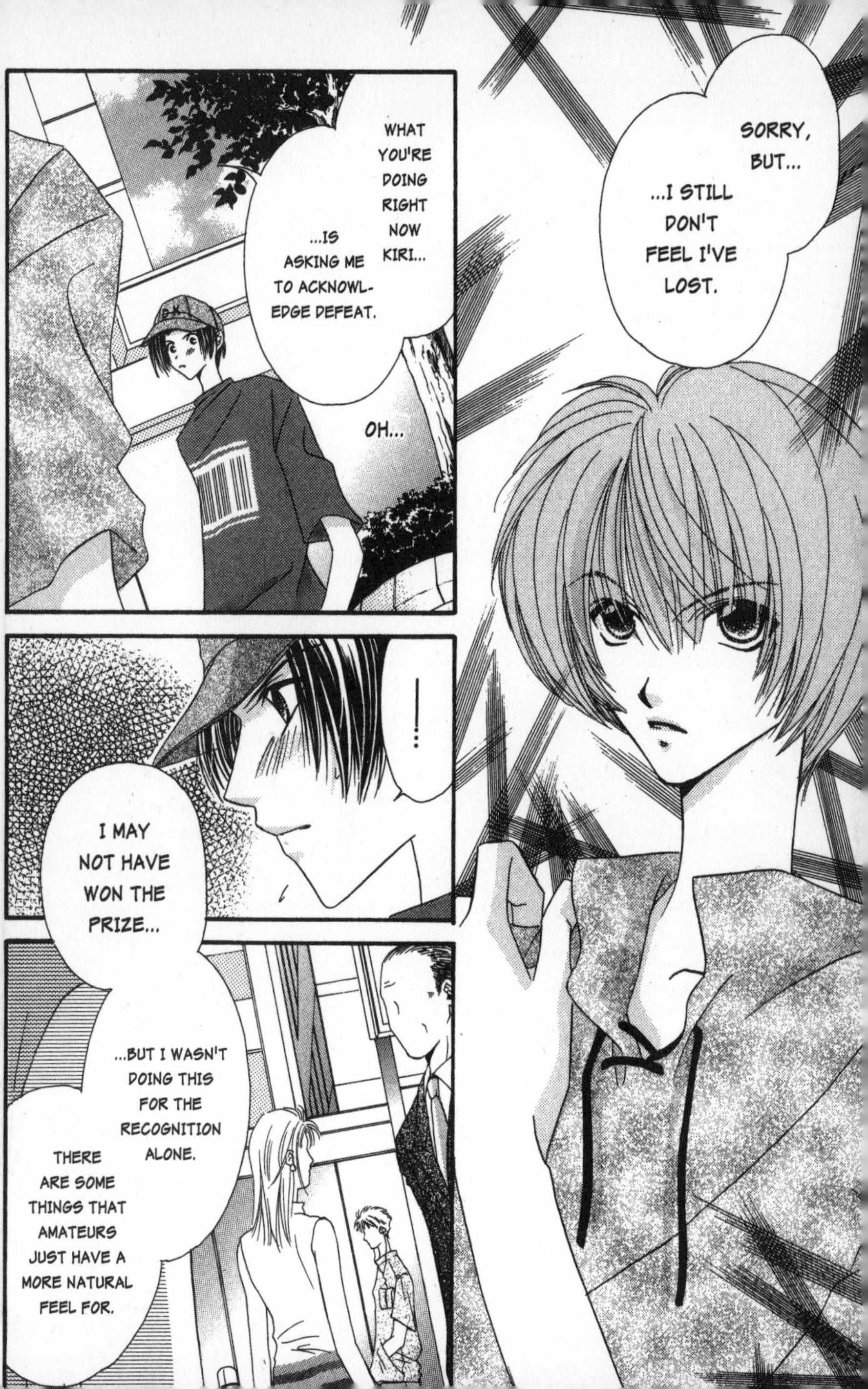
SORRY, BUT...
...I STILL DON'T FEEL I'VE LOST.
WHAT YOU'RE DOING RIGHT NOW KIRI...
...IS ASKING ME TO ACKNOWL-EDGE DEFEAT.
OH...
!...
I MAY NOT HAVE WON THE PRIZE...
...BUT I WASN'T DOING THIS FOR THE RECOGNITION ALONE.
THERE ARE SOME THINGS THAT AMATEURS JUST HAVE A MORE NATURAL FEEL FOR.

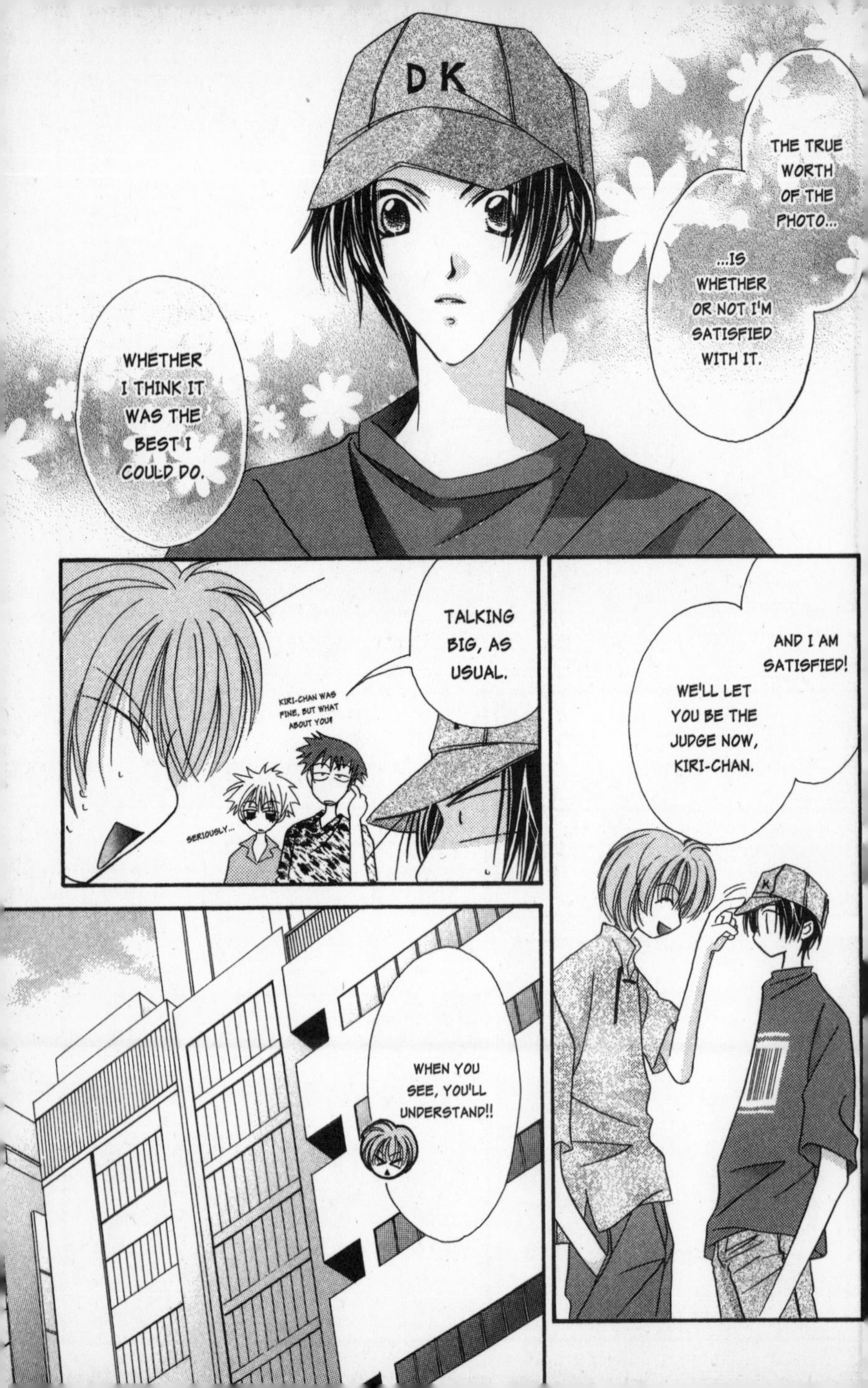
THE TRUE WORTH OF THE PHOTO...
...IS WHETHER OR NOT I'M SATISFIED WITH IT.
WHETHER I THINK IT WAS THE BEST I COULD DO.
AND I AM SATISFIED!
WE'LL LET YOU BE THE JUDGE NOW, KIRI-CHAN.
TALKING BIG, AS USUAL.
KIRI-CHAN WAS FINE, BUT WHAT ABOUT YOU?
SERIOUSLY...
WHEN YOU SEE, YOU'LL UNDERSTAND!!

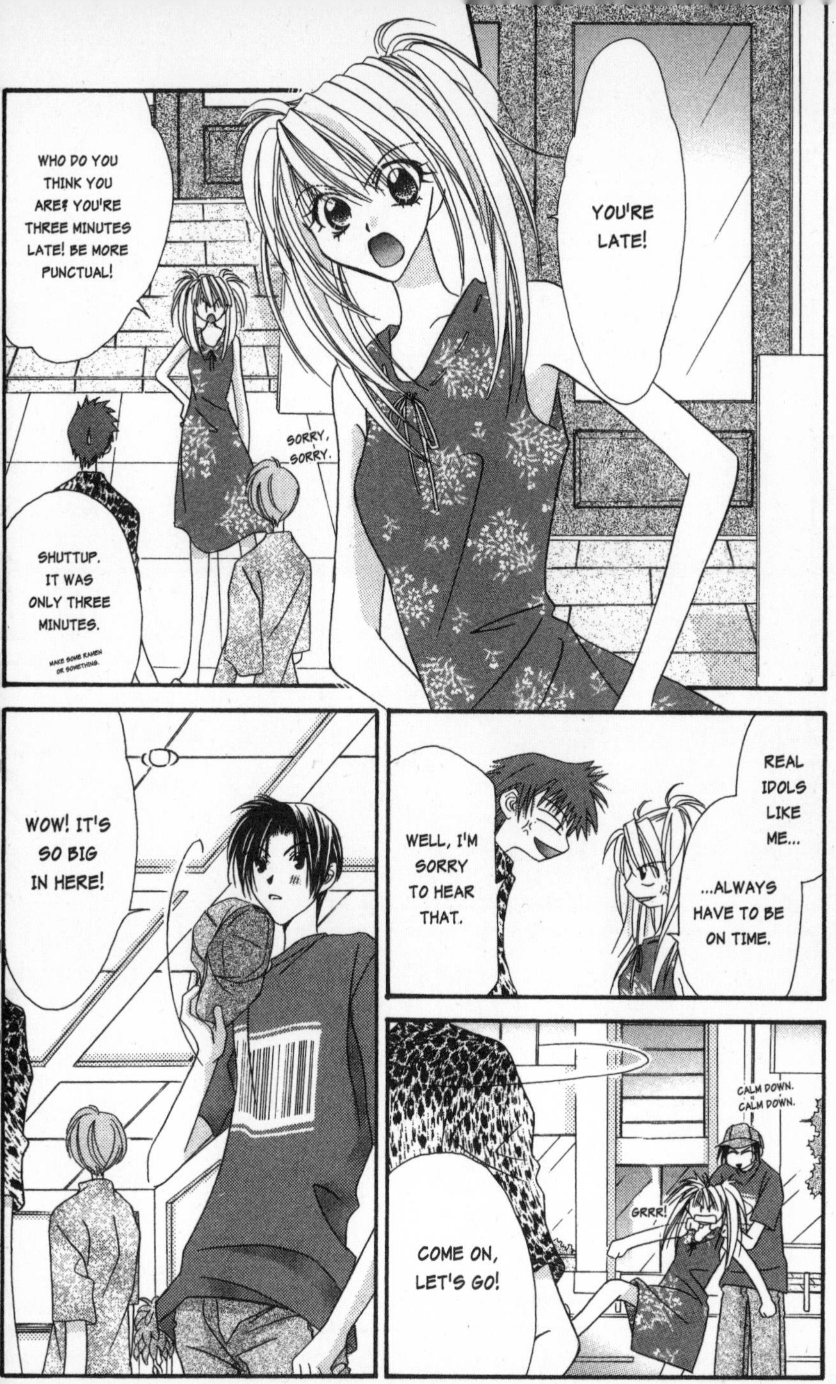
YOU'RE LATE!
WHO DO YOU THINK YOU ARE? YOU'RE THREE MINUTES LATE! BE MORE PUNCTUAL!
SORRY, SORRY.
SHUTTUP. IT WAS ONLY THREE MINUTES.
MAKE SOME RAMEN OR SOMETHING.
REAL IDOLS LIKE ME...
...ALWAYS HAVE TO BE ON TIME.
WELL, I'M SORRY TO HEAR THAT.
CALM DOWN. CALM DOWN.
GRRR!
COME ON, LET'S GO!
WOW! IT'S SO BIG IN HERE!

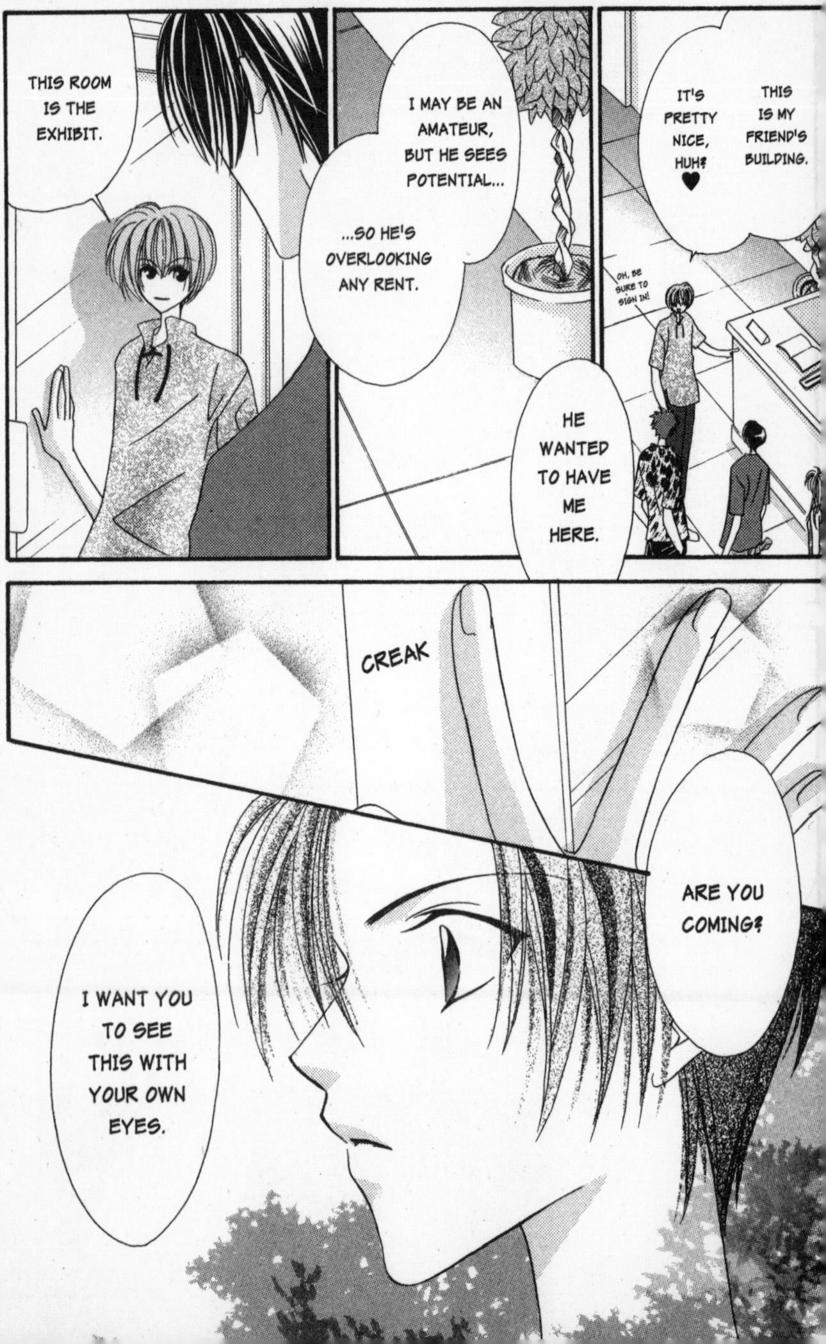
THIS IS MY FRIEND'S BUILDING.
IT'S PRETTY NICE, HUH? ♥
OH, BE SURE TO SIGN IN!
HE WANTED TO HAVE ME HERE.
I MAY BE AN AMATEUR, BUT HE SEES POTENTIAL...
...SO HE'S OVERLOOKING ANY RENT.
THIS ROOM IS THE EXHIBIT.
CREAK
ARE YOU COMING?
I WANT YOU TO SEE THIS WITH YOUR OWN EYES.

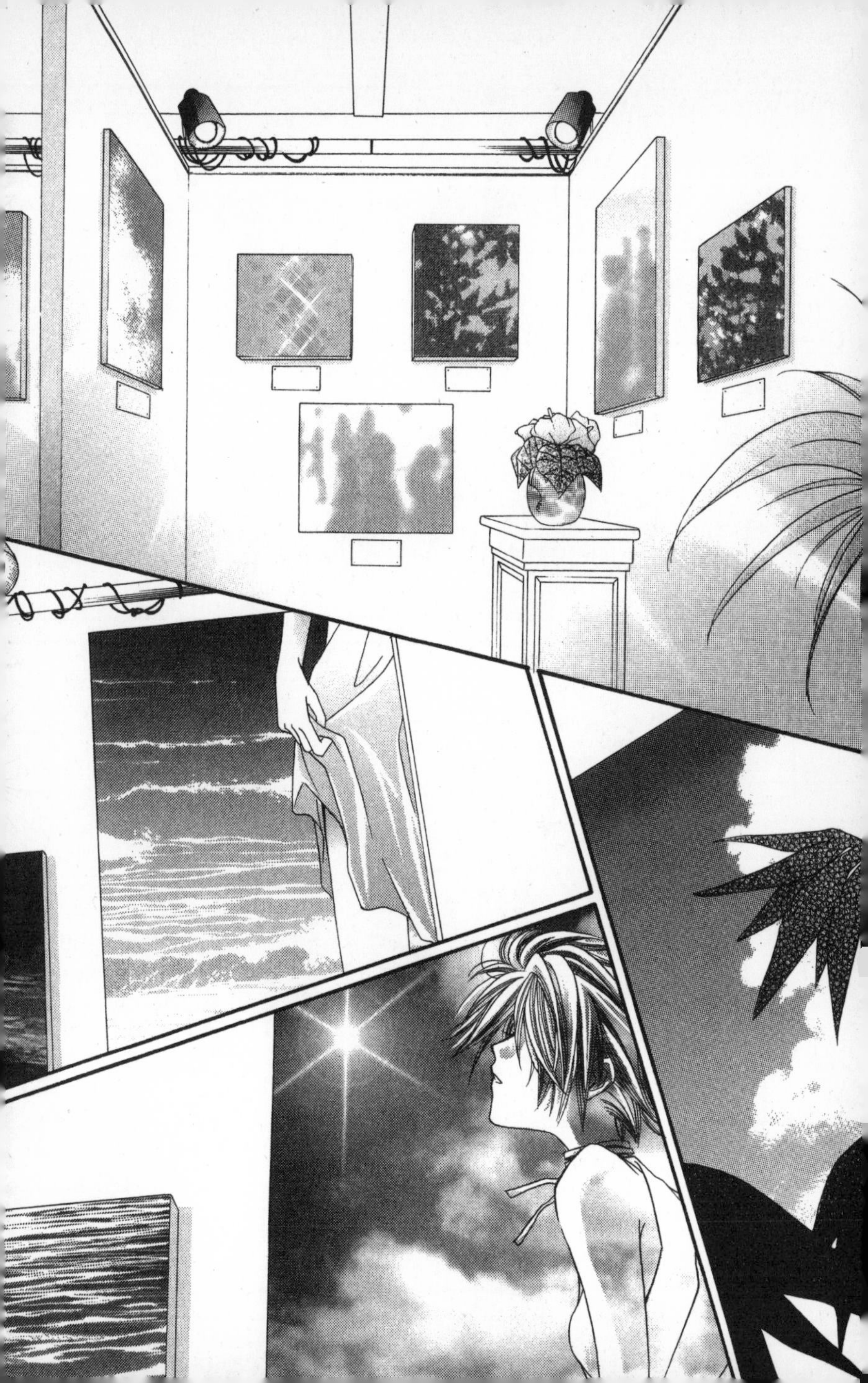

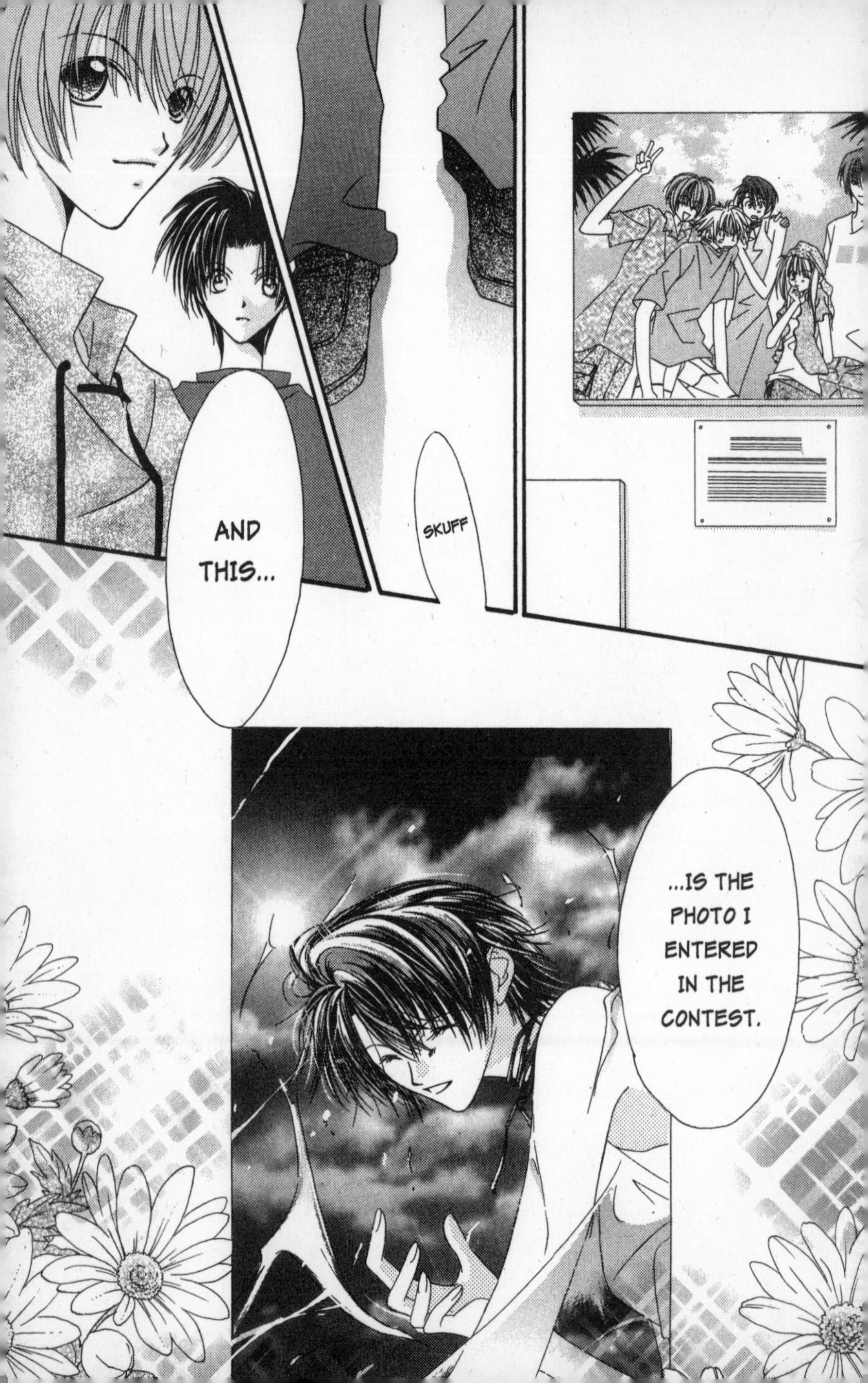
SKUFF
AND THIS...
...IS THE PHOTO I ENTERED IN THE CONTEST.

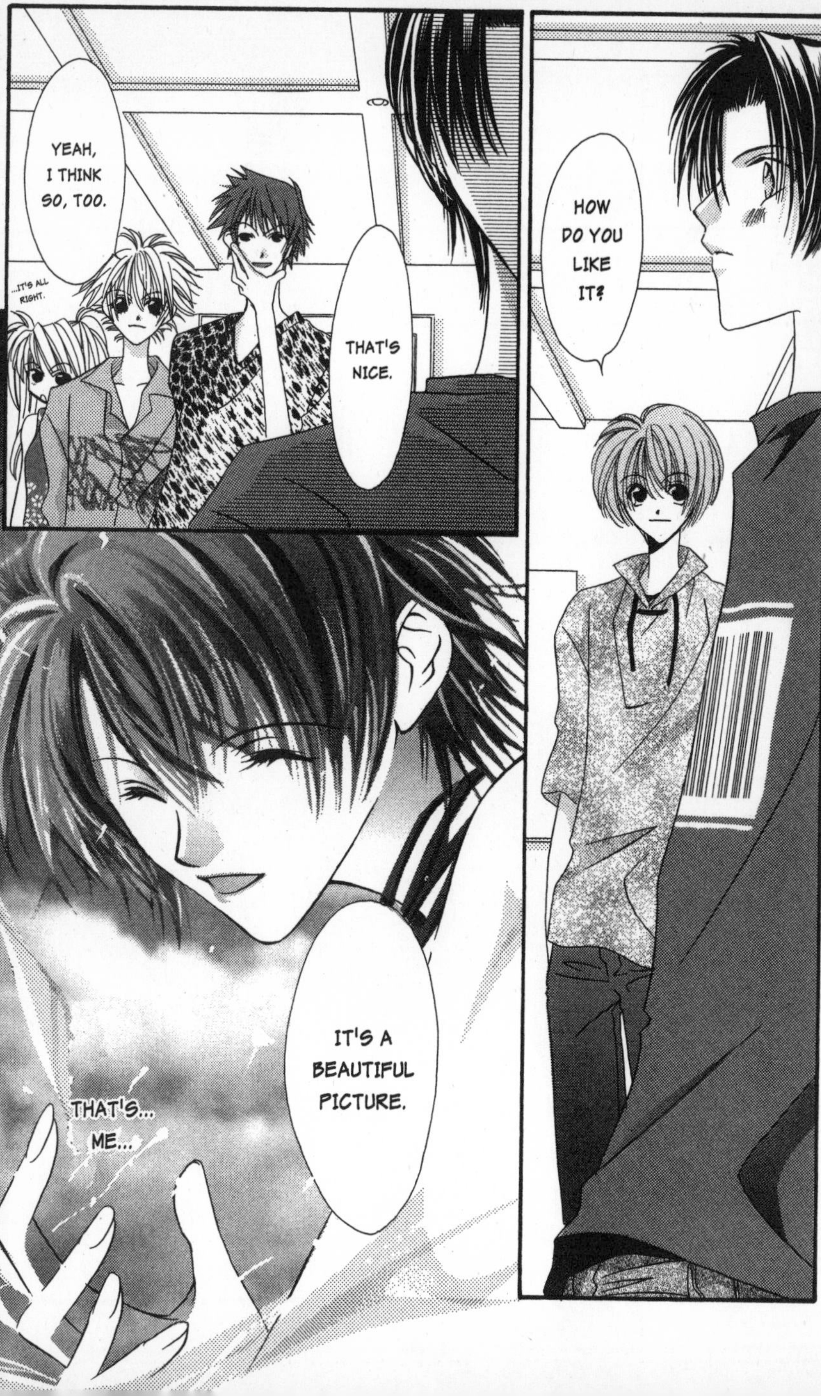
HOW DO YOU LIKE IT?
THAT'S NICE.
YEAH, I THINK SO, TOO.
...IT'S ALL RIGHT.
IT'S A BEAUTIFUL PICTURE.
THAT'S... ME...

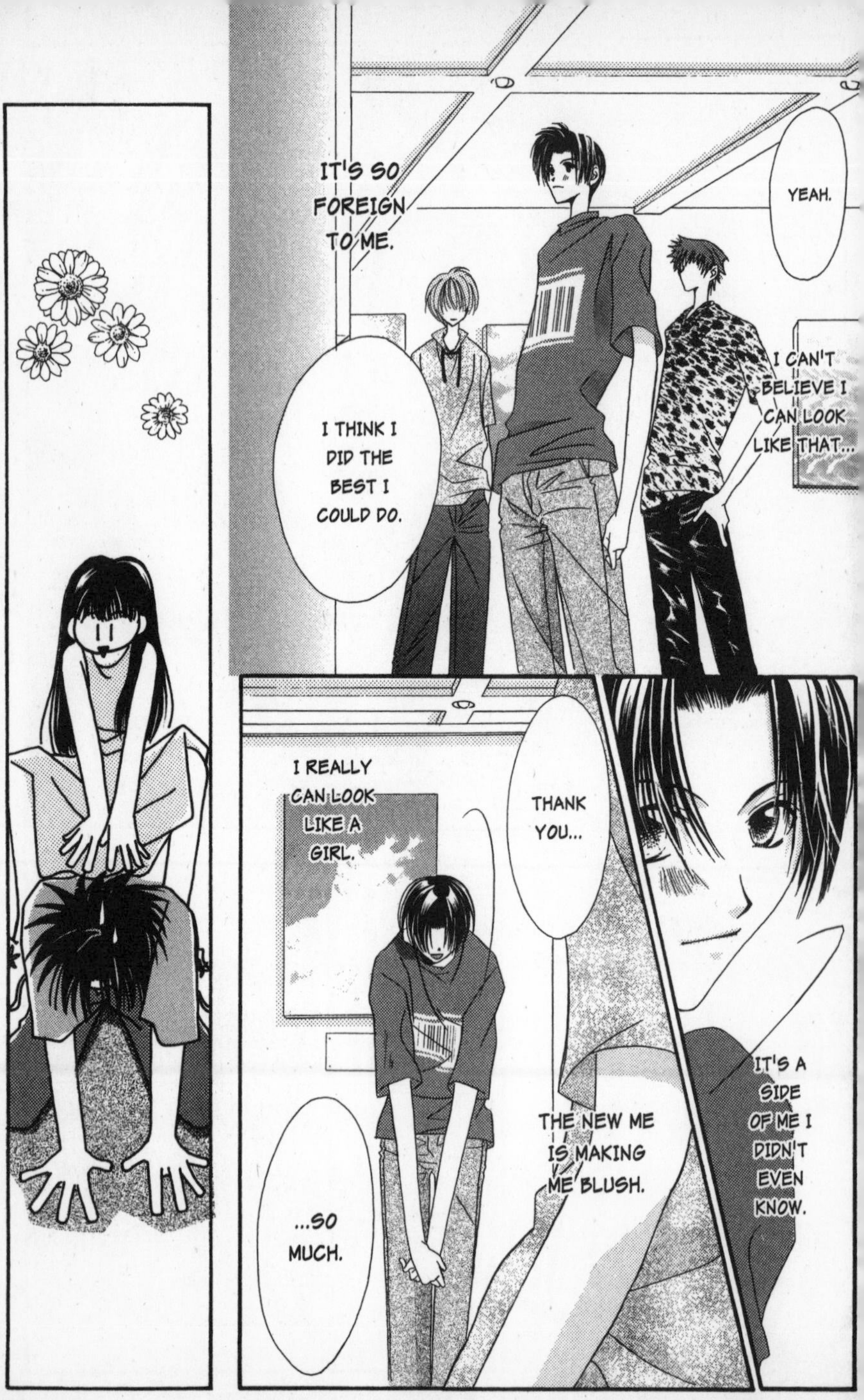
YEAH.
I CAN'T BELIEVE I CAN LOOK LIKE THAT...
IT'S SO FOREIGN TO ME.
I THINK I DID THE BEST I COULD DO.
IT'S A SIDE OF ME I DIDN'T EVEN KNOW.
THANK YOU...
I REALLY CAN LOOK LIKE A GIRL.
THE NEW ME IS MAKING ME BLUSH.
...SO MUCH.

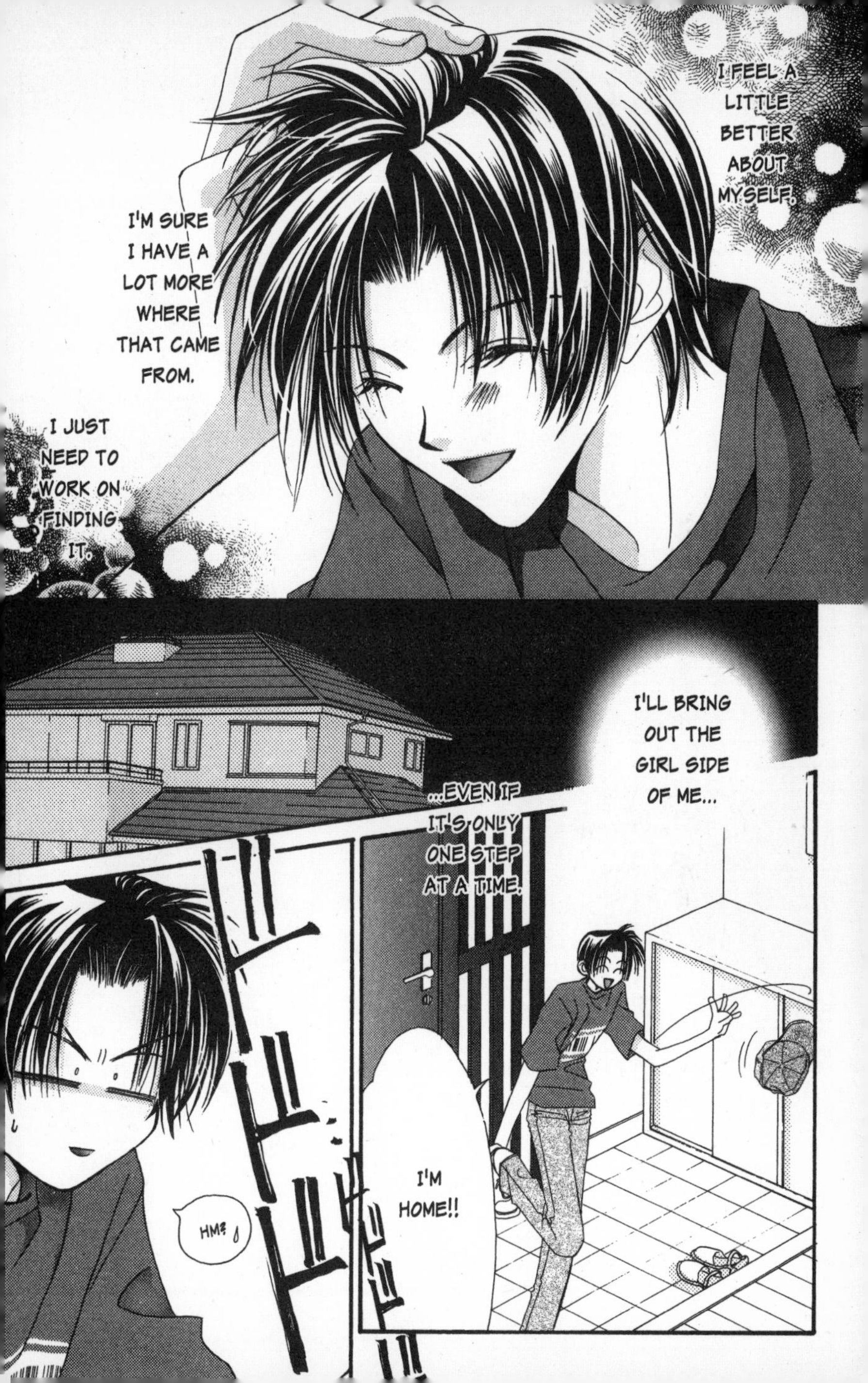
I FEEL A LITTLE BETTER ABOUT MYSELF.
I'M SURE I HAVE A LOT MORE WHERE THAT CAME FROM.
I JUST NEED TO WORK ON FINDING IT.
I'LL BRING OUT THE GIRL SIDE OF ME...
...EVEN IF IT'S ONLY ONE STEP AT A TIME.
I'M HOME!!
HM?

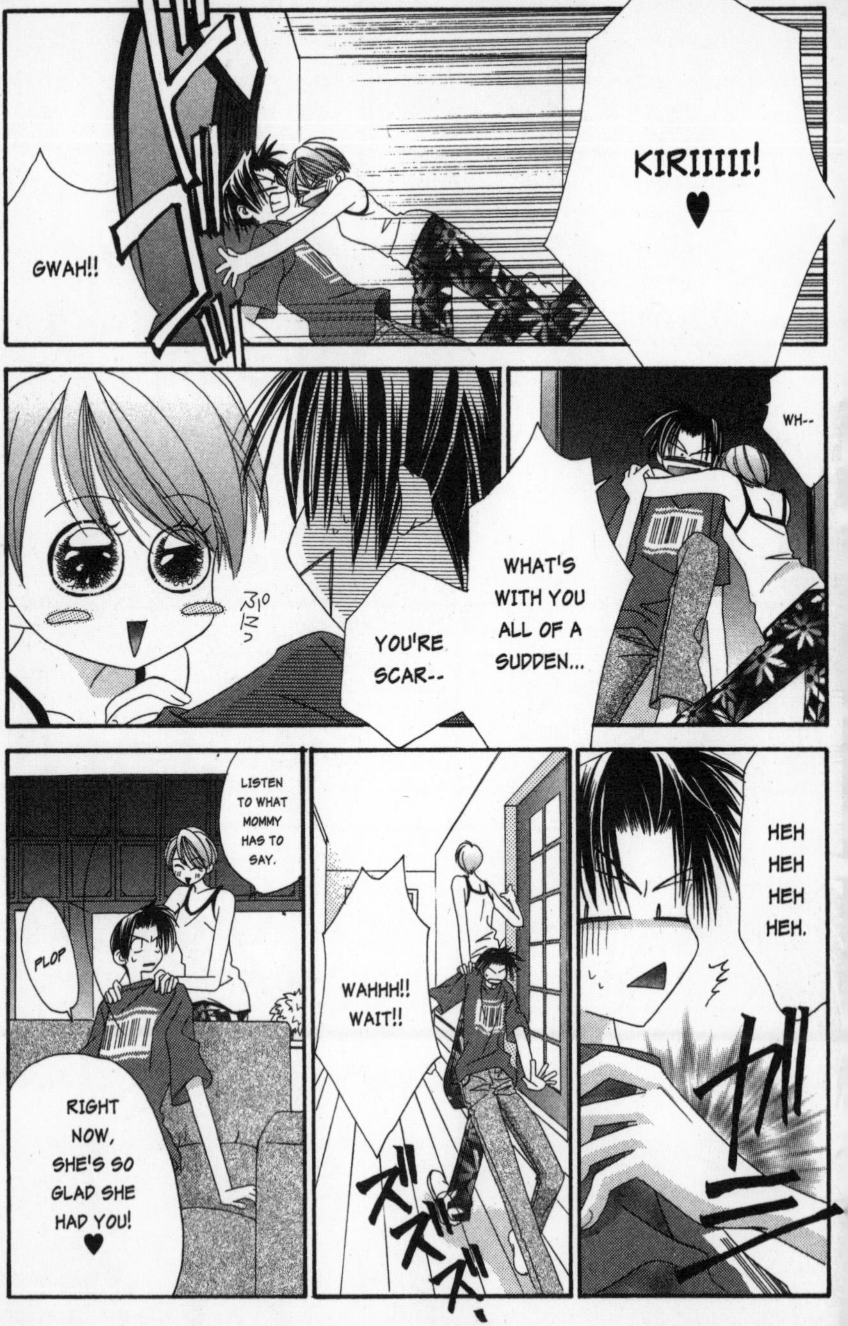
KIRIIIII! ♥
GWAH!!
WH--
WHAT'S WITH YOU ALL OF A SUDDEN...
YOU'RE SCAR--
HEH HEH HEH HEH.
WAHHH!! WAIT!!
LISTEN TO WHAT MOMMY HAS TO SAY.
PLOP
RIGHT NOW, SHE'S SO GLAD SHE HAD YOU! ♥

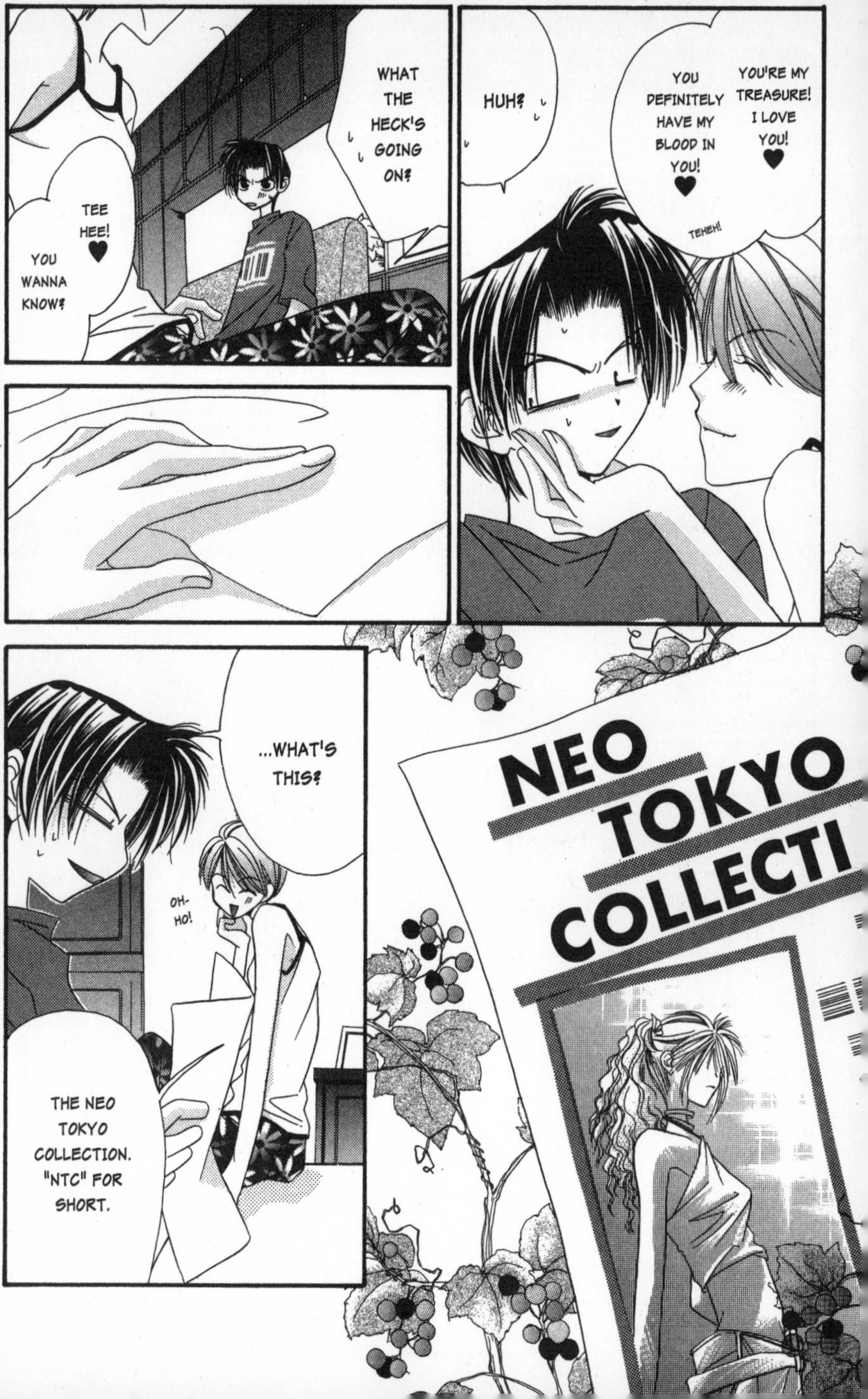
YOU'RE MY TREASURE! I LOVE YOU! ♥
YOU DEFINITELY HAVE MY BLOOD IN YOU! ♥
HUH?
TEHEH!
WHAT THE HECK'S GOING ON?
TEE HEE! ♥
YOU WANNA KNOW?
NEO TOKYO COLLECTI
...WHAT'S THIS?
OH-HO!
THE NEO TOKYO COLLECTION. "NTC" FOR SHORT.

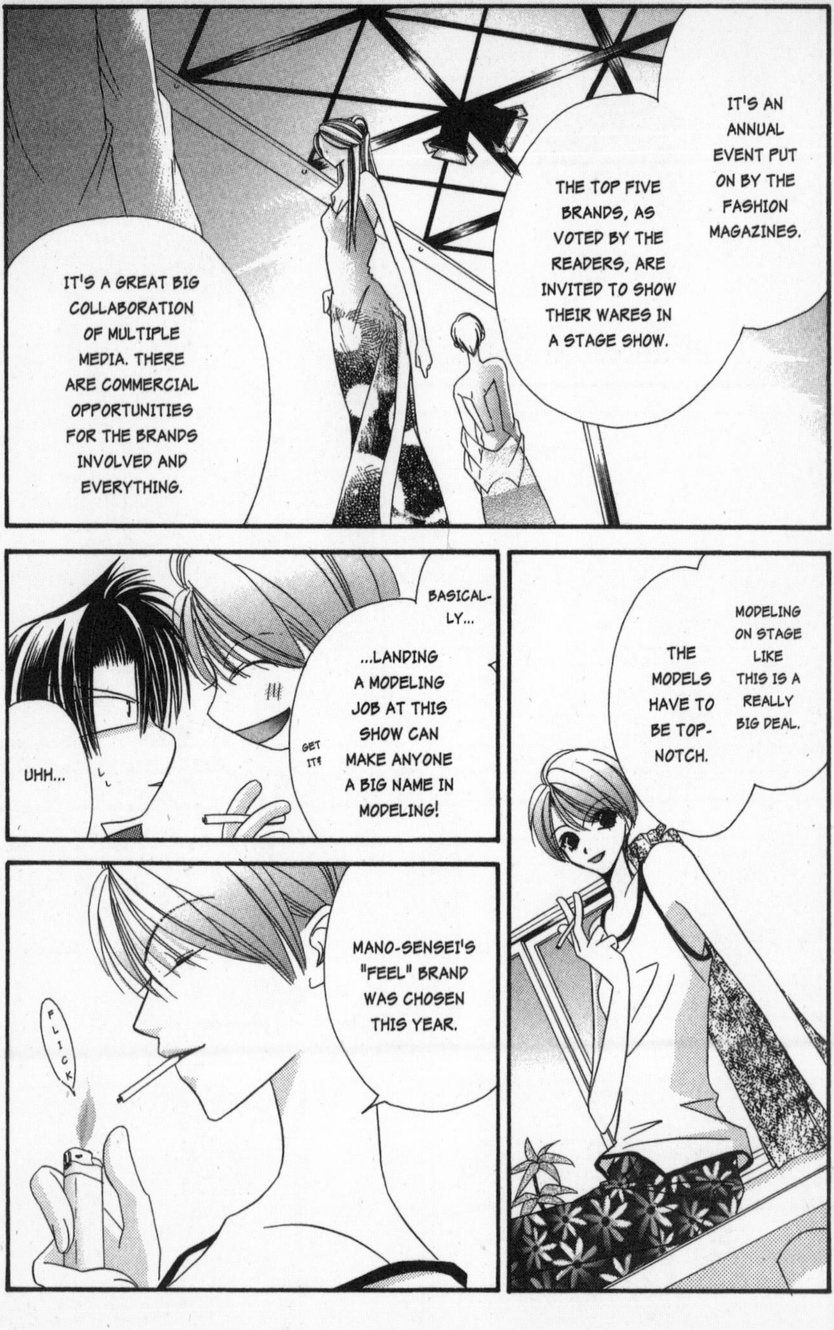
IT'S AN ANNUAL EVENT PUT ON BY THE FASHION MAGAZINES.
THE TOP FIVE BRANDS, AS VOTED BY THE READERS, ARE INVITED TO SHOW THEIR WARES IN A STAGE SHOW.
IT'S A GREAT BIG COLLABORATION OF MULTIPLE MEDIA. THERE ARE COMMERCIAL OPPORTUNITIES FOR THE BRANDS INVOLVED AND EVERYTHING.
MODELING ON STAGE LIKE THIS IS A REALLY BIG DEAL.
THE MODELS HAVE TO BE TOP-NOTCH.
BASICAL-LY...
...LANDING A MODELING JOB AT THIS SHOW CAN MAKE ANYONE A BIG NAME IN MODELING!
GET IT?
UHH...
MANO-SENSEI'S "FEEL" BRAND WAS CHOSEN THIS YEAR.
FLICK

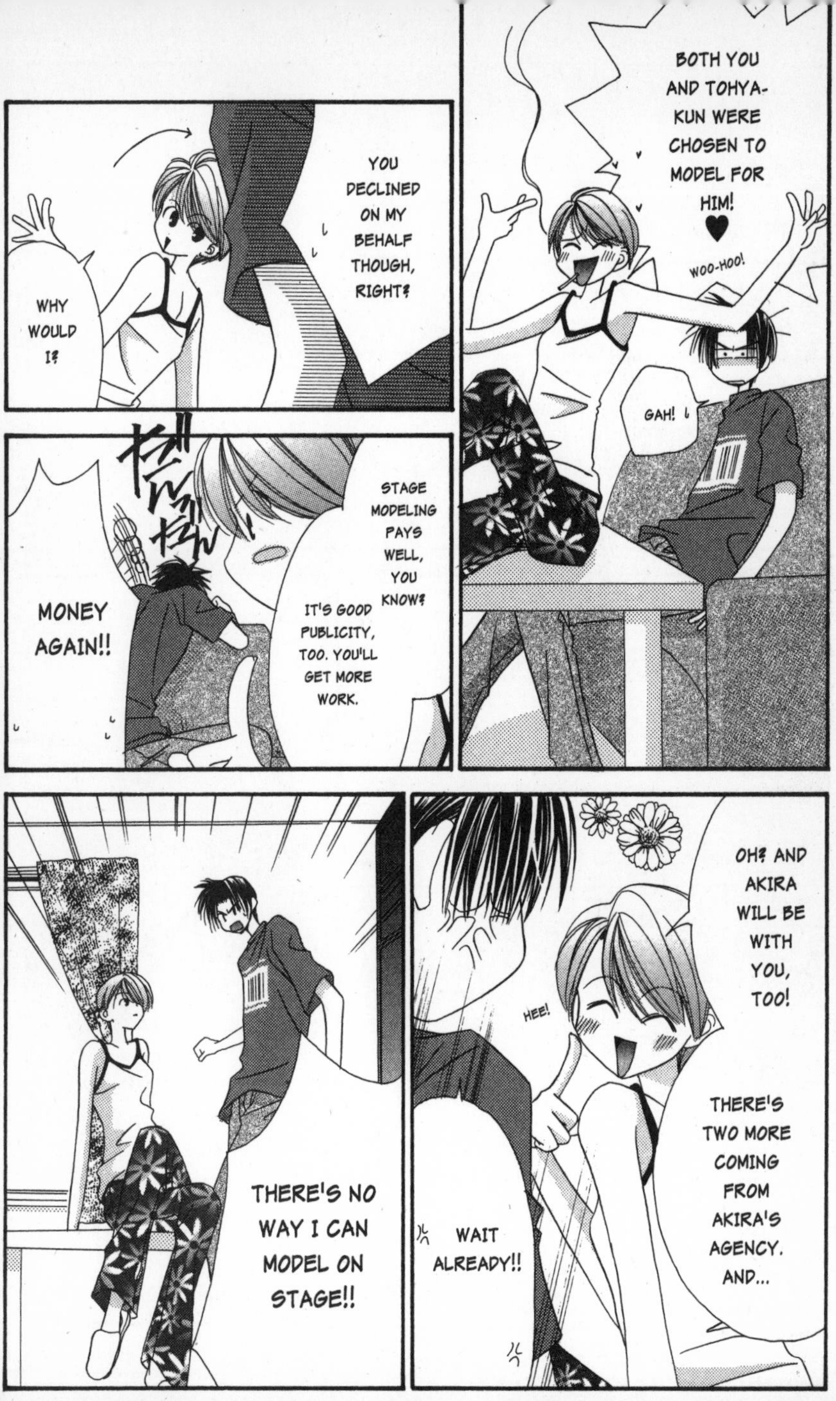
BOTH YOU AND TOHYA-KUN WERE CHOSEN TO MODEL FOR HIM! ♥
WOO-HOO!
GAH!
YOU DECLINED ON MY BEHALF THOUGH, RIGHT?
WHY WOULD I?
STAGE MODELING PAYS WELL, YOU KNOW?
IT'S GOOD PUBLICITY, TOO. YOU'LL GET MORE WORK.
MONEY AGAIN!!
OH? AND AKIRA WILL BE WITH YOU, TOO!
HEE!
THERE'S TWO MORE COMING FROM AKIRA'S AGENCY. AND...
WAIT ALREADY!!
THERE'S NO WAY I CAN MODEL ON STAGE!!

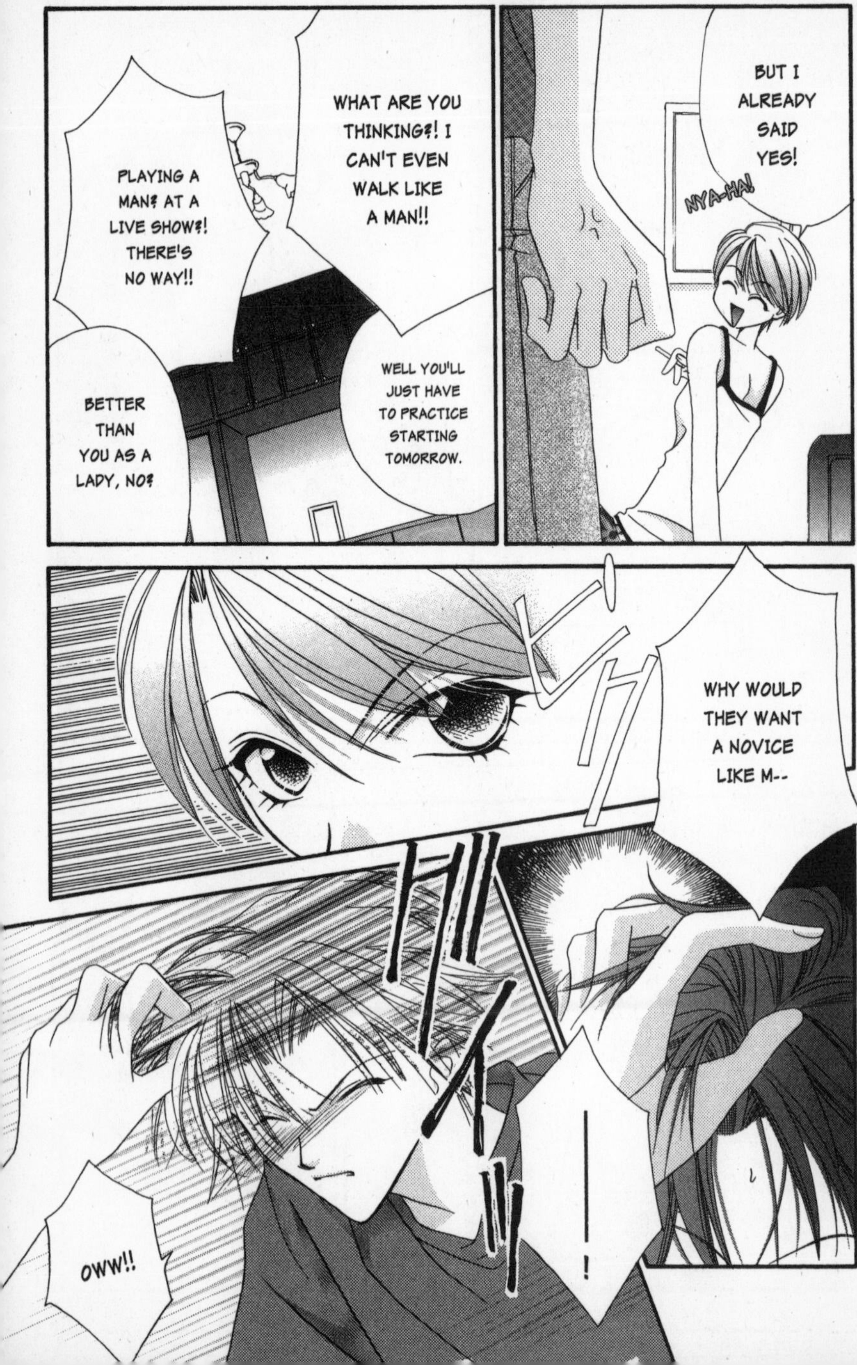
BUT I ALREADY SAID YES!
NYA-HA!
WHAT ARE YOU THINKING?! I CAN'T EVEN WALK LIKE A MAN!!
PLAYING A MAN? AT A LIVE SHOW?! THERE'S NO WAY!!
WELL YOU'LL JUST HAVE TO PRACTICE STARTING TOMORROW.
BETTER THAN YOU AS A LADY, NO?
WHY WOULD THEY WANT A NOVICE LIKE M--
OWW!!

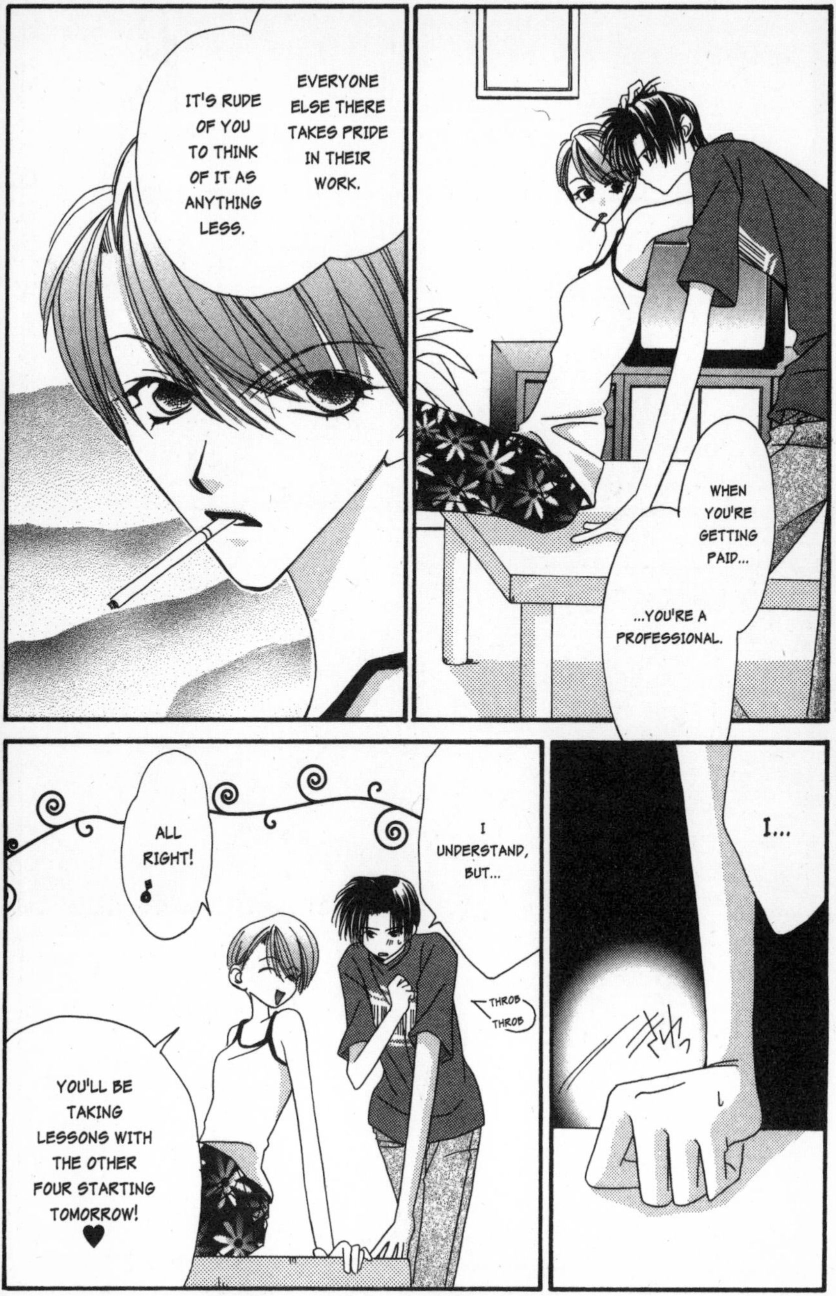
WHEN YOU'RE GETTING PAID...
...YOU'RE A PROFESSIONAL.
EVERYONE ELSE THERE TAKES PRIDE IN THEIR WORK.
IT'S RUDE OF YOU TO THINK OF IT AS ANYTHING LESS.
I...
I UNDERSTAND, BUT...
ALL RIGHT!
THROB THROB
YOU'LL BE TAKING LESSONS WITH THE OTHER FOUR STARTING TOMORROW! ♥

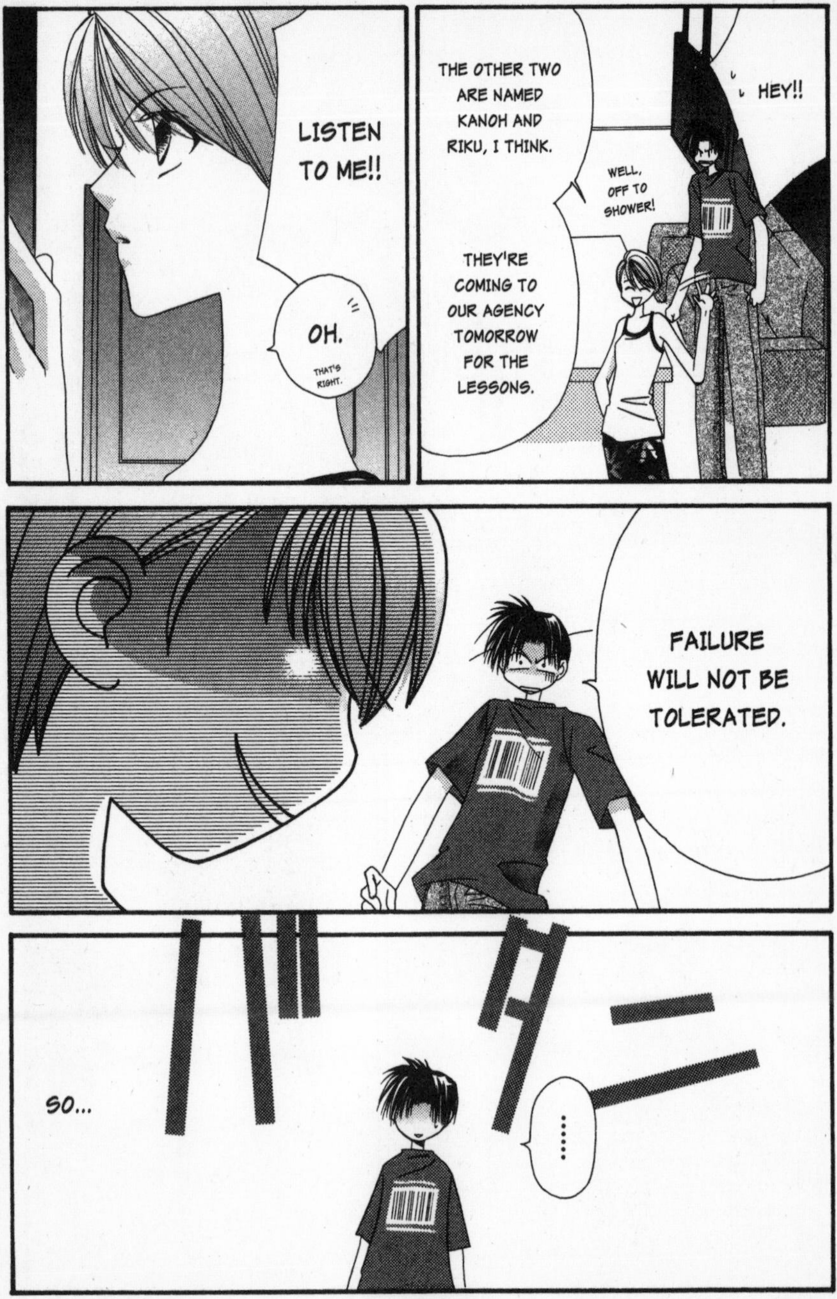
THE OTHER TWO ARE NAMED KANOH AND RIKU, I THINK.
THEY'RE COMING TO OUR AGENCY TOMORROW FOR THE LESSONS.
WELL, OFF TO SHOWER!
HEY!!
LISTEN TO ME!!
OH.
THAT'S RIGHT.
FAILURE WILL NOT BE TOLERATED.
......
SO...

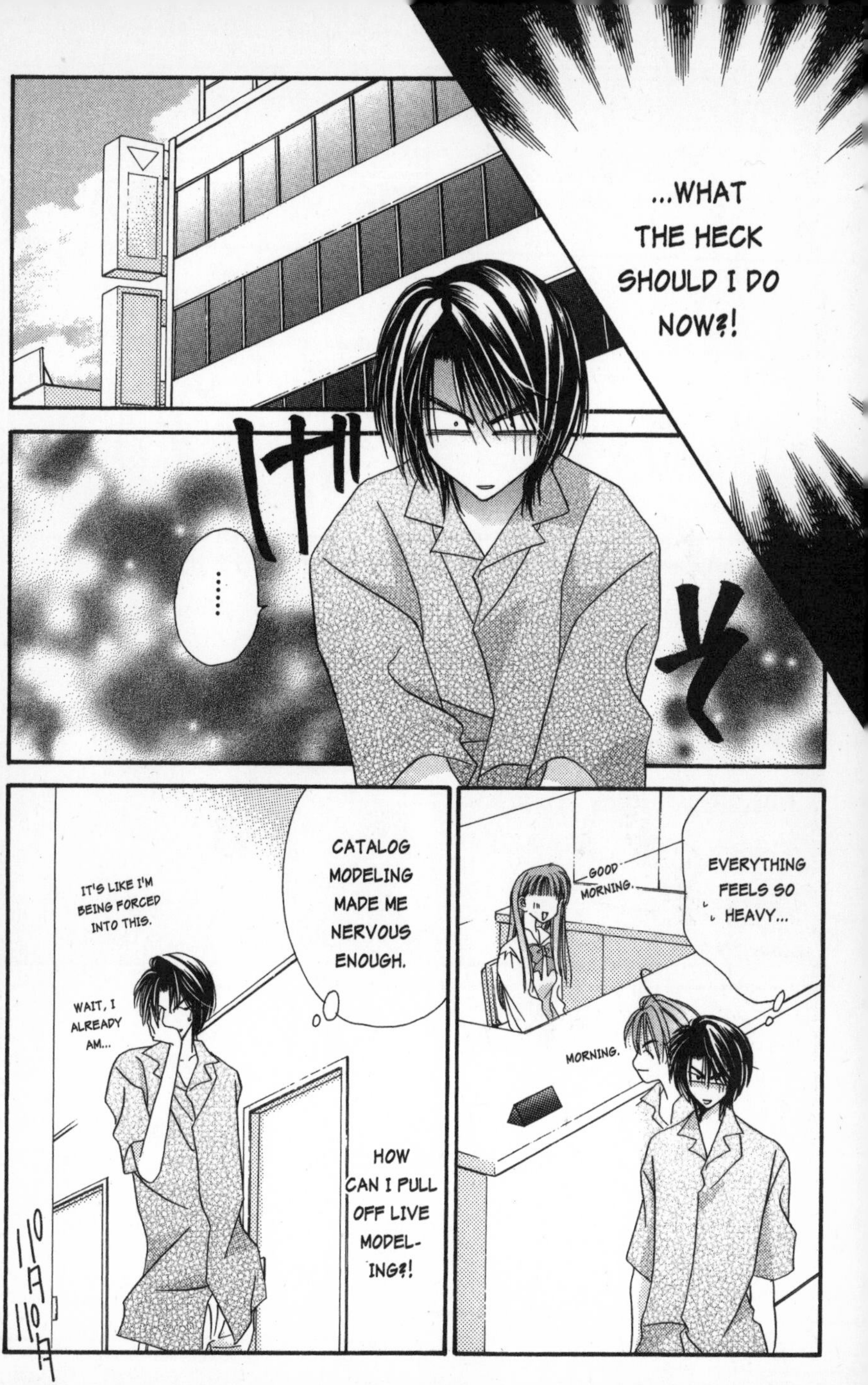
...WHAT THE HECK SHOULD I DO NOW?!
......
EVERYTHING FEELS SO HEAVY...
GOOD MORNING.
MORNING.
CATALOG MODELING MADE ME NERVOUS ENOUGH.
IT'S LIKE I'M BEING FORCED INTO THIS.
WAIT, I ALREADY AM...
HOW CAN I PULL OFF LIVE MODEL-ING?!

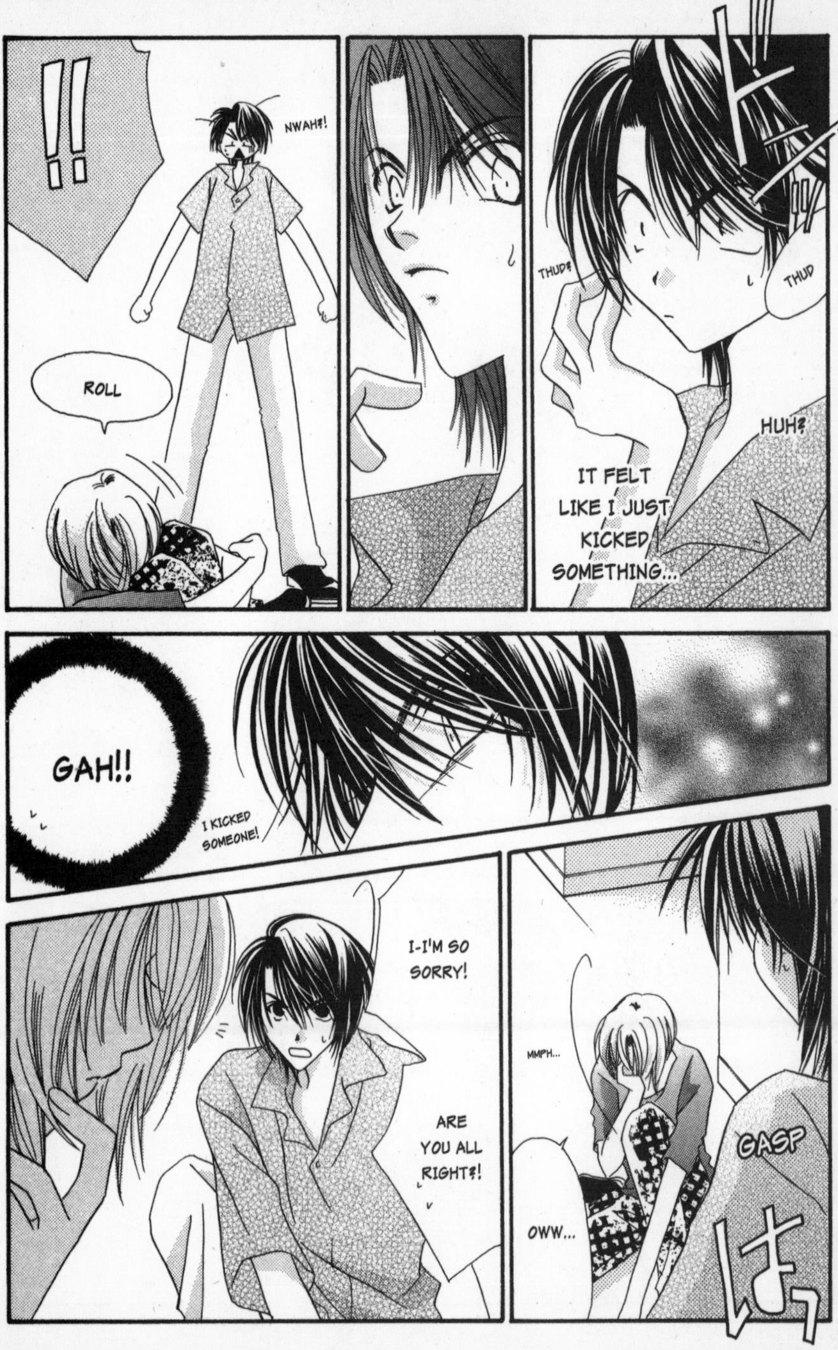
THUD
THUD?
HUH?
IT FELT LIKE I JUST KICKED SOMETHING...
NWAH?!
!!
ROLL
GAH!!
I KICKED SOMEONE!
GASP
はっ
MMPH...
OWW...
I-I'M SO SORRY!
ARE YOU ALL RIGHT?!

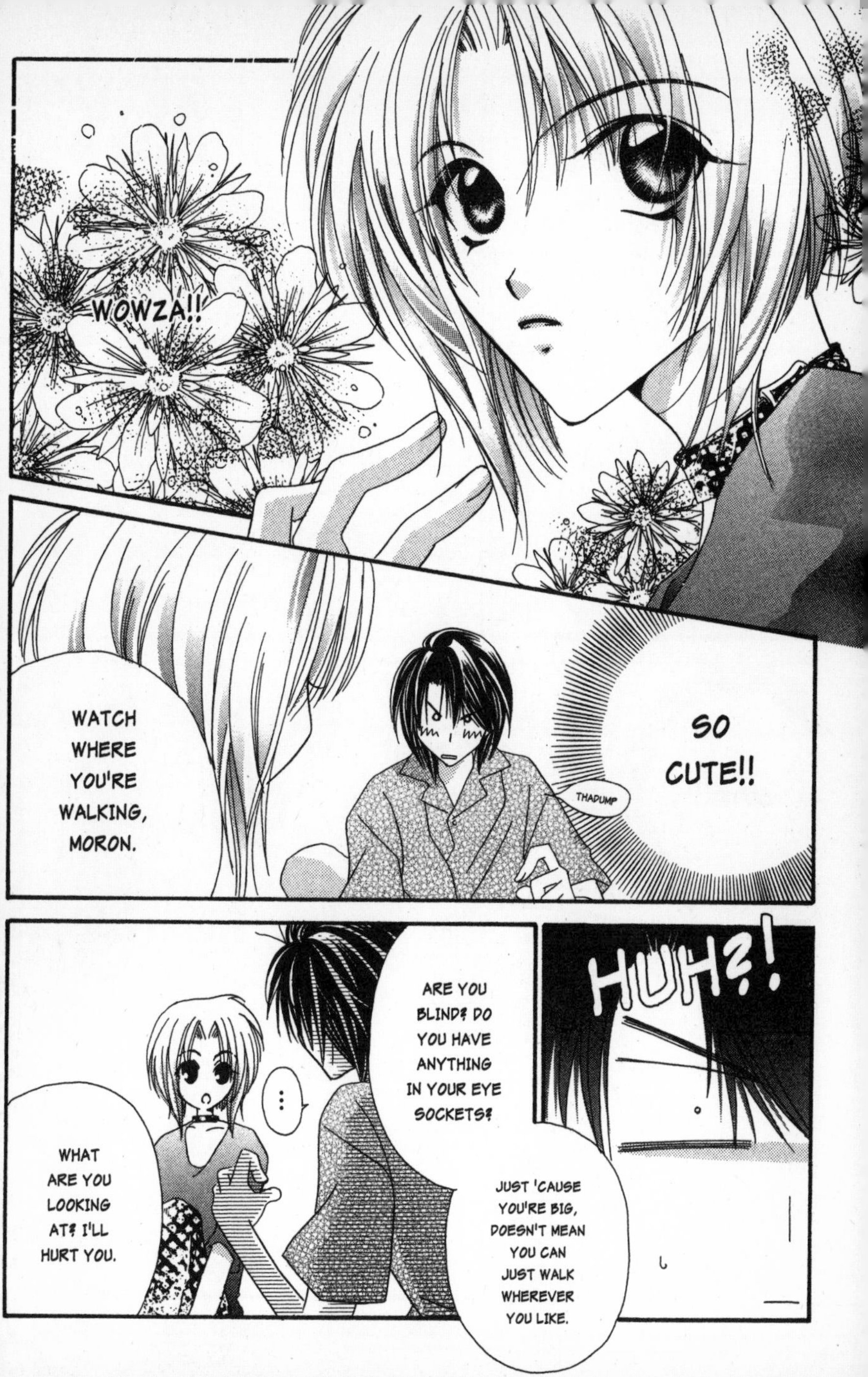
WOWZA!!
SO CUTE!!
THADUMP
WATCH WHERE YOU'RE WALKING, MORON.
HUH?!
ARE YOU BLIND? DO YOU HAVE ANYTHING IN YOUR EYE SOCKETS?
JUST 'CAUSE YOU'RE BIG, DOESN'T MEAN YOU CAN JUST WALK WHEREVER YOU LIKE.
...
WHAT ARE YOU LOOKING AT? I'LL HURT YOU.

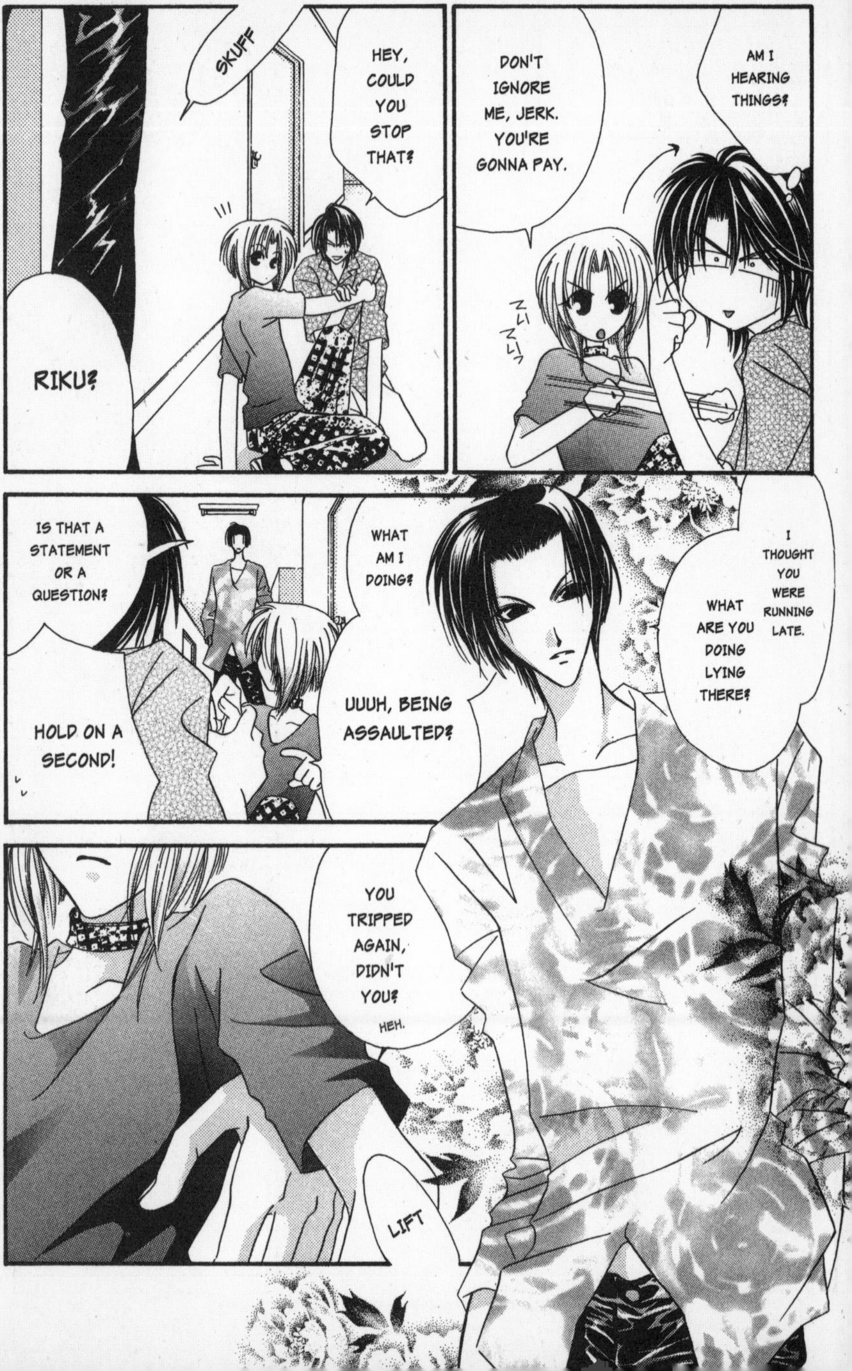
AM I HEARING THINGS?
DON'T IGNORE ME, JERK. YOU'RE GONNA PAY.
HEY, COULD YOU STOP THAT?
SKUFF
RIKU?
I THOUGHT YOU WERE RUNNING LATE.
WHAT ARE YOU DOING LYING THERE?
WHAT AM I DOING?
UUUH, BEING ASSAULTED?
IS THAT A STATEMENT OR A QUESTION?
HOLD ON A SECOND!
YOU TRIPPED AGAIN, DIDN'T YOU?
HEH.
LIFT

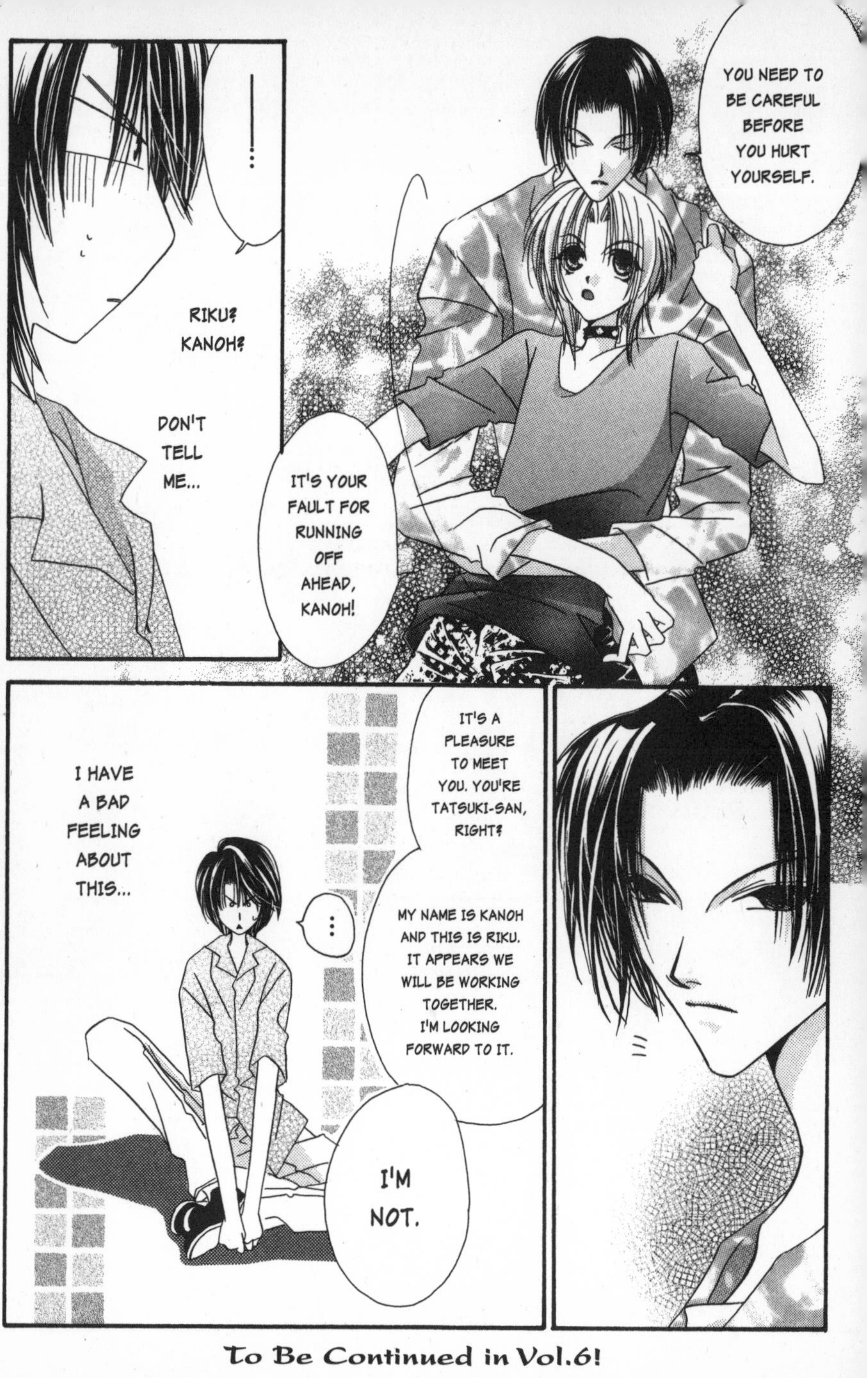
YOU NEED TO BE CAREFUL BEFORE YOU HURT YOURSELF.
IT'S YOUR FAULT FOR RUNNING OFF AHEAD, KANOH!
......!
RIKU? KANOH?
DON'T TELL ME...
IT'S A PLEASURE TO MEET YOU. YOU'RE TATSUKI-SAN, RIGHT?
MY NAME IS KANOH AND THIS IS RIKU. IT APPEARS WE WILL BE WORKING TOGETHER. I'M LOOKING FORWARD TO IT.
I HAVE A BAD FEELING ABOUT THIS...
...
I'M NOT.

To Be Continued in Vol.6!

FREE TALK

* HELLO. THIS IS MUTOU. I'M SURE THERE'S PEOPLE READING THIS WHOM I HAVEN'T INTRODUCED MYSELF TO YET (LOL) SO PLEASED TO MEET YOU. (DOUBLE LOL!) THIS IS *NEVER GIVE UP* VOLUME 5 ALREADY!! I MAY HAVE WRITTEN THIS LAST TIME TOO, BUT IT'S AMAZING HOW QUICKLY A YEAR PASSES! I GET THE FEELING I NEED TO MATCH THE SEASONS BETTER FOR KIRI AND THE GANG! IT'S STILL SUMMER IN THE SERIAL PUBLICATIONS... (SORRY). BUT I'M TRYING TO MOVE THEM ALONG A LITTLE BIT...AREN'T I? (WHO AM I ASKING? LOL) I'M TRYING HARD. THE CAST IS TRYING, TOO.

* OH, THAT'S RIGHT. I LIVE IN AICHI PREFECTURE. THE OTHER DAY, THERE WAS SOME TERRIBLE RAIN. MY TOWN WAS FINE, BUT THE TOWN ON THE OTHER SIDE OF THE RIVER, A FEW HUNDRED METERS AWAY, APPARENTLY EXPERIENCED BAD FLOODING. WAS EVERYONE ELSE FROM AICHI READING THIS OKAY? IF ANY OF YOU WERE AFFECTED BY THE FLOOD, HANG IN THERE!! I WASN'T AFFECTED, SO I CAN'T EVEN BEGIN TO IMAGINE HOW TERRIBLE IT MUST HAVE BEEN. ALL I CAN SAY IS HANG IN THERE. YEAH. PLEASE HANG IN THERE. I JUST WANTED TO PASS THAT SENTIMENT ALONG.

* SOMETIMES I ASK MYSELF, "WHAT HAVE I BEEN DOING ALL YEAR?" BUT I HAVE TO SAY I'VE BEEN HAVING FUN. KEEPING IN TOUCH WITH FRIENDS HAS MADE ME SURE OF THAT. AND IT MIGHT NOT LEAVE MUCH TIME FOR IT, BUT IT FEELS GOOD WHEN THE THINGS I DRAW AND THE THINGS I DO ACCOMPLISH THINGS FOR OTHER PEOPLE AND HELP THEM OUT. THESE ARE THE PEOPLE I LOVE, AND I'M GLAD TO SAY THEY LOVE ME BACK. EVEN AS WEAK AS I AM, I'M GLAD TO HELP PEOPLE OUT AT LEAST ONCE IN A WHILE. OR AT LEAST I TRY (LOL).

HIROMU
MUTOU 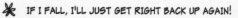 * IF I FALL, I'LL JUST GET RIGHT BACK UP AGAIN! *

Secrets of the Mutou Household

--Sexy Edition-- by Kurara

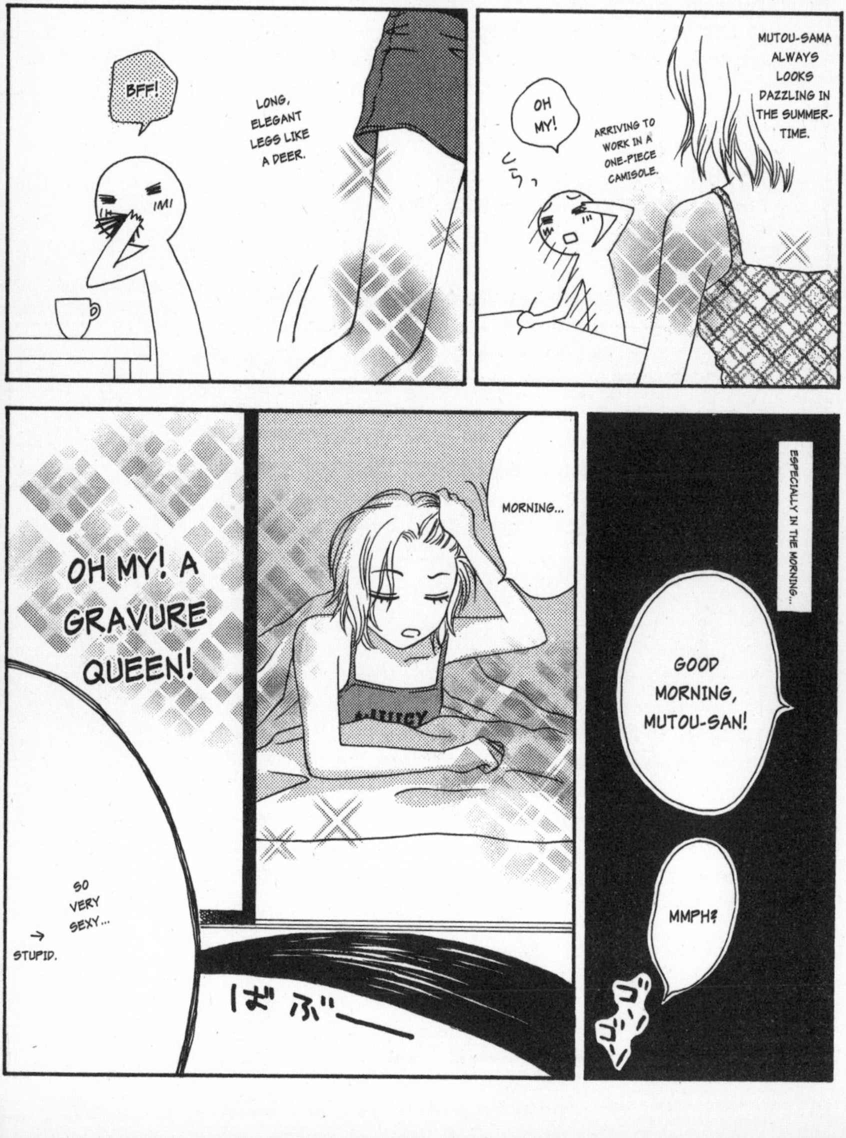

MUTOU-SAMA ALWAYS LOOKS DAZZLING IN THE SUMMER-TIME.
ARRIVING TO WORK IN A ONE-PIECE CAMISOLE.
OH MY!
LONG, ELEGANT LEGS LIKE A DEER.
BFF!
ESPECIALLY IN THE MORNING...
GOOD MORNING, MUTOU-SAN!
MMPH?
MORNING...
OH MY! A GRAVURE QUEEN!
SO VERY SEXY...
→ STUPID.
ばぶ—

Secrets of the Mutou Household

--Free Lesson-- by Takagi

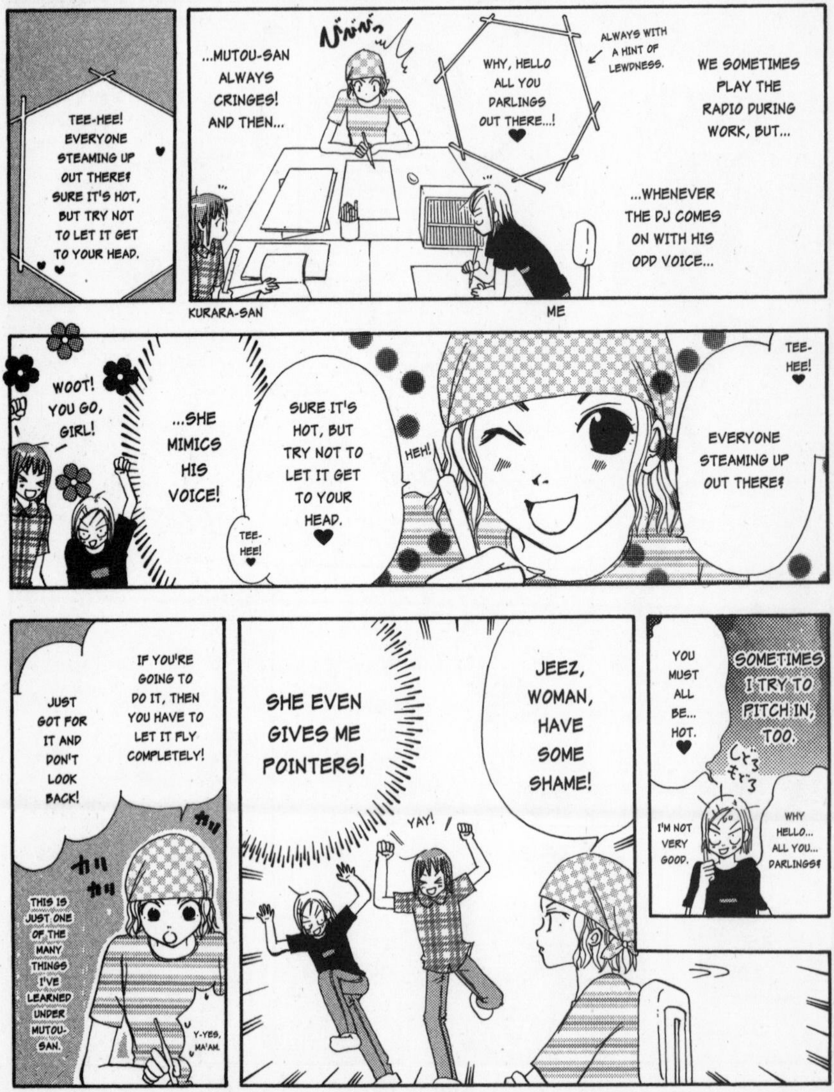
WE SOMETIMES PLAY THE RADIO DURING WORK, BUT...
ALWAYS WITH A HINT OF LEWDNESS.
WHY, HELLO ALL YOU DARLINGS OUT THERE...!
...WHENEVER THE DJ COMES ON WITH HIS ODD VOICE...
...MUTOU-SAN ALWAYS CRINGES! AND THEN...
KURARA-SAN
ME
TEE-HEE! EVERYONE STEAMING UP OUT THERE? SURE IT'S HOT, BUT TRY NOT TO LET IT GET TO YOUR HEAD.
TEE-HEE!
EVERYONE STEAMING UP OUT THERE?
HEH!
SURE IT'S HOT, BUT TRY NOT TO LET IT GET TO YOUR HEAD.
TEE-HEE!
...SHE MIMICS HIS VOICE!
WOOT! YOU GO, GIRL!
SOMETIMES I TRY TO PITCH IN, TOO.
YOU MUST ALL BE... HOT.
WHY HELLO... ALL YOU... DARLINGS?
I'M NOT VERY GOOD.
JEEZ, WOMAN, HAVE SOME SHAME!
SHE EVEN GIVES ME POINTERS!
YAY!
IF YOU'RE GOING TO DO IT, THEN YOU HAVE TO LET IT FLY COMPLETELY!
JUST GOT FOR IT AND DON'T LOOK BACK!
THIS IS JUST ONE OF THE MANY THINGS I'VE LEARNED UNDER MUTOU-SAN.
Y-YES, MA'AM.

Secrets of the Mutou Household

--Honestly Difficult-- by Sakamoto

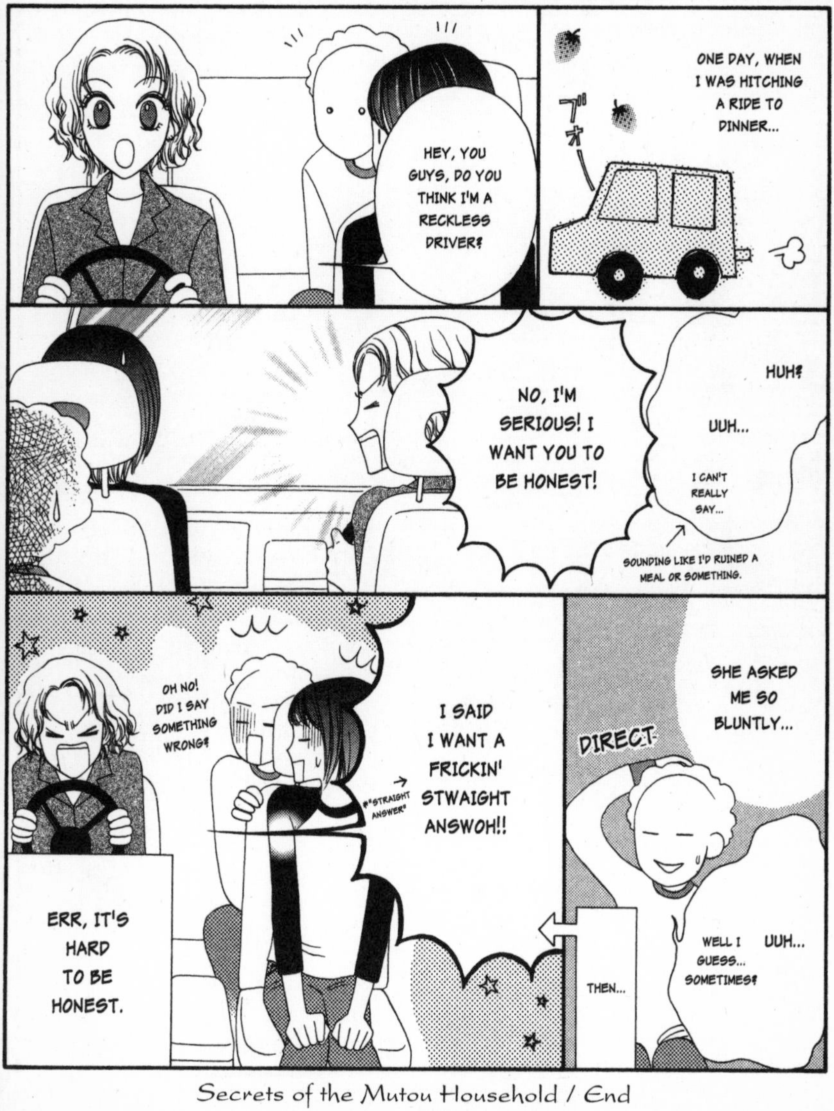
ONE DAY, WHEN I WAS HITCHING A RIDE TO DINNER...
ブォー
HEY, YOU GUYS, DO YOU THINK I'M A RECKLESS DRIVER?
HUH?
UUH...
I CAN'T REALLY SAY...
SOUNDING LIKE I'D RUINED A MEAL OR SOMETHING.
NO, I'M SERIOUS! I WANT YOU TO BE HONEST!
SHE ASKED ME SO BLUNTLY...
DIRECT
UUH...
WELL I GUESS... SOMETIMES?
THEN...
I SAID I WANT A FRICKIN' STWAIGHT ANSWOH!!
*"STRAIGHT ANSWER"
OH NO! DID I SAY SOMETHING WRONG?
ERR, IT'S HARD TO BE HONEST.

Secrets of the Mutou Household / End

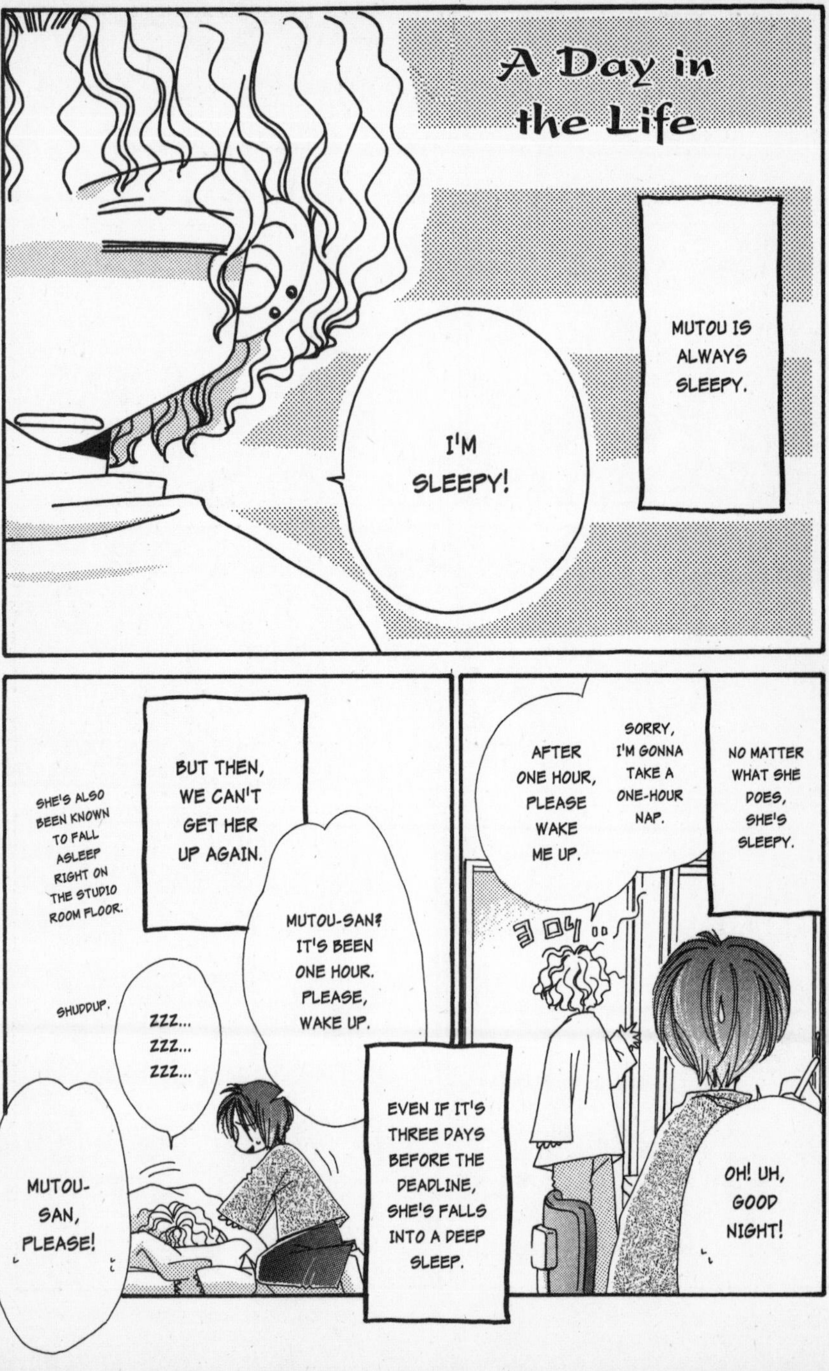
A Day in the Life
MUTOU IS ALWAYS SLEEPY.
I'M SLEEPY!
NO MATTER WHAT SHE DOES, SHE'S SLEEPY.
SORRY, I'M GONNA TAKE A ONE-HOUR NAP.
AFTER ONE HOUR, PLEASE WAKE ME UP.
OH! UH, GOOD NIGHT!
BUT THEN, WE CAN'T GET HER UP AGAIN.
SHE'S ALSO BEEN KNOWN TO FALL ASLEEP RIGHT ON THE STUDIO ROOM FLOOR.
MUTOU-SAN? IT'S BEEN ONE HOUR. PLEASE, WAKE UP.
ZZZ... ZZZ... ZZZ...
SHUDDUP.
MUTOU-SAN, PLEASE!
EVEN IF IT'S THREE DAYS BEFORE THE DEADLINE, SHE'S FALLS INTO A DEEP SLEEP.

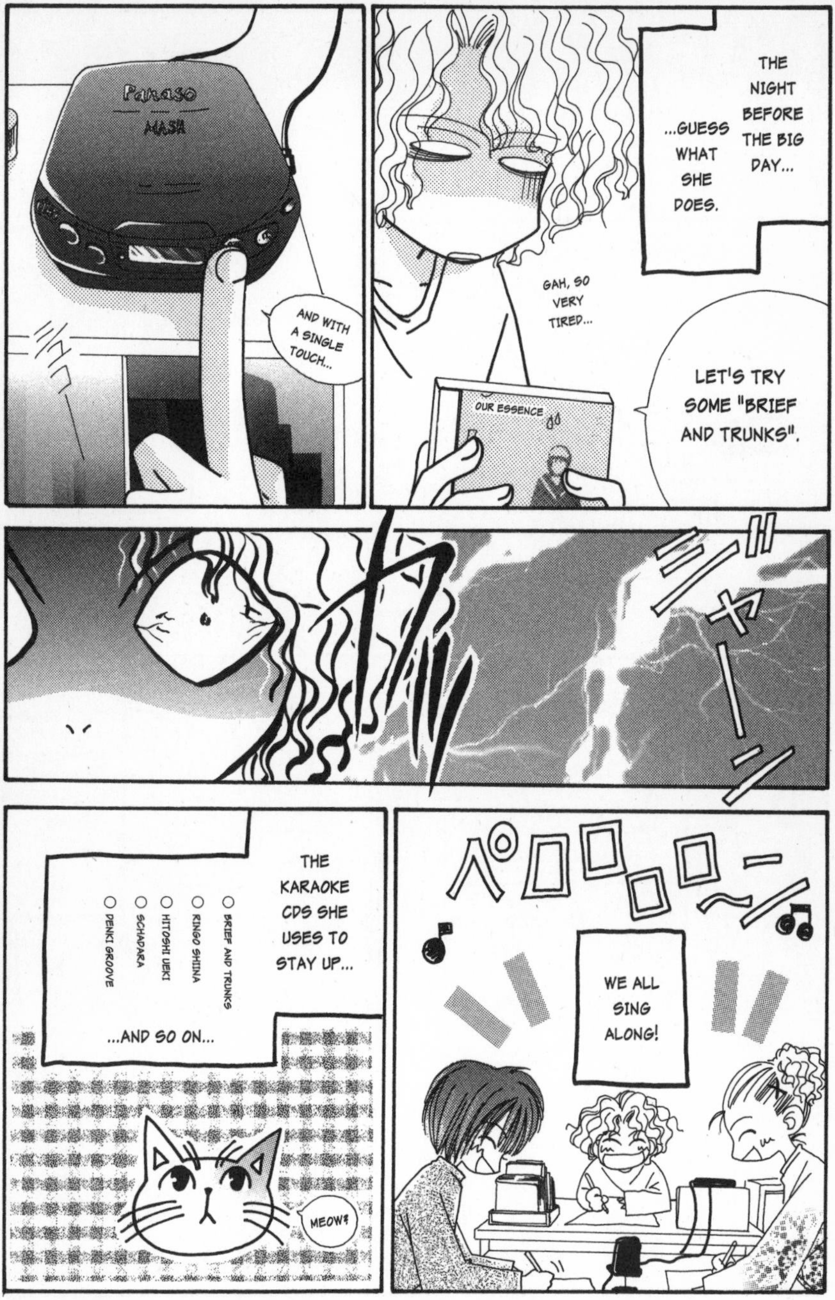
THE NIGHT BEFORE THE BIG DAY...
...GUESS WHAT SHE DOES.
GAH, SO VERY TIRED...
LET'S TRY SOME "BRIEF AND TRUNKS".
OUR ESSENCE
Panaso
MASH
AND WITH A SINGLE TOUCH...
WE ALL SING ALONG!
THE KARAOKE CDS SHE USES TO STAY UP...
○ BRIEF AND TRUNKS
○ RINGO SHIINA
○ HITOSHI UEKI
○ SCHADARA
○ PENKI GROOVE
...AND SO ON...
MEOW?

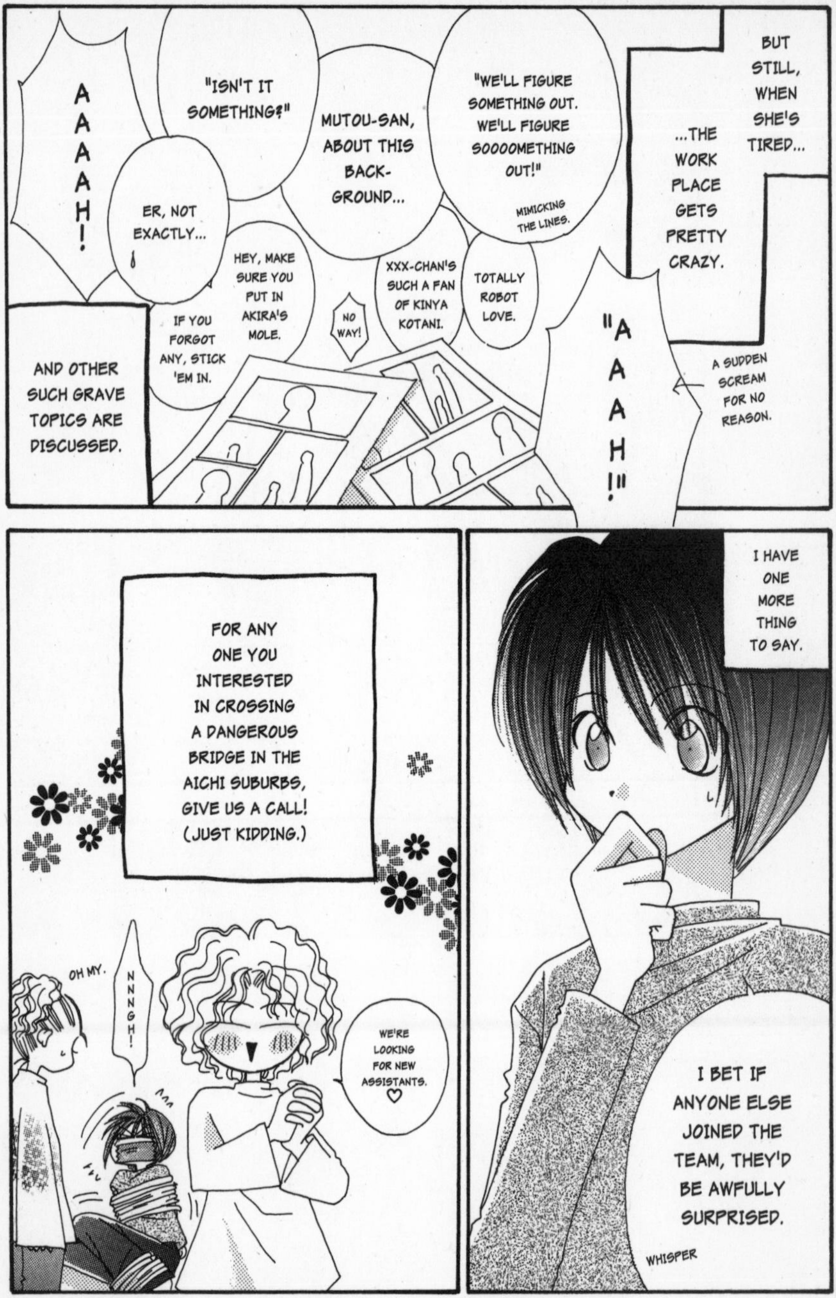
BUT STILL, WHEN SHE'S TIRED...
...THE WORK PLACE GETS PRETTY CRAZY.
"AAAH!!"
A SUDDEN SCREAM FOR NO REASON.
"WE'LL FIGURE SOMETHING OUT. WE'LL FIGURE SOOOOMETHING OUT!"
MIMICKING THE LINES.
TOTALLY ROBOT LOVE.
XXX-CHAN'S SUCH A FAN OF KINYA KOTANI.
MUTOU-SAN, ABOUT THIS BACK-GROUND...
NO WAY!
"ISN'T IT SOMETHING?"
ER, NOT EXACTLY...
HEY, MAKE SURE YOU PUT IN AKIRA'S MOLE.
IF YOU FORGOT ANY, STICK 'EM IN.
AAAAH!
AND OTHER SUCH GRAVE TOPICS ARE DISCUSSED.
I HAVE ONE MORE THING TO SAY.
I BET IF ANYONE ELSE JOINED THE TEAM, THEY'D BE AWFULLY SURPRISED.
WHISPER
FOR ANY ONE YOU INTERESTED IN CROSSING A DANGEROUS BRIDGE IN THE AICHI SUBURBS, GIVE US A CALL! (JUST KIDDING.)
WE'RE LOOKING FOR NEW ASSISTANTS. ♡
NNNGH!
OH MY.

A Day in the Life / End

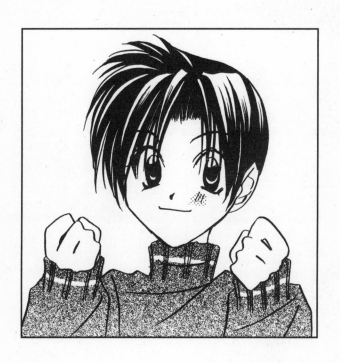

In the next volume of...

NEVER GIVE UP™

In accordance with her mother's devious ploy, Kiri's wound up training for a modeling show on stage! But she's not alone, and if she wants to survive the grueling tests before her, she's going to have to get along with her newest coworkers: Riku and Kanoh! Find out who'll be all the rage at the show in the next volume of *Never Give Up!*

GOT THE PERFECT DRESS DESIGN FOR KIRI? OR MAYBE A SUIT? SHOW THE REST OF THE FANS YOUR FASHION GODDESS IDEAS, IN *NEVER GIVE UP*'S FIRST FANART SECTION!

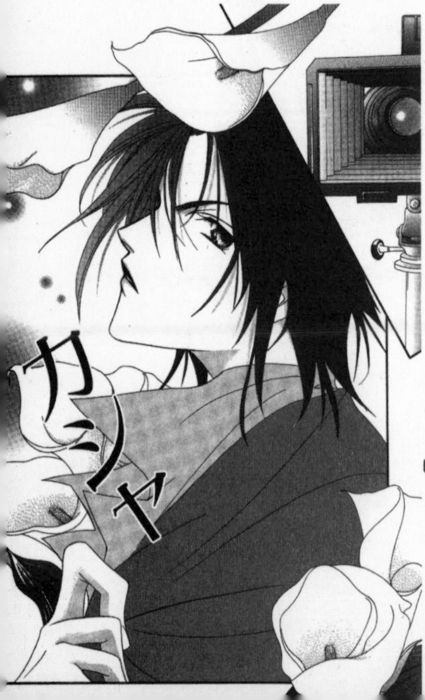
カシャ

SEND ALL SUBMISSIONS (BY MAIL!) TO:

NEVER GIVE UP FASHION RUNWAY
C/O TOKYOPOP
5900 WILSHIRE BLVD, SUITE 2000
LOS ANGELES, CA 90036

HOW TO SUBMIT:

1.) ALL WORK SHOULD BE IN BLACK-AND-WHITE AND NO LARGER THAN 8.5" X 11". (AND TRY NOT TO FOLD IT TOO MANY TIMES)! 2.) ANYTHING YOU SEND WILL NOT BE RETURNED. MAKE A COPY IF YOU WANT TO KEEP THE ORIGINAL. 3.) PLEASE INCLUDE YOUR FULL NAME, AGE, CITY AND STATE FOR US TO PRINT WITH YOUR ARTWORK. PENNAMES ARE FINE, TOO. 4.) **IMPORTANT:** IF YOU'RE UNDER THE AGE OF 18, YOU MUST HAVE YOUR GUARDIAN'S PERMISSION INCLUDED WITH THE WORK, IN ORDER FOR US TO PRINT IT. NO PARENTAL CONSENT MEANS NO USE. 5.) FOR FULL DETAILS, PLEASE CHECK OUT:

HTTP://WWW.TOKYOPOP.COM/70.HTML

Never Give Up
Fashion Runway

Only two submissions for our first "cycle" of *Never Give Up*'s Fashion Runway, that both go to the extreme to cover the spectrum of fashion!

Kristi G.
Age 22
Wesumpka, AL

Kristi goes for a minimalism look for Kiri's next summer apparel. Leaving the dress free of a model, we can juxtapose our own bodies into this light dress. Excellent use of smudging along the hem to give the effect of velvet or maybe even fur.

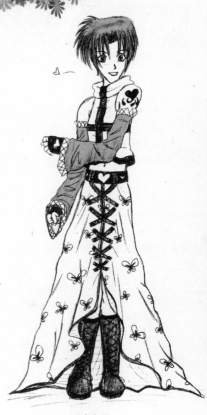

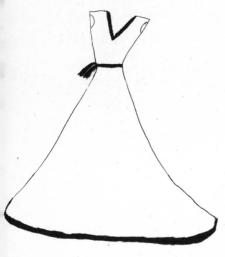

Ashyln Y.
Age 16
Monterey Park, CA

At a ripe, young age, Ashyln's showing us some serious skills as a fashion designer! And Kiri seems quite happy with her trend-setting outfit that perfectly blends the fire of punk/gothic with the elegance of a princess. The heart and butterfly motifs also really bring out Kiri's femininity.

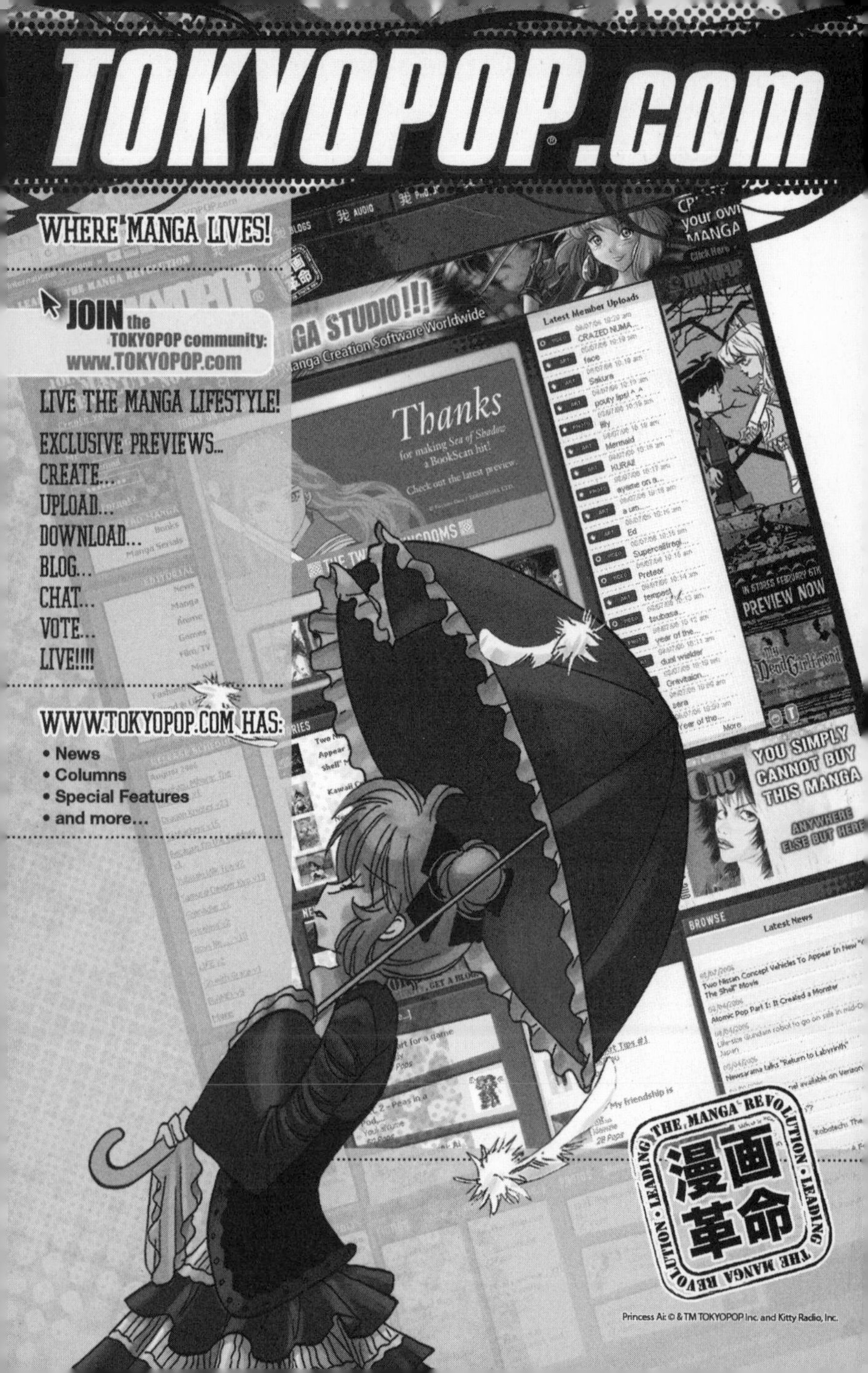
TOKYOPOP.com
WHERE MANGA LIVES!
JOIN the TOKYOPOP community: www.TOKYOPOP.com
LIVE THE MANGA LIFESTYLE!
EXCLUSIVE PREVIEWS...
CREATE...
UPLOAD...
DOWNLOAD...
BLOG...
CHAT...
VOTE...
LIVE!!!!
WWW.TOKYOPOP.COM HAS:
• News
• Columns
• Special Features
• and more...
YOU SIMPLY CANNOT BUY THIS MANGA ANYWHERE ELSE BUT HERE
THE MANGA REVOLUTION · LEADING · 漫画革命
Princess Ai: © & TM TOKYOPOP Inc. and Kitty Radio, Inc.

TOKYOPOP MANGA SUPPLEMENT

RISING STARS OF MANGA RUNNER-UP MAXIMO V. LORENZO LAYS THE
SMACK DOWN IN HIS FIRST FULL-LENGTH ACTION-PACKED MANGA!

BOMBOS VS EVERYTHING

ONLY THE SURVIVORS OF AN EPIC SHOWDOWN WITH THE MYSTERIOUS QUALIFIERS MAKE IT TO THE INCREDIBLE CITY OF BOKONON! MEET BOMBOS, THE MOST AWESOME PAPERBOY EVER TO GRACE THE PROVINCIAL BACKWATER. MORE THAN ANYTHING, HE WANTS TO

TO BE KNOWN AS THE BEST, YOU GOTTA KICK THE BUTT OF EVERYTHING!

GET TO THE CITY AND HE KNOWS HOW TO DO IT—WITH ATTITUDE AND A BAT. IT WON'T BE EASY. STANDING BETWEEN BOMBOS AND A TICKET OUT OF HIS LITTLE TOWN? IS EVERYTHING!

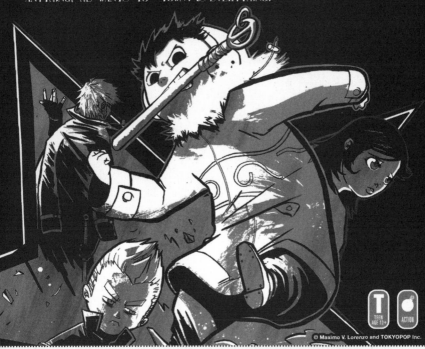

© Maximo V. Lorenzo and TOKYOPOP Inc.

FOR MORE INFORMATION VISIT: WWW.TOKYOPOP.COM

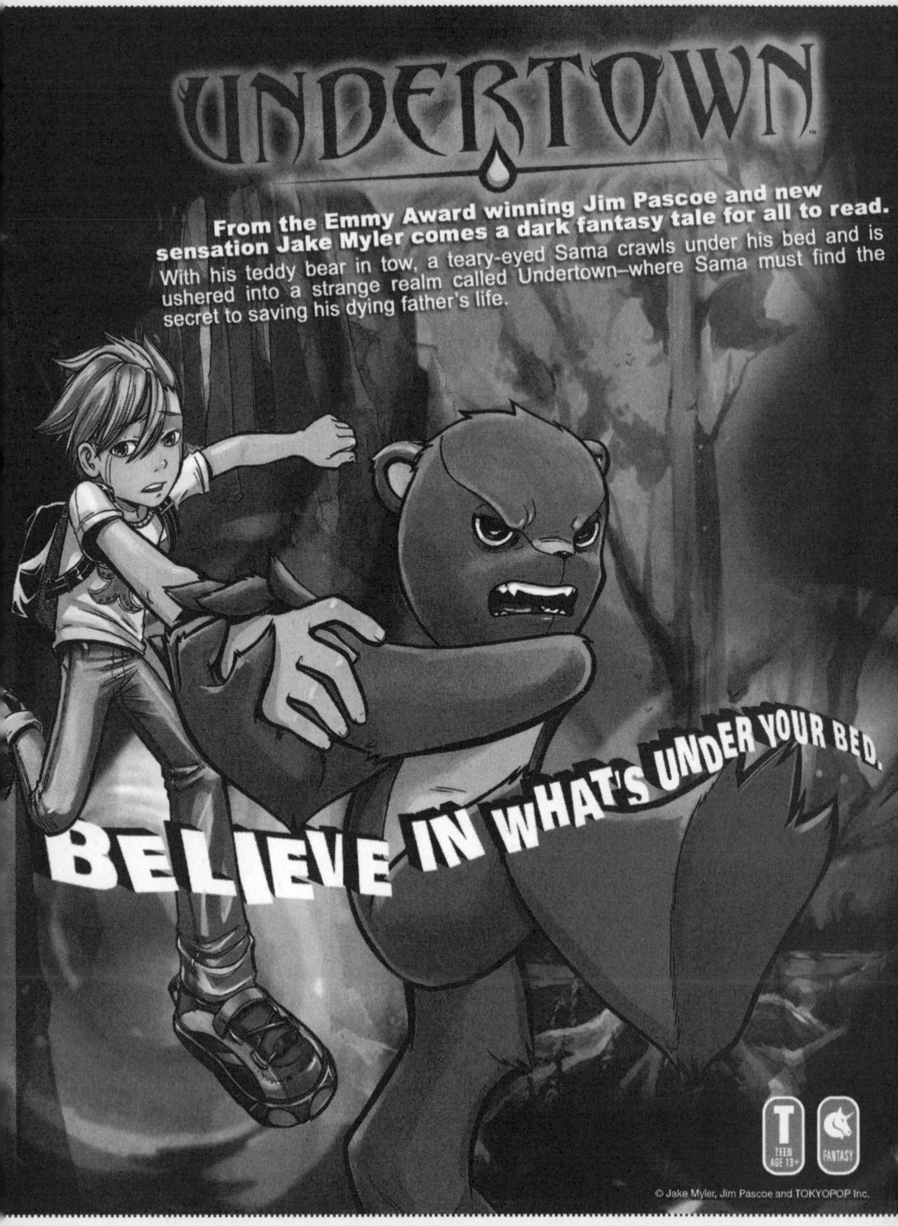

UNDERTOWN

From the Emmy Award winning Jim Pascoe and new sensation Jake Myler comes a dark fantasy tale for all to read. With his teddy bear in tow, a teary-eyed Sama crawls under his bed and is ushered into a strange realm called Undertown—where Sama must find the secret to saving his dying father's life.

BELIEVE IN WHAT'S UNDER YOUR BED.

© Jake Myler, Jim Pascoe and TOKYOPOP Inc.

FOR MORE INFORMATION VISIT: WWW.TOKYOPOP.COM

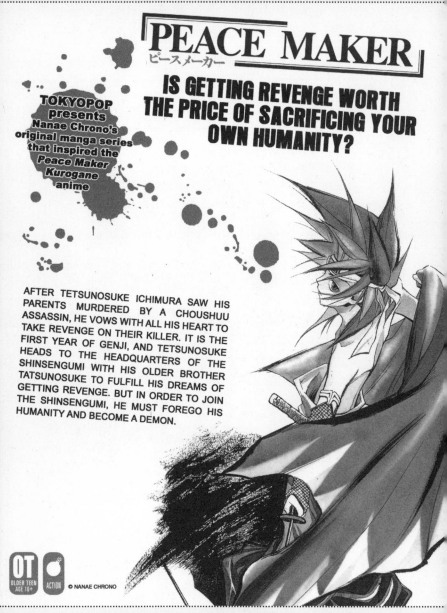

PEACE MAKER
ピースメーカー

IS GETTING REVENGE WORTH THE PRICE OF SACRIFICING YOUR OWN HUMANITY?

TOKYOPOP presents Nanae Chrono's original manga series that inspired the Peace Maker Kurogane anime

AFTER TETSUNOSUKE ICHIMURA SAW HIS PARENTS MURDERED BY A CHOUSHUU ASSASSIN, HE VOWS WITH ALL HIS HEART TO TAKE REVENGE ON THEIR KILLER. IT IS THE FIRST YEAR OF GENJI, AND TETSUNOSUKE HEADS TO THE HEADQUARTERS OF THE SHINSENGUMI WITH HIS OLDER BROTHER TATSUNOSUKE TO FULFILL HIS DREAMS OF GETTING REVENGE. BUT IN ORDER TO JOIN THE SHINSENGUMI, HE MUST FOREGO HIS HUMANITY AND BECOME A DEMON.

OT OLDER TEEN AGE 16+

ACTION

© NANAE CHRONO

FOR MORE INFORMATION VISIT: WWW.TOKYOPOP.COM

TOKYOPOP MANGA SUPPLEMENT

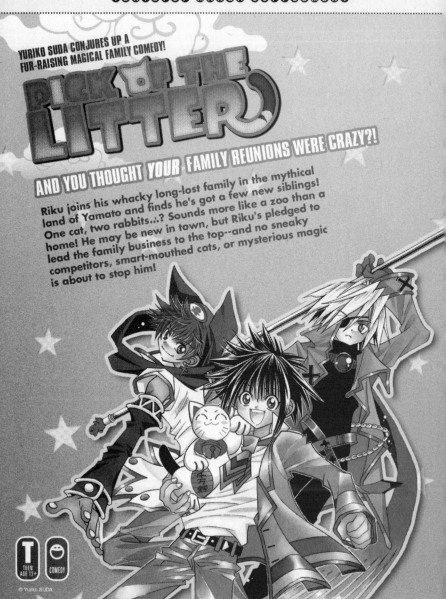

YURIKO SUDA CONJURES UP A
FUR-RAISING MAGICAL FAMILY COMEDY!

PICK OF THE LITTER

AND YOU THOUGHT *YOUR* FAMILY REUNIONS WERE CRAZY?!

Riku joins his whacky long-lost family in the mythical land of Yamato and finds he's got a few new siblings! One cat, two rabbits...? Sounds more like a zoo than a home! He may be new in town, but Riku's pledged to lead the family business to the top--and no sneaky competitors, smart-mouthed cats, or mysterious magic is about to stop him!

T TEEN AGE 13+

COMEDY

© Yuriko SUDA

FOR MORE INFORMATION VISIT: WWW.TOKYOPOP.COM

Sonny Strait--television's Dragonball Z actor, writer and director--takes on the world of manga in this magical and mischievous fractured Faerie tale...

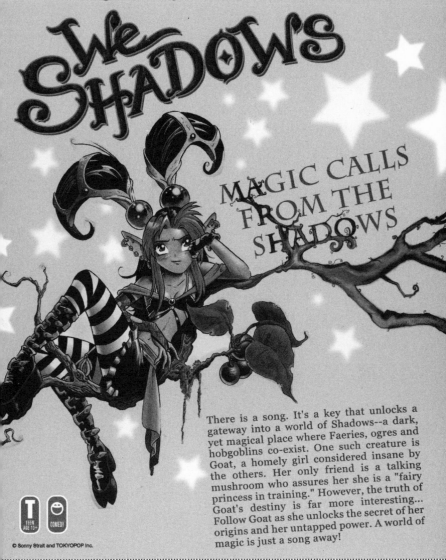

We SHADOWS

MAGIC CALLS FROM THE SHADOWS

There is a song. It's a key that unlocks a gateway into a world of Shadows--a dark, yet magical place where Faeries, ogres and hobgoblins co-exist. One such creature is Goat, a homely girl considered insane by the others. Her only friend is a talking mushroom who assures her she is a "fairy princess in training." However, the truth of Goat's destiny is far more interesting... Follow Goat as she unlocks the secret of her origins and her untapped power. A world of magic is just a song away!

T TEEN AGE 13+   COMEDY

© Sonny Strait and TOKYOPOP Inc.

FOR MORE INFORMATION VISIT: WWW.TOKYOPOP.COM

TOKYOPOP MANGA SUPPLEMENT

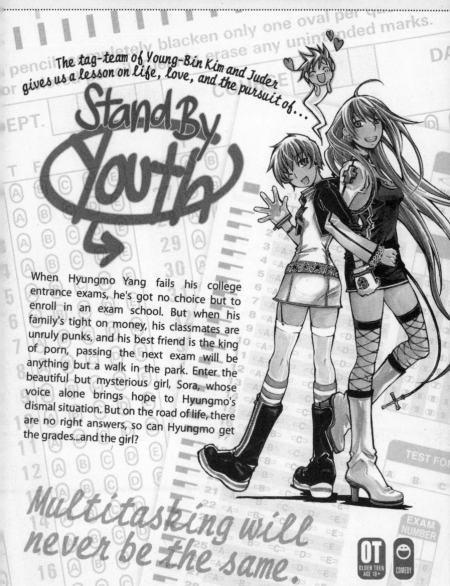

The tag-team of Young-Bin Kim and Juder gives us a lesson on life, love, and the pursuit of...

Stand By Youth

When Hyungmo Yang fails his college entrance exams, he's got no choice but to enroll in an exam school. But when his family's tight on money, his classmates are unruly punks, and his best friend is the king of porn, passing the next exam will be anything but a walk in the park. Enter the beautiful but mysterious girl, Sora, whose voice alone brings hope to Hyungmo's dismal situation. But on the road of life, there are no right answers, so can Hyungmo get the grades...and the girl?

Multitasking will never be the same.

OT OLDER TEEN AGE 16+

COMEDY

© YOUNG-BIN KIM AND JUDER, DAIWON C.I. INC.

FOR MORE INFORMATION VISIT: WWW.TOKYOPOP.COM

TOKYOPOP MANGA SUPPLEMENT

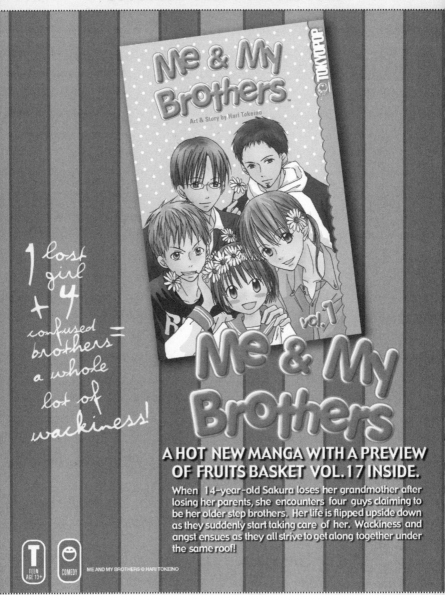

FOR MORE INFORMATION VISIT: WWW.TOKYOPOP.COM • WWW.MYSPACE.COM/TOKYOPOP

TOKYOPOP MANGA SUPPLEMENT

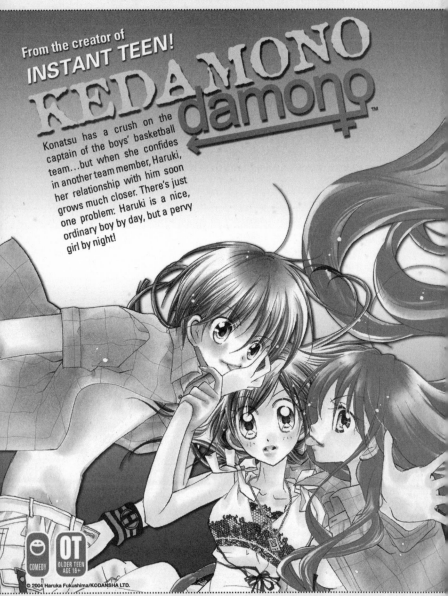

From the creator of
INSTANT TEEN!

KEDA MONO
damono™

Konatsu has a crush on the captain of the boys' basketball team...but when she confides in another team member, Haruki, her relationship with him soon grows much closer. There's just one problem: Haruki is a nice, ordinary boy by day, but a pervy girl by night!

COMEDY

OT
OLDER TEEN
AGE 16+

© 2004 Haruka Fukushima/KODANSHA LTD.

FOR MORE INFORMATION VISIT: WWW.TOKYOPOP.COM

S0-ABQ-414

STOP!

This is the back of the book.
You wouldn't want to spoil a great ending!

This book is printed "manga-style," in the authentic Japanese right-to-left format. Since none of the artwork has been flipped or altered, readers get to experience the story just as the creator intended. You've been asking for it, so TOKYOPOP® delivered: authentic, hot-off-the-press, and far more fun!

DIRECTIONS

If this is your first time reading manga-style, here's a quick guide to help you understand how it works.

It's easy... just start in the top right panel and follow the numbers. Have fun, and look for more 100% authentic manga from TOKYOPOP®!

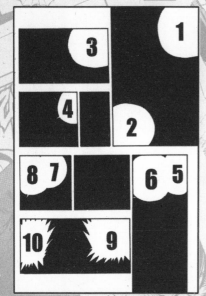

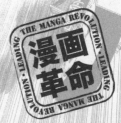